Caroline —

Best wishes to you!

PhD

The Mark of Cain

The Mark of Cain

Psychoanalytic Insight and the Psychopath

Edited by J. Reid Meloy

THE ANALYTIC PRESS

2001   Hillsdale, NJ   London

Published by
The Analytic Press, Inc., Publishers
Editorial Offices:
101 West Street
Hillsdale, New Jersey 07642
www.analyticpress.com

Set in Palatino 10.5/12 by
Christopher Jaworski, Qualitext
qualitext@earthlink.net

Index by Leonard S. Rosenbaum

Library of Congress Cataloging-in-Publication Data

Reid Meloy, J., 1949–
The mark of Cain : psychoanalytic insight and the psychopath /
edited by J. Reid Meloy.
        p.   cm.
Includes bibliographical references and index
ISBN 0-88163-310-0
1. Antisocial personality disorders. 2. Psychopaths.
        I. Meloy, J. Reid.

RC555.M37 2001
616.85′82—dc21
200122679

Printed in the United States of America
10 9 8 7 6 5 4 3 2 1

This book is dedicated to
the students and faculty of the
John Jay College of Criminal Justice

Cain said to his brother Abel, "Let us go into the open country."

While they were there, Cain attacked his brother Abel and murdered him.

The Lord said, "What have you done? Hark! Your brother's blood that has been shed is crying out to me from the ground . . . You shall be a vagrant and a wanderer on earth."

So the Lord put a mark on Cain, in order that anyone meeting Him should not kill him. Then Cain went out from the Lord's presence . . .

Genesis 4:8–16

Two traits are essential in the criminal: boundless egoism and a strong destructive impulse. Common to both of these, and a necessary condition for their expression, is the absence of love, the lack of an emotional valuation of (human) objects.

Sigmund Freud, "Dostoevsky and Parricide"

CONTENTS

(Continued)

Preface

J. Reid Meloy, Editor

When I was a young man, a newly licensed psychologist in the State of California, Kathy Wachter-Poynor, the local public mental health director, offered me a position that was to change my life and my career. She asked if I would consider developing an acute psychiatric inpatient program for mentally ill offenders in a maximum security setting. My excitement, composed equally of a tremendous naivete and a fierce ambition, both now tempered by years of experience, carried me into this valley of the shadow of death. Thankfully, I did come to fear evil.

I fairly quickly arrived at the realization that little was clinically known about some of the men I began to encounter. In those days of the *ancien régime*—DSM III had just been published—the application of specific criteria to arrive at a reliable, descriptive diagnosis was the coin of the realm. Little thought was given to the notion of *psychopathy;* no contemporary psychoanalytic writers used the term (although a few still clung to the anachronistic word *sociopathy);* and the word *psychopath* was central only to the empirically rigorous, and nonanalytic, psychological research of Robert Hare and his students at the University of British Columbia, unheralded at that time.

Unable to shake my undergraduate major in history at the College of Wooster, I began to peruse the older psychoanalytic literature for hints of clinical wisdom concerning the psychopath. I began also to search for contemporary psychoanalytic theorists who were at least obliquely interested in the internal life of such untreatable persons. I found a vein of data: gems from the past and a few diamonds from the present.

This book crystallized in my mind about six years ago, when I realized that my private intellectual labor of love might be of use to others; it could possibly become a published anthology of psychoanalysts' approaches to various facets of the psychopath, a book informed and balanced by what is currently known about psychopathy from a social, psychological, and biological research perspective.

My search for a publisher was met with several rejections. In addition, I found a daunting economic problem: reprinting published papers meant purchasing the reprint permissions, and no publisher wanted such costs to be added to the risk of printing a book that would have a small audience. The problems were solved when I received the generous support of the John Jay College of Criminal Justice Foundation and won Paul E. Stepansky's enthusiasm as Managing Director of The Analytic Press, in my opinion the premiere publishing house for psychoanalytic books.

I have organized the book into two sections: development and psychodynamics, and psychodiagnosis, treatment, and risk management. In the attempt to bring some clinical order to a varied literature, I have placed each chapter in chronological order within each section. All papers appear in their original form except for minor editorial changes. The organization reflects my belief that most of the authors were familiar with, and had read the work that had come before them, an optimism that may be more wishful than empirical; but this approach also lends a certain historical thread to the book. I begin each of the two sections with an introduction, which is my attempt to flesh out what can be psychoanalytically known about psychopaths at present. I then introduce the authors to follow and integrate our combined knowledge into other, nonanalytic domains of work, such as neurobiology, clinical psychiatry, and experimental psychology. It is illuminating to hear what analysts have said about psychopathy over the past decades and the success they have had—despite the difficulties of studying psychopaths—in applying the analytic way of knowing to discover important facets of this character pathology. As we shall see, there is an important psychoanalytic tributary feeding this cresting river of knowledge concerning the psychopath.

The mature and informed reader will nevertheless discover that certain authors or papers are missing. I offer only two weak excuses: the need for economy of size and my discovery that there is much repetition in the literature. For example, Phyllis Greenacre (1958) wrote a paper entitled "The Impostor," which was published in *Psychoanalytic Quarterly* three years after Helene Deutsch's paper of the same name appeared in the same journal. For the sake of brevity and equanimity, I decided to publish another paper of Greenacre's, "Conscience in the Psychopath" (chapter 4), and forego her expansion of the work of Deutsch. Likewise, I originally intended to include two papers by Otto Kernberg but found that "Clinical Aspects of Severe Superego Pathology," a chapter in his 1984 book of reprinted articles, *Severe Personality Disorders,* was almost completely contained in a subsequent paper, "The Narcissistic Personality Disorder and the Differential Diagnosis of Antisocial Behavior," published five years later in *Psychiatric Clinics of North America* (chapter 21).

Some authors, however, are notable for their absence: Otto Fenichel, Melita Schmideberg, Franz Alexander, and Melanie Klein, to name a few. Although each of these psychoanalysts is historically linked with the topic of this book, I did not include them, as well as others, for one of several reasons: their salient work was not contained in a representative scientific paper, but instead was dispersed throughout books and difficult to extract; their work may have provided a theoretical or clinical foundation for others' more specific writings on psychopathy but, when considered alone, was too far removed from the topic; or their work was earnest but, in the light of subsequent writings and research, generally wrong. For example, the thesis of Franz Alexander's (1930) paper, "The Neurotic Character," in which he attempted to fit the psychopath into his Procrustean bed, has not been borne out; subsequent research has shown that psychopaths are typically organized at a borderline, rather than a neurotic, level of personality (Gacono and Meloy, 1994).

I am also a great admirer of the work of Robert Lindner. His hypnoanalysis of a psychopath in *Rebel Without a Cause* (1944) and his compilation of case studies, *The Fifty-Minute Hour* (1954), remain classics in our field. He also did much to strengthen the role of psychology in psychoanalysis and made substantial contributions to Rorschach research concerning antisocial personalities. Although I did not include a selection from his writings in this book, he remains an influential source in my understanding of psychopaths. He captured quite eloquently the lure and the danger of this character disorder in his own words: "Psychopaths sparkle with the glitter of personal freedom, the checks and reins of the community are absent, and there are no limits either in a physical or a psychological sense" (Lindner, 1944, p. 13).

What matters to the psychopath is risk and reward. What matters to us who encounter the psychopath in our hospitals, prisons, jails, and communities is safety and understanding. I hope this book contributes to our endeavors.

REFERENCES

Alexander, F. (1930). The neurotic character. *Internat. J. Psycho-Anal.*, 11: 292–311.
Gacono, C. & Meloy, J. R. (1994). *Rorschach Assessment of Aggressive and Psychopathic Personalities*. Hillsdale, NJ: Lawrence Erlbaum Associates.
Greenacre, P. (1958). The impostor. *Psychoanal. Quart.*, 27:359–382.
Kernberg, O. (1984). *Severe Personality Disorders*. New Haven, CT: Yale University Press.

Lindner, R. (1944). *Rebel Without a Cause*. New York: Grune & Stratton.
Lindner, R. (1954). *The Fifty-Minute Hour*. New York: Dell.

Acknowledgments

If writing and editing books were a crime, I would be an unrepentant serial offender. This particular criminal conspiracy, moreover, could not have been completed without the enormous help of three individuals. Marilyn Clarke provided the typing and formatting to translate hundreds of pages of original journal articles into this carefully organized anthology and patiently tolerated my additions, corrections, and critiques. Esti Stevens doggedly pursued the reprint permissions for this book to literally the four corners of the earth; fortunately, email now makes such world travels so much easier. And, lastly, John Kerr provided an editorial brilliance and tenacity that made a good book much better. He would not settle for anything less than my best. I am deeply indebted to all of them.

J. Reid Meloy

Acknowledgments

Section I

Development and Psychodynamics

1

Introduction to Section I

J. Reid Meloy

A re psychopaths born or made? Robert Hare (personal communication, January 2000) told me this question was akin to attempting to describe a soccer field by its length *or* its width; both dimensions are necessary to capture the expanse, or expansive personality, that we see before us. When this question is posed to me by others, I point out that the more realistically based question is how nature and nurture shape each other over time, since a child comes into the world with a certain genotype that is phenotypically expressed according to the vagaries of personal experience.

ATTACHMENT, AROUSAL, AND ANXIETY

"The house of psychopath" is built on a psychobiological foundation of no attachment, underarousal, and minimal anxiety. I think these are necessary and related, but insufficient, characteristics that provide certain predispositions for the development of a psychopathic character.

Attachment is a biologically rooted, species-specific behavioral system that maintains close proximity between child and caretaker. It was first conceptualized and investigated by John Bowlby, James Robertson, and Mary Ainsworth at the Tavistock Clinic in London (Robertson and Bowlby, 1952; Bowlby, 1953; Ainsworth and Bowlby, 1954). Attachment is deeply rooted in both birds and mammals but is generally absent in reptiles.[1] It begins with goal-directed but objectless behaviors, such as sucking or crying, which seek to maintain physiological homeostasis in the human infant by securing warmth, touch, and food. Over time—the length of which is one of the contentious debates in developmental psychology—the proximity-seeking behavior becomes more object related and emotionally nuanced as the child attaches to the maternal

---

[1]Sometimes people with reptiles as pets will misinterpret their thermotropic (heat-seeking) behavior as an emotion related to attachment (S. Gecks, personal communication, January 2000).

3

object. Attachment is often defined as a strong affectional bond in both children and adults. Ainsworth (1989) termed it "a relatively long-enduring tie in which the partner is important as a unique individual and is interchangeable with none other" (p. 711). One of the reasons that attachment has been so thoroughly researched is the ease with which it can be behaviorally measured: proximity seeking to an object, distress when the object leaves, and the nature of the reunion behavior when the object returns. According to Miller (chapter 10, this volume) and Bursten (chapter 17, this volume), mastering mother's return may be the central task of consolidating one's healthy narcissism. A pathology of attachment is an acute or chronic disturbance in the bond that exists between infant and caretaker. Ainsworth (1989) labeled one of these disturbed patterns of attachment behavior *anxious avoidant attachment* and described it as a child's attempting to live in a pseudo-autonomous manner, chronically displaying a pattern of detachment, or indifference, to the rejecting or intrusive, but also abandoning, object. The anxious avoidant child, however, is chronically stressed but still attached. Ainsworth paralleled this finding with the third stage of attachment disruption proper, *detachment;* but subsequent research indicated that detachment is a different pattern characterized by apathy, self-absorption, preoccupation with nonhuman objects, and no displays of emotion (Bowlby, 1969). After prolonged separation, or a series of attachment disruptions, this attachment pathology may usher in *affectionless psychopathy,* well illustrated by Bowlby's 1944 paper on "Forty-Four Juvenile Thieves" (chapter 3, this volume). Bowlby (1988) later theorized that the attachment pattern seen in juvenile thieves is caused by constant maternal rejection. Current clinical wisdom supposes that future psychopaths are recruited chiefly from either the avoidant or the detached types.

Bartholomew (1990) developed a corresponding model of adult attachment based on positive and negative concepts of self and other. Her first three types—secure, preoccupied, and fearful—propose a certain positive and negative valence for the self and object; but most salient to psychopathy is her fourth type, *dismissing attachment,* which is analogous in some ways to the avoidant pattern of infancy.[2] Here is an easily

---

[2]In Bartholomew's work both dismissive and fearful are considered to derive from the avoidant strategy. An avoidant strategy is based on either a fear of rejection by the object or a dismissal of the value of the object. This distinction is impossible to make in infancy, but it is valid and important in adulthood—and also in particularizing the attitude of the psychopath.

understood pathology of attachment in which the self is viewed as positive and objects are viewed as negative. In a more psychodynamic frame, a narcissistic homeostasis is maintained through the idealization of the self and the devaluation of others. The dismissing attachment pattern relies on a strategy that minimizes distressing thoughts and affects associated with rejection by maintaining emotional distance from others (Rosenstein and Horowitz, 1996). Research has shown that dismissing attachment is correlated with conduct disorder and antisocial personality disorder (Allen, Hauser, and Borman-Spurrell, 1996), where it is assumed that acting-out behaviors are aimed at alleviating internal distress. In two related studies, Raine, Brennan, and Mednick (1994, 1997) demonstrated in a large cohort of Danish adult males that birth complications and maternal rejection in the first year of life predisposed them to an early onset (before 18 years) of violent crime (robbery, rape, murder, assault, or domestic violence). Having been reared in a public-care institution and a documented attempt to abort the fetus were among the data measuring their rejection by mother and obviously underscore the severity of the attachment disruption for these men.

The second corner of this psychobiological foundation is an arousal problem: autonomic hyporeactivity, especially to punishment or aversive consequences. The evidence for this variable extends back to the early work of Hare and his colleagues (Hare, 1970), which demonstrated peripheral autonomic irregularities among psychopaths, most notably through the use of skin conductance (SC) or GSR measures.[3] Although his work focused on adult Canadian criminals, the finding of autonomic hyporeactivity to punishment has since been replicated in other samples, including noncriminals, by other independent research groups throughout the world (Raine, 1993). What appears to be implicated in these studies is an attentional deficit among antisocial and criminal populations, which is further validated by the power of attention deficit disorder in childhood to predict criminality (Gittelman et al., 1985; Weiss et al., 1985).

The research, however, is not without its inconsistencies. For instance, one area of study argues for the importance of *schizotypy*, or schizotypal personality disorder (DSM-IV: American Psychiatric Association, 1994), as a moderator variable for orienting deficits across samples of criminal,

---

[3]A mild electrical current is passed across the finger, and, depending on how much the subject is perspiring—a direct measure of autonomic activity—skin conductance varies.

antisocial, and psychopathic individuals: high schizotypy in these groups increases their orienting deficits (Raine et al., 1999). Other research has shown *enhanced* orientation to a task among antisocials when it is seen as positive and interesting (Raine, 1989), while the orienting deficits appear limited to neutral or unpleasant stimuli.

The most important body of work related to arousal, however, and one that implicates the relationship between arousal, attachment problems, and violent criminality, is the biosocial research that finds "chronic cortical underarousal" to be a cause of early onset, and serious, habitual criminality (Raine et al., 1997). Not only do measures of chronic cortical underarousal, suggested by low resting heart rate, poor skin conductance, and slow wave (theta) EEG activity, correlate with habitual criminality, but together they have a predictive power that can override the influence of the environment, especially when the latter is what we would consider normal, nurturing, and "good enough."

Raine, Venables, and Williams (1990) demonstrated that these three measures of low CNS and ANS arousal at age 15 in a nonrandom sample of London male adolescents predicted habitual criminality when the men reached age 24. In a test of a reversal of their hypothesis—that elevated levels of CNS and ANS reactivity would *protect* individuals who were raised by criminal fathers from habitual criminal behavior—Brennan et al. (1997) studied four samples of Danish males and did find significantly higher reactivity among the noncriminals raised by criminal fathers: even higher than the reactivity of the noncriminals raised by noncriminal fathers!

Extending their work on the relationship between cortical underarousal and aggression, Raine and his colleagues have published several studies of a large sample of Mauritian[4] children (N = 1795) who are being followed longitudinally and were first examined at age three. The researchers' first published study tested the hypothesis that low resting heart rate, the best replicated biological correlate of childhood antisocial and aggressive behavior (Raine, 1993), measured at three years of age, would predict aggression at age 11 years. They supported their hypothesis, and gender and ethnicity made no difference. Eleven different biological, psychological, and psychiatric mediators and confounds also did not change the significant group differences (Raine, Venables, and Mednick, 1997). In their second study, the same large sample of Indian

---

[4]Mauritius is an island in the Indian Ocean off the coast of Africa. This cohort includes almost the entire population of that age in the two towns of Quatre Bornes and Vacaos born in 1969.

and Creole children from Mauritius were tested in a prospective longitudinal design, and aggressive children at age 11 were found to have had increased measures of stimulation-seeking, fearlessness, height, and weight at age three years when compared with the nonaggressive children (Raine, Reynolds, et al., 1998). In their third study of the same children from Mauritius, a developing tropical country very different from our Western culture, Scarpa et al. (1997) showed that children designated inhibited at age three showed significantly higher heart rates and skin conductance arousal when compared with uninhibited children. Studies have shown that such inhibition is related to the development of future anxiety disorders (Kagan, Reznick, and Snidman, 1987; 1988), and reduced inhibition is related to future antisocial behavior (Farrington, 1987).

Which brings me to the third corner of this psychobiological foundation: minimal anxiety. When anxiety is felt, such inchoate unpleasant emotion may signal danger from within or from outside, and, when it is specifically object related, we refer to it as fear. When the object is fantasy based, or patently unreasonable, we may see the patient as phobic or delusional. Fear and anxiety appear to have distinct physiological substrates (Dien, 1999; Rosen and Schulkin, 1998).

From a developmental attachment perspective, interpersonal anxiety emerges, typically in the service of safety and survival when a child perceives a stranger, since distress in the infant in the presence of someone who is unknown may be a signal to the caretaker that real danger may exist. Bowlby (1960) noted that the evolutionary basis of the causes of anxiety—the appearance of a stranger, actual separation, the anticipation of loss—keeps the maternal object in close proximity to the child and the child out of the grasp of predators; society still punishes parents as "grossly negligent" who drift out of range of their infants' distress calls, as if predators, in their contemporary metamorphosis as abductors[5] and child molesters, lurk around every corner and in every park.

In the realm of antisocial behavior, particularly psychopathy, however, anxiety is minimal or absent. This conclusion was first noted in Lykken's (1957) study, which found that anxiety differentiated secondary (anxious) psychopaths from primary (nonanxious) psychopaths. Blackburn (1975, 1998) has also identified these secondary psychopaths as being socially anxious, withdrawn, and moody, in contrast to primary

---

[5]Most child abductors, in fact, are family members, for example, estranged spouses.

psychopaths, who are hostile, extraverted, self-confident, and low-to-average anxious. Other laboratory studies support the clinical observation that anxiety is low in psychopaths (Ogloff and Wong, 1990), but self-report measures typically show a weak or neutral relationship between psychopathy and anxiety (Hare, 1991). Negative correlations between anxiety and psychopathy are more evident if the "aggressive narcissism" (Meloy, 1992) aspect of psychopathy is factored in. This component appears in children at risk of becoming psychopaths in adulthood and is referred to as a "callous/unemotional" factor or grouping of traits (Frick et al., 1994).

There is, however, a problem. Rates of anxiety disorders in conduct-disordered children range from 22% to 33% in community samples (Russo and Beidel, 1993), and significant correlations are found between antisocial behavior and anxiety on various childhood behavioral rating scales. Even the diagnosis of antisocial personality disorder in adulthood (DSM-IV: American Psychiatric Association, 1994) highly correlates with a variety of Axis I anxiety disorders (Boyd et al., 1984). How do we reconcile these findings with the low-anxiety hypothesis as a foundation for psychopathy? The answer appears to lie in separating the callous/unemotional traits of the psychopathic child from his impulsivity/conduct problems. When this is done (Frick et al., 1999), there emerges a strong negative relationship between these traits and anxiety in the psychopathic child: as subjects become more callous and unemotional, their anxiety dissipates. And, if the presence of conduct problems is controlled, a significant positive correlation between fearlessness and callous/unemotionality is seen. In other words, when the internal life of the child at risk for psychopathy, or what Lynam (1996) refers to as the "fledgling psychopath," is carefully studied and his acting-out behaviors are viewed as secondary to his emotional and defensive construction, a clear picture emerges of a developing youngster who has minimal anxiety and is essentially fearless.

No attachment, underarousal, and minimal anxiety biologically anchor the foundation of the psychopath. As we see later in adulthood, these substrates manifest in a fearless and sensation-seeking lifestyle, one that is unfettered by the constraints of an affectional bond, excitability or worry, or fear of violating the rules of others.

David Levy (chapter 2, this volume), John Bowlby (chapter 3), Lauretta Bender (chapter 5), and Kate Friedlander (chapter 6) are the early pioneers who charted the unknown territory of attachment pathology in psychopathy. Although they did not have knowledge of the inherited and acquired biological defects that provide the foundation for the "house of psychopath," their insights into the phenomenology of these patterns—and their thoughtful speculation as to etiology—are quite remarkable. For example, most of our earliest authors focus on the impact of neglect in fostering anger, impeding the formation of an object relation to the mother, and stimulating a pseudo-autonomous striving that we label pathologically narcissistic. They also stress the centrality of the joy of loving, and the pleasure derived from it, for both mother and child. Perhaps most important, the beginnings of character disturbance may be concealed by a surface adaptation, what Cleckley (1941) would later call a "mask of sanity."

FAILURES OF INTERNALIZATION

Psychological failures parallel the biological deficits of the "fledgling psychopath" (Lynam, 1996). These are failures of internalization, which Hartmann (1939) originally described as the evolutionary and phylogenetic transfer of functional-regulatory mechanisms from outside to inside. Piaget (1954) called this process assimilation, and Schafer (1968) noted that this transfer can be either reality based or fantasy based.

Within traditional psychoanalytic theory, failures of internalization begin with an organismic distrust of the sensory-perceptual environment and selective early incorporative deficits. Incorporation is the most developmentally primitive form of internalization, as the infant attempts to take in an object through the mouth; and, depending on the nature of the object—whether hard or soft—the consequent behavior will be to suck or to bite, to swallow or to sever. If normal development proceeds, these incorporative experiences are mostly hedonic, psychologically gratifying, and physiologically stabilizing. The emotional background of these incorporative experiences is a basic trust of the holding environment (Erikson, 1950).

In psychopathy, however, these incorporative failures[6] predict subsequent problems with two kinds of internalization: identifications and introjections. Identifications are modifications of the self or behavior to increase resemblance to the object (Schafer, 1968). Introjections are objects that are internalized but maintain a relationship to the self. When an introjection is conscious, it may be "seen" or "heard" in the mind,

---

[6]On occasion, forensic cases are tried in which psychopathy and cannibalism are both present, such as that of Jeffrey Dahmer, the Milwaukee man who ate body parts of his victims. This behavior may represent a very primitive psychotic attempt to master these early incorporative failures.

but it is not considered part of the self. It is subjectively experienced as "not-I" (Meloy, 1985). Borderline personality-disordered patients often complain of such powerful persecutory "voices," and these introjects may be misdiagnosed as auditory hallucinations.

In psychopathy, objects desired for internalization as either identifications or introjects are completely absent, not available when wanted, or harsh and unpleasant. There results a dearth of soothing internalization experiences. Through various kinds of conditioning, such as punishment (the presentation of an unpleasant stimulus) or negative reinforcement (the withdrawal of a pleasant stimulus), the child may come to anticipate hard, aggressive objects and may identify with such objects for both adaptive and defensive reasons.

Grotstein (1982) referred to an associated identification as the *stranger selfobject* and defined it as a normal preconceived fantasy that helps the infant anticipate the presence of the predator in the external world. I refer to this fantasy in the fledgling psychopath as the *predator part-object*. It is the primary archetypal internalization and a core narcissistic identification of the grandiose self-structure (Kernberg, 1984). It will later become the ideal self of the adult psychopath and will manifest in the positive emotional valence he attaches to his criminal versatility. As one psychopathic inmate said with disdain when he was handed his lengthy rap sheet by a television interviewer, "This isn't my complete body of work!"

The predator part-object of the psychopath as a primary unconscious identification is also evident in Rorschach research. We have noted (Meloy and Gacono, 1992) the degree to which psychopaths, both men and women, will often transform benign percepts into predatory ones: "It's a butterfly . . . with claws"; "It's a whale . . . with a shark fin"; "I see two carnivorous wolves . . . I wish I could see doves mating"; "A bat or evil moth, a furry animal that doesn't suckle to its mom." Such predatory identifications are also interpersonally evident in the pleasure psychopaths take when dominating others in real life, instead of experiencing any joy in affectional relating. This is a dominance–submission paradigm or power gradient—the seeds of sadism—which is often felt by clinicians as being "under the thumb" or being controlled by psychopathic patients. This prey–predator dynamic is also experienced with psychopathic children, adolescents, and adults in countertransference responses that are atavistic, visceral, and often felt as spontaneous autonomic arousal while one is in their presence: piloerection on the back of the neck is most common. This autonomic arousal signals a phylogenetically old fear of being prey to the predator, which internally for the psychopath is surmounted by a complete identification with the latter and the disavowal of the feared introject of the predator. He becomes what he fears the most.

The etiology of failed internalizations and, instead, a primary identification with the predator part-object is unknown. The other papers in our first section, especially those by Phyllis Greenacre (chapter 4), Adelaide Johnson (chapter 7), Helene Deutsch (chapter 8), and Donald Winnicott (chapter 9) are clearly biased toward a nurturing failure; but the importance of biology in habitual criminality and psychopathy should not be dismissed (Raine, 1993; Cooke, Forth, and Hare, 1998), nor should its likely impact on internalizations. Studies have shown that psychopathy has a negative curvilinear relationship to neglectful and abusive childhood family experiences (Marshall and Cooke, 1999). In other words, those persons who are severely psychopathic were less influenced by family factors when they were growing up; whereas those with low-to-moderate psychopathy were strongly influenced by family experience. Neuroimaging (PET) also suggests that functional deficits measured by radioactive glucose among samples of murderers with extensive criminal histories are *more* pronounced among those from good rather than poor home environments (Raine, Stoddard, et al., 1998).

THE GRANDIOSE SELF AND OMNIPOTENT FANTASY

Internalizations are most relevant to the structure of the self. Central to psychopathy is a variation of the grandiose self-structure, first formulated by Kernberg (1976) in his theoretical understanding of narcissistic personality disorder (see chapter 21). The grandiose self-structure, a pathological formation rather than a developmental fixation,[7] has three fused, or condensed, components: a real self, the actual specialness of the child; an ideal self, a fantasized self-concept, which compensates for severe oral frustration, rage, and envy; and an ideal object, a fantasized image in the child's mind of a completely loving and accepting parent, often at odds with the actual behavior of the real parent. A psychopathology of narcissism is the functional and affective core of psychopathy.

---

[7]It is difficult to advance a theoretical understanding of psychopathy if pathological narcissism is considered only a developmental fixation. Hence, Heinz Kohut and the self psychologists make virtually no reference to psychopathy in any of their writings.

The development of the grandiose self-structure—an unconscious construct filled with conscious images—is the scaffolding that continues the construction of the "house of psychopath." Conscious articulations of the self as predator, a dominant idealization, and others as prey, a submissive devaluation, are the clinical observations we make that bring us closest to the grandiose self-structure in the patient.

A psychopathic sexual murderer articulated his response to Card VIII of the Rorschach, usually seen as one or two animals: "In the grey, it looks like some kind of monster eating the winged humanoid. What was Rorschach thinking? That's it."

There continues to be intact reality testing in psychopaths, the ability to separate perceptually internal from external stimuli, yet he *conceives* of others as extensions of the self. Objects, both as internal representations and as real people, exist for the purpose of gratification of sexual or aggressive impulses and do not *conceptually* otherwise exist. This distinction may seem unimportant, but it becomes clinically and forensically very relevant when the presence or absence of psychosis in psychopathy is considered. As research has shown (Gacono and Meloy, 1994), most psychopaths are organized at a borderline level of personality with intact reality testing; nevertheless, psychosis can exist in a psychopath, reality testing or the perceptual differentiation between self and others can dissolve, and his motive for predation can become delusional.

The psychopathic grandiose self-structure is maintained as a primary identification through the behavioral devaluation of others in the real world. Although omnipotent fantasy is a clear byproduct of the grandiose self-structure, and partially maintains it, it is my observation that psychopaths must aggressively devalue others in real life to shore up their idealized identifications of the self as Predator. Fantasy alone is insufficient, unlike the more benign narcissistic personality disordered person who can nurture a private omnipotent fantasy of himself without actually damaging or degrading other people. Although this clinical observation is verifiable and forensically notable—it is one reason why psychopaths cause such destruction—the basis of this failure of fantasy, the impotence of omnipotence, is unknown. The most parsimonious theory is that psychopaths will habituate, or desensitize to their own fantasies of omnipotence. The specter of deflation haunts the edges of their psyches; autonomic arousal, already low to begin with, further ebbs; and emotions of boredom and envy begin to reach consciousness. Therefore, psychopaths act on others to derogate, devalue, dismiss, and, in some cases, destroy to once again maintain their peculiarly dependent narcissistic equilibrium.[8]

Omnipotent fantasy has a role, of course, in normal childhood development. In the fledgling psychopath, it has gone awry for any number of reasons: first, the parental environment may be so neglectful (see chapter 8) that omnipotent fantasy provides a compensatory retreat for the pain and deprivation suffered by a disregarded child; second, the environment may be so directly abusive—whether aggressively, sexually, or in some malignant, classically conditioned combination—that the child internalizes and strongly identifies with the abusive parent as a predator for whom he will eventually no longer be prey but will instead prey on others; or, third, the environment may be quite adequate and loving for most children, but in the fledgling psychopath a combination of biological predispositions makes containment and modulation of aggression impossible (Lykken, 1995). Such dispositions could range from hyperactivity, impulsivity, and attentional deficits (Lynam, 1996), through a largely heritable callousness and lack of emotion (Patrick, 1994), to a neurologically based life course of persistently antisocial behavior (Moffitt, 1993).

PRIMITIVE INTERNALIZED OBJECT RELATIONS

When one gazes upon a psychopath, there is less there than meets the eye; for example, his internalized object relations are relatively simple and primitive (ontogenetically young). The fledgling psychopath remains at a preoedipal or borderline level of personality organization. There is no tripartite (ego, id, superego) structure to his personality. Internalized objects remain part-objects in the sense that good and bad qualities are not integrated into a whole representation. The self is either good or bad; others are either good or bad. The development of a grandiose self-structure, however, allows for the maintenance of a tenuous narcissistic equilibrium in which self-representations are always positive and other

---

[8]In other work (Gacono and Meloy, 1994) we have noted that psychopaths will produce a plethora of narcissistic mirroring as well as violent symbiosis responses to the Rorschach, a combination that suggests a developmentally young transference to others and a need to aggressively separate from others at the same time. This response combination may psychodynamically give us some clues to answer the paradoxical question, if psychopaths are so detached from others, why do they keep interacting with them in such destructive ways?

representations are always negative. Unpleasant affects associated with self-representation, such as envy, are quickly evacuated through projection onto, or through projective identification *into*, others. Predatory idealization is maintained; prey devaluation is maintained. A dyadic self- and object world exists without the oedipal defenses, such as repression, or more mature structuring of a superego.

This state of mind is fundamental to the work of Kernberg (1980) and of his muse, Jacobson (1964), and is often misunderstood in failed attempts to reconcile a tripartite theory of personality structure with those authors' dyadic theory of primitive object relations. Repression must activate if there is to be a differentiated ego and id, and ideal self-representations must integrate with ideal object representations as an *ego ideal* if the differentiation between ego and superego is to begin. In the preoedipal personality of the fledgling psychopath, which continues into adulthood, there are only dyadic self- and object representations, which are either condensed (the grandiose self-structure; see Kernberg, 1984) or displaced somewhere else, usually outside the self.

> One 34-year-old serial murderer I evaluated, although both moderately psychopathic and pathologically narcissistic, could not completely rid himself of his bad objects. He was clinically depressed and had very low self-esteem. He had abducted, raped, and killed two young women and readily referred to the "sick, twisted" part of himself that committed these acts. He hated his mother owing to her abandonment of him and her drunken promiscuities with many men. He selected intoxicated victims his mother's approximate age when she left him and had rape fantasies toward his mother beginning at age 13 or 14. He believed he should be executed and wished his father had killed him when he beat him as a boy.

The simplicity and primitiveness of the psychopath's dyadic world may be masked by the patient's higher than average IQ. Clinicians may delude themselves into assuming a more complex, tripartite structure than actually exists and invest more therapeutic optimism, especially in an adult psychopathic patient, than is warranted. Gross contradictions in the observed state of mind of the psychopath may be the first clinical clue that integration of the emotional valence of self- and object representations has not occurred. These contradictions may frighten and confuse the clinician, but the psychopath, when confronted, does not see a problem.

The same serial murderer had an affectionate, loving relationship with his pregnant girlfriend while he nurtured his subterranean paraphilic fantasies and raped and murdered his two victims over the course of four months. He had also carried on a consensual relationship with another girlfriend 10 years earlier, during which he had serially raped two stranger females. When asked about this seeming contradiction, he said, "One is taking, the other is sharing."

SUPEREGO ABNORMALITIES

Without the biological substrate of normal attachment and the anxiety concomitant with the loss of the maternal object (or the more developmentally mature fear of loss of the love of the object), internalizations largely fail, along with the ability to internalize *values*. The adult psychopath is a valueless person.

Kate Friedlander refers to this in her notion of "latent delinquency" (chapter 6); and Adelaide Johnson began to explore this blighted territory with her concept of "superergo lacunae" (chapter 7). Moral responsibility is a moot question in psychopathy. Not only is there an inability to compare good and bad objects—the cognitive beginning of superego development and morality—there may be a complete "reversal of values" and a consequent identification with badness or evil.

One very bright 60-year-old psychopath, in prison for life, could argue quite convincingly that people in prison were all victims and those in society were the victimizers. Nevertheless, he believed, and incorrectly quoted Solzhenitsyn to bolster his argument, that the greatest freedom of all was incarceration.

A probation officer once characterized to me this reversal of values as the psychopath's ability to "monkey with your mind." It also gives the psychopath a tactical advantage, since internal constraints do not inhibit moment-to-moment gratification of impulse.

The psychopath's vestigial burden of conscience, however, is located in Jacobson's (1964) concept of the first layer of normal superego development: the sadistic superego precursors, which are projected aspects of early persecutory objects, cast out to deny aggression in the midst of frustration. Kernberg (1984) referred to this superego layer as the first of his six levels of superego pathology. The observed clinical manifestation of sadistic superego precursors is the psychopath's use of sadism to achieve pleasure. Sexually sadistic criminals evidence this behavior most readily in their propensity to abduct and torture victims (Dietz,

Hazelwood, and Warren, 1990). The identification with sadistic persecutory objects is very different from that of the borderline patient, who
may feel tortured "in his mind", by such sadistic introjects; borderline
patients are much more amenable to treatment.[9] We have found in our
research a significant relationship of some magnitude between various
measures of sadism–pleasure derived from the suffering and domination of another person—and psychopathy (Holt, Meloy, and Strack, 1999).

Sadistic superego precursors in the preoedipally organized fledgling
psychopath are most clinically evident in cruelty to animals, particularly domestic pets. This infliction of suffering on a dependent and
affectionate animal is the child's attempt to evacuate his own helpless
rage and instead feel pleasure through omnipotent control. The memory
of helplessness is obliterated through mastery of, and identification
with, the sadistic superego precursors. Although all children feel helpless rage at times, and the defense against this emotion is the psychodynamic basis of the sadistic impulse, it is fully acted out by only a select
few children who lack the internalized ability to constrain it. Felthous
and Kellert (1986) showed a significant correlation between cruelty to
animals in childhood and protean violence in adulthood.[10]

AFFECTS AND DEFENSES

Psychopaths live in a presocialized emotional world. Psychopaths possess an emotional range and depth and object relatedness similar to—although not identical with—those of a young toddler prior to sustained
interaction with his peers. Emotions that are consciously felt include
excitement, rage, boredom, envy, frustration, dysphoria, and shame.
These feelings do not require whole-object relatedness, that is, the
representation of self and others as whole, real, meaningful, and separate. They are part-object emotions and are felt quickly, expressed
coarsely, and dissipated rapidly. The process or phenomenon of feeling,

---

[9]Recent research, however, suggests that sexual sadists will role play being the
victim, thus assuming a masochistic position, in autoerotic activities or with a
consensual partner (Hazelwood and Warren, 2000). This finding suggests that there
is an intrapsychic oscillation between the sadistic object as an introject and as an
identification, a point conveyed by the very term sadomasochism in earlier psychoanalytic writings (Stekel, 1929).

[10]The State of California recently passed a law requiring psychological counseling
as a condition of probation for those convicted of cruelty to animals.

what is clinically referred to as modulation of affect, remains this way into adulthood; psychopathic men typically modulate affect as five-to seven-year-old children do (Gacono and Meloy, 1994).

Once again, what is absent is most important. The fledgling psychopath, partially due to his preoedipal personality organization, will not evidence the more mature feelings that necessitate whole-object relatedness and a capacity for attachment. These emotions include anger, guilt, fear, depression, sympathy, empathy, remorse, gratitude, sadness, loneliness, and reciprocal joy—a range of feeling that is broad, deep, and complex. For example, the popular notion of empathy, to "put yourself in the other person's shoes," is a welcome behavior when first seen in a child. It also correlates with a developing ability to separate reality from fantasy, as defenses such as repression mature which do not require the perceptual distortions inherent in such preoedipal defenses as projection and denial (Vaillant, 1993). There is also no requirement that the other person's shoes be the same size as that of the empathic one; empathy requires the ability to recognize the uniqueness and separateness of the other. All this is lacking in the psychopath.

In our research with adult antisocial and psychopathic males and females, we found a predominance of preoedipal defenses, most commonly devaluation, denial, splitting, omnipotence, and projective identification (Gacono and Meloy, 1994). Although more mature "neurotic" defenses, such as rationalization, will occasionally appear, the defenses cluster at a borderline level of personality organization (Kernberg, 1975). The dynamic nature of defenses (change over brief periods of time) has been demonstrated in a series of Rorschach studies (Meloy et al., 1997).

The more primitive the defense, the more obvious it is to the clinician. Projection, for example, maintains the demarcation between inside and outside, but the origin of the stimulus is relocated. A young psychopath might feel envy toward a psychotherapist who is desperately trying to be as empathic as possible in the treatment sessions. The patient's envy is stimulated by his perception of the therapist's "goodness," something the patient does not see in himself. The patient quickly defends against this intolerable insight, although it is perhaps accurate, by attributing to the therapist his felt "badness" through cruel and repeated verbal devaluations of her. Envy subsides in the midst of his rage because he has damaged her "goodness," and it is no longer there to be possessed, at least momentarily. His conception of her as a part-object allows him to maintain his projection since other remedial aspects of her personality do not come into his awareness to dilute his derogation of her as a psychotherapist.

Jealousy is a more developmentally mature and complex emotion than envy; it is triadic (two competing for the love of one) and requires the capacity for attachment and therefore the threat of loss of the love of the object. Jealousy is more apparent in males and likely serves reproductive success (Berke, 1988; Buss, 2000). It is typically not an emotion felt by psychopaths and is more likely to be seen in such common pathologies of attachment as stalking and in ordinary sexual pair bonds.[11]

The most troublesome question, and one that is not yet resolved, is whether such affective and defensive primitiveness is solely adaptive, in the sense of facilitating the search for gratification from the environment, or instead wards off low (if not despicable) self-esteem. Willock (1986, 1987), adopting the latter interpretation when clinically treating less disturbed but conduct-disordered children, has written elegantly on this topic. We (Gacono and Meloy, 1994) researched a sample of 60 conduct-disordered children, ages 5–12, and found low self-esteem, chronic emotional detachment, and minimal anxiety in comparison with normal children. Two-thirds of these children were the solitary-aggressive subtype, a DSM-III-R (American Psychiatric Association, 1987) grouping of conduct-disordered children at highest risk for psychopathy in adulthood. Their object representations, moreover, were significantly more likely to be categorized as sources of narcissistic mirroring or overwhelming and malevolent forces than in our normal comparison group: a typical example of the latter is (Rorschach Card II), "an explosion, volcano, eruption, the cut away side of molten lava blowing out all over the place . . . red, looks like a man crawling because his feet got tore off" (Gacono and Meloy, 1994, p. 32).

Again, are such thoughts and feelings defensive, adaptive, or both? There does not appear to be a general theoretical answer to this question, but from a clinical perspective, the resolution is easily found. Psychological testing will usually differentiate a primary psychopathic child (who often has been raised by prosocial parents) from a much more defensive and treatable child with conduct disorder (whose parents are often both abusive and neglectful) in that the latter child will show evidence of both attachment and anxiety. Behaviorally, in children with conduct disorder, there will also be an absence of repetitive acts of

---

[11]Recent research (Meloy, 1998) has found that most people who stalk are not psychopaths, a finding consistent with their chronic emotional detachment. Those who stalk form an intense, preoccupied attachment to their objects of pursuit and are quite obsessive and relentless.

cruelty toward domestic animals. Intensive psychoanalytic treatment will also show gains in these children (Fonagy and Target, 1996), especially if anxiety is present.

The remaining chapters in this section, by Milton Miller (chapter 10), Seymour Halleck (chapter 11), and myself (chapter 12), attempt to shed further light on the hypothesized psychodynamics of psychopaths. In his poetic chapter, Miller speaks to the discontinuity in the sense of time of psychopaths, but in a more subtle manner, he also speaks to the superficiality of psychopaths and their inability to deepen their relationships to objects. A paucity of identifications means there is no grief when there is loss and therefore no depth of attachment. Halleck depicts psychopathy as a defensive search for painless freedom from objects. Although I disagree, his argument is provocative and illustrates our propensity to idealize certain perceived characteristics of psychopaths as we struggle with our own anxieties and attachments. My chapter, which concludes the first section, is an attempt to comment on the interface of evil and psychopathy, with appropriate deference to a psychodynamic that is often denied because it frightens—sadism.

REFERENCES

Ainsworth, M. (1989). Attachments beyond infancy. *Amer. Psycholog.*, 44: 709–716.

Ainsworth, M. & Bowlby, J. (1954). Research strategy in the study of mother–child separation. *Courr. Cent. Internat. Enf.*, 4:105.

Allen, J., Hauser, S. & Borman-Spurrell, E. (1996). Attachment theory as a framework for understanding sequelae of severe adolescent psychopathology: An 11-year followup study. *J. Consult. Clin. Psychol.*, 64:254–263.

American Psychiatric Association (1987). *Diagnostic and Statistical Manual of Mental Disorders, 3rd ed. rev. (DSM-III-R).* Washington, DC: American Psychiatric Association.

American Psychiatric Association (1994). *Diagnostic and Statistical Manual of Mental Disorders (DSM-IV).* Washington, DC: American Psychiatric Association.

Bartholomew, K. (1990). Avoidance of intimacy: An attachment perspective. *J. Soc. & Pers. Rel.*, 7:147–178.

Berke, J. (1988). *The Tyranny of Malice.* New York: Summit Books.

Blackburn, R. (1975). An empirical classification of psychopathic personality. *Brit. J. Psychiat.*, 127:456–460.

Blackburn, R. (1998). Psychopathy and personality disorder: Implications of interpersonal theory. In: *Psychopathy: Theory, Research and Implications for Society*, ed. D. Cooke, A. Forth & R. Hare. London: Kluwer, pp. 269–302.

Bowlby, J. (1953). Some pathological processes set in train by early mother–child separation. *J. Ment. Sci.*, 99:265–272.

Bowlby, J. (1960). Separation anxiety. *Internat. J. Psycho-Anal.*, 41:89–111.

Bowlby, J. (1969). *Attachment and Loss, Vol. 1: Attachment*. New York: Basic Books.

Bowlby, J. (1988). Developmental psychiatry comes of age. *Amer. J. Psychiat.*, 145:1–10.

Boyd, J., Burke, J., Greenberg, E., Holzer, C., Rae, D., George, L., Karno, M., Stolzman, R., McElvoy, L. & Nesdadt, G. (1984). Exclusion criteria of DSM-III: A study of the co-occurrence of hierarchy-free symptoms. *Arch. Gen. Psychiat.*, 41:983–989.

Brennan, P., Raine, A., Schulsinger, F., Kirkegaard-Sorensen, L., Knop, J., Hutchings, B., Rosenberg, R. & Mednick, S. (1997). Psychophysiological protective factors for male subjects at high risk for criminal behavior. *Amer. J. Psychiat.*, 154:853–855.

Buss, D. (2000). *The Dangerous Passion*. New York: Free Press.

Cleckley, H. (1941). *The Mask of Sanity*. St. Louis, MO: Mosby.

Cooke, D., Forth, A. & Hare, R. D., eds. (1998). *Psychopathy: Theory, Research and Implications for Society*. London: Kluwer.

Dien, J. (1999). Differential lateralization of trait anxiety and fearfulness: Evoked potential correlates. *Personal. & Individ. Differences*, 26:333–356.

Dietz, P., Hazelwood, R. & Warren, J. (1990). The sexually sadistic criminal and his offenses. *Bull. Amer. Acad. Psychiat. & the Law*, 18:163–178.

Erikson, E. (1950). *Childhood and Society*. New York: Norton.

Farrington, D. (1987). Implications of biological findings for criminological research. In: *The Causes of Crime: New Biological Approaches*, ed. S. A. Mednick, T. E. Moffitt & S. A. Stack. New York: Cambridge University Press, pp. 42–64.

Felthous, A. & Kellert, S. (1986). Violence against animals and people: Is aggression against living creatures generalized? *Bull. Amer. Acad. Psychiat. & the Law*, 14:55–69.

Fonagy, P. & Target, M. (1996). Predictors of outcome in child psychoanalysis: A retrospective of 763 cases at The Anna Freud Centre. *J. Amer. Psychoanal. Assn.*, 44:27–78.

Freud, A. (1936). *The Ego and the Mechanisms of Defense*. New York: International Universities Press, 1966.

Frick, P., Lilienfeld, S., Ellis, M., Loney, B. & Silverthorn, P. (1999). The association between anxiety and psychopathy dimensions in children. *J. Abn. Psychol.*, 27:383–392.

Frick, P., O'Brien, B., Wootton, J. & McBurnett, K. (1994). Psychopathy and conduct problems in children. *J. Abn. Psychol.*, 103:700–707.

Gacono, C. & Meloy, J. R. (1994). *Rorschach Assessment of Aggressive and Psychopathic Personalities*. Hillsdale, NJ: Lawrence Erlbaum Associates.

Gittelman, R., Mannuzza, S., Shenker, R. & Bonagura, N. (1985). Hyperactive boys almost grown up. *Arch. Gen. Psychiat.*, 42:937–947.

Grotstein, J. (1982). Newer perspectives in object relations theory. *Contemp. Psychoanal.*, 16:479–546.

Hare, R. D. (1970). *Psychopathy: Theory and Research*. New York: Wiley.

Hare, R. D. (1991). *Manual for the Psychopathy Checklist—Revised*. Toronto: Multihealth Systems.

Hartmann, H. (1939). *Ego Psychology and the Problem of Adaptation*. New York: International Universities Press.

Hazelwood, R. & Warren, J. (2000). The sexually violent offender: Impulsive or ritualistic? *Aggress. & Violent Behav.*, 5:267–279.

Hofer, M. (1987). Early social relationships: A psychobiologist's view. *Child Devel.*, 58:633–647.

Holt, S., Meloy, J. R. & Strack, S. (1999). Sadism and psychopathy in violent and sexually violent offenders. *J. Amer. Acad. Psychiat. & the Law*, 27: 23–32.

Jacobson, E. (1964). *The Self and the Object World*. New York: International Universities Press.

Kagan, J., Reznick, J. & Snidman, N. (1987). The physiology and psychology of behavioral inhibition. *Child Devel.*, 58:1459–1473.

Kagan, J., Reznick, J. & Snidman, N. (1988). Biological bases of childhood shyness. *Science*, 240:167–171.

Kernberg, O. (1975). *Borderline Conditions and Pathological Narcissism*. New York: Aronson.

Kernberg, O. (1976). *Object Relations Theory and Clinical Psychoanalysis*. New York: Aronson.

Kernberg, O. (1980). *Internal World and External Reality*. New York: Aronson.

Kernberg, O. (1984). *Severe Personality Disorders*. New Haven, CT: Yale University Press.

Lykken, D. (1957). A study of anxiety in the sociopathic personality. *J. Abn. Soc. Psychol.*, 55:6–10.

Lykken, D. (1995). *The Antisocial Personalities*. Hillsdale, NJ: Lawrence Erlbaum Associates.

Lynam, D. (1996). Early identification of chronic offenders: Who is the fledgling psychopath? *Psycholog. Bull.*, 120:209–234.

Marshall, L. & Cooke, D. (1999). The childhood experiences of psychopaths: A retrospective study of familial and societal factors. *J. Personal. Dis.*, 13:211–225.

Meloy, J. R. (1985). Concept and percept formation in object relations theory. *Psychoanal. Psychol.*, 2:35–45.
Meloy, J. R. (1986). On the relationship between primary process and thought disorder. *J. Amer. Acad. Psychoanal.*, 14:47–56.
Meloy, J. R. (1988). *The Psychopathic Mind: Origins, Dynamics and Treatment.* Northvale, NJ: Aronson.
Meloy, J. R. (1992). *Violent Attachments.* Northvale, NJ: Aronson.
Meloy, J. R., ed. (1998). *The Psychology of Stalking: Clinical and Forensic Perspectives.* San Diego: Academic Press.
Meloy, J. R., Acklin, M., Gacono, C., Murray, J. & Peterson, C. (1997). *Contemporary Rorschach Interpretation.* Hillsdale, NJ: Lawrence Erlbaum Associates.
Meloy, J. R. & Gacono, C. B. (1992). The aggression response and the Rorschach. *J. Clin. Psychol.*, 48:104–114.
Moffitt, T. (1993). Adolescence limited and life course persistent antisocial behavior: A developmental taxonomy. *Psycholog. Rev.*, 100:674–701.
Ogloff, J. & Wong, S. (1990). Electrodermal and cardiovascular evidence of a coping response in psychopaths. *Crim. Just. & Behav.*, 17:231–245.
Patrick, C. (1994). Emotion and psychopathy: Startling new insights. *Psychophysiology*, 31:319–330.
Piaget, J. (1954). *The Construction of Reality in the Child.* New York: Basic Books.
Raine, A. (1989). Evoked potentials and psychopathy. *Internat. J. Psychophysiol.*, 8:1–16.
Raine, A. (1993). *The Psychopathology of Crime.* San Diego: Academic Press.
Raine, A., Bihrle, S., Venables, P., Mednick, S. & Pollock, V. (1999). Skin-conductance orienting deficits and increased alcoholism in schizotypal criminals. *J. Abn. Psychol.*, 108:299–306.
Raine, A., Brennan, P. & Mednick, S. (1994). Birth complications combined with early maternal rejection at age 1 year predispose to violent crime at age 18 years. *Arch. Gen. Psychiat.*, 51:984–988.
Raine, A., Brennan, P. & Mednick, S. (1997). Interaction between birth complications and early maternal rejection in predisposing individuals to adult violence: Specificity to serious, early-onset violence. *Amer. J. Psychiat.*, 154:1265–1271.
Raine, A., Reynolds, C., Venables, P., Mednick, S. & Farrington, D. (1998). Fearlessness, stimulation-seeking, and large body size at age 3 years as early predispositions to childhood aggression at age 11 years. *Arch. Gen. Psychiat.*, 55:745–751.
Raine, A., Stoddard, J., Bihrle, S. & Buchsbaum, M. (1998). Prefrontal glucose deficits in murderers lacking psychosocial deprivation. *Neuropsychiat., Neuropsychol. & Behav. Neurol.*, 11:1–7.

Raine, A., Venables, P. & Mednick, S. (1997). Low resting heart rate at age 3 years predisposes to aggression at age 11 years: Evidence from the Mauritius Child Health Project. *J. Amer. Acad. Child Adolesc. Psychiat.*, 36:1457–1464.

Raine, A., Venables, P. & Williams, M. (1990). Relationships between CNS and ANS measures of arousal at age 15 and criminality at age 24. *Arch. Gen. Psychiat.*, 53:544–549.

Robertson, J. & Bowlby, J. (1952). Responses of young children to separation from their mothers. *Courr. Cent. Internat. Enf.*, 2:131–142.

Rosen, J. & Schulkin, J. (1998). From normal fear to pathological anxiety. *Psycholog. Rev.*, 105:325–350.

Rosenstein, D. & Horowitz, H. (1996). Adolescent attachment and psychopathology. *J. Consult. Clin. Psychol.*, 64:244–253.

Russo, M. & Beidel, D. (1993). Co-morbidity of childhood anxiety and externalizing disorders: Prevalence, associated characteristics, and validation issues. *Clin. Psychol. Rev.*, 14:199–221.

Scarpa, A., Raine, A., Venables, P. & Mednick, S. (1997). Heart rate and skin conductance in behaviorally inhibited Mauritian children. *J. Abn. Psychol.*, 106:182–190.

Schafer, R. (1968). *Aspects of Internalization.* New York: International Universities Press.

Stekel, W. (1929). *Sadism and Masochism, Vols. 1 & 2.* New York: Liveright.

Vaillant, G. (1993). *The Wisdom of the Ego.* Cambridge, MA: Harvard University Press.

Weiss, G., Hechtman, L., Milry, T. & Perlman, T. (1985). Psychiatric status of hyperactives as adults: A controlled prospective 15-year follow-up of 63 hyperactive children. *J. Amer. Acad. Child Adolesc. Psychiat.*, 24:211–220.

Willock, B. (1986). Narcissistic vulnerability in the hyperaggressive child: The disregarded (unloved, uncared-for) self. *Psychoanal. Psychol.*, 3:59–80.

Willock, B. (1987). The devalued (unlovable, repugnant) self—a second facet of narcissistic vulnerability in the aggressive, conduct-disordered child. *Psychoanal. Psychol.*, 4:219–240.

2

Primary Affect Hunger

David M. Levy

Written by a pioneering New York psychiatrist and psychoanalyst, David Levy, this seminal statement on affect hunger was published in the *American Journal of Psychiatry* in 1937. Affect hunger is defined as "an emotional hunger for maternal love and those other feelings of protection and care," which Levy illustrates through a number of adoption cases in which maternal rejection appeared to be causative. The importance of this work lies in its being the first paper to suggest the paucity of relational affects in psychopathic disturbance, such as love, and perhaps object-related anger; and it warns us that a surface adaptation may mask a fundamental deficit in, or loss of, a capacity to bond. This is the chronic emotional detachment of psychopathy.

In a previous study of maternal overprotection, an investigation was made of a mother–child relationship featured by an excess of maternal love. This excess was demonstrated overtly in maternal behavior through physical and social contact with the child, infantilization, extra precautions and protective behavior. Definite criteria of a relationship were set up, and cases selected, out of a large number, in which the criteria were satisfied. Case studies were thereby utilized in the form of an experiment, as though to say: If we could make an experimental study of such a relationship, we would have to satisfy certain conditions. Let us see if in a large body of case material such conditions are already satisfied. Naturally, the more definite and numerous the criteria the fewer the number of cases that can be filtered out by this process. The advantage, however, is that the greater the selectivity, the "purer" the relationship to be studied.

During the study of maternal overprotection, it was necessary to select, for the purpose of contrast studies, cases of maternal rejection. In the latter group, however, selective criteria were never adequately worked out. Since the investigation of the overprotective groups was terminated by the closing of the Institute for Child Guidance, a staff was no longer available for study of the numerous details that were part of the undertaking. In the absence of such aids to a companion study of maternal rejection, it is necessary to have recourse to a simpler method. I must therefore, in this paper, utilize illustrative cases to indicate certain basic dynamic principles, without statistical aids. Furthermore, this study is limited in its orientation to the child who suffers the rejection. It is also limited to the experience of a certain type of rejection, to which I am applying the name "affect hunger."

The term affect hunger is used to mean an emotional hunger for maternal love and those other feelings of protection and care implied in the mother–child relationship. The term has been utilized to indicate a state of privation due primarily to a lack of maternal affection, with a resulting need, as of food in a state of starvation. Since the symptoms of affect hunger are clearly manifested in children who receive maternal care and direction to a high degree in a physical and intellectual sense, though without any evidence of affection, the analogy is more accurately related to a vitamin deficiency rather than to a gross starvation. The use of the term affect hunger, rather than affection or love hunger, opens the possibility, also, of a privation of other sources of the emotional life, even possibly of hostility, though this is yet to be investigated. A child who has been overprotected and later, through the birth of another child, thrown into a rejected state, may also suffer affect hunger. In the present paper, however, I am using the term to apply only to individuals who have suffered lack of maternal love in the early years of life. Assuming for the moment the value of maternal love as an essential component in the development of the emotional life, what happens when this element is left out of the primary social relationship? Is it possible that there results a deficiency disease of the emotional life, comparable to a deficiency of vital nutritional elements within the developing organism?

My first example is an eight-year-old girl who was adopted a year and a half before referral. After an illegitimate birth, the child was shifted about from one relative to another, finally brought to a child placing agency, and then placed in a foster home for two months before she came to the referring foster parents. The complaints were lying and stealing. The parents described the child's reaction to the adoption as very casual. When they brought her home and showed her the room she was to have all for herself, and took her on a tour of the house and grounds, she showed apparently no emotional response. Yet she appeared very vivacious and "affectionate on the surface." After a few weeks of experience with her, the mother complained to the husband that the child did not seem able to show any affection. The child, to use the mother's words, "would kiss you but it would mean nothing." The husband told his wife that she was expecting too much, that she should give the child a chance to get adapted to the situation. The mother was somewhat mollified by these remarks, but still insisted that something was wrong. The father said he saw nothing wrong with the child. In a few months, however, he made the same complaint. By this time, also, it was noted that the child was deceitful and evasive. All methods of correction were of no avail. A psychoanalyst was seen. He recommended that the parents stop all correction and give the child a great deal of affection. This method was tried, according to both parents, with no result. The school teacher complained of her general inattention, and her lack of pride in the way her things looked. However, she did well in her school subjects, in keeping with her good intelligence. She also made friends with children, though none of these were close friendships. After a contact of a year and a half with the patient the father said, "You just can't get to her," and the mother remarked, "I have no more idea today what's going on in that child's mind than I knew the day she came. You can't get under her skin. She never tells what she's thinking or what she feels. She chatters but it's all surface."

I have selected this case as my first illustration of a type of difficulty that is familiar to everyone who works with children, because I feel reasonably sure that the parents were distinctly affectionate with children, and also because their own child, aged 12, was affectionate and well adjusted.

Repeated experience in the treatment of the type of child referred indicates a poor prognosis. Before considering this phase of the problem, I would like to cite further examples.

An unmarried woman, aged 40, adopted a child aged two years and eight months, through private arrangement. The child was the illegitimate son of a woman of high economic and social status. The family history was negative. The child was turned over to an agency very soon after birth, placed in an orphanage from age 12 to 27 months and then transferred to a boarding home, where he remained until the period of adoption. After a year, the mother gave up the possibility of getting any emotional relationship with the child. She had never been able to get any sign of affection from him. He never accepted her fondling. In the household there was a doting and indulgent grandmother, to whom the child also did not respond. The mother felt she had been taking punishment for a year and could stand it no longer. Besides the lack of emotional response, she complained chiefly of his negativistic behavior. According to tests, the child had superior intelligence, and the physical examination was negative.

The third example is that of a boy adopted at the age of three. The previous history was unknown, except that he was illegitimate and had been shifted around from place to place. A Wassermann test and physical examination made at the time were negative. I examined him at the age of eight years. There was a good health history, and the physical examination was negative. According to tests, the intelligence was adequate. He was referred because he had been twice suspended from school for poor work, and the fact that he made a general nuisance of himself. The mother had given up hope of making any relationship with him. He showed no affectionate response. Although she made several trips away from home, he never asked about her when she was away. Punishment or ordinary methods of correction had no effect. He would "forget" too easily. His behavior in the office was quite infantile, I thought like that of a three-year-old boy. He showed a complete lack of appreciation of his difficulties at school and at home. There was no question of some distinct emotional deficiency in his response.

The fourth case is another example of an adopted child, a girl aged nine years and ten months at the time of referral to the Institute for Child Guidance. She was referred for general incorrigibility. She had been adopted at the age of seven months into a home in which the foster mother could give little affection, but demanded highly conventional behavior. Before the referral, she had been seen by two psychiatrists, one in consultation and the other for a series of about twelve interviews. She had also received thyroid treatment for a period of time, though our findings showed no evidence of physical difficulty. Our examination revealed, besides the problems for which she was referred, fantastic lying, difficulty in making any friendly relationships with children, and school retardation. The parents noted especially her "failure to profit by experience" and "unresponsiveness to affection." The problem was complicated by the fact that the home was of superior type in a cultural sense—requirements that were too high for a child with an I.Q. of 80. The entire history led to the conclusion that the patient had some inadequacy in her emotional response and was an unfavorable subject for therapy. The parents were, throughout the long contract that ensued, conscientious in cooperating with every therapeutic effort. The patient was treated by the psychiatrist, utilizing chiefly a psychoanalytic method, for a period of two years. The behavior of the patient during the process of over 200 sessions was markedly negativistic. There were some interesting periods of improvement. Nevertheless, the result of the entire therapy was practically nil.

At the end of the treatment, the parents were willing to consider another therapeutic adventure before referring the child to foster care.

Through special circumstances, it was possible to send the child to Vienna, where she was treated by a psychiatrist of the Adlerian school, with whom she lived for a period of three years. The results were essentially negative; indeed, the child's problems became more alarming because of her greatly increased aggression. She was thereupon sent to her own mother and very quickly got into difficulty because of her incorrigibility and because, somehow or other, she had managed to collect five revolvers. From there she was sent to an orphanage, from which she ran away on two occasions, and then to a detention home, from which the psychiatrist wrote that he considered the patient an excellent prospect for intensive psychotherapy. At the last notation patient was 18. It is interesting that the typical attitude of the psychiatrist was that she would respond to psychotherapy. I have cited this case especially to show the failure of psychotherapy to meet these problems.

These case illustrations are given as examples of emotional pathology caused by primary affect hunger of a severe degree. The symptom-complaints are of various types. They include, frequently, aggressive sexual behavior in early life, stealing, lying, often of the fantastic type, and, essentially, complaints, variously expressed, that indicate some lack of emotional response in the child. It is this lack of emotional response, this shallowness of affect, that explains the difficulty in modifying behavior. The inhibitions to the instinctive impulses, normally strengthened by the response to maternal affection, are no longer in operation. As an instrument in modifying behavior, the power of maternal love may be seen most clearly in life histories where it is absent—a kind of ablation experiment in social life. That the difficulty in these cases is due to a primary affect hunger seems a reasonable assumption, even though not proven by any direct experiment or by statistical checks. Does it follow, necessarily, that any child who suffers complete loss of maternal love, during the infantile period, will develop into a psychopathic personality of the type described? Further, in a number of cases in which a child was given presumably normal maternal love, in the first two years of life, the same difficulties may occur when an attempt at adoption is made at this age. Such cases were sufficiently numerous in my experience to warrant the advice that adoptions be made either in the first year of life, or after the infantile period. It was assumed that when the early emotional attachments were made by the child, as the personality began to grow, a break at this stage caused a situation similar to one in which the child could make no emotional attachment to start with.

There is an interesting bit of evidence on the prognosis in cases of primary affect hunger in a recent issue of the *American Journal of Orthopsychiatry* (Powdermaker, Levis, and Touraine, 1937). Eighty-one delinquent girls were treated by a combination of social and psychotherapy. Successes and failures were tabulated by follow-up studies varying from one to five years after discharge from the home. One of the investigators independently analyzed the parent–child relationships and classified them into four groups. The successes and failures were then checked against these classifications. They illustrate a finding already determined in previous studies, to wit that the cooperation of the parent is the most important item in prognosis. One finding, however, is especially striking, namely, that the 17 cases in which there was evidence of complete rejection showed 100 per cent failure in response to therapy. This is in contrast with the general result of 50 per cent success for the group. The case examples of complete rejection cited are extreme and convincing.

In contrast with the extreme cases of affect hunger, we have, at the other end of the scale, a series of children whose difficulties are solved by the restoration of maternal love. In such cases psychotherapy may be either unnecessary or merely a complementary therapy. There are a number of children who do well with affectionate foster parents, or with a psychiatrist who renders the therapeutic relationship primarily supportive. This type of treatment, to which the name supportive therapy has been given, is recognition of the fact that in certain cases the child's hunger for love must be gratified. It is recognized that in every therapeutic relationship the patient receives some support of this type (transference) but there are cases in which the treatment must be primarily, even exclusively, supportive; a treatment in which the worker acts *in loco parentis*. Favorable results with such children are often utilized to prove the particular merits of this or the other type of psychotherapy, whereas it matters little what technique is used as long as the child feels loved.

A patient was referred to the Institute for Child Guidance at the age of nine years, with a complaint of enuresis and temper tantrums. A visitor to the foster home wrote a letter to the Institute from which the following excerpt is taken: "He is starved for affection. His mother rarely visits him, although she is urged to do so frequently. When she is there, he acts very infantile, climbing up on her lap, always wishing to be with her, and showing off. Then as time elapses after her visit, he becomes more unmanageable and disagreeable." The history of the case is featured by the child's affectionate response to grown-ups, his making up to any stranger, explosive and dangerous temper tantrums, and marked jealousy of the other children in the foster home. The "hunger" element in the difficulty is seen in the response to grownups and to the mother, with whom he acts in complete disregard of what is usually a strong inhibiting influence—the presence of other boys. When his mother is about he is always sitting in her lap; he holds his face up to be kissed and puts his arms around her neck. According to the foster mother, he acts in these situations quite like an infant. Though affectionate to the foster mother, he makes no such display with her. The severity of the temper tantrums must be mentioned. On one occasion he tried to break up a game which the other boys were playing. The foster mother sent him to his room, whereupon he tore up the bedding and pulled all the pictures off the walls. On another occasion he attempted to hit a boy with an axe. On another, he chased the teacher and the children out of school.

The patient lived with his father and mother in the first year of life. After the death of the father he was placed in an institution for a year, then for two years in a boarding home, from which he was removed by his mother. He was placed again with the previous boarding mother. He was moved again to a foster home in which he had been living for a year and four months at the time of referral. There are certain elements in the history that indicate a certain modicum of affection from the mother and in the homes in which he was placed. In one boarding home there was an affectionate mother. The foster mother also was affectionate with him. Furthermore, his own mother, though very spasmodic and infrequent in her visits, was affectionate while with him.

In this case, treatment consisted in getting placement with a foster mother who could give him a great deal of affection. There were only four interviews with the psychiatrist. They consisted largely of chats about the foster home. Marked improvement in behavior occurred and continued for two years. A follow-up study, made when the patient was twelve years six months old, showed complete cessation of the temper tantrums, good school adjustment, growth in responsibility, though no improvement in the enuresis.

The case described illustrates a very frequent problem for social agencies. A number of cases in the Institute for Child Guidance series show a growing adjustment under the care of an affectionate foster mother. Such therapeutic benefit may occur even in the adolescent group. However, the stumbling block is often the mother of the child, who continues sporadic contact. She visits the child once a week, more commonly once in several weeks, and thereby prevents the building up of a stable relationship with the foster parent. Furthermore, the fact that the child is under foster care while his own mother is still in contact with him, stimulates various fantasies of abandonment, confusion about his own place in the world, sometimes even a confusion of self-identity, often an illusion that the mother who has really abandoned him is a loving and protecting mother. Agencies seem to foster this illusion on the part of the child, because otherwise they would feel guilty of encouraging hostile feelings toward the mother. The mother who has given the child to foster care, yet refuses to give up the child for adoption, is motivated by her feelings of guilt over the rejection and thereby acts as a great handicap to the child's stability. Frequently, also, we have instances in which the mother removes the child from one boarding home, has the child live with her for a week, and then through the agency gets another placement. Because of her own guilt, also, she may find all kinds of fault with different foster mothers. It is not unexpected, therefore, that a recent follow-up in the case of this patient, now age 18, shows this type of history: discharged from a foster mother to his own mother, back to another foster mother, truancies to his own mother, then placement in a farm school.

In a similar case, presented by Dr. Blanchard at the last meeting of the American Orthopsychiatric Association, the main psychodynamics are clearly discernible. (1) A group of activities representing responses to the primary need. They are manifested in various maneuvers to hold closely to a person, to win demonstrations of affection, to plead for love, to utilize pathetic appeals and states of helplessness, in order to stimulate a love response from a mother-person. The kissing-bug reaction represents an avidity for physical affection, as illustrated in the previous case, and belongs in this category of responses. So also a number of the whiners and pleaders and naggers for attention, for closeness and for guarantees that the maternal sustenance will never be withdrawn. Out of this group, also, are derived the mechanisms of constant begging for gifts, also of making overwhelming demands from a friendship later in life, to insure against any possible break in the relationship. (2) A group of activities that represent various hostile acts designed to punish the one who denies love and to prevent the possibility of its withdrawal. The mother who denied or withheld stimulates a hostile rejoinder in the form of wishes for her death, various sadistic fantasies, even threats to her life, also threats of suicide if she will not respond. The conscious level of these performances varies, but they may be overtly expressed. The temper tantrums, possibly also the enuresis, may be manifestations in this group, as may all types of "bad" behavior. (3) A group of symptoms that are based on the child's fear of the hostile impulses. These represent the source of the emotional conflicts and neurotic derivatives of the original state of privation. Fear of death is a manifestation. In fact, for every hostile move there is a retaliatory fear. There are a number of interesting derivatives from this state that have to do with the feeling of being deprived, and its consequences. These have to do with various forms of self-pity, the creation in the individual of helpless states, and even depression, but time does not allow these elaborations.

So far I have cited two types of response to affect hunger: one, the extreme instance in which the emotional development of the child has been adversely affected from the start, with a resulting pathology of affect; the other, an instance in which the renewal of maternal love has a successful restorative function. There now remains a large mid-group of cases in which the problems derivative of the early affect hunger are marked by special and usually persistent relationship difficulties. They follow along the lines in which the denials of maternal love and affection are especially marked.

In the last case cited, a boy who made up to every adult, we have an example of what may become a characteristic of every relationship. Such examples are better seen in those adults whose social life represents a series of relationships with older people, every one of whom is a substitute mother. They may be single or in combination, the point being simply that the patient must, throughout life, be in contact with a person from whom the same demands are made that were thwarted in the original experience with the mother. The life pattern then becomes dependent on maintaining such relationships. When one of them is broken there is a period of depression, or a feeling that "something is terrifically lacking," until another relationship is made.

Another type of reaction is seen in the form chiefly of excessive demands made on the person who is selected to satisfy the privations of early life. Such examples also represent a distinctive cluster of cases seen in social agencies, especially in children who have difficulty in adapting to the foster home. The story is typically that the child makes a good impression, the foster parents are delighted, and then, within a week or two, the demands of the child become so excessive that the foster parents are worn out and insist on release from their charge. The problem is always the same—excessive demands for food, for money, for privileges. Attempts to satisfy them end always in disaster. They represent, it seems to me, the child's need of proof that the adult is a loving parent because he satisfies every requirement that is made, also a hostile motive to destroy by getting things out of them. It is as though the child has to repeat the original frustration. A recent example comes to me of a delinquent boy who, in relation with the social worker, tried to get money from her. It was put on the basis that "if you love me you will do this for me." If the demand was not satisfied, the refrain would be "then this shows that you don't care for me." Every attempt made at giving insight into the relationship failed. The patient showed initiative in getting a job but quit in a short time because he thought he deserved more money, they should give him more time for lunch, etc., etc. Other jobs were terminated for the same reasons. The patient was able to respond only to stern necessity. He was never modified by therapeutic methods.

No doubt there are a number of children who feel a distinct lack that is related to an original privation, who, nevertheless, are in a state of externally good adjustment. Such children naturally are not referred for treatment, since it is rare that a child is not brought to treatment through an adult. There are, certainly, numerous examples of adults, well adjusted according to the criteria of overt behavior, with complaints of various dissatisfactions, chiefly in the form of futility, or depression, that have their origin primarily in affect hunger. How much of the difficulty is related to a true deficiency in the infantile period, and how much is due to neurotic mechanisms is a question that the psychoanalyst is in the best position to solve, but I feel sure that there are numerous instances in which the deficiency is covered by neurosis, and the difficulty mistakenly attributed to the overlying structure. At least, a recognition of this fact will compel a reorientation to the life history.

The responses described seem to pick out special elements of privation in the mother–child relationship. In the social relationship the protective phase of maternal care may be sought; or the giving function in maternal care may be the special point of attack. In others, it may be the mere demonstration of affection, including also genital satisfaction. These elements represent special incompleteness in the early emotional development of the patient and must be demonstrable in numerous phases of the life history, of which this account can only be a rough sketch.

I have tried in this study to indicate certain basic responses to affect hunger showing a group of cases in which there are pathologic residues due to an extreme deficiency; second, a group in which the restoration of maternal love has marked therapeutic effect; and third, a group which demonstrates specialized difficulties in social relationships that are derivatives of a primary affect hunger.

REFERENCE

Powdermaker, F., Levis, H. & Touraine, G. (1937). Psychopathology and treatment of delinquent girls. *Amer. J. Orthopsychiat.*, 7:58.

3

Forty-Four Juvenile Thieves
Their Characters and Home-Life
John Bowlby

The following chapter is a small portion of a two-part paper published in the *International Journal of Psychoanalysis* in 1944 by John Bowlby, a British psychoanalyst and past supervisee of Melanie Klein. It ushered in his discovery of human attachment and foretells the enormous contributions of his subsequent career. Bowlby notes the affectionless nature of a carefully studied sample of juvenile thieves and here elaborates on the inhibition of love by rage, stimulated by parental neglect, and the consequent fantasies of badness that come to define internalized representations of self and others. This indifference, or *dismissive* pattern of attachment, eliminates "any risk of letting our hearts be broken again."

(V) NOTES ON THE PSYCHOPATHOLOGY OF THE AFFECTIONLESS CHARACTER

The foregoing statistical analysis has demonstrated that a prolonged separation of a child from his mother (or mother-figure) in the early years commonly leads to his becoming a persistent thief and an Affectionless Character. An understanding of the detailed psychopathology must await the analysis of a few typical cases. Nevertheless an outline of the probable pathology may be sketched.[1]

First we may note the parts played by libidinal and aggressive impulses, both of which will inevitably have been excessively stimulated by the frustration of separation. By stealing the child hopes for libidinal satisfaction, though in reality it proves ineffective, because the

---

[1] In these brief notes there has been no occasion for a detailed discussion of the theories of Freud, Klein and other psycho-analysts and in consequence references are omitted. My debt to other analysts will however be obvious.

symbol of love has been mistaken for the real thing. From earliest days libidinal satisfaction is associated with obtaining possession of things. In infancy it is milk, in later years toys and sweets; and even in adult life a drink, a box of chocolates, a cigarette or a good meal are the bearers of kindly feelings from one person to another. Food and other objects thus become symbols of affection. A child separated from his mother comes to crave both for her love and for its accompanying symbols and this craving, if unsatisfied, later presents itself as stealing. The fact that most of these children stole food or money to buy food and that these thefts were often from their mothers, was clearly no accident. The food they stole was no doubt felt to be the equivalent of love from the mother whom they had lost, though probably none was conscious of the fact.

The violence which these desires assume when untoward circumstances lead to their being thwarted is illustrated by several cases. Despite repeated and severe punishments these children persisted in pilfering from their mothers' bags and boxes. Norman K. broke into his mother's money box, whilst Nansi F. pried open a Salvation Army collecting box with a knife. The need to gain possession of all their mother's good things, if necessary by attacking her, is evident.

These libidinal cravings commonly take an oral form, sometimes of a very primitive kind. Again and again one hears that milk is stolen. Such early oral desires were particularly noticeable in an adult thief of Schizoid or Affectionless Character whom I have treated: she had the habit of taking her morning tea from a baby's bottle. These excessive libidinal cravings may, of course, be expressed in any of the typical forms, oral, anal, urethral or genital, and it will be surprising if investigation does not confirm the impression that a close association exists between chronic stealing and promiscuity, a topic which is discussed in the next section. Such an association is clearly to be expected if we are right in postulating a strong though distorted libidinal component in the make-up of persistent thieves.

Important though libidinal factors are in driving children to steal, the part played by aggression must not be forgotten, for stealing not only enriches oneself, but impoverishes and hurts others. Revenge is unquestionably a very powerful driving force towards stealing. If one has suffered great deprivation oneself, one will feel inclined to inflict equal suffering on someone else.*

---

*Editor's Note: This is, of course, an example of lex talionis, the law of talion or revenge, a primitive impulse that provides a psychobiological underpinning for retributive justice.

Now the children whom we are discussing have suffered great deprivation and it is not to be wondered at that they are impelled to inflict
similar suffering on others. Derrick O'C., whom I was able to see
regularly, reluctantly admitted (after interpretation) that much of his
stealing had been done out of revenge. He had been extremely jealous
of his brother Johnny, four years younger, and consciously felt that
Johnny's presence had robbed him of much affection and many presents. The fact that he had been farmed out for most of his first three
years must have added poignancy to Derrick's vision of his mother
lavishing affection on Johnny. At any rate he was jealous of Johnny and
felt that he would have got more love and better presents if Johnny were
not there. His stealing, therefore, was motivated partly by a desire to
make up to himself and partly by a desire to revenge himself on his
mother, who admitted herself that she favoured Johnny. He recalled that
he had often deliberately stolen after his mother had shouted at him or
punished him and that his motive in stealing the two bicycles had been
partly to get his father fined in the Police Court. The story was that many
other boys had bikes, and Derrick had asked his father to give him one.
His father refused, so in revenge Derrick took the bikes, knowing he
would get caught and expecting and hoping his father also would get
into trouble.

Still there is nothing pathognomonic about excessive libidinal and
aggressive impulses directed towards parents. They are found in one
form or another in all cases of functional mental illness. What characterize these particular cases are (i) that they lack the usual inhibition of
these impulses and (ii) that they are unable to make permanent personal
relationships owing to their inability to feel or express love; in other
words there is an extreme degree of the impaired capacity to make
object-relationships which is present in some degree in every neurotic
and unstable person. In these Affectionless Characters it amounts to a
massive inhibition of object-love combined with excessive and relatively uninhibited libidinal and aggressive impulses. This combination
is clearly no accident. On the contrary the lack of inhibition is the
necessary result of the lack of a love-relationship, a result which is
explained by a theory of the origin of the superego and the development
of object-love which, though implicit in psychoanalytic literature, has
not, so far as I know, been the subject of a detailed exposition.*

Editor's Note: See Arnold Modell (1968). *Object Love and Reality.* New York:
International Universities Press.

Observations on infants show that they become clearly aware of their mothers' individuality during their first year of life. By the end of this year they not only recognize and value her as the person from whom love and all good things emanate, but have come to take pleasure in reciprocating her love. Object-love, a mixture of the selfish and the altruistic, is already developed to a considerable degree. Normally, through the processes of identification and introjection, there then comes to be formed in the child's mind a pattern of feeling and behavior, the superego, which is designed to maintain this relationship with the object by inhibiting impulses inimical to it. The superego, although often experienced as a foreign body, an agent of the loved object, is in reality the expression both of the need for the object and of love for it, and this remains so despite its frequent use of aggressive measures to attain its ends. Without some measure of object-love the whole structure of the superego, whether it operates by violent inhibition or moderate control, could not exist, since both the purpose which it serves and the needs which it expresses would be non-existent.

Now it is precisely these affectionate relationships with loved objects which are lacking in the case of the Affectionless thieves; the lack of any properly developed superego, with its regulation of the libidinal and aggressive impulses, is the direct result. The problem thus resolves itself into elucidating the reasons for the absence of object-love. Several factors are almost certainly responsible and the difficulty is to know what weight each should be given, especially as it is extremely probable that their influence varies with different cases.

In the first place, especially in the younger children, lack of opportunity may well play a part in the failure of object-love to develop. The growth of object-love is normally rapid during the second six months of life and it is not unnatural to suppose that if there is no opportunity for its exercise it will fail to grow. Such a state of affairs exists when an infant or small child is in a hospital, since it is rare for nurses to remain long enough in a ward for tiny children to become attached to them. The likelihood of a simple process of this kind operating is strengthened by the familiar observation that dogs need to be in the hands of one person during the critical period of their training and that if they are not they grow up lacking attachment to a master and consequently wild and disobedient. Since experiment would be possible, it is perhaps not altogether fanciful to suggest that a study in the social development of dogs or monkeys might be of value in this connection.

A second fairly simple factor which almost certainly plays a part is the swamping of affection by rage. This was obviously important in those cases who at a rather later age were reft from homes where they were happy and then expected to settle down cheerfully with strangers. It is hardly unexpected that the reaction to such a situation is often one of intense hatred for the new mother-figure, a hatred which effectively inhibits any growth of love. It is not unlikely that such emotions may also be called up towards a mother who places her child in a hospital or foster-home. The child does not know the reason for this event, but may well interpret it as a particularly hateful act on the part of the mother. This hypothesis is supported by the well-established observation that in certain cases children so deserted refuse to have anything to do with their parents when they visit, treating them with active avoidance, unlike their treatment of strangers. Betty I. was an example; she refused to have anything to do with her mother when she visited her in her foster-home and continued to avoid her when at length she returned home. Love is impossible if hate is entrenched.

In the human mind, unlike the dog's, such a mood of hatred tends to perpetuate itself through phantasy. To hate a person is to conjure up a picture of him as bad and evil and bent on enmity towards oneself. For a child to hate his mother is for him to picture her as not merely frustrating but filled with emotions of animosity and revenge. Phantasy, born of rage, thus distorts the picture of the real mother. A kindly mother who has to put her child in a hospital, a frustrating yet well-meaning mother and a really unkind mother can, by this process, alike come to be regarded as malicious and hostile figures. The dreadful nightmares of a horrifying dream-lady which beset Norman K. probably originated in this way. The child thus comes to be haunted by bad objects, with the familiar result that he comes to regard himself also as a bad object. Whether this is wholly through the process of introjection or whether primary self-reproach for having hateful feelings towards the loved object also plays a part is at present not clear, though I incline personally to the view that both factors operate. In any case the child's picture of himself becomes as distorted as his picture of his mother. He comes to see himself as a bad, unloveworthy child and interprets circumstances accordingly.

One of the Affectionless thieves, Derrick O'C., showed this tendency very strikingly. Over a long period he came regularly to see me once a week. He proved unexpectedly co-operative and did much to unearth the causes of his own stealing, but he was always pathetically anxious to please and was obviously worried when he was unable to answer some query I might make. One day when he came his presence was overlooked in the hall and I was told he had not arrived. This was not surprising as he had slunk in so quietly with other patients and re-mained so quiet that the doorkeeper had simply not seen him. However, on going into the hall 45 minutes later I found him patiently waiting, and, since I had a little time to spare, arranged to see him. The analysis soon got on to his fear of people punishing him, and I asked him if he sometimes felt I might punish him. To this he replied that he thought his being kept waiting so long in the hall was my way of punishing him for not always answering my questions. Such a misinterpretation implies not only that the analyst is a bad and hostile person, but also that the patient is bad and worthy only of punishment.

Now such misconceptions regarding both the motives of others and of their own unloveworthiness, in each case the result of phantasy, are common to all neurotics. Normally, however, these misconceptions coexist with other, more realistic conceptions of the situation, with the result that object-relationships continue possible, though disturbed. The Affectionless thief on the other hand seems to be dominated by these phantasies; the real situation is obliterated. This, it would appear, is the result of the separation they have suffered being a prolonged one. Normally when such phantasies arise in children they are soon corrected to some degree by contact with the real mother, who, whatever her shortcomings, is never so bad as the bad mother which the child pictures to himself when he is in a rage. The mere presence of the real mother, therefore, almost irrespective of what she does, will go far to offset the phantasy figure and so will reassure the child as regards both her and himself. But where a child does not see his mother for many months there is no opportunity for this correction of phantasy by reality-testing to operate. Extravagant phantasies of the kind described then become so entrenched that, when the child returns to the real situation, he can see it in no terms but those of his phantasies. The progressive modification of phantasy by contact with reality is thus stultified and the child is doomed to see both himself and the world of people as reflections of his own angry and horrifying conceptions of them. And the result is that both he and they appear untrustworthy and unloveworthy.

The presence of such phantasies goes far to account for the suspicion, secrecy and guilt which characterize these children. For instance, Betty I. and Derrick O'C. were said never to ask for anything, which suggests that they expected to be given nothing and felt they deserved nothing. Moreover, several patients gave their spoils away to other children, again suggesting a feeling that they ought not to have anything.

Two principal causes of an inability to form and maintain loving relationships have been proposed, the failure of development of the capacity owing to absence of opportunity at a critical period and the inhibition of love by rage and the phantasies resulting from rage. There is one other factor which is probably also important, perhaps particularly so in the child who suffers separation at the age of two or three. This is the determination at all costs not to risk again the disappointment and the resulting rages and longings which wanting someone very much and not getting them involves. If we are indifferent to others or dislike them we disarm them of any power to hurt us. Now this *indifference* was absolutely characteristic of every one of these children, although in some cases it was little more than skin-deep. They neither showed affection nor appeared to care whether they got it. "Whatever we do," we might imagine them saying, "do not let us care too much for anyone. At all costs let us avoid any risk of allowing our hearts to be broken again." This, I think, is the explanation of much of their hard-boiledness and apparent indifference, traits which puzzle and irritate almost everyone who has to deal with them. It is a policy of self-protection against the slings and arrows of their own turbulent feelings.

4

Conscience in the Psychopath

Phyllis Greenacre

Phyllis Greenacre's paper, first read at a New York conference on April 26, 1945, and subsequently published in the *American Journal of Orthopsychiatry*, established the critical groundwork for the later superego theories of Jacobson and Kernberg. She emphasizes two psychodynamics: first, the projected aggressive impulses of the child in response to frustration as a part-object of the parent; and second, the pathologically narcissistic milieu of the family in which the child takes on a "show window display role." What *seems* to be is more valued than what *is*. If remnants of conscience appear in the psychopath, they are often isolated and useless. As she concludes, it is "a gossamer substance, shot with magic, valued only as an adornment."

This paper will discuss the faulty structural development of the conscience in a group of patients within the larger one generally designated as *constitutional psychopaths* or *psychopathic personalities*. This diagnostic classification has tended to be a catch-all for patients who show repeated evidence of antisocial behavior without symptoms belonging to the classical neurotic or psychotic pictures. The behavior of the patients here described is primarily characterized by impulsiveness and marked irresponsibility, intense but labile emotional states, and generally quixotic and superficial love relationships. These patients are not deliberate offenders; they lie and steal impulsively, especially under pressure. They sign bad checks or impulsively forge another's name, marry on the spur of the moment, and as often impulsively run away from a marriage or a job. Characteristically, they appear to live in the moment, with great intensity, acting without plan and seemingly without concern for the consequences. Indeed, the lack of practical appreciation of time and the inability to learn from experience stand out as cardinal symptoms. They are the living antithesis of the saying, "A burnt child dreads the fire," since they repeat the same fiascos time and again in an impressively self-destructive fashion. There is usually poor tolerance of pain. Alcoholism, drug addiction, polymorphous sexual

43

perversions may be associated secondary symptoms. Homosexual tendencies appear in a high percentage of cases, and there appears to be a special predisposition to homosexuality inherent in the very structure of the personality.* This group was formerly described as moral imbeciles.

The cases which I have especially scrutinized belong to the private patient group; they are all patients seen in consultation or in private psychiatric hospitals with which I was associated. While this is obviously a selected subdivision of the entire group, and may not be generally representative, it is one which presents better opportunity for investigation because there is a higher degree of cooperation and less concealment on the part of both the patient and his relatives than in groups composed of patients who are hospitalized because they are already in practical conflict with the law. Further, the psychopath seen in private practice generally comes from a relatively secure economic background, and there is not the same mass of socio-economic factors forming a backdrop and complicating the picture, factors which, in my opinion, are generally secondary reinforcing involvements, which may be used as rationalizations by the patient; they assume an undue prominence in the patients seen in city hospitals and court clinics.

All private practitioners of psychiatry see a few psychopaths in consultation. Since they generally are not amenable to treatment, they pass from view fairly quickly and it is seldom possible to study them intensively. Psychoanalysis rarely has turned its microscope upon them as they generally have neither patience, willingness nor emotional capacity to be analyzed. The present study, utilizing freely psychoanalytic concepts and knowledge, is based on the investigation of the detailed biographical records of fourteen patients, the data being given by relatives, friends, and the patient.

It is my intention to indicate the essentially defective character of the conscience of these patients, and to point out the location and origin of the special defects, coming as they do from a pervasive infiltration of certain unfavorable products of the earliest narcissism, which distorts the sense of reality and devitalizes and degrades the conscience in characteristic ways.

Editor's Note: This is not true among psychopaths. Their sexuality is more accurately described as "polymorphously perverse" wherein their sex-object choice is dictated by opportunity rather than by emotion or attachment.

If one examines from a purely descriptive angle the irresponsible behavior of the psychopath, one is struck not only by the unplannedness and lack of deliberation of the untoward behavior, but especially by the total practical disregard of consequences even though these are clearly known to him. He behaves as though such consequences were meant for the other man, but not for him; as though he will in some way be exempt, or will be miraculously saved. He seems to live only in a series of present moments, without real consideration for past or future. Such consideration as is expressed smacks generally of lip-service and lacks emotional tone, depth, and conviction. This same lack of emotional depth, the substitution of the symbol of gesture or word for the accomplished act seems to characterize the behavior throughout. Such patients are frequently verbalistic, plausible, and charming. They commonly make a very good first impression but lack perseverance and become impatient. They behave repeatedly *as if* they had accomplished some intention, and are offended or non-understanding when others do not accept the intention as the deed, especially if it has been accompanied by the gesture. For example, such a patient, who may have "borrowed" money without asking, states that he intends to repay, and then acts exactly as though the restitution were already accomplished, and is righteously outraged when he is called to account. If punished, he not infrequently regards the punishment as unfair in view of his having behaved so properly, and is no way deterred from a repetition of the same situation. It is characteristic, too, of such patients that they rarely deliberately evade punishment except by flight, though they cleverly talk themselves out of many predicaments by their plausibility.

It has been said that the conscience is the heir of the oedipus complex, that is, with the relinquishment of the demand for sexual gratification from the parent at the beginning of the latency period, the process of incorporation of the parental standards which has been going on for some time is given a special integrative impetus, through the identification with the parent of the same sex, and the more definite formation of ideals based on the parental images. All this occurs at a time when, with the first experiences in school, there is some practical separation of the child from the parents and the addition of a new set of adults, chiefly teachers, as quasi-parent figures. This, too, is the time when conspicuously there is a special reinforcement and vitalization of the child's concept of the future, of the relinquishment of immediate satisfactions in the interest of future gain. This is an area in which there is special damage to the future psychopath, damage resulting not alone from the trauma or other unfortunate influences which may befall the child at this time, but also from the reaction of these on an already specially distorted sense of reality and impaired emotional reactivity.

Obviously the conscience does not spring fully formed from the oedipus situation. Children, long before the age of five or six, have some standards of right and wrong, of property possession, of restraint in activities which will harm others, and in other particulars. Probably the main sources of the pre-oedipal conscience lie first in the almost automatically established control of uncomfortably large amounts of infantile aggression, and second in the semi-organic conception of code and order which is crystallized in the formation of habits, especially those meeting the bodily needs of ingestion and of excretion. The early roots of the conscience in the erection of threatening fantasy parental figures countering and reproducing the young child's own increased aggression was indicated by Freud when he stated in *Civilization and Its Discontents* that "the original severity of the super-ego does not—or not so much—represent the severity which has been experienced or anticipated from the object, but expresses the child's own aggressiveness toward the latter." (This was early indicated in the analysis of Little Hans.) We can understand this as stemming from a time in the infant's development when its realization of its own separateness from the mother is incomplete, and as part of this the operation of the introjection-projection mechanism is prolonged and strengthened.[1] Any influences which tend to increase the quantity of the infantile aggression (such as illness, discomfort, frustration, and restraint) or to delay the sense of separateness will then tend to strengthen this original root of the conscience. As has been pointed out by Melanie Klein (1944) and others, these primitive parental images are monstrous and terrifying and arouse in themselves great anxiety. "They call out violent defensive mechanisms—which are unethical and asocial in their nature." I would agree with Klein that this heightened aggression of earliest childhood with its reflected severity of primitive threatening figures is of the utmost importance in the development of schizophrenics. I believe that

---

[1]Gesell has noted that children between two and one-half and three and one-half, at first tentatively, then with considerable elaboration, often develop imaginary companions, sometimes human, sometimes animals, and that these serve as alteregos, genuine scapegoats on occasion. This seems to coincide with the child's own definite awareness of his own identity, which is not accomplished, however, without regret and recapitulation of the past, as though he had to reassimilate the fact of his growth from babyhood to this stage. (Cf. Gesell, Ilg, et al, *Infant and Child in the Culture of Today, etc.*, pp. 210–211.) Interestingly Gesell also remarks that this is a time especially when authority about any specific situation should not be divided between father and mother.

it may also be one of the important contributing factors in some psychopaths, only, however, if it combines with certain later elements which form the essential nucleus for the character deformation of the psychopath. One must quite clearly recognize that these reflected or projected images are at the time of their inception in no way a conscience, but are reacted to by the child as though they were totally outside of himself. Their strength, however, does influence the intensity of that part of the later conscience development which is based on the fear of punishment and of authority. These primitive conscience roots will be further dealt with in this paper in the discussion of the feelings of guilt of the psychopath.

While disturbances of character formation springing from attitudes developed in response to toilet and feeding training may occur in the psychopath, and seem in some instances to determine the special form of sexual perversions, they are not in themselves more characteristic of the psychopath than of many other psychic disturbances.

In reviewing the life stories of a number of psychopaths, certain configurations of parent–child relationship recurred with considerable frequency. I shall attempt to give first a kind of composite picture, and then illustrate them with specific clinical examples.

It is a little startling to note how many of the psychopaths seen in private practice come from families in which the father or the grandfather has been an unusually prominent and respected man. This is strikingly obvious when one compares a group of psychopaths with a similar number of schizophrenics or of manic-depressives. I think, therefore, that this observation is of true significance and not merely an artifact due to the selectiveness of private practice in contrast to the situations of the public clinic or hospital. Indeed, among the parents or near forebears of these patients are a large number of people whose very work or professions put them in positions of conspicuous public trust and authority, as clergymen, judges, heads of schools, civic leaders, or in humbler walks of life, policemen, detectives, truant officers. They are the "fathers" to their communities as well as to their children, and stand out as symbolic collective paternal figures. An old proverb that ministers' sons and deacons' daughters come to no good end is probably a general recognition of this frequent occurrence of the irresponsible child in the families of the conspicuously righteous.*

---

*Editor's Note: As a "preacher's kid" myself, I certainly react to this statement personally, but research indicates that socioeconomic status is *not* related to the "aggressive narcissism" or interpersonal-affective component of psychopathy. Unfortunately, the influence of religious upbringing upon psychopathy has yet to be studied.

Further, investigation of the biographical data generally reveals marked discrepancies and conflicts in the parental attitudes in regard to authority, independence, and the goals of achievement. In my experience there is most frequently a stern, respected, and often obsessional father who is remote, preoccupied, and fear-inspiring in relation to his children; and an indulgent, pleasure-loving, frequently pretty but frivolous mother who is often tacitly contemptuous of her husband's importance. While there may be a different distribution of character traits between the parents, there is generally a marked discrepancy or definite conflict in the parental ideals and attitudes toward the child's immediate experiences. The contrast, too, between the brave façade presented to the world and the conflict and misery behind it is often most conspicuous.

In such family configurations, generally both parents are highly narcissistic in their more than ordinary dependence on the approval or admiration of their contemporaries. There is further basically a poor relationship between the parents and the infant from its earliest days. Pride, or its dark counterpart of shame, plays too big a part between parents and child, and substitutes for or counterfeits love. In the groups of patients whose biographies I studied it was appallingly evident that these children were not greatly loved, and that what might appear as an excess of love was generally an excess of indulgence of solicitude.

Both the inner and outer psychic situations of the parents, with their overvaluation on external appearances, tends to promote a kind of show window display role for the child, with a premium on formally good behavior for the sake of reflecting favorably on the parents. Where, as is often the case, the mother has an even deeper narcissistic attachment to the child, essentially regarding it always as though it were still only a part of and manifestation of herself, it is obvious that the sense of separateness and individuation is delayed in the child. In consequence of this there may be a strengthening of the introjective-projective stage of development and (seemingly paradoxically) an intensification of the externalized punitive figures as already indicated. The longer the child is treated as though only a part of the parent, the greater will be the aggression against the parent reflected commensurately in exaggerated fear-inspiring parental figures. This aggression of need for separation is different in origin and probably in quality from the aggression arising in response to early physical discomforts or illness. The family situation I am describing tends to increase very much the exhibitionistic component of the child's narcissism, to exaggerate grotesquely its fear and awe of the parents, and to dilute or stunt the development of healthy love impulses.

Further than this, the actual position of the father in "typical" situations tends in reality to comply with and verify the frightening images which the child has raised, in as much as the father is often distant, awe inspiring and something of a frightening demi-god, lacking the substance and vital warmth which are part of good object-relationships. Such children are treated as though they must not fail. They are habitually on show, and failures are either denied, concealed, or explained away. Thus they are robbed of the full measure of reality testing[2] and performance even in the earliest years becomes measured largely by its appearance rather than by its intrinsic accomplishment. One sees in miniature the attitudes which later are so characteristic of the psychopath, i.e., what *seems* to be is more valued than what *is*. This characteristic, together with the essential emotional impoverishment, tends to create a very thin stage-property vision of reality in which the façade at any given time is the prime consideration.

Under these circumstances a highly ambivalent attitude toward the parents and toward all authority inevitably develops. The magic father is feared by the child but at the same time there is an extension of the magic over-valuation to the child himself, and the frequent actual exemptions from consequences of his behavior because he is his father's son; or on the positive side, his acceptance as his father's son rather than because of attainment of his own. Here again actual experience may promote and seem to accede to just those narcissistic fantasies of magic omnipotence which have already grown to undue proportions.

The degradation of the sense of reality by the opportunistic need to be pleasing seems in these children to develop early a charm and a tact which gives the semblance of responsiveness and consideration for others, but which generally later is unmasked in all its superficiality, and may be the foundation of a later adroitness in managing people which savors of blackmail.

The Oedipus period is a particularly vulnerable time in these developing personalities. The contradictory maternal indulgence and paternal austerity tend to bind the child unduly to the mother and at the same

---

[2]Aichhorn has described well the way in which the indulgent mother protects the child from reality, out of self-indulgent vanity. He further mentions almost precisely the configuration I have described of the stern father and the indulgent mother, and the way in which the child flees from one to the other to escape reality and ends by rebelling against both (*Wayward Youth*, Viking Press, 1935, p. 203). Wall (1936) and Heaver (1944), working with psychopaths treated in hospital setting, have also been impressed with this family configuration and its resulting influences.

time to promote the formation of peculiarly unreal and gauzy ideals. The psychopath generally has very "high" ideals but they are especially expansive, and utterly detached from reality. There is an unsuccessful effort on the part of the boy to identify with the father, but this is not possible because of the severity and remoteness of the paternal image, and tends to promote a bisexual identification. At the same time the boy remains in a prolonged emotional subjugation to the mother and never clearly comes through the Oedipus struggle. Many psychopaths, in their later life, seem to be repeatedly reenacting this stage of their life in one relationship after another. Even so the apparent Oedipus struggle is conspicuously superficial, presenting a kind of surface show, simultaneous or alternating with strong homosexual tendencies, reproducing the inverted elements in the original Oedipus situation. All this is quite striking in the clinical examples which follow.

The bisexuality of these patients has been thought by some to be due to disturbances of the sexual development arising at a time when there was already awareness of special pleasure from the genital area, but when appreciation of the anatomical differences between the sexes was not yet secure (the protophallic stage of Jones). This may be true but the biographical material which I have does not contain sufficiently detailed data to warrant a conclusive interpretation of this as a primary site of disturbance.[3] Certainly, so it seems to me, children with a delayed sense of separateness from the mother, may as part of this general condition, have also a delayed and uncertain appreciation of sexual differences, the prolonged confusion on this score being part of the broader based disturbance of reality differentiation between *what is I* or *what belongs to*

---

[3]Wittels (1938) develops this as the central point of the psychopath's sexual pathology, and believes that there is a secondary fixation in the oedipal phase. He considers the disturbances of behavior as desexualized displacements. His presentation is persuasive but his interpretations seemingly are arrived at largely by theoretical deduction, and since his illustrations are almost exclusively from characters of literature or mythology which he considers as exaggeratedly "pure" examples, there is little detailed supporting clinical evidence. His paper is "based on the principle that the structure of the sex life gives shape to the neurosis and also to the psychopathy." It seems to me rather that the psychopathy like the psychosis is given shape primarily by the distortion of the ego development and that the structure of the sex life is accordingly disturbed and then gives rise to additional complicating factors. My findings differ from Wittel's in respect to the latency period. He states that the latency period in the pure protophallic psychopath shrinks almost to nothing. My cases differ from this. I was, in fact, impressed with how smooth the latency period was or seemed to be in many cases.

me and *what is his/hers,* or *belongs to him/her,* which includes others than the mother. I believe, however, that such a confusion is very much increased and generally gains significance by the difficulties of identification mentioned and which were uniformly present in the cases I studied.

Case I. This was a young woman of twenty, in her second year of college. She had made a suicidal gesture by taking a non-lethal overdose of sedatives. This occurred when the patient felt rejected and gossiped about in connection with a homosexual triangular affair with two fellow students. She was unusually attractive, obviously bright, quite animated, and at the time I saw her, only a day or two after the suicidal attempt, she was not really depressed.

The patient has been recognized as presenting especial problems since about her sixteenth year, when she had been expelled from preparatory school for a rather harmless prank. This was the only point on which she showed her contempt for the school authority. She had had the sympathy of her family at this time as her mother and sister felt the punishment had been overly severe. In the boarding school where she next went she made a brilliant record scholastically and was a class leader. She graduated at eighteen. In this period she experienced her first homosexual arousal, which appears to have come about spontaneously; at least, not through seduction. After a few months at college, which she chose in order to be close to her best girl friend (with whom there had been no overt homosexual relationship), she ran away with a boy from an adjacent college, intending to marry him, and representing herself as having done so. The upshot of this was that both were expelled from college and were married shortly thereafter. A few months later the patient had a brief intense infatuation for her husband's best friend, and divorced her husband.

All this died down quickly and the following fall she re-entered college. Here, while she did quite good academic work, she launched into a homosexual affair with a conspicuously masculine girl, then changed to another homosexual partner, and at the same time carried on an affair with a young doctor by whom she became pregnant. During the summer of that year (she was then 19) she attached one man after another. She conspicuously chose married men, and seemingly preferred men who were married to her female relatives. At one time, then, she took an overdose of sedatives in a suicidal attempt. On returning to college in the fall, she found her two earlier homosexual partners united in an alliance from which she was excluded. It was in this setting that she made the suicidal attempt which caused her to be brought to me. This was a repetition of the suicidal attempt a few months earlier.

I next heard of her a year and a half later when she again made a suicidal attempt. In the meantime, she had developed a sudden infatuation for a paternal cousin, who was then living with another woman. She succeeded in displacing this woman and set up an establishment with her cousin, spending more than half of a recent inheritance to furnish their place. She showed more attachment to him than to any of the previous men, stayed with him for more than a year in spite of some discomforts. She made two suicidal gestures, one by attempting to throw herself into a river, and the other by cutting her wrist, when she was piqued and made jealous by this man's waning interest in her.

This girl was the younger of two sisters by six and a half years. The parents were outstanding. The father's family contained several members who were sufficiently well known that the surname itself brought some recognition. The father was a brilliant man, an educator who had attained an unusual position of trust and respect early in life, but had somehow not sustained his early promise. This grandfather of the patient had thrown over a position of considerable prestige in a fit of pique, and not long thereafter withdrew from his marriage with apparent suddenness, divorced his wife, remarried, and died, all within the course of a few years.

The mother was a brilliant, aggressive woman of a substantial family. First a teacher, she later became interested in educational psychology. During our patient's early childhood the mother was building up a position of considerable note in well-publicized but creditable efforts to bring precise scientific methods into child psychology.

Our patient was a healthy baby, active, pretty and precocious. She always had to be coaxed to eat, but otherwise was not thought to show any early problems. She talked early with remarkable facility. According to her own recollection, she did not see a great deal of her busy mother except in the evening. During her fourth and fifth years her father was away at service in the first World War and she missed him greatly, especially as she felt she was his favorite rather than her exceedingly brilliant older sister whom she imagined her mother preferred. From her third to sixth year she was a special visitor in the first grade of a school in which her mother was interested. She was both proud and jealous of her sister, whom she tormented consistently in a way which the parents considered cute. She was photographed much, and was frequently used as illustrations for her mother's lectures. Later, in temper outbursts, she spoke in frank resentment of feeling she had been displayed "as a guinea pig." Always in the background were her godparents, a childless couple who were her own parents' best friends. At nine when she was vaguely ill (coincident in time with the more obvious disruption of the home) she was taken care of by this couple, but their home was not any warmer than her own. The godfather, a man of considerable repute as a scientist, was capricious, erratic, and rather uncertainly stern, while his wife was a worried, indulgent, fretful woman, unhappy with her husband and overprotective with the child.

The following year her own father seceded from the family and she saw little of him afterward. When patient was thirteen, her mother received considerable public notice because of certain attainments, and almost at once collapsed in a severe melancholia which was to last for some time. The child was again sent to the godparents to be cared for, but her unhappiness there caused her to be placed in a boarding school. It was here that her overt rebellion against authority began. It should further be mentioned that the patient's father died very shortly before her elopement with the college student, the beginning of her frantic series of sexual alliances. While she herself did not express any awareness of the connection between these events, the timing of relationship was striking.

This history is given in great factual detail in order that it may speak for itself in regard to the emotional impoverishment of this girl, overlaid by displays of attention which really promoted her exhibitionism and made it, perhaps, her most dependable adaptive function. The indulgence and austerity were not allocated so precisely to mother and father, respectively, as I have somewhat schematically described in a "typical" situation, but the contrast was there, involving the character of both parents and reinforced by the quite "typical" godparents. The further complete collapse, not only of the parental relationship but of the parents themselves during the girl's adolescence appears as a tragic enlargement of the shadowy part of the earlier picture. Especially striking, too, in this case, is the triangular character of the sexual relationships in which the patient became progressively involved, and in which she generally ended as the excluded third member.

Case II. An unusually handsome young man in his late twenties came to psychiatric attention because of periodic alcoholism, especially marked during the preceding four years. In addition, he seemed unable to hold a job beyond a few weeks or months, habitually borrowed money which he did not return, and on a number of occasions removed money from the cash drawer wherever he happened to be working. He had held jobs varying in character from ditch digging to clerical work, had never been able to support himself, much less his wife and child. He had married his wife in an elopement while drunk, but seemed fond of her and was considered to be extremely devoted to his young son. In general he was genial, easy going, optimistic, made friends readily, but generally lost them through "borrowing" from them. When he was drunk he talked about leaving his family and sometimes of killing himself, but made no gesture of carrying it out. After the birth of his child, he became more irresponsible.

His irresponsible behavior was the more striking in that he was the son of a father who was interested in all aspects of education. The father, a quiet, thoughtful man, showed in his statement about the boy that he had a pretty clear but detached descriptive idea of the boy's shortcomings, but surprisingly little thought of their origin. The patient was the youngest of a fairly large family, "spoiled by the mother" and, according to the father, had never developed any serious purpose in life, had seemed always to have things made easy for him, and expected to have things done for him. He seemed to have an unjustified confidence in his own ability, evaded rather than lied outright, and was a chronic procrastinator. He was respectful to and afraid of his father, and very much attached to his mother who felt the bond between them was so close that each could sense how the other would feel in any given situation. The father had been especially severe with his son in order to counteract the mother's indulgence, but it had never done any good. The father was now inclined to resort to the old explanation that the boy had a congenital deficiency of character, had been born soft, as it were. One felt from the father's account, that he had long been disappointed in his son or that he was himself an habitually withdrawn, emotionally detached man. The mother, on the other hand, was a voluble, fulsome woman, rather exhibitionistic in appearance and in the vivid dramatic quality with which she gave her account of her relation to her son. The biographical facts given are put together in chronological form from the statements of all three: mother, father and patient.

The patient was a healthy baby. His mother prided herself on her abundant maternity and clung to his babyhood especially as he was the youngest. A rather sensual appearing woman in general, she spoke directly of the very special pleasure which nursing gave her and of her efforts to prolong his nursing for her own gratification. She had frequently appeared nude before the boy since he was a baby and encouraged him to do likewise, regarding this as evidence of their freedom from any unhealthy inhibitions. When he was about five, the patient had a period of nocturnal enuresis. When he wet his bed, he would then get into his mother's bed, cuddle up to her and attempt to nurse. She repulsed him, insisted on his staying in his own bed, and the enuresis cleared up. During the years until he was twelve, the family traveled much, and he went to many different schools both here and abroad. The mother felt "that it was a liberal education for the boy simply to be his parents' son, as there were always so many distinguished people around and that to be able to go to a man like his father and ask questions was to get a sensible education of real value."

The emptiness of this conception is further emphasized by the facts that the boy was chronically afraid of his father's sarcasm, and that he was not permitted to eat at table with his father until he was twelve, after which he was sent away to school. His later retaliative exploitation of these cultural advantages was clear when on one occasion in his early twenties he telephoned his parents who were then entertaining the President of the United States at dinner to tell them that he had stolen a hundred dollars from the cash drawer of his employer and was in immediate danger of apprehension. In the period from age six to twelve there was no conspicuous trouble with this affable charming boy except that he was indolent. On being sent to a rather formal school at age twelve, he began to truant. He was then sent to a boarding school, where he became attached to both the headmaster and his wife.

He had respected his father, but stood in awe of him. His mother had disciplined him by spanking even up to age fourteen. For major offenses he was sent to his father whose scornful sarcasm he dreaded. In pre-paratory school he made quite a good relationship with the headmaster whom he found both fair and approachable. It was the one place he liked to return to later. In this period, he barely passed academically, but did somewhat better in the extramural activities, dramatics, and athletics, which were more akin to his mother's interests. He did not really care very much for any of it. He failed his first year in college, and was withdrawn and "put to work."

Then the underlying instability began to flower. He truanted from work—loafing or sleeping instead, began to drink somewhat and fre-quented rather low saloons. Sexually, he was rather prim. At nine he had been made the subject of a sexual demonstration by a little girl of twelve. In his preparatory school and college days he was less experi-mental sexually than most of his classmates. He had many very thinly veiled incestuous dreams about his mother toward whom he regarded himself as so commendably free. She dissuaded him from an engage-ment at twenty which she considered socially inappropriate. When he married, it was only accomplished under the influence of liquor. In his marriage, he was a cunnilinguist, and this seemed to him so much the height of sensual pleasure that he believed any man who said he did not do this was a liar!

The special neurotic shape of the symptoms, with the fixation on the oral sucking interest is glaringly obvious in this patient's history. I am more concerned now, however, with the broader influences of his relationship to his parents which seems to me to follow quite typically the pattern which was indicated at the beginning of this paper: the fear-inspiring remote father, the indulgent, extraordinarily vain mother, who not only indulged this boy but used him as a kind of specially provided organ for her own gratification; the complete façade of the emotional relationships to both parents and the ridiculous mockery of education which resulted. While this situation undermines the capacity for love relationships, and in so doing further defrauds the sense of reality and impairs the development of the conscience as already described, one must also realize that these influences exist continuously in the patient's life from his earliest days until he leaves his parents' home. The character changes which have their inception early are generally fostered by the continuation of these very same influences later and there is no need or even opportunity for change until the patient feels it from the encroachment of the world's demands. It might be said that the charming opportunistic versatility of this type of psychopath is the best adaptation possible if the world consisted only of his parents. Quite often his overt disturbances of stealing and lying appear in troubling proportions only when he is forced by growth or accident to make a pretense of responsibility. In this respect this group of psychopaths differs from those in which there is a larger schizoid element, with the predominance of early, semiorganically aroused aggression and a different configuration of the conscience, due to a greater reaction to the underlying sense of guilt.

This brings us to the consideration of the sense of guilt. It is not my intention to deal exhaustively with the complicated subject of the sense of guilt or to try to trace out all of the source of the neurotic and psychotic guilt feelings, which like anxiety form the center of so many vicious circles of psychic disturbance; but rather to limit my discussion so far as possible to what seems to me characteristic of the group of psychopaths I have described. It has been said that the psychopath has no guilt feelings, no conscience (the potentialities of a conscience have never been internalized and what remains is only a fear of external punishment), and no psychic mechanisms of defense; some descriptions state that he has no anxiety. If all this were true, I believe that the psychopath would not live very long, but would explode from the force of his own primitive aggression. It would seem that these characterizations may be due either to attempts to place the psychopath too precisely as a clinical entity in psychiatric nosology and psychoanalytic theory, or to see a special group as representing the whole group; and in general to therapeutic discouragement on the part of the doctor with a consequent retreat to a descriptive point of view. Certainly many psychopaths behave at times as though they had almost no conscience, no defense restraints, and no anxiety. In my own clinical experience I have yet to see the patient who was as completely primitive as such a conscienceless fearless creature would be.

The sense of guilt presumably is a product of and roughly commensurate with the strength of the self-critical faculties of the conscience. These in turn, are based on the internalized controls (commands, punishments, and rewards of discipline) reinforced by the primitive fantasies, which had appeared originally as projections of the child's own aggression before the precipitation of the conscience. The origin of this very early aggression has already been described as coming from the somatic discomforts and frustrations of the infant, but especially in the psychopath from the increased need for separation from the mother due to the specific type of maternal narcissistic attachment to the infant. The very attitude of the mother which arouses this aggression also tends to retard and impair the internalization process. Consequently the psychopath often has vivid and fantastic threatening authoritative figures which are only comparatively little internalized with which he seems to play hide and seek both inside and outside himself.[4]

There are two other very early conditions which seem to influence the formation of the conscience and especially to promote the tendency to the formation of strong guilt feelings: (1) the predisposition to anxiety which heightens the anxiety pitch in the later vicissitudes of life; and (2) a special negative narcissistic relation to the parents which *is* prominent in the histories of many psychopaths. These two factors sometimes cooperate, though it is the second which is most characteristic of the psychopath. In regard to the first, the same conditions of somatic frustration and discomfort in early infancy which produce such a heightening of infantile aggression, may produce also a degree of infantile tension which subsequently combines with current anxiety in disastrous proportions. Anxiety in itself carries with it the psychic element of anxious anticipation, which in these cases then becomes expanded into a kind of expectation of doom, as it is amalgamated with guilt feelings. One sees this commonly in the psychotic, both the depressed patient and the schizophrenic who confess themselves the greatest sinners on earth. More characteristic of the psychopath's guilt feelings is the factor of the negative narcissistic relation to the parents. Where

---

[4]It is interesting, too, that under fever or intoxication the psychopath readily breaks down in delirious episodes in which such primitive figures run rampant.

this is true, the child is also overly attached to both parents, especially to the mother; but instead of being a specially favored part or organ of the mother, it is regarded by her with shame and as evidence of her guilt. The child seems to imbibe this from its earliest days and takes over this guilt and generally both rebels against and succumbs to it.

This was quite clear in the cases of two young women patients who were psychopathic prostitutes. Both had been the object of shame on the part of their mothers, and reproach from their fathers; in the one instance because the father knew, and in the other because he suspected that the child was not his. In both cases the mother indulged, favored, and defended, but was indubitably ashamed of the little one in a way which built up a striking but dark counterpart of the magic distinction so clear in the second case given in detail in this paper. In one instance the father was a detective, and in the other a court bailiff; both were alcoholic. Thus here again was the exaggerated paternal authoritative figure, but inconsistent in its rightness, and feared rather than respected.

Helen Deutsch (1942) in an article on some forms of emotional disturbance related to schizophrenia describes several patients who present clinical pictures somewhat similar to what has been described in this paper. Since her paper deals largely with the nature of the disturbance of the sense of reality rather than with the conscience of the patients, the focus is different. She remarks that the "emptiness and . . . lack of individuality so evident in the emotional life appear also in the moral structure" and sees the ideals and convictions of such patients as being "simply reflections of another person, good or bad." In my patients I have been more impressed by the remoteness and unusability of their ideals than by their changing suggestible character. The ideals seemed reproductions of the fantasies of the magic grandeur of the parent(s) but unattached to the everyday life and exerting no leverage on it. Her description of the disturbed sense of reality in her patients is very similar to my own observations: these patients do not suffer from depersonalization because they have never been really personalized.

A number of recent writers, including Levy (1937), Bender and Yarnell (1941), Powdermaker (1937), Lowrey (1940), Goldfarb (1943), Ford (1938), as well as such older investigators as Healy (1929) and the Gluecks (1934), have pointed with varying degrees of intensity to the essential early emotional deprivation of psychopaths and delinquents. My own findings verify this. It seems, however, that there may be some differences in the special symptom pictures between those cases where this deprivation was by and large the *main* and very far-reaching disturbance as is the case in children reared from birth in institutions, and those here described who suffer an actual love deprivation even though camouflaged by indulgence.

An article by Dunn (1941) gives a good picture of the protean manifestations of the psychopathic personality and contains a survey of much of the recent literature. Henderson's (1939) lectures on the psychopathic states recognize the primary affect hunger, but in the broad basis of his description he appears to me to shy away from any deep understanding of the questions which he raises. He does bring up the question of the finely balanced trigger-reaction of many psychopaths. This is outside the scope of this paper, but it is an exceedingly interesting problem bearing on the relation of some psychopathic states to creative ability.

Cleckley (1941) in an engagingly vivid account of his clinical experiences with psychopaths proposes the term *semantic dementia* for the empty "as-if" behavior and especially for the speech of these patients, emphasizing that they make the proper gestures and say the proper things but without emotional depth or rootedness. He does not interpret the origin of this disturbance but appears to regard the state as regressive. While many of his clinical histories suggest the very problems of the parent–child relationship which I have pointed out, his reports do not contain detailed facts of the early childhood, and he seems to have been impressed by the goodness and respectability of the parents without recognizing the high degree of narcissism involved. In his cases, the overt symptoms had been long existent and the more remote history was obscured by the florid events of the recent past.

A recent book by Lindner (1944) gives a detailed and enthusiastic account of the hypnoanalytic treatment of a criminal psychopath. His presentation stresses certain early traumata, especially a single primal scene experience before the age of eight months. There was a resultant fear and hatred of the father, overattachment to the mother, and latent homosexuality followed by excessive masturbation and a classical fear of castration at the hands of the father. I cannot agree with all of Lindner's interpretations, nor with the validity of his skipping as unimportant so much of the material presented by his patient. Aside from this, he does not deal adequately with the development of the sense of self (ego development) and its defects, but appears to consider distortions as being due primarily to focal traumata. I think that his emphasis on the primal scene experience may have importance in the understanding of criminal psychopaths in a different way than the one in which he has presented it: the patient was exposed not to a single primal scene experience, but according to his own account, to a series of them.

It has long been my impression that repeated exposure of this kind in early childhood might be an additional source of overstimulation of infantile aggression and so play into other accumulations of early frustration, as well as causing a neurotic scoptophilia and other symptoms. How frequent and wide-spread such experiences are in families living in crowded conditions is readily apparent when one looks at the actual sleeping arrangements.[5] It may be an unrecognized psychological factor in slum life from which criminals so often emerge.

The monograph of Reich (1925) on the psychopath seems to me still the most valuable study of the structure of the character of the psychopath. While I would not wholly agree with some of Reich's differentiations of types nor perhaps with his statement of the way in which the conscience (superego) of the psychopath becomes isolated, his emphasis on the combination of the indulgence and severity of the parental figures and on the practical isolation of the conscience are quite in accord with the character structure which I have been describing. It appears to me that the isolation and unusability of the conscience in these patients is due largely to its gossamer substance, its being shot with magic and being valued as an adornment rather than for its utility. In other words it is as much the content of the conscience as its arrest before it is thoroughly introjected that is responsible for its lofty remoteness, even though the introjection itself is conspicuously poor.

REFERENCES

Bender, L. & Yarnell, H. (1941). An observation nursery. *Amer. J. Psychiat.*, 97:5.

Cleckley, H. (1941). *The Mask of Sanity.* Philadelphia: Mosby.

Deutsch, H. (1942). Some forms of emotional disturbance and their relationship to schizophrenia. *Psychoanal. Quart.*, 11:301–321.

Dunn, W. H. (1941). The psychopath in the armed forces. *Psychiatry*, 4: 251–259.

Ford, C. A. (1938). Institutional rearing as a factor in delinquency. Presented at Fourth Conf. on Education & the Exceptional Child. Child Research Clinic of the Woods School, May.

---

[5] An unpublished study by Judith Silberpfennig on sleeping arrangements in the families of adolescent patients on the psychiatric service at Bellevue [Hospital in New York City] reinforces my own impression of the inevitable constant sexual stimulation in the families of children in this social group.

Glueck, S. & Glueck, E. T. (1934). *Five Hundred Delinquent Women*. New York: Knopf.

Goldfarb, W. (1943). Infant rearing and problem behavior. *Amer. J. Orthopsychiat.*, 13:2.

Healy, W. (1929). *Reconstructing Behavior in Youth*. New York: Knopf.

Heaver, W. L. (1944). A study of forty male psychopathic personalities. *Amer. J. Psychiat.*, 100:342–346.

Henderson, D. K. (1939). *Psychopathic States*. New York: Norton.

Klein, M. (1944). The early development of conscience in the child. *Psycho-Anal. Today*, p. 66. New York: Covici-Friede Publishers.

Levy, D. (1937). Primary affect hunger. *Amer. J. Psychiat.*, 94:643–652.

Lindner, R. (1944). *Rebel Without a Cause*. New York: Grune & Stratton.

Lowrey, L. G. (1940). Personality distortion and early institutional care. *Amer. J. Orthopsychiat.*, 10:3.

Powdermaker, F. (1937). Psychopathology and treatment of delinquent girls. *Amer. J. Orthopsychiat.*, 7.

Reich, W. (1925). *Der Triebhafte Charakter*. Vienna: Internationaler Psychoanalytischer Verlag.

Wall, J. H. (1936). A study of alcoholism in men. *Amer. J. Psychiat.*, 92: 1389–1401.

Wittels, F. (1938). The position of the psychopath in the psychoanalytic system. *Internat. J. Psycho-Anal.*, 19:471–488.

5

Psychopathic Behavior Disorders in Children

Lauretta Bender

Lauretta Bender's paper was first published in the *Handbook of Correctional Psychology* in 1947. A psychiatrist, psychoanalyst, and inventor of the Bender-Gestalt test, Bender reviews the important observations of others concerning the psychopathologies of institutionalized children during World War II. She then offers her own cogent, experience-near observations of children at Bellevue Hospital. The beauty of this work, although she discounts biological contributions, is her insight into the interplay of attachment, identifications, affect, and intellectual development and her understanding of how aberrations in one domain of personality will dynamically change others.

In 10 years (1935–44) over 5000 preadolescent children (under 13 years of age) have been under observation on the Children's Ward of the Psychiatric Division of Bellevue Hospital. The majority (65% to 75%) of these children have presented problems in behavior with neurotic mechanisms. The causative factors have been conflicts and aggressive reaction to frustrations common to all of us in our culture but exaggerated in these children. Unsatisfactory experiences in their personal relationships are due to (1) inadequate and distorted parent–child relationships in the early childhood period (before five or six years of age), because of at least one absent or seriously asocial, psychotic, defective, or otherwise unsuitable parent; (2) social-economic-emotional deprivation in social minority groups; (3) serious language handicap, such as a language disability, including reading disability and intellectual limitations or a relatively alingual home. Usually only one of these factors is not enough to cause a serious behavior disorder in a child, so wide is the margin of safety in the developmental urge for normalcy.

Another 10% to 20% of the children are handicapped by some organic brain disorder, such as developmental defects or one of the degenerative, inflammatory or traumatic encephalopathies. The brain disorder alone may account for the behavior disorder if it is associated with a considerable disturbance in brain tissue or a progressive process, or if it is associated with epilepsy. However, in many of the traumatic encephalopathies and non-progressive inflammatory encephalopathies and developmental deviations, a behavior disorder, if it is present, will be found to be related to the conflicts, frustrations and deprivations subsequent to the pathological process and any related or incidental disturbance in family, social and language background. Children with progressive encephalitis or encephalopathy (especially with epilepsy) may present a psychopathic type of personality. In contrast to the psychopathic behavior disorders, however, they usually manifest some neurotic reactions such as anxiety, feelings of guilt, and inadequacy in response to the frustration imposed upon them by the organic pathology, especially if the frustration involves their interpersonal relationships. Such neurotic features are an aid in diagnosis, make the prognosis more favorable and offer the therapist an approach to the child that is often very gratifying in its results. Schizophrenia in childhood appears to be closely related to the progressive encephalopathies.* A neurotic response with anxiety to the frustrations which the schizophrenic personality must face is evident in the early stages and often confuses the diagnosis. However, this neurotic reaction is at present our only means of a therapeutic approach to the personality while the patterned functions are being disorganized by the schizophrenic process.

There still remains a group of children representing 5% to 10% of the whole which we will refer to as psychopathic behavior disorders in children. This group of children presents a clinical picture which forms a syndrome in that the causative factors in the early life of the individual are known, the developmental course may be anticipated, the behavior pattern is typical and closely resembles the classical description of the so-called constitutional psychopathic personality. Moreover, psychological tests for personality show a specific patterning and the response to various treatment programs is known.

The study of these children has resulted in important contributions to modern psychopathology. It not only has thrown light on the question of the psychopathic personality, but has made possible a preventive program and also has brought new data to some controversial problems about the normal personality structure and the development of various personality functions and dysfunctions.

Editor's Note: Subsequent research has not supported this idea.

The cause of the condition is emotional deprivation in the infantile period due to a lack or a serious break in parent–child relationship, for example, the child who has spent considerable time in infancy or early childhood in an institution without any affectional ties, or a child who has been transferred from one foster home to another with critical breaks in the continuity of affectional patterns. The defect is in the ability to form relationships, to identify themselves with others and, consequently, in conceptualization of intellectual, emotion and social problems and asocial or unsocial behavior. The developmental processes in the personality become fixated at the earliest stage; there are no satisfactions derived from human experiences and no anxieties because there are no conflicts. The ego is defective and there is no superego. After a certain period this fixation in the development of the personality can no longer be overcome or corrected because a therapeutic or transference relationship can not be obtained. This is the reason for the difficulties in treatment. Prevention is possible by avoiding such deprivation in the early infantile period and insuring against critical breaks in the continuity of close personal relationships in a family circle, from the early weeks of life until the child is well out of the infantile period and in the middle childhood period.

Once a child can exhibit independent behavior, enter into new relationships with adults and children—as the child does when he goes to school at the age of 5 or 6 years—he can show that his personality has safely developed beyond the period when such breaks or deprivation will any longer be critical. Freud originally placed the superego development at 3 1/2 to 5 years. Melaine Klein (1932) shows that there is evidence of superego formation well inside of the first year. In general, it seems that the younger the child at the time of the deprivation, the more serious the effect upon the personality. The first year is, therefore, the most vulnerable, although prolonged or critical breaks in the continuity in parent–child relationship during the second, third and fourth years often distorts the personality in the direction of a social agnosia rather than in a neurotic reaction type. A critical break is one in which the child completely forgets the parent, or in which the relationship is completely broken and the new one does not establish itself on a similar pattern.

Margaret Ribble has shown the need of mothering to the new-born and young infant for its immediate well being and its future personality development. It has been known for a century that the hospitalized or institutionalized child might suffer even death, or marasmic physical states, and pronounced deficiencies, or deterioration in mental and personality development. Hans Christoffel (1939) (Switzerland) has quoted Parrot, a great infants' clinician of the 19th century (1839–1883) in France, to this effect. Emperor Frederick the Second was said to have experimented in the fifteenth century with an attempt at raising infants without demonstrations of affection; and they all died because they were "without the appreciation, the facial expression, friendly gestures and loveable care of their nurses" (quoted from Salin Benes, the monk). Hildegard Dufree and Kathe Wolf (1934) found that infants raised in proletarian infants' and children's homes in Vienna could be in good physical condition where the emphasis was on physical hygiene, but suffered in mental and emotional development.

A large number of problem children at all ages have been brought to Bellevue for observation from the different child-caring institutions and foster home agencies. They have represented almost a laboratory experiment in personality structure. In many children there has been a profound inhibition in personality development, while in others various degrees of a similar personality defect. In children who have been in institutions for the first two or three years of their lives without a parent who visits frequently and takes an interest in them, we find the most severe type of deprived, asocial, psychopathic personality deviation. There is a lack of human identification or object relationship and an inability to experience such when therapeutic efforts are made to offer such a relationship to the child. There is a lack of ego or superego awareness. There is a lack of anxiety or any neurotic structure as a reaction pattern to conflicts or to frustration. There are no conflicts, and frustration is reacted to immediately by temper tantrums. There is an inability to love or feel guilty. There is no conscience. The unconscious fantasy material is shallow and shows only a tendency to react to immediate impulses or experiences, although there often are abortive efforts to experience an awareness of the ego or to identify the personality.

Their inability to enter into any relationship makes therapy or even education impossible. There is an inability to conceptualize, particularly significant in regard to time. They have no concept of time, so that they never keep pace with any schedule, have no attention span, cannot recall past experience and cannot benefit from past experience or be motivated to future goals.

This lack of time concept is a striking feature in the defective organization of the personality structure or patterned behavior. The biological instinctual needs and tendency to normal development drives the child to activity which never satisfies him and is the chief source of frustration. There is a drive to use perceptual patterns as a mode of experience, and it is thus that they tend to imitate the behavior or ideology or art expressions of other children. This gives us our best lead as to the care and training of such children.

They should be placed in a benign institutional setup, organized with well routinized and patterned social and educational activities, in small groups of children where they can fall into a routine and imitate other children. They should not be expected to take any responsibility for their behavior, to make any decisions, to profit by their or others children's mistakes, or to be motivated to future goals. Corrective discipline or insight therapy have no place in their training.

Helen Yarnell and I (Bender and Yarnell, unpublished ms.) in a survey of 250 children under the age of six years who had been on the Children's Ward during the five year period from 1934 to 1939, found that about 10% or 12% of this group were referred from child placing agencies because of this type of problem. One agency was without psychiatrically trained workers at that time. The boys were placed in foster homes and there was no effort to make them feel emotionally secure. In fact, it was felt that an attachment between the child and the foster parent should be discouraged, and frequent changes in foster home placement was a part of the program. These boys were usually referred to us between five and seven years of age when they failed to become part of a school or community group because of their extreme infantile behavior, the wild disorganized activity, their inability to relate themselves to anybody or any group, or to become satisfactory members of a foster home or school room.

Another group consisted of children who were placed in infancy in an infants' home of one agency. The children were given the best physical and pediatric care and were well developed and healthy, but they were deprived of all affectional ties, social contacts and even play materials. As a result, they all appeared retarded in speech, in patterned behavior, even in motor functions, and in social and personality development. At a little over three years they were transferred to foster homes in which they usually could not adjust and were then moved to several other trial homes; each time they became more difficult. They appeared to be unable to accept love or the pattern of life in a home situation because of the deprivation of institutional life for the first three years. There were instances in which the deprivation was limited to within the first year, but these children showed the same personality retardation and distortion. It appears that some children of this type may be acceptable to a very tolerant foster mother if she either can give all her attention to the child or if she is insensitive to his unpatterned, impulsive, infantile, unresponsive behavior, and if there is no other child of a similar age with whom he must compete in the home. Even such children do not mature and their behavior never becomes patterned or acceptable when they reach school age.

These children do not develop a play pattern; they cannot enter into group play with other children, but abuse any child near them as frustrating objects to the satisfaction of their own impulses. They seek adults for constant contact but are never gratified by the contact and have temper tantrums when any impulse arising from instinctive needs is frustrated, or when any type of cooperation implying either interpersonal relationship or patterned behavior is expected. They are hyperkinetic, distractible, short in attention span, subject to uncontrolled mood swings, lacking any concepts of human relationships. They speak of having many mothers and fathers and say that everybody is their brother and sister. They love themselves or "God" or the nearest person to them, or "all the mothers and fathers and brothers and sisters." These children do not respond to the group nursery care on the ward as children do who have had some sort of parent–child relationship.

Our follow-up study on 10 of these children in 1939 showed that some of them had settled down during the latency period in orphan homes and some had been accepted by particularly tolerant and undemanding foster mothers. All remained infantile, unhappy or affectless, and unable to adjust to children in the schoolroom or other group situation. At that time we classified these children as psychopathic personalities which had been caused by emotional or social deprivation during the formative infantile period. A failure to identify themselves in an interpersonal relationship was the essential psychopathological mechanism.

We also observed a characteristic curve of the Stanford-Binet intelligence quotient during the childhood period, indicating a specific intellectual retardation which results from the non-stimulating experiences of their infancy and the inability to utilize identification processes for psychic development. For example, Harry was placed at birth in the infants' home. His physical development was normal. At three years he was examined in the home before placement and scored an I.Q. of 78. At four years, after failing to be accepted in two foster homes, his I.Q. was 83. At five he was back on our ward following six foster home experiences, and his I.Q. was 85. At eight years (in our 1939 follow-up study) his I.Q. was 88; he was failing to do any work in school. At eleven years his I.Q. was 75, and institutional care was the only possible recommendation. Albert's I.Q. was 68 at four years when he was leaving the infants' home; it was 75 at five years, 86 at six-and-a-half, 95 at nine, when he was placed in an institution, and 82 at 11. The child shows clear evidence of retardation as a result of three or four years of socially depriving institutional care, and then shows accelerated development of intelligence under the more stimulating influence of the foster home, community and school life to the eighth or ninth year, and then a retardation again because of his inability to apply himself to school work and to acquire learned techniques or social or verbal insight.

Maizie Becker (1941) made a follow-up study of 25 boys who had been on our ward and presented psychopathic behavior problems. Half of these boys came from the same infant home experience described above, the rest from other agency-type of care for the dependent child. Their ages were nine to fifteen at the time of the follow-up, and five to thirteen at the time they were first seen on the ward. Her conclusions were that the study confirmed Dr. Yarnell's and my observations on the nursery-age children that

> children who have been brought up in institutions where personal stimuli are lacking (or have experienced repeated breaks in affectional ties through frequent shifts in foster home placements), and are emotionally under-privileged, have no feelings for human relationships, are asocial in their behavior, and have no capacity for anxiety or guilt.

She found that

> an institution regime seemed to afford the best facilities for the care of this type of child. In the majority of cases no change in the emotional structure had occurred. In a few instances boys had been able to form attachments to foster parents. In all these cases it was possible to confirm that the child had had a relationship throughout his institutional experience with a mother. There was one exception that could not be accounted for.

In 1940 Lawson G. Lowrey made a report on the children from this same agency under the title of "Personality Distortion and Early Institutional Care." He reported 28 children from the same infants' home who were subsequently referred to him for psychiatric advice because of serious problems in social adjustment. He stated that

> the conclusion seems inescapable that infants reared in institutions undergo an isolation type of experience with a resulting isolation type of personality characterized by unsocial behavior, hostile

aggression, lack of pattern for giving and receiving affection, inability to understand and accept limitations, marked insecurity in adapting to environment. These children present delays in development and intensification as well as prolongation of behavior manifestations at these levels. At the time of transfer (from institution to foster home at 3 1/2 years of age) they are at a stage where they can form only partial love attachments.

Lowery concluded that, if the transfer was to occur at this time, it should be cushioned by the experience of being in a small group intimately in contact with warm adults genuinely interested in them, but that preferably they should not be transferred from an institution to a boarding home when negativism is at its peak. More significant seems his conclusion that "infants should not be reared in institutions, or at least for the shortest possible time; otherwise the institutions should furnish such intimate personal planned contact with at least one adult."

It is of interest that Anna Freud (1944), in her experiences with young children in nurseries in England during the war, also came to the conclusion that serious personality disorders in children might be prevented by creating a family-like situation in the institution with one adult relating herself closely with an expressed mother relationship to only two or three children. It is apparently true that some children are raised in institutions through the early infantile period and show a normal personality development. Usually it is possible to show that such children have been regularly visited by a parent (in one instance, at least, this was the father), or that someone in the institution took a warm and continuous interest in the child, acting as a satisfactory parent substitute. David Levy in 1937 used the term "affect hunger" in describing a group of problem children brought to his attention by the Child Guidance Clinic, a number of whom had suffered similar deprivations in their earlier lives, although some had been "rejected" children and others "spoiled" children of over solicitous mothers.

William Goldfarb (1943a, b) has made most important contributions to the study of the personality deviations in children by studying children who in their infancy had been in the same infants' home we have referred to above. His first study was in 1943 on "Infant Rearing and Problem Behavior." He based it on the

suggestive data that in 1938 children were referred by the foster home agency to Bellevue Hospital for observation because of extremely poor personal and social adjustment. Investigation of their background disclosed the startling fact that all had spent their infant years in an infant institution. The problem was described in six cases as a behavior disorder with symptoms of aggression, hyperactivity, quarrelsomeness, disobedience, destructiveness, restlessness, stubbornness and shallowness of affect. In one the problem was stubbornness and ease of emotional upset.

Goldfarb made a series of carefully planned and controlled studies of children who had spent their first three years in this institution and then were placed in foster homes under supervision of trained psychiatric social workers, comparing them with matched children who had been placed in foster homes from their earliest infancy. His studies included behavior, personality and intellectual development, using the case records and questionnaires of the social workers, interviews, observation, and clinical psychological tests on the children. He found important and sharp contrasts between the children who had spent their earliest years in infants' homes and those who had been from the beginning in foster homes. The first group were more retarded in general. Behavior was characterized by destructiveness, consistent failure regarding privacy rights, antagonism and cruelty to other children as infantile modes of expression. There was speech retardation, relative mental retardation, poor school adjustment. It was noted that those children who had been cared for entirely in foster homes also had problems, but they were more heterogeneous and, specifically, there was more "passive anxiety" as compared to aggression in the institutional children. This may be interpreted to mean that there were more neurotic features or mechanisms in children who had always been in a home or family situation, and that the unpatterned impulsive overactivity of the institutional children showed no neurotic or anxiety mechanisms.

In Goldfarb's (1943b) comprehensive paper, "The Effects of Early Institutional Care on Adolescent Personality," he compared two groups of adolescent children then in foster homes, but the first group had been in an infants' home for the first three or more years. He says,

it would appear as though the early group experience of the institution children was a highly isolating one. The emotional and intellectual deprivation resulting from the absence of adults produced a series of distinctive personality traits. These children continue to be different from a group of children with continuous family experience even as late as adolescence and even after a long period of foster family and community contact. They remain less well adjusted to the demands of the community group, more simple in their mental organization, less capable of making reflective and complex practical adjustments at school and more important, less capable of normal human relationships.

He attempted a general theoretical formulation, but his most important conclusions dealt with the

specific implications for the field of child care since all of the institutional children were reared in early infancy in what the field of child care has regarded as one of the better infant institutions and it is unlikely that other institutions have been supplying a more personalized type of care.

Significantly, the mean I.Q. (Bellevue-Wechsler) for the "institution" group was 72, and for the foster home group was 95, the difference being greater for verbal function than performance function. Conceptual thinking was especially defective and proportionally more so than in mentally defective children of a similar functioning level. Rorschach tests on this same group of children demonstrated that the "institution" children showed more deviations from the norms in that they were more concrete and inadequate in conceptualization, which indicated an apathy in relationship to the environment, behavior that is unaccountable and without conscious purpose.

From these children we have learned that the emotional deprivation which results from spending the first three years in an institution may produce an irreparable distortion of the personality with the features of infantilism, lack of patterned behavior with an aimless hyperkinesis, apathy, relative retardation in intellectual development most severe in the fields of conceptualization, language development, and inability to make an object relationship or to give and take in any human relationship.

It is needless to say that on the Children's Ward at Bellevue Psychiatric Hospital there have been many other children with psychopathic behavior disorders besides those coming from this particular infants' home. Some, indeed, may have spent no time in an institution, but may have been changed frequently in foster homes, so that the child was unable to maintain any continuous relationship or identification with any one parent or parent substitute. It appears that there may be two different causative factors. One is the absence or inadequacy of emotional, social or cultural stimuli which is a part of the institutional life of children and which is related to the intellectual retardation, apathy and lack of patterned behavior.

The other factor is the absence of, or critical or repetitious breaks in, an identifying close adult–child relationship. This alone may produce a severe and irreparable distortion in personality of the psychopathic type. In these children the intellectual retardation may not be so marked, but the children will never function intellectually at their maximum because of inability to identify themselves with a teacher or a school room situation or with social concepts, due to lack of motivation, poor attention span, poor work habits and techniques and defects in patterned behavior and conceptualization. Unsuccessful satisfaction-seeking behavior and a complete infantilism in personality is most characteristic of these children. They are overactive and socially and physically destructive without being hostile in their aggression. They show no neurotic features and are therefore without anxiety, guilt, or any positive or negative human emotions of love or hate.

From several children such as these, we have learned that the critical age is certainly under two years (the period of language development is undoubtedly critical); in some cases it is definitely under one year. A serious deformity in personality might occur in a child in whom there had been a critical change in parent relationship before the latter part of the first half year of life, because that is the period when children first identify their parents and show a definite and individual relationship to the people around them. However, it also appears that a very critical break in total family identification during the second, third, and fourth years may produce the same personality distortion. If there is no chance to carry on any of the earlier identification processes, all memory of them is lost or distorted and the normal processes of personality development cannot continue. It is probably true that in these instances severely traumatic experiences such as abusive or neglectful care, long periods in impersonal shelter care, or severe illnesses with hospital care, may be contributing factors. But these only serve to make the really critical factor, namely the break in identification processes, a telling one. Patterned behavior, conceptualization, depth and reality in object relationship in normal human development, are therefore dependent upon the continuation of such experiences through the early critical years of personality development.

Psychopathic behavior disorders are quite common among adopted children when the child has been adopted in this early childhood period especially from institutions, or after a period of neglectful care or too long a period in a hospital. This type of behavior disorder is also seen in children of the upper economic and social levels when the child has been left in the care of rapidly changing servants, and when the relationship to the mother and father due, in part perhaps, to their many business and social obligations, has been too scant to permit of any real opportunity for identification, normal interpersonal relationships, and personality development. The first case in Helene Deutsch's (1942) paper on the "As if Personality" is an example.

SUMMARY

(1) These children impress us with their diffusely unpatterned impulsive behavior. At all levels it is unorganized and it remains unorganized. It is exceedingly difficult to find any educational or psychotherapeutic method whereby it can be modified into organized or patterned behavior. The child is clearly driven by inner impulses which demand immediate satisfaction; these impulses or needs show the usual changes with physical and chronological growth of the child, but even they do not add much pattern to the behavior. Motivation, discipline, punishment and insight therapy have little effect. Controlling the environment in which the child may act, to which he may respond by imitation, seems the only means of producing social patterns and even this is superficial.

(2) The behavior remains always infantile. It is true that there are some differences in different individuals as to the level of the infantile fixations. It is certainly pre-oedipal, pre-superego, and usually pre-narcissistic. It is as though a newborn infant had urgent needs which must be satisfied. Screaming, kicking or temper tantrums or disturbed behavior of which the larger child is capable continues when frustration occurs, as it must a good deal of the time. All kinds of oral activity, clinging, wetting, soiling, senseless motor activity, and genital manipulation may be observed. These are not neurotic traits and do not indicate regression but retardation in personality development. In some instances they may be given up through a quiescent period only to recur again when inner drives are great or outer satisfactions less. Psychopathic behavior disordered children are often attention-seeking, clinging, passively dependent, seductive and, with it all, amiable. This may be mistaken for an attachment or interpersonal relationship. Actually, there is no warmth, and the relationship can stand no separation or disappointments or demands: it shifts for the nearest new object as soon as the recipient is out of sight. It seems probable, however, that they finally find such a relationship upon which they can depend, especially after the strongest of the youthful impulses have subsided, as the psychopathic individual seems to disappear in early adulthood.

(3) The primary defect is an inability to identify themselves in a relationship with other people, due to the fact that they experienced no continuous identification during the early infantile period from the first weeks through the period when language and social concepts, and psychosexual and personality development, were proceeding. Related to this lack of capacity to identify or to form an object-relationship is a lack of anxiety and inability to feel guilt. It would thus appear that anxiety and guilt are not primary or instinctual qualities, but that they arise in reaction to threats to object relationships and identifications. This is of great theoretical significance in the whole area of the psychology and psychopathology of personality.

(4) There is a serious defect in language development. In the youngest child this is the whole field of language. Later it concerns itself more with the semantic function of language and especially with conceptualization and social concepts. Cleckley emphasized this semantic defect, while Reich referred to a "social agnosia." Goldfarb has studied the conceptual difficulties and general interference in intellectual development. The earliest identification with the mother and her constant affectional care during the period of habit training, formation of concepts of the family unit, and language development, are necessary for the later higher semantic and social development.

(5) There are tendencies to rhythmical fluctuations in behavior which may be looked upon as mood swings and may sometimes be confused with manic–depressive states. This is particularly true of the adolescent period. The mood swings are related to internal biological drives which always tend to show some rhythmical behavior. It is as though the biological unit under the pressure of inner drives or needs could move along at a certain rate only so long before swinging into a new pace.

(6) There is an imitative, passive "as if" quality to the behavior of the older children and adolescents. This is because there is an inner drive to behave like a human being. Whereas behavior in the normal child arises from internal mechanisms, such as identification processes, object relationships, anxieties and symbolic fantasy life, the psychopathic child has no such inner life but still has the physiological or intellectual capacity to perceive and use symbols and patterned behavior. It, therefore, copies the behavior of other children, according to its maturation level and ability. This is done in an effort to understand what other children are experiencing. Confabulations have the same meaning. Ridiculing and caricaturing behavior of others is on the same basis.

(7) Once the early childhood has been passed without the adequate opportunity for normal relationships and personality development, the organization of the personality permits no modification. These children do not show a change in behavior by sudden confinement to a restricting institution as all other children do. Their behavior is not modified (in part because of the semantic defect) by insight therapy or transference therapy because they cannot relate themselves to anyone. Our experience has led us to the opinion that in early childhood there should be patient efforts to establish habit training, socially acceptable behavior and language by one attentive mother figure in the home situation. Once the defect is present, however, this will only accomplish a superficial effect, the underlying defect in personality will persist and assert itself. From about the eighth or ninth year into middle adolescence, the best program is a small closed institution with other children of a similar age. Here the psychopathic child can be expected to fall into the carefully controlled routine and to imitate the behavior of the other children about him. He need have no responsibility for making decisions about his behavior. Nothing is expected in regard to goals or ideologies. Later, if he can become attached in a dependent role to some institution, or person, it may be that he will not be socially destructive.

(8) The defect in time concept is one of the most significant problems.* This may be related to the lack of identification as a continuous temporal process. Even in those children where the problem was a lack of a continuous personal relationship, the same may be said. It appears that we develop our time concept from the passage of time in our earliest love relationships. These children do not remember the past, they cannot benefit from past mistakes; consequently, they have no future goals and cannot be motivated to control their behavior for future gains. There is a somewhat similar defect in spatial concepts. Thus, even when they become momentarily attached to a person, they loosen the attachment when the person is absent. This defect in time concept may be tested by suitable clinical tests. It is related to the problem of lack of pattern in all behavior.

(9) Finally, we come again to the origin of this specific defect in personality development in children. It is not a hereditary or constitutional defect. It is caused by early emotional and social deprivation, due either to early institutional or other neglectful care, or to critical breaks in the continuity of their relationships to mother and mother substitutes.

---

*Editor's Note: They are prisoners of the present. See Milton Miller, chapter 10.

We know that the critical time is the first three years, especially the first year; any sufficient break in parent relationship or period of deprivation under five years may be sufficient to produce this personality defect. Once the defect is created, it cannot be corrected. However, we know a good deal about what we should do to prevent such psychopathic behavior disorders.

No child during the first years of its life should be placed or left in an institution for any period of time, even a few weeks in the first year of life is probably too long. If an institution is to be used, it should furnish for each individual child an individual adult who will enter into a continuous, warm, human relationship with him and replace his parents in this relationship. When hospitalization is necessary for infants, it should be as brief as possible, and should provide regular parental visits. Babies put out for adoption should be accepted for adoption in the first weeks of life. They should not be placed in institutions or other foster homes for a period of observation and "preparation." Changes in foster homes or any other radical changes which sever all relationships should be avoided for children under school age. Children who have had any of these experiences should not be considered adoptable until they have reached school age and have shown normal personality development and school adjustment. The care and treatment of such children, once the psychopathic personality defect is established, should not be therapeutic, corrective or punitive: it should be protective and should aim to foster a dependent relationship.

REFERENCES

Becker, M. (1941). *Psychopathic Personality*. A follow-up study of twenty-five boys of the Children's Ward of the Psychiatric Division of Bellevue Hospital. A professional project completed in partial fulfillment of the requirements for diploma from the New York School of Social Work. Unpublished.

Bender, L. & Yarnell, H. (unpublished manuscript). *An Observation Nursery*. A study of two hundred and fifty children on the Psychiatric Division of Bellevue Hospital, New York City.

Christoffel, H. (1939). On some foetal and early infantile reactions. *Internat. Z. Psychoanal. Imago*, 24.

Deutsch, H. (1942). Some forms of emotional disturbance and their relationship to schizophrenia. *Psychoanal. Quart.*, 11:301–321.

Dufree, H. & Wolf, K. (1934). *Image*, 20:253.

Freud, A. (1944). *Infants Without Families*. New York: Medical War Books.

Goldfarb, W. (1943a). Infant rearing and problem behavior. *Amer. J. Orthop-sychiat.*, 13:249–265.
Goldfarb, W. (1943b). The effects of early institutional care on adolescent personality. *J. Exp. Educ.*, 12:106–129.
Klein, M. (1932). *Psychoanalysis of Children.* London: Hogarth Press.
Levy, D. M. (1937). Primary affect hunger. *Amer. J. Psychiat.*, 94:643–652.
Lowrey, L. (1940). Personality distortion and early institutional care. *Amer. J. Orthopsychiat.*, 10:576–585.

6

Latent Delinquency and Ego Development

Kate Friedlander

Psychiatrist Kate Friedlander's paper first appeared as a chapter in Kurt Eissler's *Searchlights on Delinquency*, published in 1949. In this work she emphasizes the importance of Aichhorn's concept of "latent delinquency," that is, an arrested personality disposition still under the dominance of the pleasure principle. She ties it closely to a narcissistically disturbed relationship with the mother during early childhood and points to the centrality of object relations in character pathology. Friedlander correctly presumes that the earlier the disturbance in developmental object relations, the more severe the "conduct disorder"—our current psychiatric term—may be. She also integrates findings from earlier studies of the abnormal attachment histories of antisocial children. She does not disavow inheritance but instead emphasizes areas of development where prevention may work.

In 1925, Aichhorn (1935) introduced the concept of "latent delinquency" into the psychoanalytic literature. This is, in my view, one of the most decisive contributions to an understanding of the personality deviations of offenders. Aichhorn recognized that delinquent behavior is often released by experiences which are in themselves not traumatic and he realized that these experiences lead to antisocial behavior if a disposition thereto already exists. He saw this disposition in an arrested personality development. He maintained that the ego of the delinquent is still under the dominance of the pleasure principle and that for this reason impulses are acted out more easily than with a personality whose ego is governed by the reality principle.

This conception is of importance from various aspects. It is fully recognized that a decisive change in delinquency figures can only result from an effective program of prevention. Therefore, if there is a disposition to anti-social behavior and if this disposition is to be found in the personality structure rather than in inherited characteristics, the factors contributing to this development must be understood before effective preventive measures can be devised. From the point of view of treatment, only methods which deal with the underlying disposition will eventually effect a cure.

The conception of "latent delinquency" has not been given the attention it deserves and it therefore seems justified to show its implications in some detail. Aichhorn himself, although working with this hypothesis, never studied the early disturbance in itself, but only stated its implications.

I should like to examine further the hypothesis that environmental factors lead to a disturbance in early instinct modification and object relationships, which results in what I have called the "antisocial character formation" (Friedlander, 1945). The findings of those cases which have been analyzed as well as the findings of a larger number of cases which have been examined, seem to show that this character deviation was the result of a disturbed ego development. This occurs when for various reasons the modification of primitive antisocial instinctive drives has not taken place, or has only partially succeeded. During the first three years of life, a process of education takes place which is more far-reaching than any other educational effort later on, although normally it comes about almost unnoticed. Owing to the child's absolute dependence on the mother and the strong emotional tie which unites them, the mother's demands are fulfilled without undue stress, even though each of them imposes a frustration on one or another instinctive drive. Changes in two different directions are being brought about by this early handling. First, the child learns to wait for the gratification of instinctive drives and does so even in the most lenient environment. Second, it learns to accept substitute gratifications, and, slightly later, a deviation of instinctive energy into reaction formation takes place. All these factors are essential for ego formation. We assume that the first distinction between the ego and the non-ego occurs when gratification is not forthcoming and tension rises and causes unpleasant feelings. Each further frustration, if administered by the person whom the child loves and if handled in a way the child can easily endure, contributes to a deviation of energy from the instincts to the ego.

Any factor which interferes with the establishment of a firm mother–child relationship and with consistent handling of primitive instinctive drives will hinder this process of ego development. Separations of any length of time before the age of three, lack of interest or lack of time on the mother's side, personality defects in the mother which make her inconsistent during the periods of feeding, weaning and the training for cleanliness, all may lead to a disturbance in ego development, which will be the more severe, the graver the environmental defect and the stronger the child's instinctive drives. This disturbance in ego development runs parallel to the disturbance in establishing object relationships. The relationship to the mother is highly gratifying and this gratification leads to an outward flow of libido and thereby to a strengthening of the object relationship. If the gratification derived from the love object is insignificant or followed by too much displeasure, the self remains cathected to a much larger extent. We observe this result constantly in counseling mothers of children under the age of three. The mother of a one-year-old child, for instance, is exasperated because her child will not eat, and she feels that all her efforts are in vain. She has no influence over the child. The child's needs are explained to her and this effects a change in her way of handling him. In the majority of cases she comes back after a fortnight very happy not only because the child now eats but because she feels that the child's relationship to her has changed, not necessarily from hostility to love but from withdrawal to interest.

Normally the child's ego at the age of three is strong enough to enable him to endure a certain amount of tension and to cope with primitive instinctive urges, the expression of which is not favored by the environment. Object relationships also have to some extent become more important than direct instinct gratifications, at least at certain times and when there is a conflict between the two.

In cases where this early education has failed, a three-year-old child cannot stand tension and easily withdraws to autoerotic activities if the object relationship becomes frustrating. The child then freely expresses undesirable urges, such as aggression.

If a child enters the oedipal phase with an ego thus undeveloped, and, as Aichhorn points out, still more or less fully under the dominance of the pleasure principle, it is very unlikely that this phase can pass without further disturbance. The most important outcome of the decline of the oedipal phase is the consolidation of the superego by a process of internalization and desexualization, which together lead to the oedipal identifications. This process of identification is based on the slow renunciation of oedipal desires. These wishes have to remain active and unrepressed for some time and the ego has to be sufficiently strong to stand the tension of ungratified desires and castration anxiety. If the ego is weak, castration anxiety is unbearable and the oedipal desires are quickly repressed.

But such an ego is not strong enough to maintain an effective defense. The tension of ungratified desires becomes unbearable and the instinctual drives then seek gratification by regressing to a pregenital level. In contrast to the mechanisms at work in obsessional neurosis, for instance, this defective ego permits the gratification of these desires without building up new defenses against them. The relationship to the parents or other adults remains sexualized, usually on the anal-sadistic level and as a result of this the superego is defective. Contact with adults outside the family circle does not lead to the usual identifications of the latency period, which enrich the personality, but remains on the same level as the sexualized relationship to the original love objects. The people in the environment are loved as long as they gratify and hated as soon as they frustrate. The usual reaction of the latency period to the demands of adults is lacking. Since there is no functioning superego, there is no internal demand and consequently no tension between ego and superego to produce guilt feelings. The child's actions are governed by the pleasure principle, so that only direct prohibition of instinctive drives is successful, and that only temporarily. Although there is intellectual insight into the result of actions, there is no emotional insight. The pleasure of the moment is more important than the threat of displeasures in the future.

This character formation is identical with what Aichhorn called the state of latent delinquency, and our understanding of the antisocial personality has greatly gained by it. I believe that basically it is this character formation which determines whether a person reacts with neurotic or delinquent behavior to inner or outer stress (Friedlander, 1945). The unconscious conflicts which we find in neurotic or delinquent children and adults are identical and so far no specific conflict constellation has been described to explain why one particular person becomes delinquent and not neurotic and vice versa. Even the conflict underlying the actions of the "Criminal from a Sense of Guilt" (Freud, 1916) is found in masochistic character disturbances without antisocial tendencies. Elsewhere I have made a classification of delinquent behavior on the basis of this underlying character disturbance (Friedlander, 1945).

I believe that the age at which the delinquent behavior becomes manifest and the form in which it expresses itself depend both on the degree of this character disturbance and the degree of the neurotic admixtures. There are many delinquents whose behavior is based solely on this disturbed character development. There are others, of a later age, near puberty, who show this character disturbance with an admixture of neurotic conflicts which color the picture. This category includes the cases of obsessional stealing, or wandering, or firesetting. Here the superego functions in relation to certain instinctive urges but not with others. And finally this category also includes those cases of antisocial behavior whose conduct is the result of an emotional conflict of recent origin. The conflict is much easier to unravel in these latter cases than in those with a neurotic disturbance, but the recent conflict is not the sole determinant of their behavior. It was the basic character deviation which prevented the delinquent from making a further elaboration of the conflict and drove him instead into immediate action.

If we are correct in assuming that it is an antisocial character formation which is the basic disturbance underlying delinquent behavior, we should expect to find in the early history of delinquents those environmental factors that are apt to cause the specific disturbance in ego development.

In recent years some observations have been made which seem to confirm the correctness of this assumption. The authors (Carr and Mannheim, 1942) of a statistical investigation, carried out in this country for the purpose of finding the significant environmental factors contributing to delinquent behavior, concluded that their data can only be understood if a "susceptibility" to delinquency exists before it becomes manifest.

Of more significance are van Ophuijsen's (1945) observations. He states that in his cases of "primary conduct disorders" antisocial behavior starts very early in the form of unmanageableness at home, truancy from school, lying and pilfering. In all those cases he finds gross disturbances in the early family setting, resulting in rejection and neglect of the child. According to his findings, children with conduct disorders are characterized by "abnormal aggressiveness, absence or defective development of guilt feelings and narcissistic self-evaluation." He connects the absence of guilt feelings with a defective superego development, again due to adverse environmental influences. Van Ophuijsen described another type of delinquent behavior which is related to the influence of one particular person or displayed in one situation only, as for instance at school. These cases, especially the ones in which the delinquency first manifests itself at puberty, have a different pathology, according to van Ophuijsen. Their etiology lies in a disturbed oedipal development or in neurotic conflicts.

I should be inclined to a different interpretation of the causation of these delinquencies. When antisocial behavior is manifest from the age of four or five onwards, the character defect is very pronounced and superego formation is therefore correspondingly defective. In such cases the environmental disturbances are always obvious. In other cases where delinquent behavior occurs only in relation to certain persons, the character defect is less pronounced and a partial superego development has taken place. When the delinquent conduct does not appear until puberty, the character defect is slight and normal or abnormal conflicts lead to anti-social behavior instead of to neurotic manifestations. I have usually found that the conflicts leading to the antisocial manifestations are the usual ones met with in adolescence: severe frustrations of the desire to be grown up, events in the home which tend to increase incestuous desires, such as the birth of a sibling, and so on. Despite the fact that the home environment of these cases is not a severely disturbed one, nevertheless we usually find typical antisocial rather than neurotic reactions in their early histories.

Lauretta Bender (1947) describes "psychopathic personalities" among children seen at Bellevue Hospital, whose main characteristic is their inability to fit into any community. Her own investigations and those of her co-workers confirm the fact that this personality development pre-dominates in those children who, up to the age of five, were unable to establish object relationships because they were separated from their mothers and were in institutions or foster homes where there was frequent change of the adults in their environment. Lauretta Bender maintains that the disturbance occurs very early, before the oedipal phase, and that it is closely linked to separation from the mother at this early age.

Bowlby (1944), investigating the early family setting, with special emphasis on the mother–child relationship, of 44 juvenile thieves, found that in a highly significant number of cases there were early separations from the mother with a subsequent disturbance of the establishment of object relationships, while in his control group of otherwise disturbed but non-delinquent children this factor played a very minor part.

A recent study at a child guidance clinic of the home backgrounds of delinquent children and adolescents showed that of 34 cases, 12 had been separated from their mothers before the age of four, or had never known them, and were living in institutions or foster homes. In all these cases there was a frequent change of adults in the child's environment before the age of five. In a further series of 12 cases there were gross disturbances in the family setting before the age of five, such as psy-chotic mothers, desertion by the father, separation from the mother and living away from home after the age of six, illegitimacy and so on. In 10 cases only were the children living at home and had not been separated from their mothers, and of these homes only two could be regarded as stable. In these two cases the delinquent behavior became manifest in adolescence for the first time, under provocation, and disappeared after management of the environmental and inner disturbance. The factor common to the other eight homes was the lack of interest in and the inconsistent handling of the child, a lack of tradition in the home and frequent changes of residence, which is rather rare in the rural popula-tion of the clinic district.

In most of the cases we had difficulty in getting a detailed social history covering our essential data of the first five years, not so much because the parents were uncooperative (although this factor played a part as well), but also because the mother did not remember what was to her quite unimportant. This attitude is in great contrast to that of parents of neurotic children, where with very few exceptions the parents are as interested in providing us with facts of the early history as we are in receiving them. The same contrast exists in the actual home background. Out of 33 cases of neurotic children, 32 cases showed a stable home background and an uninterrupted mother–child relationship.

In recent years the study of the early mother–child relationship has received such attention, and it is to be hoped that follow-up studies of children observed during the first years of life will contribute substantially to the elucidation of this problem. Spitz's (1945) investigations have already shown the relationship between ego development and the presence or absence of the mother or a mother substitute during the first year of life.

A further confirmation of the basic character disturbance in delinquents can be found both in the treatment results and in the recommendations for treatment of those who deal with large numbers of delinquents. Aichhorn (1935) has always maintained that the first step in the treatment of delinquent personalities was the establishment of an object relationship, and he draws attention to the difficulties of doing so because of the delinquent's inherent inability to form relationships which can endure frustrations. Van Ophuijsen (1945) states that in all cases of "primary conduct disorder" the treatment plan consists in the establishment of a relationship with the child. He maintains that this may take a long time but that it must be the essential part of every treatment plan.

We would expect that a character disturbance of the type described can only be rectified by a process of re-educating the child by means of an emotional relationship to an adult who represents a parent substitute. If the assumption of a basic character disturbance is correct, the result of this process of re-education will depend on the age at which the child is diagnosed as being antisocial, regardless of whether treatment is undertaken by working with the parents, with the child or with both, or whether it is being done in a foster home or an institution. Naturally, treatment can be more effective before or at the beginning of the latency period than at any later time.

We are all familiar with the picture of the antisocial child during the late latency period and prepuberty, with his narcissistic self-evaluation, his impulsiveness and his inability to establish object relationships which endure frustrations. It would be valuable to be able to diagnose the disturbance at a much earlier age, between four and six years. This may appear difficult, as at this age both normal and neurotic children are also still narcissistic and impulsive. But the history of the primary antisocial child even at this early age is very typical. The parents complain that such children have always been disobedient, destructive and unmanageable. They lie with unconcern, pilfer, run away and tend to stay out later than is permitted. In addition to this there may be other behavior disorders, but it is the combination of the unmanageableness with lying and running away, and the attitude of the parents towards the child which point to an antisocial character disturbance.

In most cases the diagnosis can also be established by examining the child. Between the ages of four to six, the difference between a neurotic and an antisocial child is rather striking, especially if the diagnostic procedure includes observation in the treatment situation, either individually or in a group.

I should like to illustrate certain points regarding early diagnosis by a short case history which is typical of the early manifestation of an antisocial character formation.

We first heard about Peter when he was five and one-half years old. His mother had come for advice about the feeding difficulty of her second son, aged one. After a few weeks when this had disappeared, she confided to us that she was also worried about the older boy, whom she had previously described as perfect. He had started school but was having reading difficulties although he appeared to be intelligent.

At this stage the mother did not admit any difficulty at home and it was not until much later that we heard about certain behavior disorders which had existed ever since early days. He was dry and clean before 18 months, but at that time he began smearing with feces. Threats and punishment succeeded in putting a stop to this habit but nothing could prevent him from being destructive. Toys were so promptly destroyed that the mother no longer bought him any, and he could not be left alone in a room for fear he would damage everything in it. In further interviews with the mother it appeared that the destructiveness had not disappeared at the age of four, as she told us at first, but that he still had phases when he would destroy his own toys and everything else he could lay his hands on. He had always been very disobedient and his behavior had now reached a stage where neither friendliness nor strictness was of any avail. His behavior had become more difficult at four-and-a-half after the birth of a younger brother.

We also learned in time that the teachers were not so much concerned about the boy's inability to read as about his behavior in class. He was a disturbing influence in the group because he prevented other children from learning either by drawing attention to himself or by being aggressive to them.

When Peter was first seen at the clinic, this information was not available and therefore his difficulty in learning to read (he had an I.Q. of 140) appeared from the description as a neurotic learning inhibition.

During the first interview the boy gave the impression of being a friendly, uninhibited child. He came into the room with great pleasure and without any embarrassment, and immediately concentrated on the toys, talking quite freely while doing so. He did not settle down to any play activity, but investigated everything in the room, as is not unusual in a first interview. The only salient features during this interview were that his free and easy behavior, his lack of embarrassment and his free talk did not fit into the picture of a neurotically disturbed child and that his talk and behavior were on a superficial and social level, and had no relationship to the interviewer.

During the following interviews he displayed two different attitudes. During most of the interview he was friendly on a very superficial level and talked freely, revealing fantasies and ideas about religion which were very much in the foreground at that time. He maintained that ghosts urged him to be naughty, but that he was always very good. At the end of the second hour he suddenly decided that he wanted to take one of the toys home with him, and when it was explained that toys remained at the clinic he became aggressive and threatening, saying that he would not come again if he could not have it. He admitted that this was the way in which he behaved at home, but he took the toy with him when he left, without my noticing it. This aggressive behavior repeated itself during the following sessions, appearing sometimes at the beginning, but more often at the end of the session, when he declined to leave. On many occasions he would empty the content of all the toy shelves on the floor in one quick sweeping movement, usually after he had helped to put the toys back. Invariably when it was time for him to leave he would invent many things which he had to do before going.

While there was still no relationship to me during his friendly behavior, the first sign of an object relationship revealed itself in these brief episodes when he became aggressive and unmanageable.

It was months before Peter established a relationship to me which was genuine and not intended to deceive me. When that stage was reached the mother stopped his coming. Half a year later we heard that he had stolen outside the home.

During the interviews we were able to observe closely the boy's behavior at home and at school, his relationship to his parents and brother, as well as the other inter-family relationships, and could confirm the diagnosis which was made after the third interview before the pertinent facts of his history had been made available. The diagnosis was based on this failure to establish an object relationship as well as on the way he behaved toward the instinctive desires aroused in the treatment session, namely to take home a toy. This desire is universal in children who come to the clinic, but only antisocial children express it in this way, by stealing what they cannot get by bribery. Sometimes, during the course of treatment, neurotic children may insist on taking something home with them, but they are then easily satisfied with a substitute and their reaction relates only to material brought forward in one particular session.

The attitude of children with a pronounced degree of antisocial character formation is so typical even at an early age that we have postulated a definite diagnostic entity for them, namely, that of "Primary Antisocial Conduct." In some cases, especially with children under the age of five, there are still doubts about the future development. These we would classify as "primary behavior disorders with antisocial traits."

Although Peter's home background was one of the least disturbed in our group of cases, it was not difficult to understand how the boy's ego development had been disrupted. His mother was a young and attractive woman, with little emotional control. She had a good relationship with her husband, who shared her attitude of unconcern about the children whenever their own emotions were involved. They had both very much wanted the oldest child and were glad that he was a boy. But the mother's handling was very inconsistent from the beginning. She smothered the child with affection one moment and was very harsh with him when he was tired or when he annoyed her. Her husband had grown up with a very strict stepfather and his only interest in the boy was to punish him. Both parents had high ambitions for the older boy until the younger child was born. Then the father openly preferred the baby and Mrs. X had very little time to spend on Peter. She also told him that now he would not be able to go to the university because there would not be enough money for both of the children.

Mrs. X's attitude toward the clinic was also rather typical. She was superficially co-operative and did not break appointments as long as she mainly came for advice about the baby's feeding difficulty. But as soon as Peter started to come regularly, she was late for her appointments and often failed to come. She was more interested in showing off the younger boy than in giving information about the older one, and it became clear that she was quite unable to avoid having scenes with Peter. She was insincere with us and induced the boy to lie for her. In the end she kept the boy away just when he had established a relationship with me and was himself very eager to come and frightened that he might not be allowed to continue. Half a year after the end of the observation, when the boy had stolen from a neighbor and the school became aware of his pilfering, the headmaster informed us that the mother had rejected his suggestion that she should come to the clinic but had asked him whether he could see her regularly. He agreed, but she never came again.

The relationship of this mother to her child was not one of simple rejection. She certainly had a strong emotional relationship to him, but one which was based first and foremost on her own narcissistic needs. She was not only unaware of the child's needs, she disregarded them as soon as they ran counter to her own desire of the moment. The father's relationship was very similar to hers, with the added difficulty that he openly preferred the younger child. The mother's relationship to the younger child was the same as that to the older. She showed him off as part of herself and was impatient when he presented any difficulty. Peter was, of course, very jealous of his younger brother, but this acted only as an aggravation of his already existing disturbance.

Under these conditions the early instinct education could not proceed satisfactorily because of the constant oscillation between too much frustration and too much gratification, which disturbed the ego development. The correspondingly defective superego development is shown in the boy's inability to conform to rules at school and at home, and in his lack of guilt feelings when he was destructive. Peter could not learn because his interest was still centered round the direct gratification of pregenital instinctive drives.

In summary, I should like to emphasize that Aichhorn's conception of "latent delinquency" has directed attention to the study of the underlying basic disturbance in the delinquent personality. The most important result of these studies is the elucidation of the effect of gross environmental disturbances on the child's ego development, and the subsequent disturbance of superego function. Studies of the early home background of later delinquents have already given ample proof that the cause of the antisocial character formation lies largely in the environment. Any effective program of prevention will have to make use of these observations, and plans for treatment should be based on the idea of helping the offender to establish a relationship with one adult who can then undertake the process of education which has not taken place in infancy. In those cases where there is a neurotic admixture as well, the treatment of this condition will have to be deferred until after the education process.

One rather interesting conclusion could be tentatively drawn, namely, that the idea current in the literature of delinquency that constitutional factors play such an important part in the development of antisocial behavior may be fallacious. We can point to the early environmental factors responsible for the faulty development underlying delinquency with even greater certainty than to those which cause neurotic disturbances.

REFERENCES

Aichhorn, A. (1935). *Wayward Youth*. New York: Viking Press.
Bender, L. (1947). Psychopathic behavior disorders in children. In: *Handbook of Correctional Psychology*, ed. R. Lindner & R. Seliger. New York: Philosophical Library, pp. 360–377.
Bowlby, J. (1944). Forty-four juvenile thieves: Their characters and home life. *Internat. J. Psycho-Anal.*, 25:107–128.
Carr, S. & Mannheim, R. (1942). *Young Offenders*. New York: Cambridge.
Freud, S. (1916). Criminals from a sense of guilt. *Standard Edition*, 14: 332–333. London: Hogarth Press, 1957.
Friedlander, K. (1945). The formation of the antisocial character. *The Psychoanalytic Study of the Child*, 1. New York: International Universities Press.
Spitz, R. (1945). Hospitalism. *The Psychoanalytic Study of the Child*, 1. New York: International Universities Press.
van Ophuijsen, J. H. W. (1945). Primary conduct disorders. In: *Modern Trends in Child Psychiatry*, ed. N. D. C. Lewis & B. L. Pacella. New York: International Universities Press.

7

Sanctions for Superego Lacunae of Adolescents

Adelaide M. Johnson

Adelaide Johnson, a psychiatrist and psychoanalyst, presented this monumental paper to the Chicago Psychoanalytic Society on March 25, 1947. It was subsequently published in Kurt Eissler's edited book, *Searchlights on Delinquency*. Her phrase *superego lacunae* has been embedded in psychoanalytic thought ever since. Central to our memory of this paper is Johnson's clinical argument that certain immoral and antisocial behaviors are intergenerationally transmitted from parents to children through the parents' unconscious feelings, impulses, attitudes, and acts. What is not always remembered about this paper is equally important: the gradual identification of the child with the image of him in his mother's mind. In health, the mother's object representation of him as an honest and moral character, and her firm confrontation of him without guilt and anxiety when he is not, shapes his destiny.

The problems discussed in this paper are not peculiar to adolescents, although most of the material will be drawn primarily from my experiences with that age group.

It is essential to define the character problems involved: those of adolescents in conflict with parents or some other external authority because of an acting out of forbidden, antisocial impulses. There is rarely a generalized weakness of the superego in the cases under consideration but rather a lack of superego in certain circumscribed areas of behavior, which may be termed *superego lacunae*. For instance, a child may be entirely dependable about regular school attendance or honesty at work, but engage in petty stealing or serious sexual acting out. Frequently, mild or severe neurotic conflicts accompany such superego lacunae.

I shall attempt to illustrate that the parents may find vicarious gratification of their own poorly integrated forbidden impulses in the acting out of the child, through their conscious, or more often unconscious, permissiveness or inconsistency toward the child in these spheres of behavior. The child's superego lacunae correspond to similar defects of the parents' superego, which in turn were derived from the conscious or unconscious permissiveness of their own parents. These conclusions are the result of the collaborative study and treatment of the significant parent as well as the adolescent patient as reported briefly by Szurek in 1942.

The literature reveals a variety of descriptions and discussions of the etiology of such superego defects. Reich (1925) was the first to introduce the term "impulsive character" into psychoanalytic literature. Alexander (1930) introduced the concept of the need for self-punishment as a motive for "acting out." Other authors stress the patient's receiving insufficient love and warmth so that a strong identification with the unloving parents is impossible. This lack of love is commonly considered the basic cause of superego defects.

Schmideberg (1938) believed that people who act out their conflicts have a greater constitutional inability to tolerate frustration than the more inhibited persons. Greenacre (1945) reported in some detail a number of cases of psychopathic personality but without concomitant study of the parents. She found that the fathers of such patients were usually ambitious and prominent, and the mothers usually frivolous and superficial, giving little attention to the home. She discussed the interrelationships of such parents with the child in respect to its superego development, but did not speak of defects in the parents' superego.

Aichhorn (1935) and Healy and Brenner (1936) stated that some antisocial children have identified themselves with the gross ethical distortions of these parents. These observers saw the gross pathological correlations but apparently did not stress the implications in the subtler cases with which we are concerned in this paper. Healy and Brenner attributed the child's inability to develop a normal superego to the coldness and rejection of the parents, so that one child in a family may steal and another will not, depending upon the one being unloved and the other loved. Even granting that unloved children may not develop a "normal superego," it does not follow that coldness of parents alone can lead to the superego lacunae under discussion. Some very cold parents create such great guilt in children that a punitive, hostile superego is developed. On the other hand, there are warm parents whose child may act out antisocially.*

---

*Editor's Note: The presence or absence of loving affect does not necessarily translocate specific values from parent to child.

At the Institute for Juvenile Research our collaborative therapy of purely neurotic children and their parents revealed certain unmistakable but subtle parent–child interrelationships in which one provided the other with an unconscious impetus to the neurosis. The confusing literature on delinquency and the dissatisfaction with our results in treating delinquent children stimulated a research into the subtle family relationships for a clue such as we had found in the purely neurotic cases. It seemed logical to seek some hidden links between the superego of the parent and the child, even in cases where the parent himself did not act out.

Szurek (1942) stated the problem briefly and brilliantly in an understandable and simple way for both the gross *and* the subtler pathologies. Due to limitations of space he could not present the large amount of available evidence for his thesis. He saw the problem as a defect in personality organization—a defect in conscience:

Clinical experience with children showing predominantly behavior which is a problem to others and *concurrent therapeutic effort with the parent* leaves the impression that the genesis of some of the human characteristics included in the definition of psychopathic personality is no greater mystery than other syndromes in psychopathology. Almost literally, in no instances in which adequate psychiatric therapeutic study of *both* parent and child has been possible has it been difficult to obtain sufficient evidence to reconstruct the chief dynamics of the situation. Regularly the more important parent—usually the mother, although the father is always in some way involved—has been seen *unconsciously* to encourage the amoral or antisocial behavior of the child. The neurotic needs of the parent whether of excessively dominating, dependent or erotic character are vicariously gratified by the behavior of the child, or in relation to the child. Such neurotic needs of the parent exist either because of some current inability to satisfy them in the world of adults, or because of the stunting experiences in the parent's own childhood— or more commonly, because of a combination of both of these factors. Because their parental needs are unintegrated, unconscious and unacceptable to the parent himself, the child in every instance is sooner or later frustrated and thus experiences no durable satisfactions. Because the indulgence or permissiveness of the parent in regard to marked overt hostility, or to some mastery techniques, for example, is uncertain and inconsistent, control over the former or acquisition of the latter by the child is similarly uncertain and confused. If a discipline of the parent is administered with guilt, it permits the child to exploit and subtly to blackmail the parent until the particular issue between them is befogged and piled high with irrelevant bickerings and implied or expressed mutual recriminations.

The astonishing observation emerging repeatedly in our studies was the subtle manner in which one child in a family of several children might unconsciously be singled out as the scapegoat to act out the parent's poorly integrated and forbidden impulses. Analytic study of the significant parent showed unmistakably the peculiar meaning this child had for the parent and the tragic mode in which both the parent and the child were consciously, but much more often *unconsciously*, involved in the fatal march of events. As therapists we could not avoid feeling sympathy for these consciously well-intentioned parents whose unconscious needs were unwittingly bringing disaster down on the family. This was strikingly illustrated in several families that had an adopted child as well as one or more children of their own. The acting out of the parent through the adopted child was always rationalized as inherited behavior.

Although not emphasized by Szurek, another fact that became obvious was that not only was the parent's forbidden impulse acted out vicariously by the unfortunate child, but this very acting out, in a way so foreign to the conscious wishes of the parent, served often as a channel for hostile, destructive impulses that the parent felt toward the child. In many cases, parents may reveal blatantly the child's acting out to schools, family friends, and neighbors in a way most destructive for the child's reputation. This becomes one of the greatest sources of rage in the child. The press recently reported a young adolescent girl hanging herself because her mother, missing $10.00, telephoned the school authorities to search the girl's purse.

Thus the parent's unconscious condoning of the acting out of asocial impulses by the child may serve the two-fold purpose of allowing the parent vicarious gratification of forbidden impulses as well as the expression of hostile destructive impulses felt toward the child.

Similarly the child consciously but more often unwittingly exposes the parent to all degrees of suffering through acting out. This acting out may often be an exaggerated picture of the unconscious impulses of the parent.

We must first understand the behavior of a well-integrated parent, and the subtle conscious and unconscious ways in which this behavior directs the child's superego development in order to be able to recognize the evidences of such destructive sanctions in less integrated parents.

To be sure, the dissolution of the Oedipus conflict puts the real seal on the superego, but it is well to be aware of all the preoedipal and oedipal subtleties in the family which are part and parcel of this development. To the child in the early and middle latency period there may be alternative modes of reacting on an ego level, but when the superego is involved the child normally is reared as if there could be *no* alternative reaction in regard to the suppression of the impulses to theft, murder, truancy, etc. The well-integrated, mature mother issuing an order to a child does not immediately check to see if it has been done, or suggest beforehand that if it is not done, there will be serious consequences.

Such constant checking or such a warning means to the child that there is an alternative to the mother's order and an alternate image of *him* in the mother's mind. Identification with the parent does not consist merely of identification with the manifest behavior of the parent. It necessarily includes a sharing by the child of the parent's conscious and unconscious concept of the child as one who is loved and honest or sometimes unloved or dishonest.

It is essential to appreciate this fact if we are to understand the etiology of superego defects and plan a rational therapy. Angry orders or suspiciousness or commands colored by feelings of guilt convey to the child the doubtful alternative image of him in the parent's mind. The mature mother expects the thing to be done, and later if she finds the child has side-stepped her wishes, she insists without guilt on her part that it be done. The mother must have this undoubting, firm, unconscious assurance that her child will soon make her intention his own in accordance with her own image of him. This, however, produces a rather rigid and inflexible attitude in the young child. As Fenichel (1941) says: "After the dissolution of the Oedipus complex we say the superego is at first rigid and strict . . . and that later in normal persons it becomes more amenable to the ego, more plastic and *more sensible*."

In adolescence the superego is normally still fairly rigid and the child is greatly disturbed when adults express doubts about it. Nothing angers adolescents more than to be warned about or accused of indiscretions of which overtly they were not guilty. Such lack of good faith in them threatens to break down their repressive defenses and lowers their self-esteem and feeling that they would do the right thing. It suggests an alternative mode of behavior which at that age frightens them.

With these simple basic concepts in mind it becomes relatively easy to see what is happening in some rather simple cases of superego defect and to present the evidence for what Szurek stated in his article. It should be made clear that it is not within the scope of this paper to discuss the multiple determined types of character defenses which the child may evolve and use. Nor can the particular mode of therapy dealing with such character defenses be here included. These topics have been discussed in previous papers (Fenichel, 1945; Greenacre, 1945).

Let us return to our simple cases of superego defect. How is truancy initiated? It is not just that parents are cold and rejecting as so many authors imply. How does the specific idea of leaving home originate? At six the little girl may say angrily: "You don't love me—nobody loves me—I hate you all." Quite often the child will receive such replies as: "Well, why don't you just pack your bag and go live some place else if you think we're so awful?" We know that some parents even follow this up by packing the little one's suitcase, which at first may terrify the child. The suggestion to leave home comes more frequently from inside the home than outside, for not many small children tell others at school that their parents are mean or get suggestions from other children to leave home.

If little children (especially up to the age of 11 or 12) let the thought that they are unloved come into consciousness at all, they then do not express that thought outside the family circle from feelings of both guilt and pride.

When we carefully examine the cases of a first or a repeated running away, we often find that it was the parents who unconsciously made provocative suggestions from a variety of motives such as hostility, or a need of vicarious gratification or both.

As, for example, six-year-old Stevie, who had been running away since he was four. His father seemed to know an inexplicable amount of detail concerning the boy's episodes of exploration. He reported that during these same two years he himself had been unable to continue his work as driver of a transcontinental truck, a job in which he revelled. Instead his present job confines him to the city. It was striking to observe this father with the little boy. He asked Stevie to tell of his most recent running away. When the child guiltily hesitated, his father started him on his way with an intriguing reminder. As the boy gave his account, his father was obviously fascinated—even occasionally prompting the child. Toward the end, the father suddenly and angrily cut the child off, saying, "That's enough, Stevie; now you see what I mean, Doctor?" Stevie could not help but see his father's great interest and pleasure when he told his tale each time he returned home, even though at the end of his account he received his whipping. The father was a kind, well-intentioned man who rightly feared for his little son's safety, but he was quite unconscious of the fact that the stimulus of his own thwarted need to travel was easily conveyed to the small, bright boy of whom the father said: "Stevie's really a good kid—he would follow me around the top of a wall 50 feet high."

No better example of how an adult can initiate such running away can be found than the story of how Aichhorn (1935) deliberately resorted to such provocation as a technique of treatment. In handling the transference, he consciously used a simple provocative mechanism to get a boy to run away from the institution, since he could not make any positive contact with the adolescent. This very narcissistic boy, with no positive feeling for Aichhorn, constantly complained about the institution. Aichhorn made subtle suggestions about the attractiveness of the outside world and an hour later the boy ran away. As Aichhorn had anticipated, some days later the boy returned, having found the outside world uninviting and then entered at once into a positive relationship with Aichhorn.

Let us now attempt to discover how stealing is initiated.

One of my patients, a woman who had been in analysis for nine months, came in very angry at her nine-year-old daughter. The reason for the anger was that the child had been found stealing some money from the teacher's desk the day before. The patient stated that she knew Margaret had taken nickels from her purse off and on since she was six or seven but had said nothing, feeling that "she would outgrow it." When I asked why she had said nothing, she said it was never serious, so she had felt the less said the better. It was stated earlier in this paper that the mature mother does not anticipate trouble nor check up constantly on her child. On the other hand, neither does she let something amiss go by when she observes it, but instead handles it promptly without anxiety or guilt. She can neither be the nagging, checking detective, nor the permissive, lax condoner.

During this hour, my patient told me a dream she had had over the weekend. In the dream she went into Saks and stole a beautiful pair of slippers. In the discussion I commented that I was struck with the fact that in her dream she did not even project the theft onto someone else and wondered if possibly her mother had been permissive with little thefts. Then my patient told me, for the first time, of numerous thefts all through her childhood and adolescence and that her mother had always protected her. For instance, during one year of her adolescence she had stolen at least two dozen lipsticks from stores. The prohibitions which had been so poorly integrated in her own life were unconsciously permitting and condoning her daughter's stealing. It was a revealing experience for my patient when three months later her mother came for a visit, to observe her mother's little deceptions and permissions with the two grandchildren, such deceptions as my patient had herself hitherto ignored. She did what she could to stop them and decided to limit long visits from her mother until the children were much older. In a very short time her daughter stopped all thefts as my patient, through her analysis, was able to make a definite stand without anxiety or vacillation. The child, formerly so unhappy and unpopular, later became an outstanding pupil in her school.

We see in this mother's behavior an attitude commonly found among parents of children who steal. The parent whose own superego is defective is the one who will say "He will outgrow it," and often the parent who is not involved in the acting out is the one who finally insists upon bringing the child to treatment. "He will outgrow it" is the permissive, protective attitude that keeps the problem active.

There are many such parents whose own poorly integrated prohibitions permit them to let slight offenses go by, only to react with sudden and guilty alarm at the first signs of criticism from outside the home by then angrily accusing and punishing their child. The child, confused and angry, in turn feels betrayed, and may in his own mind review his parents' similar deceptions. If he has the courage and is not too ashamed, he may point this out to the parent, and in this way the vicious circle of hostile, mutual blackmail and corruption is started.

The fantasies, hopes and fears which parents express in reaction to some behavior of their child is one of the commonest ways in which a child is influenced toward a healthy or a maladapted career. The horrified comments or anxiety over some behavior of the child are well known to everyone. How commonly we hear the parent of the little child, caught in some minor offense, angrily say, "You are beyond me—I can't handle you any more—if this doesn't stop, you will end in the reform school." Or the child who is just beginning to misbehave is likened to his uncle who came to a bad end. We become "good" or "bad" depending upon our parents' fantasies about us.

A professional worker recently told me that 17 years ago she visited her friends who had a nine-month-old baby boy. The worker took the little boy on her lap and when he reached up and put his hands around her neck, the child's mother with a really frightening expression said, "I hope my son won't be a killer." The worker told me that by the age of 15 years that boy had committed murder.

However, I do not intend to use evidence here of the more tragic cases, which have come to our attention, but will confine the discussion to fairly simple examples.

In *Psychoanalytic Therapy* (Alexander et al., 1946), written by the staff of the Institute for Psychoanalysis of Chicago, I reported the case of 17-year-old Ann, who suffered from great anxiety and whose mother had written fraudulent excuses for the girl's absences from the school. The girl refused treatment and I treated only the mother. It was possible to analyze not only much of the mother's destructive hostility to Ann, but also in the transference, to manage and thwart the mother's attempts to corrupt the analyst and pull her into the vicious circle. Two years later, Ann is in college and making an excellent adjustment.

Another case is that of a 16-year-old girl who came to treatment because of several years of severe depression and the occasional idea that she was being poisoned at the school cafeteria. As her depression subsided and her anger toward me came out, she went home one day and told her mother she was so angry at the therapist, she was going to kill her.* The mother said, with horror, "Oh, Marion, don't bring any more tragedy on the family." Marion rushed back to me greatly frightened saying, "My mother actually believed I would murder—what is wrong with her?" At that point I succeeded in also getting the mother into treatment with another analyst. It was fortunate that I did so, for Marion's father had died psychotic, and the maternal grandmother had been promiscuous, so Marion's mother was acting out ominous impulses through this girl, and blaming them all on Marion's heredity from her father.

When one parent advises a child to keep something from the other parent, it is a frequent and destructive factor in creating deceptions and stealing. "Here, I'll give you $2.00, but don't tell your father." One could list an endless array of such sanctions. In treatment these children will always try to get the therapist to lie to the parents. The parents' "more sensible superegos" unconsciously overlook the fact that to the rigid superego of a six- or nine-year-old, this does not look "sensible" but dishonest.

If we break a promise to a child without a sincere statement of the facts and a regretful apology, we undermine his ability to identify with us as adults of sound integrity.

In work with neurotic adolescents and young people, all therapists at times unwittingly ask questions which the child interprets as a

---

Editor's Note: This is an expressive, rather than an instrumental, threat. The former is used to regulate affect in the threatener; the latter is used to control the target of the threat through fear or intimidation. This mother's gross misinterpretation is evident. Most people never act on their threats.

permission. For instance, one frequently hears of analysts in a consultation with a 20-year-old ask, "Have you ever had intercourse?" One young colleague told me he learned only too well the unwisdom of such a question. In the initial interview he asked a 19-year-old college student if he had had intercourse and the patient said, "Yes." Several months later his patient confessed that at the time the therapist had questioned him, he had *not* had intercourse. He felt guilty that he had lied and ashamed that he was so unmanly, so he had sex relations to undo the lie and prove his manliness. Probably all therapists unwittingly make some of the same errors in the treatment of children which some of the parents make to a greater degree. It is just these errors that led me to consider carefully Freud's meaning and intention when he made his suggestion for offsetting "acting out" in analysis, by interpreting and warning ahead of time.

Some analysts, dealing with cases of perversions or even more serious antisocial behavior, warn the patients ahead of time that they may have the impulse to act out in some manner. Certainly, *this* was not Freud's thinking on the matter. When he spoke of revealing to the patient, at the correct time, the possibility of his acting out and the meaning of it, he had in mind the so-called acting out of the neurotic patient on the couch who was repeating in the transference the salient episodes of his earlier life. This is an entirely different matter from warning a patient about some antisocial impulsive behavior. In fact, if I understand Freud correctly, he warned analysts against mobilizing and interpreting too rapidly any impulses that might be dangerously expressed outside the analytic hour—particularly sadism. A loose and unclear concept of what is meant by "acting out" has led a number of analysts to carry over Freud's suggestions about transference "acting out" to the "acting out" in a serious antisocial way. A warning to a patient with a defective superego can act as a destructive force, disrupting what one has attempted to build up, namely, the patient's belief in the therapist's ethical concept of him. Any warning or questioning without factual justification may be interpreted both as a humiliation and a permission.

There is an additional etiological factor in these cases which is puzzling. In work with adolescents from all social strata, I was impressed, as was Szurek, with the fact that sometimes the child's parents had a similar partial superego defect, that is, the mother was promiscuous or the father committed some thefts, etc. But there are other cases in which the parents had never actually done any of this acting out so far as we could find, and yet we could see them unconsciously initiating this with the child. These parents, let us say, had some neurotic conflicts about thefts, promiscuity, etc., like many of us, but why did such parents permit themselves to act these conflicts out through the child, while many neurotic parents do not? With this question in mind, whenever I had a parent in treatment, I explored the relation to her own parents very closely.

Where did the parent get the permission to act out through the child? Since the parent did not act out herself, she must have had a fairly strong conscience. Yet what caused this poorly integrated prohibition to appear in the next generation?

I frequently found that the present parent had gone along for years developing a good conscience, was secure about controlling her own impulses and then something arose that led her parents to surprising suspicions and accusations. Since the parent under treatment already had a good conscience, he or she could not respond to this permissive accusation by acting out, yet was enraged at the injustice and defamation. The rage and the permission would then come out unconsciously by being displaced onto the daughter or son. The parent's acting out through the child may also occur when the parent, with a well-developed conscience, *later* observed dishonesty, erotic acting out, or some other disturbing behavior in *her* parents and felt much pain and confusion about their actions. Our parent in question already had a good conscience and too much guilt to do likewise herself, but the confusion, anger, and permission cannot be normally integrated into her personality and appears later through her own child. For several years I have found increasing evidence to substantiate this statement, but I am not satisfied that this is the final answer.

With this understanding, it could be seen more clearly why at the Institute for Juvenile Research we had failed so repeatedly with even relatively mild cases of acting out, although we had seen some of them frequently (four to five times a week), for one or two years. We had given a great deal of consistent warmth and affection, but the child continued to steal or act out sexually. Any guilt developed toward us with regard to an act was met with unconscious permission at home and the child was only confused and frequently became more fearful toward us and finally stopped coming. We succeeded with even mild cases only if we could get the significant parent into treatment or could remove the child from the home during the therapy. Treatment of such parents, whose role is so often unconscious, is a miserable ordeal for them and the greatest sensitiveness and skill is necessary in carrying them through. Many break away in spite of our best efforts to go slowly. Where the sanction was perfectly conscious on the parent's part, treatment of him was almost always futile. If neither treatment of the parent nor placement is possible, then any treatment in a severe case is not only futile, but often dangerous, because the parent can unconsciously act out through the child and make the therapist "responsible," just as parents make heredity the scapegoat in some adoptive cases.

My first experience with such a serious hazard came a few years ago. A young woman therapist who did not share our conviction of these dangers insisted on trying treatment of a 10-year-old boy who stole and had set a few fires three years earlier.

Neither parent had been interviewed with the idea of considering treatment. A few weeks later a serious fire occurred at the home. The mother particularly was enraged at the therapist. To relieve the tension and clarify the situation, I talked with her. She told me that she had been downtown shopping; that she was a woman who trusted her premonitions and she had become uneasy about something vague and hurried home. A few blocks from home she heard the fire department and, "I just knew it was our house." When I asked her why she should have been so uneasy and certain, since there had been no fire for three years, she flushed, stiffened and maintained, "I always trust my hunches." I asked her if the boy had mentioned fires at any time recently. She thought for a while and then told me that he had become angry at his little sister a few days before. When the mother interfered, he shouted that he hated them all and would kill them or burn them all up. This is a frequent threat of many angry children and the average parent pays no attention to it. This mother had told him then that if he tried anything like that, he would end in the reform school. Like most of these threats by parents of antisocial children, they are not carried through and the child knows the parent will protect him until he does something far worse. I spoke reassuringly of our interest in helping in some way, but she angrily withdrew herself and child entirely from the treatment situation, blaming the child's therapist.

In treating younger children and adolescents with conscience defects, one of the great errors commonly made is that of too energetic attempts to liberate the child from the permissive parent, especially by telling the child that the parent is dishonest, or sexually unstable. These children often know these facts consciously, but it is a frightening and humiliating thing to the insecure young patient to be told such things. If he is not conscious of such facts, this knowledge early in treatment is devastating to the child and utterly cruel to the parent who is unconscious of the implications in his or her permissive behavior or attitude. When the children become more secure in handling their own impulses, these patients if they observe them, bring up these tragic facts themselves and they can be discussed at that time.

I wish to emphasize certain facts about the treatment of the young and older adolescents who are not too seriously handicapped. With the exception of one girl who lied and stole, all were able to develop a fairly *positive transference* within a month or two. To be sure, some were seen five and six times a week for the first few months and were permitted many additional telephone contacts. I spent over a year developing a good relationship with one girl. There were two girls and one boy whom I never saw, but whose mothers I treated—one by psychotherapy for nine months and two in analysis. All of these cases were adolescents who in certain areas of behavior had excellent conscience formation but nevertheless showed other symptoms of defect such as stealing, lying, cheating, running away, or sexual acting out. I cannot emphasize too strongly that the successes I have had are not with very severe cases such as the highly narcissistic children with widespread superego defects. Also, when I have been successful, the parents have been cooperative and well enough to enter treatment themselves or allow me to place the adolescent in a school or a club.

To make for a simpler presentation of some of the principles of the direct treatment of an adolescent with a conscience lacuna, I shall confine the discussion more or less to one group, namely those children in whom stealing was the essential problem. I can think of none whom I have treated who did not also have neurotic conflicts which likewise had to be resolved when the time was propitious.

In the literature such brilliant therapists as Aichhorn and Schmideberg speak of more or less long periods of education and re-education of such children preparatory to analysis or along with analysis of their neurotic symptoms. This preparatory "educational" phase apparently has to do with strengthening the superego, but I have always wished they would write in more detail of the therapeutic technique which brings this about. Aichhorn deals rather extensively with the need to change the urge for living by the pleasure principle into a more realistic attitude, but there are few specific details of the ways and means he employed.

Aichhorn never began by asking a child to give an account of his misdemeanors because he felt quite sure he would only weaken the relationship by forcing the child into more falsifications. Many therapists, however, approach an adolescent boy who steals by trying to get him to give an account of his misdemeanors and difficulties. When they are asked why they force the child to recount these facts, they reply that it is to see if he has "insight" into why he is brought for therapy. Usually he would not give a frank confession, but even if he did, this has nothing to do with "insight." If he were deeply deprived early, then the therapist might say he hopes to help the patient to see some connection between the consciously or unconsciously permitted stealing and his emotional deprivation. But by proceeding this way their patients' thefts usually increase for reasons which will soon be clear.

How does the patient react to such an approach? By evasions, rationalizations and outright falsifications and the ensuing anger, fear and humiliation will now present an even greater obstacle to therapy.

The primary difficulty is a partial superego lack—a lacuna. If a normal superego is developed through identification with mature parents who automatically believe in and are certain their child will have integrity, then it would seem logical that the correction of such a lacuna (even at so late a period as adolescence) must proceed by having the therapist assume that there are the same potentialities for identification with himself as he would see in his own child. This attitude is essential or all the warmth in the world will not repair a conscience defect in the child. I cannot emphasize too strongly that this attitude and a deep feeling of respect for the adolescent are absolutely basic in the treatment of these cases.

I have no great optimism about success with a very severe superego defect, but with the milder lacunae, the success of our treatment depends on our understanding of the child's relationship to the therapist.

At the initial interview, regardless of the transference, I do take into account a factor which Aichhorn does not elaborate. Since the adolescent for a long period probably has been consciously or unconsciously protected and his conduct ambiguously condoned by his parent or parents, he has therefore developed a definite pattern of expectation of some degree of whitewashing from other adults. As soon as the therapist gives in to that, the vicious circle of blackmail begins. Therefore, at the initial interview I merely say I know he has had these misunderstandings and difficulties about money which we need not go into but that I have the feeling as he becomes more sure of me, and we understand each other this will eventually subside. I feel that the child must be spared humiliation and given hope for the future without burdening him by excessive standards of good behavior. His past must not be held against him, yet too great a whitewashing of his conduct would be permissive.

Let us remember that the battle at home has gone on through mutual corruption and blackmail, albeit often subtly. This is true in stealing, having the parents write false excuses, lying, etc. Keeping this in mind, if the therapist begins by asking for an account of past misdemeanors, the patient will at once be humiliated and angry. Every patient soon tests the analyst over and over to see if he is corruptible, and if the therapist begins by humiliating him, that testing out will come much more quickly and often more seriously and the whole case may get out of hand before it is well started.

The first thing that should be verbalized casually to the child is the therapist's confidence that with the growth of mutual understanding, all of these old troubles in time will subside. Doubts, accusations or warnings that the child may be tempted to steal will rapidly destroy any possible identification with the adult's superego, the therapist's good understanding of the patient's potentialities notwithstanding.

If a therapist cannot sincerely feel that this child can eventually become thoroughly honest in relation to her without at the same time burdening the child with therapeutic expectations, no improvement will occur no matter how hard she strives to follow the suggestions given here. Many workers will say: "How can I have confidence in the child when he has stolen for years or set several fires? I shall feel duped if after months of treatment, I find he was pulling the wool over my eyes all along." This is a very real countertransference problem. The therapist, without conflict in this area, would not mind if he finds he has been fooled for a time. Resistance and relapse are to be expected in the analysis of a neurosis, and similar lags and relapses are to be expected in treating superego defects. If despair or annoyance overwhelms the therapist at these points, all is lost. Misdemeanors should be neither overlooked nor whitewashed but be frankly discussed with the patient.

In several instances I have come into the picture after a crisis when the parents were terrified by the risks of the child's future and the child knew this. Feeling that for once an adult had to express to the child a sound expectation of him, I have casually but definitely and in the child's presence, expressed my complete assurance of success.

I remember the cases of a boy and a girl who precipitated near tragedies in the home by setting fires just before they were to leave for summer camps. I think the fact that the parents expressed their doubts in the children's presence and that I answered promptly and with conviction, made it possible for the children to feel safe. There was little time to develop strong contacts with these adolescents before camp, but the summer was successful. This is not to say that the task of the treatment had gone beyond a mere beginning. Many therapists may feel that in such a situation the child may "call your bluff" for his parents have usually threatened him with punishment for future misdemeanors only to give ground when the child put them to the test. The difference in these two cases was that I made no threats and said nothing to invite a threat.

Treating these cases calls for the greatest flexibility. At the beginning I may see them five or six times a week and answer their telephone calls every night for months. Especially with the narcissistic child it may need many hours a week to stir up any positive feeling. Broken appointments are frequently followed by a friendly telephone call from the therapist, and this may go on for weeks and months. So much flexibility and time for unpredictable calls and appointments are necessary that I avoid carrying more than two or three of these adolescents at a time on my schedule.

All analysts know how carefully and frankly they must deal with the ego problems of a paranoid patient. Similarly, a great amount of care must be taken with these patients, to avoid any possibility of the patients seeing the therapist as deceptive or evasive in any way. I make it clear that if anyone should ever talk of him to me, I shall tell him at once and if possible get his permission before talking to anyone about him. As an adult in these matters, I do not display the "sensible superego" of Fenichel but to many of my colleagues may give the impression of being childlike in my care to have everything above board. I am extremely careful about promises since to a small child a promise is part and parcel of the whole matter of superego development. Some of these adolescents will beg you to promise they can go home in three months—but I use great care in never over-promising just to ease temporary pain.

I make it a point to catch little, off-color, dishonest things immediately, even though a good positive transference may not yet have developed. The child so often, consciously and unconsciously, makes these little slips early to test the therapist's corruptibility. I try to do this before many of these events have occurred or before the child has too much tension about seeing where I stand. This has to be done in a very comfortable and friendly manner. During the war the commonest technique was to offer to get me extra ration stamps. My own response was to smile and comment that I guessed I could stand the government regulation without dying. At first the patient may be wary about lying and cheating since he knows that is the reason for coming, but often he unwittingly lets slip some matter about cheating because there is little guilt.

Twelve-year-old Jerry had been in to see me about four times and had quickly developed a strong attachment. One day as he was leaving he said, "Well, I'm off to the movies. Sure lucky I'm little and can get by at half price." I laughed and said, "It isn't the size you know, Jerry. When you are 21 years old, whether you are six and one-half feet tall or five feet tall, you will get to vote. The law goes by age, not by size. But, by the way, speaking of age, when you became 12, did your social worker increase your allowance since at 12, by law, you have to pay more for movies and street cars?" Jerry said, "No, should she?" I replied, "I'm sure she would have if she had thought a minute, for it's the only fair arrangement for boys and girls when they become 12. Let's try to telephone her about it now and get her O.K. to my lending you the extra today and when she sees you Saturday, you can repay me." He was eager to call her and, of course, she agreed. A few weeks later Jerry said, "The kids think I'm a sucker to spend double for movies." He was silent a while and then said, "I crashed the gate last Saturday with the kids, but it's no go. No more of that."

I never moralize nor act too grave about the matter but comment casually and good-naturedly that I guess we had better stick fairly closely to the rules of the game. Very early, they watch you closely for any slip. I recall a young social worker, just beginning treatment of an adolescent girl who stole. The worker parked her car by a "no parking" sign. When she stepped out of her car and saw this, she commented that she would have to move the car. The girl said, "I noticed the sign and wondered what you would do." There is often a decrease in anxiety and increase in positive feeling when one of these small episodes has been handled definitely and good-naturedly. Complicated character defenses magnify the therapeutic problem greatly, but a therapist's own guilt or anxiety in dealing frankly with the child can frequently greatly intensify the child's defensiveness.

In her second hour, an adolescent girl who had been stealing and who lived in a boarding club, showed me $5.00, which she had just received from her mother and said, "I'm not going to turn this in to my Club Mother." I asked her to describe the setup at the club, and she explained that the girls turned in their money and then asked for it when they wanted to spend it. I merely commented that it sounded similar to the arrangement I have with the bank which I found very satisfactory and safe. The girl said that she was going to spend 50¢ and not report it, to which I replied the rules probably irked her somewhat, but that it was a simple matter to report spending the 50¢. She then asked if I would report it, and I casually answered, "Why should I? You will report it, and let's drop the subject." The next hour she asked if I had checked up with the Club Mother; I appeared rather blank for I had forgotten the incident. She reminded me and then added: "Well, I turned in the report."

But suppose the child returned and defiantly told the therapist she had not reported the 50 cents? What is the therapist to do then? My own experience has been that if I then became an accomplice, in the end the child's need to test me further would drive him to increasing excesses and I would lose the patient. Therefore, my own procedure is again casually to try to work with the patient toward making a collaborative report as well as talking over her basic uneasiness about whether I will protect her in small or large misdemeanors.

A 12-year-old boy once said to me, "That new foster mother of mine won't work out." When I asked why, he replied, "She has no respect for me—she's a snooper. I told her I was going to the 'Y' and that I would take the bus. When I was waiting for the bus, I saw her following in her car, so I slipped into a building and later went out and got my bus to the 'Y.' She told me I didn't go to the 'Y' and when I asked her how she knew, she said she had a seventh sense. She's just tricky and it won't work."

I would rather be deceived for a time than raise such doubts of my belief in the child. I have seen foster mothers give great warmth only to ruin it all by such doubting.

As soon as the patients consciously or by a slip give me facts of misdemeanors or facts come to me by other routes, I take them up with the patient frankly at once. When the therapist lets little things go by, and this is observed by these patients, their anger at the seeming treachery of being severe only when a serious misdemeanor arises, is justified. This is exactly what happened at home in their past experience where they were protected in small deceptions. If the first attempts to corrupt the therapist are handled correctly, then very soon one may begin to see more superego strength in the patient. I find that handling such attempts along with warmth makes for a more rapid, confident and positive transference. I think that this has been one of the greatest obstacles and pitfalls in the therapy of these patients. Either its real meaning is overlooked at the beginning or it is mishandled. I have had to deal with several mothers with relatively good superegos in certain areas who nevertheless made attempts to corrupt me. It took only a few hours to work through these attempts with firmness. The change in their child, whom I never saw, was striking enough for others as well as the mother, to report it.

It is important when a relapse occurs that every effort be made to help redress a wrong to someone else, but at the same time to maintain the patient's confidence in his growing strength. I usually help the patient to see that some lack of security may still be leading him to thoughtless and impulsive behavior but that a large part of him would prefer to avoid this. In returning stolen goods or adjusting some wrong, I make it clear to the adolescent that we must return the article with as little fuss as possible, for I do not want the patient to suffer unfair and exaggerated criticism. It is important to help the patient with regard to correcting any injustice done to someone. No young child and usually no adolescent should have to go back to the store alone to return some stolen article or to adjust some serious infringement of a rule with the head of a boarding school. However, if the therapist is willing to help in such situations, the child might take it as suspicion on the analyst's part that the child will not carry through and this must be watched for and reassurance given.

The therapist's position has to be one of helping to make amends to the injured party even though punishment may still come about in contrast to the parent's attitude. Yet the therapist should make clear to the patient that she will do everything possible to help the authorities to understand the plan of therapy. Many times the young child or adolescent will agree to do this. What if they do not agree? The therapist may feel afraid that the patient will turn against her if she exposes him. If, however, she maintains silence, she certainly has laid herself irrevocably open to blackmail by the patient and may never undo this. This course would be similar to the vicious family circle of mutual evasion and permissive protection where the parents give in to the child's promises or threats of suicide.

Aichhorn writes in detail of this giving in by the parents and of his own capacity to avoid being overwhelmed by such threats. If the therapist is frightened of taking a stand here out of self-protection sooner or later she will lose the patient who will try to push her into a worse situation in his vain attempt to find someone who has the courage to set limits to his forbidden impulses. I believe that the craving to have limits set to their forbidden impulses is often why children and adolescents arrange things so they will be caught. This reason, I believe, to be more often determining than the motive of guilt.

By this time it has become clear why any questioning of the patient or any accusation without facts, or any warnings of possible impulsive acting out of an antisocial nature will weaken that confidence the patient achieves from the therapist's confidence in him. If this occurs, then the adolescent for instance, feeling hurt and spiteful, will react rapidly and try to enmesh the analyst quickly in the old family net of attempted corruption. Unless he is alert the therapist very soon can be pulled into an embarrassing and destructive situation by the angry child. Then the less experienced therapist is apt to be corrupted by his own anxiety and guilt and the fat may be in the fire.

I recall one gifted social worker who had been making splendid progress with a 16-year-old girl who had been stealing for years. No stealing had occurred for nine months. The girl was on a clothes allowance. One day the worker irritably told the child she should not have bought an article of clothing without asking her. They were walking in the suburbs and in two minutes the patient had the worker picking some flowers inside a private yard. The worker soon got hold of herself and said it was not the thing for them to do. Now the girl pitifully tried to excuse the worker, for she wanted her worker to be honest and said there were not any "no trespassing" signs. The worker, however, made it clear that she had been doing wrong even if there were not any signs forbidding trespassing. The girl agreed, "That is right—people do not have signs in their homes saying 'do not take the furniture.'" The worker also made it clear to the patient that she (the worker) had no justification for being so incensed about the articles of clothing, since the girl had her own budget for clothes. Actually the worker had for a moment succumbed to the girl's spiteful corrupting influence because the worker was guilty over her irritable outburst toward her patient.

After a therapist has put a great deal of effort into the treatment of one of these difficult patients, one can see how she might over-react to a report that the child has been stealing for months while the therapist had believed things were going well. Some therapists are so hurt and humiliated that they see themselves as "duped." One young man therapist said to me, "I feel like a soft fool taken in by that kid." We usually do not react with any such feeling of abuse in the analysis of a neurotic if our patient has a serious relapse after long and hard work with him. This male therapist had overlooked many small signs of ominous import before this major evidence shattered his self-esteem. His personal need to do so had been sensed by his patient, who had been well aware of the small ways in which he was getting by before he acted out more dangerously. This is one of the great hazards in treating such patients, namely, to avoid accusations without good evidence, but to see little off-color things when they *do* arise and to handle them immediately with frankness and without anxiety on the part of the analyst.

It is important to stress again the adolescent's reaction to feeling that his therapist has a deep respect for him. He must gradually see himself as a personality endowed with the many facets which his therapist has spread before him. A ragged 11-year-old boy came in beaming one day. I asked him why he was so happy and he said, "I love my new teacher, she respects me." Therapists must not overlook the many small opportunities for stressing their confidence in their neurotic or delinquent patient's sense of good taste and correctness. That adult who can sincerely make an insecure adolescent feel that his ideas have significance, can hope for success in his treatment.

Handling transference and counter-transference problems involved in treatment of the partially developed superego is extremely complex and relatively little explored. I have touched on only a few aspects of our experience with such cases.

In most of these cases there are also neurotic problems that must be analyzed. One should analyze only that transference neurosis which interferes with therapy until the particular defect in the superego has been strengthened. If the latter is not achieved before the therapist begins intensive analysis of the neurotic conflicts, the acting out of the mobilized deeper impulses will get out of control. While our experience in treating these cases was still limited, this mistake occurred often.

Suppose one is dealing with a 16-year-old girl who stole and who had too much responsibility for the care of younger siblings. To begin analyzing this girl's dependency needs before the superego had been strengthened with regard to property would lead to such a flood of stealing as to defeat any therapeutic efforts. After this patient's intense guilt about her hatred of her younger siblings had been analyzed, we could see how the mother's unconscious condoning of the stealing had made possible this less painful mode of expressing both her hatred and her own needs. When stealing is an acting out of the oedipal conflict, if one starts to analyze the conflict before the prohibition about stealing is fairly firm, the problem will certainly get out of hand as I saw happen all too often in my early IJR days.

This is the sort of "insight" I think many therapists have in mind when they begin therapy by saying "Let us see why you take things," and the more they probe, the worse matters become. But it is true that these conflicts often boil up too rapidly even before the analyst made any attempt to mobilize them, so that treatment is extremely difficult if not impossible outside of a controlled environment. *Treatment of the adolescent always involves his total family and environmental relationship.** When he is secure enough in his own self-esteem he will, himself, come to the more painful aspects of his parents' personalities which confuse and shame him. When this happens, the therapist must avoid both permissiveness and any moralistic condemnation. I usually stress that this seems to be the parent's problem, that it is not an innate defect, but that had the parent had an easier life and been more secure with his own parents, and had had a helpful counselor outside the home, matters might have been different. I speak of my regret that one of us could not have helped long ago to make this parent's life a little easier. Although

---

Editor's Note: My emphasis.

this approach makes the young patient more guilty toward the parents and more neurotic, in such cases this is better than to cut him off from the parent.

In summary I should like to state briefly the significant features in this paper:

(1) I aimed to elaborate on the evidence for the etiology of conscience defects as presented by Szurek in 1942.

(2) More detailed clarification of the subtleties involved in preoedipal and oedipal and latency superego formation was given with the emphasis on the child's seeing the parent's concept of himself as part of the mother with whom he is identifying.

(3) Using this concept as the basis for treatment, the doubting, accusations and policing of the child's developing superego were seen as illogical to any rational therapy. I have emphasized the difference between the warning given in the analysis of a neurosis, the acting out of the transference and the effects of warning a patient about antisocial behavior involving a superego defect.

(4) I have enlarged upon the therapist's role in setting the limits of permissible behavior as soon as test situations arose in the treatment. I have pointed out that his own unanalyzed guilt feelings can prevent him both from quick recognition of such situations and deftness in meeting them. It was stated that it is necessary to set definite limits regardless of threats by the patient in order to avoid repetition of the mutual blackmail and permission of the family constellation. An attempt has been made to depict a few of the details of how certain incidents in the relationship with reference to the superego were handled. This represents only a limited amount of material, should not be accepted dogmatically, and represents possibly only the manner in which certain therapists might operate.

(5) The cases reported where the treatment was successful were not severe maladjustments. They were patients who were able to develop some positive transference, fairly soon, whose superego defect was not widespread, and whose significant parent could cooperate by also entering treatment or by permitting the child to be removed from the home during treatment.

REFERENCES

Aichhorn, A. (1935). *Wayward Youth*. New York: Viking Press.

Alexander, F. (1930). The neurotic character. *Internat. J. Psycho-Anal.*, 11: 292–311.

Alexander, F. et al. (1946). *Psychoanalytic Therapy.* New York: Ronald Press.

Fenichel, O. (1941). *Problems of Psychoanalytic Technique.* ch. V, p. 71; ch. VI, pp. 80–81. New York: Psychoanalytic Quarterly.

Fenichel, O. (1945). *The Psychoanalytic Theory of Neurosis.* New York: Norton, pp. 468–469.

Greenacre, P. (1945). Conscience in the psychopath. *Amer. J. Orthopsychiat.,* 15:495.

Healy, W. & Brenner, A. (1936). *New Light on Delinquency and Its Treatment.* New Haven, CT: Yale University Press.

Johnson, A., Szurek, S. & Falstein, E. (1942). Collaborative psychiatric treatment in parent–child problems. *Amer. J. Orthopsychiat.,* 12:511.

Johnson, A., Falstein, E., Szurek, S. & Svendson, M. (1941). School phobia. *Amer. J. Orthopsychiat.,* 11:702.

Orgel, S. Z. (1941). Identification as a socializing and therapeutic force. *Amer. J. Orthopsychiat.,* 11:119.

Reich, W. (1925). *Der Triebhafte Charakter.* Vienna: Internationaler Psychoanalytischer Verlag.

Schmideberg, M. (1935). The psychoanalysis of asocial children and adolescents. *Internat. J. Psycho-Anal.,* 16:22.

Schmideberg, M. (1938). The mode of operation of psychoanalytic therapy. *Internat. J. Psycho-Anal.,* 19:314.

Schmideberg, M. (1947). The treatment of psychopaths and borderline patients. *Internat. J. Psychother.,* 1:45.

Szurek, S. (1942). Genesis of psychopathic personality trends. *Psychiatry,* 5:1.

8

The Impostor

Contribution to Ego Psychology of a Type of Psychopath

Helene Deutsch

In this paper, first published in the *Psychoanalytic Quarterly* in 1955, Helene Deutsch spells out the behavior and psychodynamics of imposturing in a psychopath. Through the case of Jimmy, a patient whom she saw for eight years, she describes the inflated ego ideal of the impostor, fostered by a very successful and dominant father and an indulgent and anxious mother. The passive entitlement of the impostor, moreover, leads to his pretending that his grandiose fantasies have been realized, rather than choosing a course of sustained effort to achieve real success. Treatment progress for Jimmy increased feelings of anxiety at being "unmasked" and inferiority. Deutsch concludes that certain imposturing is normal, since we often "pretend that we are actually what we would like to be."

For psychoanalytic research in the field of psychopathy, the year 1925 constitutes a historical milestone, as it was then that Aichhorn (1925) published his book, *Wayward Youth,* and Abraham (1925) his paper, "The History of a Swindler." Whereas Aichhorn drew his knowledge from many years of observation and from the therapy of numerous cases, Abraham based his psychoanalytic findings on the study of one psychopath of a certain type. Abraham's paper has remained one of the classics of psychoanalytic literature. Following his example, I consider it especially valuable to single out from the many varieties of psychopathic personality one particular type and to attempt to understand him. The type I have chosen is the impostor. I will restrict myself to the undramatic kind of impostor and leave the others—more fascinating ones—to a later publication.

About 20 years ago, the head of a large agency for the treatment of juvenile delinquents persuaded me to interest myself in a 14-year-old boy and, if possible, to lead him into analysis. The boy came from an exceedingly respectable family. His father, a business magnate, was a well-known philanthropist to whom the agency was indebted for major financial assistance. A typical American businessman, he was entirely committed to the financial aspects of life. His sincerity and altruism gave him a dignity which everyone respected. He never pretended to be something he was not, and his business acumen was accompanied by a great sense of social responsibility. Son of a poor Lutheran clergyman, the manners and morals of his pious father were engrained in his character.

This father's hard work, perseverance, and—judging from his reputation—his "financial genius" had made him one of the richest men in the community. He loved to stress the fact that he was a "self-made man," and it was his great ambition to leave his flourishing business to his sons for further expansion. At home he was a tyrant who made everyone tremble and subject to his command. His wife was a simple woman from a poor family, not very beautiful, not gifted with any sort of talent. He had simply married an obedient bed companion and housewife, let her share his material goods and, in part, his social prominence, and supported various members of her family.

Jimmy, the patient, was born late in the marriage. At his birth, his older brother was 11, the next 10 years old. The mother, always anxious, but warmhearted and tender, devoted herself completely to her youngest child. She indulged him endlessly, her chief interest being to please him. All his wishes were fulfilled and his every expression of displeasure was a command to provide new pleasures. In such an atmosphere, narcissism and passivity were bound to flourish. These were the foundations, the powerful predisposing factors for the boy's further development. The growing brothers abetted the mother's coddling, and for them the little boy was a darling toy to whom everything was given without expecting anything in return.

The father did not concern himself with the boy during the first three or four years of his life. In those days Jimmy escaped the paternal tyranny, and the older brothers' battle against the despot took place outside the little boy's sphere of living. As the two older boys entered adolescence, this battle became more intense and ended in full rebellion. The younger brother, an introverted, artistically inclined boy, exchanged home for boarding school; the older, mechanically gifted, soon became independent and left the family.

The father was not a man to accept defeat. He simply renounced the older sons and with his boundless energy turned to his youngest, thus transferring the boy from his mother's care into his own. He partially retired from business but continued the pursuit of his financial and philanthropic activities from home. Jimmy, then four years old, spent the major part of the day with his father, and heard his conversations with visitors who were all in a subordinate position to his father and in many cases financially dependent on him. The father became to him a giant, and the boy reacted to his father's efforts to make him active and aggressive and to arouse intellectual interests in him with some anxiety, yet with positive signs of compliance. A strong unity developed, and the process of the boy's identification with his father, which the latter had mobilized, was in full flower.

When Jimmy was seven, his father became the victim of a serious chronic illness resulting in five years of invalidism, during which time he lived at home in a wing removed from the central part of the house. Whether this illness was pulmonary tuberculosis or lung abscess never became clear. The boy saw very little of his father and the most vivid memory of this sickness was his father's malodorous sputum. According to Jimmy's report, his father remained alive only to spit and to smell bad.

Around this time a change took place in Jimmy. He developed a condition which appears to have been a genuine depression. He stopped playing, ate little, and took no interest in anything. Then—in a striking way—he became very aggressive, tyrannized his mother, and attempted to dominate his brothers. His first truancy was to run away to a nearby woods and refuse to come home. He created for himself a world of fantasy and described in a pseudological fashion his heroic deeds and the unusual events in which he had played a prominent role. These pseudologies, typical for his age, may well have been the precursors of Jimmy's future actions. While his mother—"for the sake of peace" and not to disturb the sick father—continued giving in to him in everything, his brothers now ridiculed him and relegated him to the role of a "little nobody."

In the course of the next few years, Jimmy had some difficulties in school. Though he was intelligent and learned quickly, he found it hard to accept discipline, made no real friends, was malicious and aggressive without developing any worth-while activity—"a sissy"—as he characterized himself. Since the father's name carried weight in the community, Jimmy felt with partial justification that nothing could happen to him, his father's son. He was not yet guilty of asocial acts, not even childish stealing.

When he was 12 years old, his once beloved father died. Jimmy did not feel any grief. His reaction was manifested in increased narcissistic demands, the devaluation of all authority, and in a kind of aggressive triumph: "I am free—I can do whatever I want." Soon afterward, his asocial acts began to occur.

Before we discuss his pathology, let us say a few words about this boy's relationship to his father, which suffered such a sudden break. In this alliance with his father, which began in his fifth year, the spoiled, passive little boy became in part the father's appendage. Identification with the powerful father created a situation in which the ego was simultaneously weakened and strengthened. When he had been in competition with the father, he was forced to feel small and weak, but when he accepted as a criterion of his own value his father's verdict: "You are my wonderful boy," and his plans for the future: "You will be my successor," then Jimmy's self-conception and ego image resembled his marvelous father, and his narcissism—originally cultivated by his mother—received new powers from his relationship with his father. In his seventh or eighth year Jimmy lost this "wonderful" father (not yet by death, but by devaluation), and his *own* conception of himself as a "wonderful boy" suffered a heavy blow.

The events of later years give more understanding of what took place in this period which was so fateful for him. As mentioned before, I first saw Jimmy when he was 14 years old.

FIRST PHASE OF TREATMENT

I was determined to resist accepting Jimmy for treatment. I had never had any experience in treating juvenile delinquents, associating such cases with Aichhorn and his school, which I considered outside my sphere. I yielded, however, to the pressure of the boy's mother, whom I knew and respected, and to the pleas of the heads of the social agency. Because of the uncertainty of my approach and in contrast to my usual habit, I made notes of Jimmy's behavior. They contain the results of four to six interviews. At the time they seemed somewhat sterile to me and yet, regarding them in the light of later insights, they are extraordinarily illuminating. The interviews took place in 1935.

Jimmy was a typical young psychopath. He was increasingly unable to submit to the discipline of school. There was a repetitive pattern in his pathological acting out. At first he ingratiated himself by doing quite well; after a time he became insolent and rebellious toward his superiors, seduced his friends to break discipline, tried to impress them by the extravagance of his financial expenditures, and started quarrels and fights only to escape in a cowardly fashion under the ridicule of his companions. He forged checks with his mother's or older brother's signatures and disrupted the school and the neighborhood by his misdeeds. Every attempt to bring about his adaptation by changing schools ended in truancy. Toward me he behaved very arrogantly. With an obvious lack of respect he stated that he had not come of his own accord.

He claimed nothing was wrong with him; that it was "the others" who would benefit by treatment.

He admitted he had again run away from school, and that this had been bad for him, and insisted that his trouble started when he began to "grow very fast." He wanted to remain a little boy; when he was little he was his father's pet. His father used to say, "Just wait until you are grown-up: *we* [father and he] will show the world."

Jimmy complained that the boys laughed at him; but "You know," he said, "I can defend myself." Sometimes he was sincere and admitted that essentially he was helpless and weak: "You know, they never took me seriously at home. For my big brothers I was sort of a puppet, a joke. I was always a kid whose ideas did not count and whose performance was laughable."

School was like home. He had difficulties because not to learn meant showing them, "I can do what I want, and do not have to obey." He forgot everything he learned, so "Why learn," he asked, "if I forget it?" He told me that his father had cursed his brothers: "I will show them," he had said, "they will end up in the gutter without my help." But to his father, Jimmy was different: father based all his hopes on him. When he was a little boy he felt that nothing could happen to him because his father was very powerful. Everything was subject to his father and together they were allies against all hostile influences. His father's sickness changed all this. The big promise, "We will show them," could not be redeemed. The brothers were now stronger than he. They ridiculed him and he was waiting to be grown-up; then he would show them!

In school it was always the same story. The teachers and especially the headmasters were "no good." They pretended to be something they were not. Of course he did not wish to obey them. He knew at least as much as they did, but they refused to acknowledge it. The boys were no good. Some might have been but they were led on by the others. And all this was instigated from "above," because "they" knew that he would not let himself be put upon.

In this short period of observation I learned that Jimmy was infuriated by not being acknowledged as someone special; some of his complaints had an uncanny, paranoid character.

During our meetings, Jimmy played the undaunted hero, but with no trace of any emotion. One got an impression of great affective emptiness in him. All his asocial acts were his means of showing that he was something special. Stealing, debts were ways of obtaining money for the purpose, one might say, of buying narcissistic gratifications. He rebelled against all authority and devalued it. The moment he perceived that the methods he employed no longer sustained his prestige, his displeasure quickly mounted and drove him away.

With me he was overbearing, arrogant, cocksure. One day he came with the question: "Are you a Freudian?" He then proceeded, most unintelligently, to lecture me about analysis with catchwords he had picked up, or remarks based on titles he had seen. For instance: "That thing about civilization is particularly idiotic"; or "The old man [meaning Freud] isn't even a doctor." When I tried to point out to him that, after all, he did not know anything, and that I believed he talked so big because he was afraid, he stopped coming; as usual, a truant.

He presented such a typical picture of a juvenile delinquent that I felt concern about his future, wondering whether he would eventually become a criminal. His lack of affect, inability to form human relationships, and paranoid ideas led me to consider the possibility of an incipient schizophrenia.

SECOND PHASE OF TREATMENT

I did not see Jimmy for eight years, but remained in contact with several people close to him. Some of the news about him was reassuring. He nevertheless confronted those around him with one problem after another. These were truancies in a more adult sense. He accepted positions which he did not keep, responsibilities he failed to meet. He made promises and broke them, with serious consequences to himself and to others. He accepted financial commitments, but neglected them so that they ended in failure. He provoked situations ominous not only for himself but also for those whom he had lured into these situations with false promises which to him, however, were real. Up to the time he came of age, his misdeeds were regarded as youthful indiscretions by the executors of the family estate. At 21, he assumed that he was now financially independent and had already made financial commitments in the most extravagant ventures, when, to his fury, he was placed under legal guardianship.

With his customary bravado, Jimmy volunteered for military service during the war. He reported for duty on his new, shiny motorcycle. Soon he was the center of admiration among his comrades. Neither he nor they had any doubt that he would become one of the heroes of the war. He had, after all, volunteered to protect his fatherland, and his grandiose spending, his hints at connections with military authorities left no doubt that he was someone quite special. In this atmosphere he thrived until one day the news came that a commanding officer, noted for his severity, was to attend inspection. Jimmy had sufficient orientation in reality to realize that one cannot fool military authorities. The "hero" turned into a truant. But in military life that was not so easy. One does not desert, as one does in civilian life under the auspices of an approving family. On the contrary, one is punished for such actions, and Jimmy could never tolerate punishment. He had an attack of anxiety—which was genuine—and a delusional state—which was not. He was declared to be sick, taken to a hospital, and from there was sent home.

The anxiety had been real, and his fear frightened him. His dream of being a hero was shattered. It is quite possible that under more favorable circumstances Jimmy, like so many other heroes of wars and revolutions, might have made his pathology serve a glorious career. Now he remembered that years ago a woman had predicted just this kind of fear, and he came straight to me for help.

He was in analysis so-called, although it was actually more a supportive therapy, for eight years. The success of this treatment, while limited, was nevertheless important for him. During that period I witnessed many episodes in his pathological acting out, and gained some insight into its nature. What kept him in treatment, however, was his anxiety which had increased since the war episode. It was evident that the defensive function of his acting out had been sufficiently threatened by reality that it was no longer adequate to hold internal dangers in check.

During the eight years which had elapsed since my first contact with Jimmy, he had been put through high school and prep school by the combined efforts of tutors, teachers, advisors, the head of the child guidance clinic, and his financial managers. They had even succeeded in having him admitted to a college where he stayed half a year. His intelligence and ability to grasp things quickly had, of course, been a help, but further than this he could not go. His narcissism did not permit him to be one of many; his self-love could be nourished only by feeling that he was unique. This desire for "uniqueness" did not, however, make him a lonely, schizoid personality.* He was oriented toward reality which to him was a stage on which he was destined to play the leading role with the rest of humanity as an admiring audience. There were for him no human relationships, no emotional ties which did not have narcissistic gratification as their goal. His contact with reality was maintained, but it was not object libido which formed the bridge to it.

Editor's Note: The word lonely is a misnomer. Schizoid individuals, like psychopaths, are often *alone*, but do not feel lonesome or lonely. The latter emotions require a capacity for, if not the experience of, attachment and loss.

He was always active and he surrounded himself with people; he sent out "pseudopodia," but only to retract them laden with gifts from the outside world.

After Jimmy left college, it was necessary to find him a job, to settle him in some field of work. All attempts at this of course failed. As in his school days, he could not tolerate authority and had no capacity for sustained effort. Success had to be immediate; he had to play the leading role from the start. He decided to become a gentleman farmer. A farm was purchased for him and he worked zealously on the plans for the farm. The preliminary work was done, the livestock was in the barn, and Jimmy even behaved as a socially responsible person. He created several positions at the farm for his former cronies; the fact that they knew as little about farming as he did was to him beside the point. His adaptation to reality had come to its end, and the enterprise was doomed to failure. Jimmy, however, acquired an elegant country outfit, saw to it that his clothing was saturated with barnyard smells, dyed his hair and eyebrows blond, and appeared among a group of former acquaintances in a New York restaurant as a "country gentleman." His farm project was soon involved in various difficulties, and his protégés deserted him; he was in debt, and financial ruin seemed imminent, when his guardians came to his rescue and he was saved by his fortune.

In another episode Jimmy was a great writer. Here his pseudo-contact with others was even more intense. He presided over a kind of literary salon where intellectuals gathered about his fireplace, with Jimmy in the center. Short stories were his specialty for, of course, he lacked the capacity for prolonged, patient creativity. He knew how to make life so very pleasant for his literary admirers that they remained within his circle. He had even drawn several well-known writers into his orbit. He already visualized himself as a great writer, and brought a sample of his productivity for me to read. When I seemed somewhat critical (his writing was pretentious and quite without originality) he was furious and told me that I simply did not understand modern literature.

He soon gave up his literary career to become a movie producer. He made connections with men in the industry and spent considerable sums of money, but the result was always the same. At one time he became an inventor and even succeeded in inventing a few small things. It was fascinating to watch the great ado over these little inventions and how he used them to appear a genius to himself and to others. He had calling cards printed with the identification "inventor" on them, and set up a laboratory to work out his discoveries. This time he chose as his collaborator an experienced physicist, and within a short period succeeded in making this man believe that Jimmy was a genius. With uncanny skill he created an atmosphere in which the physicist was convinced that his own achievements were inspired by Jimmy, the genius. His pretense that he was a genius was often so persuasive that others were taken in for a short time. Jimmy's self-esteem was so inflated by these reactions from his environment that occasionally he was able to achieve things which to some degree justified the admiration which he himself had generated.

In the course of his treatment I succeeded in getting Jimmy through college. His success in temporarily impressing his teachers as an out-standing student of philosophy was almost a farce. Actually he knew little beyond the titles and the blurbs on the jackets of the books; but on this basis he was able to engage for hours in polemics, and it was some time before he was found out. In these activities Jimmy did not impress us as a real impostor. His transformations from a pseudo-impostor into a real one were only transitory. For instance, he made certain connec-tions by using the name of the above-mentioned collaborator; another time he altered his name in such a way that it was almost identical with the name of a celebrity in a particular field. He was not an extravagant impostor; his pretenses were always close to reality but were neverthe-less a sham.

For purposes of comparison, it may serve to summarize briefly the stories of impostors who are closely related to the type described. They differ only in the stability of their chosen roles. A fascinating example is the well-known case of Ferdinand Demara, which was much discussed several years ago (McCarthy, 1952). After running away from home, Demara became, in turn, a teacher of psychology, a monk, a soldier, a sailor, a deputy sheriff, a psychiatrist and a surgeon—always under another man's name. With almost incredible cleverness and skill he obtained each time the credentials of an expert, and made use of knowledge acquired *ad hoc* so brilliantly that he was able to perpetrate his hoaxes with complete success. It was always "by accident," never through mistakes he had made, that he was exposed as an impostor. In his own estimation, he was a man of genius for whom it was not necessary to acquire academic knowledge through prolonged studies, but who was able to achieve anything, thanks to his innate genius.

Reading his life history, one sees that he was perpetually in pursuit of an identity which would do justice to his narcissistic conception of himself in terms of "I am a genius," and which at the same time would serve to deny his own identity. This denial of his own identity appears to me to be the chief motive for his actions, as is true in the case of other impostors.* In the course of his masquerading, Demara did much capable work and could bask in the sunshine of his successes. His parents had wanted to finance his way through college and medical school but he was never interested in a conventional way of life. When interviewed by reporters he acknowledged his enormous ambition and his need to take "short cuts." He declared that he would like for a change to use his own name but that he could not because of all that had happened. Whenever Demara resumes his activities, one may presume it will be possible only under a usurped name or not at all. His statement that he cannot use his own name—however rational it may sound—is nevertheless the expression of a deeper motive.

Another famous impostor of recent years is the "physicist" Hewitt, who, under the name of Dr. Derry, began teaching theoretical physics, mathematics, and electrical engineering in numerous universities with great success, without ever having finished high school (Brean, 1954). Like Jimmy, he sometimes used his own name, but again like Jimmy, under false colors. He impersonated two different actual doctors of philosophy in physics, masqueraded as a nationally known man, and took responsible positions under various names. He had been unmasked twice, yet tried again to achieve success under still another physicist's name.

In Hewitt's life history there are many analogies to Jimmy's history. Hewitt's need for admiration was as great as Jimmy's, and the narcissistic motive behind his masquerading was equally evident. At the beginning of his career as an impostor, Hewitt was somewhat unsure of himself, but when he found himself being admired, his personality unfolded its full capacities. He was able to create for himself an atmosphere of power and prestige. When he felt that his masquerading was becoming too dangerous, he abandoned his project, changed his name, and embarked on another masquerade which became a new source of narcissistic satisfaction. Sometimes he was presented with an opportunity to work under his own name, as he was a gifted and really brilliant man who could have had a successful career. Such offers he always turned down: he could work only under another name, in an atmosphere of tension, in the precarious situation of imminent exposure. Like Jimmy, he regarded himself as a genius and courted situations in which he would be exposed as the counterpart of a genius—a liar, an impostor.

---

*Editor's Note: This motivation should not be confused with a dissociative fugue state, in which amnesia plays a central role. Imposturing psychopaths are conscious of their schemes.

Demara, Hewitt, and Jimmy appear to be victims of the same patho-logical process of the ego—only the level of their functioning is different. Demara changed the objects of his identifications, perhaps because he was driven by fear of impending unmasking. The objects whose names he temporarily bore corresponded to his high ego ideal, and he was able to maintain himself on the high level of the men he imperson-ated. His manifold talents and his intelligence were outstanding, his capacity for sublimation was but little impaired. It was not lack of ability, but psychopathology which made him an impostor.

Hewitt had a much more consolidated ego ideal. His interests were from the beginning oriented toward physics, his talent in this direction even made him a child prodigy; his path was marked out. But he rejected any success which he could realistically achieve through work and perseverance under his own name, and preferred *pretending* under the mask of a stranger's name. The objects of his identification were physi-cists of repute, men who already were what he would have liked to become. In this as in the other cases, I consider the incapacity to accept the demands imposed by the discipline of study, and the lack of perse-verance, to be a secondary motive for becoming an impostor.

Jimmy, in his striving for an ego ideal, appears to us like a caricature of Demara and Hewitt. In contrast to them he was unable to find objects for successful identification because his limited capacity for sublimation and his lack of talent made this impossible for him. He was able to satisfy his fantasies of grandeur only in naïve acting out, pretending that he was *really* in accordance with his ego ideal. On closer examination I was struck by the resemblance of his acting out to the performance of girls in prepuberty.

> Various identifications which later in puberty can be explained as defense mechanisms and which one meets in schizoid personali-ties as expressions of a pathological emotional condition, prove on closer inspection, to have a specific character in prepuberty. They remind us strongly of the play of small children, and seem to be an "acting out" of those transitory, conscious wishes that express the idea, "That's what I want to be like." It is noteworthy that this acting out has a concrete and real character, different from mere fantasying [Deutsch, 1944].

Jimmy too acted out his transitory ideals which never became fully established. Compared with Dr. Greenacre's (1952) "psychopathic pa-tients," Jimmy's ideals did not have the character of magic grandeur, and were not so unattached to reality. Quite the contrary. Jimmy always turned to external reality to gratify his narcissistic needs. His emptiness and the lack of individuality in his emotional life and moral structure remind us furthermore of the "as-if" personalities (Deutsch, 1942). In contrast to these, Jimmy's ego did not dissolve in numerous identifications with external objects. He sought, on the contrary, to impose on others belief in his greatness, and in this he often succeeded. His only identifications were with objects which corresponded to his ego ideal— just like the impostor Hewitt, only on a more infantile level. Another difference is that the "as-if" patients are not aware of their disturbance, whereas Jimmy, while firmly pretending that he *was* what he pretended to be, asked me again and again, sometimes in despair: "Who am I? Can *you* tell me that?"

In spite of these individual differences between the various types, I believe that all impostors have this in common: they assume the identities of other men not because they themselves lack the ability for achievement, but because they have to hide under a strange name to materialize a more or less reality-adapted fantasy. It seems to me that the ego of the impostor, as expressed in his own true name, is devaluated, guilt-laden. Hence he must usurp the name of an individual who fulfills the requirements of his own magnificent ego ideal. Later we shall see that Jimmy's fear of being unmasked as an impostor increased when he began to be successful under his own name and figure.

As his treatment proceeded, Jimmy's fears increased as his acting out lessened. With this change of behavior he entered a new phase in his therapy: the phase of anxiety. It was this phase which revealed more of the nature of the process. But this does not mean that the phase of acting out was free of anxiety. It was anxiety that brought him to me, and anxiety kept him with me. In time, his increasing anxieties assumed a more hypochondriacal character. He examined his body, his pulse, etc., and wanted to be certain that a physician could be reached. It was not difficult to assume that a man whose personality was limited by an unsuccessful identification with his father repeated his father's disease in hypochondriacal symptoms.

By and by Jimmy gave up his grotesque acting out and his behavior became increasingly realistic. First, he founded an institute for inventions. This project was still in accordance with his fantasy of being a great inventor. Because he had associated himself with a friend who, despite his naïve belief in Jimmy, was genuinely gifted scientifically and had already achieved recognition, and because of the considerable sums of money available, Jimmy gradually worked his way toward acquiring a going concern. Here, for the first time in his life, he functioned well and enjoyed a certain solid respect. He limited his acting out to founding a colony for artists in which he acted the role of a "brilliant connoisseur of art"; also he set up for himself some sort of an "altar" at home. He married a girl with an infantile personality who blindly believed in his "genius" and adored him. When she began to have doubts, he simply sent her away and threatened her with divorce. Love he never experienced; even from his children he expected gratifications for his narcissism and he hated them when they failed him in this respect.

The condition which now confronted us seemed paradoxical: the more effectively he functioned in reality, the more anxiety he developed. In the days when he had really been a swindler, he never feared exposure. Now that he worked more honestly and pretended less, he was tortured by the fear that his deceit might be discovered. He felt like an impostor in his new role: that of doing honest work. Obviously he remained an impostor after all, and in his very real personal success he now had an inner perception of his inferiority. In the beginning, we had had the suspicion that Jimmy always feared his own inferiority, and that he was hiding his anxiety behind a bloated ego ideal. It could now be better understood why he inquired after his identity, why he had the depersonalized feeling, "Who am I really?" In this he reminds us of those more or less neurotic individuals who, having achieved success, experience like Jimmy the painful sensation: "I am an impostor," stemming from the same inner motivation.

Jimmy's anxieties gradually acquired a phobic character. His professional activities were impeded by a fear of leaving town and of being too far from home. This evidently represented a counterphobic mechanism against his earlier running away.

Thus we may speak of a certain success in his treatment which was never a psychoanalysis. In my 40 years of practice I have never seen a patient as little capable of transference as Jimmy. He and I sometimes talked of "hot-air therapy," for I called his grandiose acting out, "hot-air," until it was greatly devalued. At the same time I appealed to his narcissism by showing him what he could really achieve. In this way we continued for eight years. About two years ago I passed him on to a colleague who is continuing the therapy.

Reviewing Jimmy's pathological behavior chronologically, the connection between his preadolescent delinquency and his later acting out becomes clear. By the phrase he used when he came to see me as a 14-year-old, "I became grown-up too fast," he meant to say that he did not yet feel capable of playing the role his father had assigned to him for a time when he would be grown-up. His high ego ideal, cultivated by the father and an identification with the "great father," did not permit him—despite a certain degree of insight—to wait for the process of growing up to take place. He demanded that the world treat him not according to his achievements but according to his exalted ego ideal. The refusal of his environment to do so was an attack on himself, on his grandeur, on his ego ideal. This feeling that hostile elements were aligned against him grew at times into paranoid reactions. He responded to these insults in a way which brought him to the borderline of real criminal behavior; but when he began to feel that he was defeated, he ran away.

Perhaps if he had had enough aggression at his disposal, he would have continued his career as a criminal. An appeal to his conscience was fruitless, as, after all, he considered himself to be a victim and his actions as self-defense. Maybe this is true of all juvenile delinquents. Social injustice and a desire to avenge oneself for it is often given as a reason for delinquent behavior. In Jimmy's case such a rationalization could not be used.

His passivity led him in another direction. Instead of fighting for his narcissistic "rights," he found less dangerous and more regressive methods of asserting his ego ideal. What he was not, he could become by "pretending." Only when this was made impossible for him—first through external reality (the army), then through his treatment—was he overwhelmed by anxiety and feelings of inferiority, and one could then realize the defensive function of his pathological behavior.

We suspect that Demara and Hewitt, the other two impostors mentioned, were also hiding such an ego through identification with someone else's ego, by means of what might be called a "nonego ego." In these cases of a more solidly constructed imposture, the inner anxiety is partly projected to the outside, and the impostor lives in perpetual fear of discovery. Jimmy did not fear such discovery, for he had not assumed another's name. What threatened him was that if his "pretending" were to be unmasked, he would be laughed at, as he was once ridiculed by his brothers and later by his schoolmates.* He developed real anxiety only when he gave up "pretending" so that both he and others were confronted with his "true" ego.

Let us consider the causes of Jimmy's pathology: Greenacre (1952)—in agreement with other writers—finds etiological factors in the emotional deprivation of psychopaths and delinquents. Her emphasis rests on the combination of both indulgence and severity on the part of the parental figures; this is in accordance with Wilhelm Reich's (1933) conception of the character structure of the psychopath. The emotional

---

*Editor's Note: The imposturing becomes a behavioral defense against the anticipation of shame.

climate of Jimmy's childhood was different, but evidently no less disastrous. Whereas Greenacre's patient was emotionally deprived, Jimmy was overloaded with maternal love. I knew the mother very well, and I know that she was one of those masochistic mothers who, loving and warmhearted, completely surrender themselves for the benefit of others. She was a masochistic victim not only of the despotic father, but also of her children, especially Jimmy. Her last child's every wish was granted. Any active striving he had was paralyzed through premature compliance; every need for wooing and giving was smothered by the mother's loving initiative in meeting his demands.

I believe that the emotional "overfeeding" of a child is capable of producing very much the same results as emotional frustration. It contributes to an increase of infantile narcissism, makes adaptation to reality and relationships to objects more difficult. It creates intolerance of frustration, weakens the ego's ability to develop constructive defenses, and is in large measure responsible for passivity.

Jimmy's relationship with his father was very well suited to strengthen the predisposition created by the mother. The powerful, despotic personality of the father contributed to Jimmy's passivity, and the father's narcissism prepared the ground for Jimmy's later, fateful identification with him.

These attitudes of the parents created a predisposition for the pathological development of the boy. But it was a traumatic experience which activated this predisposition. The father's sickness and isolation caused an abrupt interruption of the normal maturing process of Jimmy's ego. The frustration stemming from the fact that Jimmy was no longer able to feel himself to be part of a great father crippled his ego which was not yet strong enough to endure the brutal attack of separation. The enforced awareness of his self as being distinct from that of his father was anachronistic in his development. The normal process of identification had not yet reached that degree of maturity from which further development would have been possible.

Simultaneously with the separation from his father came the devaluation of that "powerful" figure. Consequently, the character of his identification also underwent a change. What had so far strengthened his ego was no longer available. With the devaluation of the father, a shadow fell across his own identified ego. The fact that the traumatic event occurred in the latter part of latency was decisive for Jimmy's psychopathology. As we know, this period is of utmost importance for the maturation of the ego apparatus, for the establishment of a less rigid superego, and for the capacity to cope with reality. In a normal, gradual development of a boy in latency, not harmed by trauma, Jimmy would have transferred his identification with the father onto other suitable objects. Eventually his ego would have been ready to assimilate the identifications into the self, and to achieve a reliable degree of inner stability. His ambivalent sexual relationship to the father would have yielded to tender love, and a path toward reality and toward the formation of constant object relationships would have been made.

The pathogenic force of this trauma was due to two factors: first, its suddenness; second, its daily repetition during the four years that preceded his father's death. As a result, regressive forces in the ego replaced progress in development, and the whole process of sublimation was impaired.[1] The boy was incapable of goal-oriented endeavor, because he was unable to postpone reaching an attempted goal. The fact that his relationship to the father never became desexualized was revealed in his masturbatory fantasies of a passive-feminine-masochistic character and in his fears of homosexuality. His relationship to his mother became submerged in his identification with her as his father's debased sexual object. The manifestations of this identification could be traced back from his recent masturbatory fantasies to that period of his childhood in which he had been enuretic (Michaels, 1955).

It is interesting to observe pathology in what is commonly agreed to be "normal." The world is crowded with "as-if" personalities, and even more so with impostors and pretenders. Ever since I became interested in the impostor, he pursues me everywhere. I find him among my friends and acquaintances, as well as in myself. Little Nancy, a fine three-and-a-half-year-old daughter of one of my friends, goes around with an air of dignity, holding her hands together tightly. Asked about this attitude she explains: "I am Nancy's guardian angel, and I'm taking care of little Nancy." Her father asked her about the angel's name. "Nancy" was the proud answer of this little impostor.

Having referred to "normal impostors," I should clarify my conception of the term "impostor." The pathological impostor endeavors to eliminate the friction between his pathologically exaggerated ego ideal and the other, devaluated, inferior, guilt-laden part of his ego, in a manner which is characteristic for him: he behaves as if his ego ideal were identical with himself; and he expects everyone else to acknowledge this status. If the inner voice of his devaluated ego on the one hand, reminds him of the unreality of his ego ideal, he still clings to this

---

[1] There are psychopaths endowed with great capacities for sublimation and creativeness, although their ego functioning is gravely impaired.

narcissistic position. He desperately tries—through pretending and under cover of someone else's name—to maintain his ego ideal, to force it upon the world, so to speak.

A similar conflict, though in a milder form, seems to exist also in the normal personality. In the complex development of a "normal" individual, there are certain irregularities, and only seldom can a successful harmony be attained. Perhaps the identity between the ego ideal and the self is achieved only by saints, geniuses, or psychotics. As one's ego ideal can never be completely gratified from *within*, we direct our demands to the external world, *pretending* (like Jimmy) *that we actually are what we would like to be.* Very often we encounter paranoid reactions in normal personalities, which result from the fact that their environment has refused to accept an imposture of this sort.

Both history and belletristic literature are rich in impostors. Thomas Mann's (1954) story about the impostor Felix Krull shows the most profound understanding of this type. It is amazing to consider how the psychological genius of a writer is able to grasp intuitively insights at which we arrive laboriously through clinical empiricism. The passivity, the narcissistic ego ideal, the devaluation of the father's authority, and the complicated processes of identification of the impostor Felix Krull are very well understood by Mann; and even the profound similarity between the shabby Krull and the wealthy, distinguished prince whose name and existence Krull, the impostor, takes over, is well understood by the writer.

I wish to close by repeating what I stated at the beginning. The case here discussed represents only a certain type of psychopath. I believe that such an individual typologic approach to the large problem of psychopathy may prove very fruitful.

REFERENCES

Abraham, K. (1925). Die Geschichte eines Hochstaplers im Lichte psychoanalytischer Erkenntnis. *Imago,* 11:355–370. (Trans. A. Strachey [1935]. *Psychoanal. Quart.,* 4:570–587.)

Aichhorn, A. (1925). *Verwahrloste Jugend [Wayward Youth].* Vienna: Internationaler Psychoanalytischer Verlag; New York: Viking Press, 1935.

Brean, H. (1954). Narvin Hewitt Ph(ony)D. *Life Magazine,* April 12.

Deutsch, H. (1942). Some forms of emotional disturbance and their relationship to schizophrenia. *Psychoanal. Quart.,* 11:301–321.

Deutsch, H. (1944). *The Psychology of Women, Vol. I.* New York: Grune & Stratton, p. 9.

Greenacre, P. (1952). Conscience in the psychopath. In: *Trauma, Growth, and Personality*. New York: Norton, p. 167.

Mann, T. (1954). *Bekenntnisse des Hochstaplers Felix Krull* [*Confessions of Felix Krull*]. Frankfurt: Fischer Verlag; New York: Knopf, 1955.

McCarthy, J. (1952). The master impostor. *Life Magazine*, January 28.

Michaels, J. J. (1955). *Disorders of Character*. Springfield, IL: Charles C. Thomas.

Reich, W. (1933). *Charakteranalyse* [*Character Analysis*]. Vienna: The Author; New York: Orgone Institute Press, 1945.

9

The Antisocial Tendency

D. W. Winnicott

D. W. Winnicott first read this paper before the British Psycho-Analytical Society on June 20, 1956. It was subsequently published in *Through Paediatrics to Psychoanalysis*. Although he does not acknowledge any biological contributions to the antisocial tendency—what contemporary psychiatry would label symptoms of conduct disorder—he elaborates on the important role of the mother in gratifying object seeking and containing the aggressive impulses of her child. Successful "holding" promotes a "union of the two trends" and ushers in a tendency toward self-cure. Winnicott's therapeutic optimism—an empirically verifiable finding 50 years later for the conduct-disordered child—and practical clinical wisdom are evident throughout these writings.

The antisocial tendency provides psychoanalysis with some awkward problems, problems of a practical as well as a theoretical nature. Freud, through his introduction to Aichhorn's *Wayward Youth*, showed that psychoanalysis not only contributes to the understanding of delinquency, but it is also enriched by an understanding of the work of those who cope with delinquents.

I have chosen to discuss the antisocial tendency, not delinquency. The reason is that the organized antisocial defense is overloaded with secondary gain and social reactions which make it difficult for the investigator to get to its core. By contrast the antisocial tendency can be studied as it appears in the normal or near-normal child, where it is related to the difficulties that are inherent in emotional development.

I will start with two simple references to clinical material:

For my first child analysis I chose a delinquent. This boy attended regularly for a year and the treatment stopped because of the disturbance that the boy caused in the clinic. I could say that the analysis was going well, and its cessation caused distress both to the boy and to myself in spite of the fact that on several occasions I got badly bitten on the buttocks. The boy got out on the roof and also he spilt so much water that the basement became flooded. He broke into my locked car and drove it away in bottom gear on the self-starter. The clinic ordered termination of the treatment for the sake of the other patients. He went to an approved school.

I may say that he is now 35, and he has been able to earn his living in a job that caters to his restlessness. He is married with several children. Nevertheless I am afraid to follow up his case for fear that I should become involved again with a psychopath, and I prefer that society should continue to take the burden of his management.*

It can easily be seen that the treatment for this boy should have been not psychoanalysis but placement. Psychoanalysis only made sense if added after placement. Since this time I have watched analysts of all kinds fail in the psychoanalysis of antisocial children.

By contrast, the following story brings out the fact that an antisocial tendency may sometimes be treated very easily if the treatment be adjunctive to specialized environmental care.

I was asked by a friend to discuss the case of her son, the eldest of a family of four. She could not bring John to me in an open way because of her husband, who objects to psychology on religious grounds. All she could do was to have a talk with me about the boy's compulsion to steal, which was developing into something quite serious; he was stealing in a big way from shops as well as at home. It was not possible for practical reasons to arrange for anything else but for the mother and myself to have a quick meal together in a restaurant, in the course of which she told me about the troubles and asked me for advice. There was nothing for me to do unless I could do it then and there. I therefore explained the meaning of the stealing and suggested that she should find a good moment in her relationship with the boy and make an interpretation to him. It appeared that she and John had a good relationship with each other for a few moments each evening after he had gone to bed; usually at such a time he would discuss the stars and the moon. This moment could be used.

I said: "Why not tell him that you know that when he steals he is not wanting the things that he steals but he is looking for something that he has a right to: that he is making a claim on his mother and father because he feels deprived of their love." I told her to use language which he could understand. I may say that I knew enough of this family, in which both the parents are musicians, to see how it was that this boy had become to some extent a deprived child, although he has a good home.

Editor's Note: Winnicott's excellent clinical judgment is quite apparent.

Some time later I had a letter telling me that she had done what I suggested. She wrote:

I told him that what he really wanted when he stole money and food and things was his mum; and I must say I didn't really expect him to understand, but he did seem to. I asked him if he thought we didn't love him because he was so naughty sometimes, and he said right out that he didn't think we did, much. Poor little scrap! I felt so awful, I can't tell you. So I told him never, never to doubt it again and if he ever did feel doubtful to remind me to tell him again. But of course I shan't need reminding for a long time, it's been such a shock. One seems to need these shocks. So I'm being a lot more demonstrative to try and keep him from being doubtful any more. And up to now there's been absolutely no more stealing.

The mother had had a talk with the former teacher and had explained to her that the boy was in need of love and appreciation, and had gained her co-operation although the boy gives a lot of trouble at school.

Now, after eight months, it is possible to report that there has been no return of stealing, and the relationship between the boy and his family has very much improved.

In considering this case it must be remembered that I had known the mother very well during her adolescence and to some extent had seen her through an antisocial phase of her own. She was the eldest in a large family. She had a very good home but very strong discipline was exerted by the father, especially at the time when she was a small child. What I did therefore had the effect of a double therapy, enabling this young woman to get insight into her own difficulties through the help that she was able to give to her son. When we are able to help parents to help their children we do in fact help them about themselves.

(In another paper I propose to give clinical examples illustrating the management of children with antisocial tendency; here I do no more than attempt a brief statement of the basis of my personal attitude to the clinical problem.)

NATURE OF ANTISOCIAL TENDENCY

The antisocial tendency *is not a diagnosis*. It does not compare directly with other diagnostic terms such as neurosis and psychosis. The antisocial tendency may be found in a normal individual, or in one that is neurotic or psychotic.

For the sake of simplicity I will refer only to children, but the antisocial tendency may be found at all ages. The various terms in use in Great Britain may be brought together in the following way:

A child becomes a *deprived child* when deprived of certain essential features of home life. Some degree of what might be called the "deprived complex" becomes manifest. *Antisocial behavior* will be manifest at home or in a wider sphere. On account of *the antisocial tendency* the child may eventually need to *be deemed maladjusted,* and to receive treatment in a *hostel for maladjusted children,* or may be brought before the courts as *beyond control.* The child, now *a delinquent,* may then become a *probationer* under a court order, or may be sent to *an approved school.* If the home ceases to function in an important respect the child may be taken over by the Children's Committee (under the Children Act, 1948) and be given *"care and protection."* If possible a foster home will be found. Should these measures fail the young adult may be said to have become a *psychopath* and may be sent by the courts to a *Borstal* or to prison. There may be an established tendency to repeat crimes for which we use the term *recidivism.*

All this makes no comment on the individual's psychiatric diagnosis.

The antisocial tendency is characterized by an *element in it which compels the environment to be important.* The patient through unconscious drives compels someone to attend to management. It is the task of the therapist to become involved in this, the patient's unconscious drive, and the work is done by the therapist in terms of management, tolerance, and understanding.

The antisocial tendency implies hope. Lack of hope is the basic feature of the deprived child who, of course, is not all the time being antisocial. In the period of hope the child manifests an antisocial tendency. This may be awkward for society, and for you if it is your bicycle that is stolen, but those who are not personally involved can see the hope that underlies the compulsion to steal. Perhaps one of the reasons why we tend to leave the therapy of the delinquent to others is that we dislike being stolen from?

The understanding that the antisocial act is an expression of hope is vital in the treatment of children who show the antisocial tendency. Over and over again one sees the moment of hope wasted, or withered, because of mismanagement or intolerance. This is another way of saying that the treatment of the antisocial tendency is not psychoanalysis but management, a going to meet and match the moment of hope.

There is a direct relationship between the antisocial tendency and deprivation. This has long been known by specialists in the field, but it is largely due to John Bowlby that there is now a widespread recognition of the relationship that exists between the antisocial tendency in individuals and emotional deprivation, typically in the period of late infancy and the early toddler stage, round about the age of one and two years.

When there is an antisocial tendency *there has been a true deprivation* (not a simple privation); that is to say, there has been a loss of something good that has been positive in the child's experience up to a certain date,[1] and that has been withdrawn; the withdrawal has extended over a period of time longer than that over which the child can keep the memory of the experience alive. The comprehensive statement of deprivation is one that includes both the early and the late, both the pinpoint trauma and the sustained traumatic condition and also both the near normal and the clearly abnormal.

NOTE

In a statement in my own language of Klein's depressive position, I have tried to make clear the intimate relationship that exists between Klein's concept and Bowlby's emphasis on deprivation. Bowlby's three stages of the clinical reaction of a child of two years who goes to hospital can be given a theoretical formulation in terms of the gradual loss of hope because of the death of the internal object or introjected version of the external object that is lost. What can be further discussed is the relative importance of death of the internal object through anger and contact of "good objects" with hate products within the psyche, and ego maturity or immaturity insofar as this affects the capacity to keep alive a memory.

Bowlby needs Klein's intricate statement that is built round the understanding of melancholia, and that derives from Freud and Abraham, but it is also true that psychoanalysis needs Bowlby's emphasis on deprivation, if psychoanalysis is ever to come to terms with this special subject of the antisocial tendency.

There are always two trends in the antisocial tendency although the accent is sometimes more on one than on the other. One trend is represented typically in stealing, and the other in destructiveness. By *one* trend the child is looking for something, somewhere, and failing to

---

[1] This idea seems to be implied in Bowlby's *Maternal Care and Mental Health*, where he compares his observations with those of others and suggests that the different results are explained according to the age of a child at the time of deprivation.

find it seeks it elsewhere, when hopeful. By the *other* the child is seeking that amount of environmental stability which will stand the strain resulting from impulsive behavior. This is a search for an environmental provision that has been lost, a human attitude which, because it can be relied on, gives freedom to the individual to move and to act and to get excited.

It is particularly because of the second of these trends that the child provokes total environmental reactions, as if seeking an ever-widening frame, a circle which had as its first example the mother's arms or the mother's body. One can discern a series—the mother's body, the mother's arms, the parental relationship, the home, the family including cousins and near relations, the school, the locality with its police-stations, the country with its laws.*

In examining the near-normal and (in terms of individual development) the early roots of the antisocial tendency, I wish to keep in mind all the time these two trends: object-seeking and destruction.

STEALING

Stealing is at the center of the antisocial tendency, with the associated lying.

The child who steals an object is not looking for *the object stolen but seeks the mother over whom he or she has rights*. These rights derive from the fact that (from the child's point of view) the mother was created by the child. The mother met the child's primary creativity, and so became the object that the child was ready to find. (The child could not have created the mother; also the mother's meaning for the child depends on the child's creativity.)

Is it possible to join up the two trends, the stealing and the destruction, the object-seeking and that which provokes, the libidinal and the aggressive compulsions? I suggest that the union of the two trends is in the child and that it represents *a tendency towards self-cure*, cure of a defusion of instincts.

When there is at the time of the original deprivation some fusion of aggressive (or motility) roots with the libidinal the child claims the mother by a mixture of stealing and hurting and messing, according to

---

Editor's Note: Winnicott's "holding environment." See J. R. Meloy (1985). Inpatient psychiatric treatment in a county jail. *Journal of Psychiatry and Law,* 14:377–396.

the specific details of that child's emotional developmental state. When there is less fusion the child's object-seeking and aggression are more separated off from each other, and there is a greater degree of dissociation in the child. This leads to the proposition that *the nuisance value of the antisocial child is an essential feature*, and is also, at its best, *a favorable feature* indicating again a potentiality for recovery of lost fusion of the libidinal and motility drives.

In ordinary infant care the mother is constantly dealing with the nuisance value of her infant. For instance, a baby commonly passes water on the mother's lap while feeding at the breast. At a later date this appears as a momentary regression in sleep or at the moment of waking and bed-wetting results. Any exaggeration of the nuisance value of an infant may indicate the existence of a degree of deprivation and antisocial tendency.

The manifestation of the antisocial tendency includes stealing and lying, incontinence and the making of a mess generally. Although each symptom has its specific meaning and value, the common factor for my purpose in my attempt to describe the antisocial tendency is *the nuisance value of the symptoms*. This nuisance value is exploited by the child, and is not a chance affair. Much of the motivation is unconscious, but not necessarily all.

FIRST SIGNS OF ANTISOCIAL TENDENCY

I suggest that the first signs of deprivation are so common that they pass for normal; take, for example, the imperious behavior which most parents meet with a mixture of submission and reaction. *This is not infantile omnipotence*, which is a matter of psychic reality, not of behavior.

A very common antisocial symptom is greediness, with the closely related inhibition of appetite. If we study greediness we shall find the deprived complex. In other words, if an infant is greedy there is some degree of deprivation and some compulsion towards seeking for a therapy in respect of this deprivation through the environment. The fact that the mother is herself willing to cater to the infant's greediness makes for therapeutic success in the vast majority of cases in which this compulsion can be observed. Greediness in an infant is not the same as greed. The word "greed" is used in the theoretical statement of the tremendous instinctual claims that an infant makes on the mother at the beginning, that is to say, at the time when the infant is only starting to allow the mother a separate existence, at the first acceptance of the Reality Principle.

In parenthesis, it is sometimes said that a mother must fail in her adaptation to her infant's needs. Is this not a mistaken idea based on a consideration of id needs and a neglect of the needs of the ego? A mother must fail in satisfying instinctual demands, but she may completely succeed in not "letting the infant down," *in catering to ego needs*, until such a time as the infant may have an introjected ego-supportive mother, and may be old enough to maintain this introjection in spite of failures of ego support in the actual environment.

The primitive love impulse is not the same as ruthless greediness. In the process of the development of an infant the primitive love impulse and greediness are separated by the mother's adaptation. The mother necessarily fails to maintain a high degree of adaptation to id needs and to some extent therefore every infant may be deprived, but is able to get the mother to cure this sub-deprived state by her meeting the greediness and messiness, these being symptoms of deprivation. The greediness is part of the infant's compulsion to seek for a cure from the mother who caused the deprivation. This greediness is antisocial; it is the precursor of stealing, and it can be met and cured by the mother's therapeutic adaptation, so easily mistaken for spoiling. It should be said, however, that whatever the mother does, this does not annul the fact that the mother first failed in her adaptation to her infant's ego needs. The mother is usually able to meet the compulsive claims of the infant, and so to do a successful *therapy* of the deprived complex which is near its point of origin. She gets near to a cure because she enables the infant's hate to be expressed while she, the therapist, is in fact the depriving mother.

It will be noted that whereas the infant is under no obligation to the mother in respect to her meeting the primitive love impulse, there is some feeling of obligation as the result of the mother's therapy, that is to say, her willingness to meet the claims arising out of frustration, claims that begin to have a nuisance value. Therapy by the mother may cure, but this is not mother-love.

This way of looking at the mother's indulgence of her infant involves a more complex statement of mothering than is usually acceptable. Mother-love is often thought of in terms of this indulgence, which in fact is a *therapy in respect to a failure of mother-love*. It is a therapy, a second chance given to mothers who cannot always be expected to succeed in their initial most delicate task of primary love. If a mother does this therapy as a reaction formation arising out of her own complexes, then what she does is called spoiling. Insofar as she is able to do it because she sees the necessity for the child's claims to be met, and for the child's compulsive greediness to be indulged, then it is a therapy that is usually successful. Not only the mother, but the father, and indeed the family, may be involved.

Clinically, there is an awkward borderline between the mother's therapy which is successful and that which is unsuccessful. Often we watch a mother spoiling an infant and yet this therapy will not be successful, the initial deprivation having been too severe for mending "by first intention" (to borrow a term from the surgery of wounds).

Just as greediness may be a manifestation of the reaction to deprivation and of an antisocial tendency, so may messiness and wetting and compulsive destructiveness. All these manifestations are closely interrelated. In bed-wetting, which is so common a complaint, the accent is on regression at the moment of the dream, or on the antisocial compulsion to claim the right to wet on mother's body.

In a more complete study of stealing I would need to refer to the compulsion to go out and buy something, which is a common manifestation of the antisocial tendency that we meet in our psychoanalytic patients. It is possible to do a long and interesting analysis of a patient without affecting this sort of symptom, which belongs not to the patient's neurotic or psychotic defences but which does belong to the antisocial tendency, that which is a reaction to deprivation of a special kind and that took place at a special time. From this it will be clear that birthday presents and pocket money absorb some of the antisocial tendency that is to be normally expected. In the same category as the shopping expedition we find, clinically, a "going out," without aim, *truancy*, a centrifugal tendency that replaces the centripetal gesture which is implicit in thieving.

THE ORIGINAL LOSS

There is one special point that I wish to make. At the basis of the antisocial tendency is a good early experience that has been lost. Surely, *it is an essential feature that the infant has reached a capacity to perceive that the cause of the disaster lies in an environmental failure.* Correct knowledge that the cause of the depression or disintegration is an external one, and not an internal one, is responsible for the personality distortion and for the urge to seek for a cure by new environmental provision. The state of ego maturity enabling perception of this kind determines the development of an antisocial tendency instead of a psychotic illness. A great number of antisocial compulsions present and become successfully treated in the early stages by the parents. Antisocial children, however, are constantly pressing for this cure by environmental provision (unconsciously, or by unconscious motivation) but are unable to make use of it.

It would appear that the time of the original deprivation is during the period when in the infant or small child the ego is in the process of achieving fusion of the libidinal and aggressive (or motility) id roots. In the hopeful moment the child:

1. Perceives a new setting that has some elements of reliability.
2. Experiences a drive that could be called object-seeking. Recognizes the fact that ruthlessness is about to become a feature, and so
3. Stirs up the immediate environment in an effort to make it alert to danger, and organized to tolerate nuisance.
4. If the situation holds, the environment must be tested and retested in its capacity to stand the aggression, to prevent or repair the destruction, to tolerate the nuisance, to recognize the positive element in the antisocial tendency, to provide and preserve the object that is to be sought and found.

In a favorable case, when there is not too much madness or unconscious compulsion or paranoid organization, the favorable conditions may in the course of time enable the child to find and love a person, instead of continuing the search through laying claims on substitute objects that had lost their symbolic value.

In the next stage the child needs to be able to experience despair in a relationship, instead of hope alone. Beyond this is the real possibility of a life for the child. When the wardens and staff of a hostel carry a child through all the processes, *they have done a therapy that is surely comparable to analytic work.*

Commonly, parents do this complete job with one of their own children. But many parents who are quite able to bring up normal children are not able to succeed with one of their children who happens to manifest an antisocial tendency.

In this statement I have deliberately omitted references to the relationship of the antisocial tendency to:

Acting out.
Masturbation.
Pathological superego, unconscious guilt.
Stages of libidinal development.
Repetition compulsion.
Regression to preconcern.
Paranoid defence.
Sex-linkage in respect of symptomatology.

TREATMENT

Briefly, the treatment of the antisocial tendency is not psychoanalysis. It is the provision of child care which can be rediscovered by the child, and into which the child can experiment again with the id impulses, and which then can be tested. It is the stability of the new environmental provision which gives the therapeutics. Id impulses must be experienced, if they are to make sense, in a framework of ego relatedness, and when the patient is a deprived child ego relatedness must derive support from the therapist's side of the relationship. According to the theory put forward in this paper, it is the environment that must give new opportunity for ego relatedness since the child has perceived that it was an environmental failure in ego support that originally led to the antisocial tendency.

If the child is in analysis, the analyst must either allow the weight of the transference to develop outside the analysis, or else must expect the antisocial tendency to develop full strength in the analytic situation, and must be prepared to bear the brunt.

10

Time and the Character Disorder

Milton H. Miller

Milton Miller's paper appeared in 1964 in the *Journal of Nervous and Mental Disease,* one of the world's oldest and most respected psychiatric journals. It is a poetic clinical exploration of the absence of temporal continuity in the inner life of the psychopath. He implicitly suggests that an absence of attachment may impair the capacity to choose some potentialities, while surrendering others, and therefore may fail to deepen one's relationship to objects; instead, the psychopath "seems to be walking through snow without leaving footprints." One aspect of this failure to surrender potentialities that Miller does not comment on is its usefulness in maintaining fantasies of immortality, a temporal aspect of the psychopath's grandiosity. If he loses nothing, he grieves nothing, and nothing ends.

Throughout the centuries there has been a kind of person whose way of living in the world has confounded, confused, occasionally inspired, but more typically infuriated or worried his contemporaries. We have known him by many names and currently we call him the "character disorder." He is ordinarily understood as a person with whom something is wrong or amiss and, depending upon the genesis of evil in the particular era in which he lives, that which is believed to be wrong has been variously explained. There was a time when he was thought to be suffering from "bedevilment" in the concrete sense of the word. He has been depicted as deficient in protoplasm, overly or inadequately nurtured in early years, and, in recent decades, has been described as suffering the consequences of preoedipal sexual conflicts of unresolved nature. Johnson and Szurek (1952) have suggested that he is a person who acts out the unstated wish of a parent and thereby provides for that parent the vicarious satisfaction of a desired but denied variety of experience. All of which may serve to emphasize that his behavior is easier for us to describe than truly to understand in a genetic sense.

In any given moment he may resemble his neighbor. It is in the collection of sequential moments of his life that there is the implication that something is disturbed. He may, for example, experience eloquent moments or moments of great despair, those of great sacrifice or of selfish narcissism. Yet, in the following moment, the last one may be far, far away and the time ahead may be separate *in toto*. The experience of the passage of time as one important dimension of his existence seems sharply impaired. In a certain sense, he seems to be walking through snow without leaving footprints. It is as if, for the character disorder, potentialities in the world were never lost.

To draw from clinical experience:

"You ask me what I'm going to do when I leave here, Doctor? Well, first I'm going back and talk things over with my wife. I'm going to see if maybe we can get started again. I'm ready to settle down now, and she said that if I could promise to settle down, she'd be ready to talk it over. How long since I saw her, you ask? Six years, I guess."

And another patient:

"About the career, I hope you won't laugh, but I have given serious thought to medicine. Being in the hospital all these times does teach you something. Of course, it will take some schooling and I'm no chicken any more like a lot of those kids who are doctors, no offense to you, Doctor, but there is a difference in learning from experience. I'd find school tough, but I did enjoy science. You want to know how much schooling I've had. Well, I almost finished. I was going to take the GED test in the Army but I never got to it. I imagine if I went back and talked to the principal of that high school that . . . ."

Or, the patient's lack of appreciation of the meaning of time may be seen most clearly as he talks of his parents:

"And then, Doctor, I told Mother that she would have to stop making those demands upon me. I told her that I am grown up. By God, I am sick and tired of her ruining my life and advising me. I told her that if ever I was to get anywhere in this world she'd have to loosen up. After all, I'm past 44 now and . . . ."

I speak of a very ahistoric man, one who is deprived of an understanding openness to the experience of the world by a way of living which obscures the meaningful relationship between the moment at hand and those which are past and future. Our understanding of these individuals requires that the nature or consequences of being deprived of "openness to the world" and the significance of "living in an ahistoric fashion" be further illuminated. Yet, all too obvious are the difficulties implicit in studying any individual's "way of living." Little wonder that in clinical practice we often bracket, put aside these matters of "life living," claiming that they are out of the province of psychiatry, that they are more properly considered by philosophy or religion, and that in any case, insofar as science is concerned, they represent unknowables. We are often all too willing to translate the patient's concern about life and his life into concerns about one thing or another encountered along his way.

Yet such translations must be suspect. The nature of one's knowledge about himself is inextricably rooted in knowledge about questions such as, "What is life about? What are its ground rules?" Individually, and as a society, we try to devote ourselves to explication of these questions. Insofar as we know about ourselves, we know a good deal about life, and our lives. Insofar as we are estranged from ourselves, we are estranged as well from an awareness of the ground rules and meaning of life. Others have considered psychopathology as a form of estrangement from oneself (Gendlin, 1962; Rogers, 1957). It is useful to consider psychopathology further in the light of certain commonly shared notions about the nature of our existence.

Begin with the primordial fact of human existence. I am, and, as an existing being, a myriad of feelings, thoughts, tastes, senses, potentialities are available to illuminate the objects and persons of my world. Yet, a second of the important facts of existence is its imitations. We live in limited time and space. Significantly, the meaningfulness of life seems tied to the vitality with which one recognizes both the opportunities within and the limitations of life. Our meaning becomes actualized as we select from among our potentialities and as we surrender others. The vitality of life resides in an awareness of the necessity for choosing and surrendering. By accepting one potentiality, we surrender another. By surrendering no potentiality, we lose them all.

There is a boy of 17, and his potentialities are boundless. There are so many things he can be and do and feel in the universe. As to career, his future is without limitation. He can be a doctor, a lawyer, an athlete, an engineer, a minister, and indeed, at various times in his thoughts, he is all of these. Perhaps his school will be Harvard, or Yale, or Indiana, or Stanford, or MIT, or Wisconsin, or Chicago. And then one day he chooses. Not quite with finality, however, since he thinks that, perhaps, he will spend two years at his chosen school and then go on later in his career to Harvard or Yale, or Columbia, or perhaps all three. But he chooses. And in doing so, makes certain surrender.

The broad general educational possibilities at the University allow him to sustain into his second semester the potentiality of all the careers. But then there comes another moment, a moment in which he must choose again and perhaps this time for a variety of reasons, he may choose medicine. In this choice there is much surrendering and he does not make it easily. Law, engineering, basic science, architecture, the ministry are all surrendered. Or perhaps, here again he slightly hedges the commitment by combining in his planning law and medicine in forensic medicine, hoping subsequently to take the law degree; or he resolves his conflict between the ministry and medicine by deciding to be a medical missionary; or resolves his conflict between psychology, sociology and medicine by planning to be a psychiatrist. But still he chooses.

About this time, another matter captures his attention. His determination to stay a bachelor, play the field and marry at a mature 35 is tested in his 20th year by a young woman, she also a student in the college, perhaps in music or the arts. He feels she is getting too serious, repeatedly warns her against this, and ultimately, in order to avoid dangerous foreign entanglements, suggests to her that six dates a week is too many and that they each should see other people. He urges maturity, good judgment, prudence, points to the difficulties of early marriage, even offers to help her find other dates, which she tearfully repudiates and instead arranges her own. And then, in a day, after considering the full array of potentialities, including bachelorhood to 35, playing the field, being practical, he chooses her. In this choosing, which for him represents a more or less firm commitment, he has surrendered much, though he hedges the surrendering slightly. Perhaps she will work over the years and the baby or babies will be delayed until after he is able to complete his medical training, his internship in Hawaii, his training in obstetrics at the Johns Hopkins or better, psychiatry at the Sorbonne.

The coming of the first baby, near the end of the first year of medical school and the coming of the second baby during the latter months of his internship at Wesley Hospital in Chicago were not decisive in his ultimate surrender of the possibility of studying psychiatry at the Sorbonne. This surrender followed an interview with a friendly insurance man, the one who sells those "insure now and pay later" policies to protect "that lovely wife and those two swell babies of yours."

At age 32, his training is over and he is a physician and a psychiatrist. He is in practice and now pays the insurance man for the years of coverage. There are many things that he is not. He is not an alumnus of Harvard, Yale, MIT. He is not a lawyer, engineer, minister, sociologist, physicist, anthropologist, or baseball player. Although he is alive, awake and attentive to the world, certain kinds of contacts with one billion five hundred million humans called "women" are surrendered.* Some

*Editor's Note: Population demographics are acutely time sensitive; there are now

things are not surrendered, but were rather traded. The year of internship in Hawaii was traded for Annie; the year at the Sorbonne was
substituted for by the coming of Susie. And the hypothesized and
thought-about analytic fourth year—this time with a woman analyst—
was forsaken and substituted for by a house in the suburbs.

Although there are many things surrendered, and many potentialities lost, there are many things that he is in the world. He is keenly aware
of who he is, where he has been, and he is very curious about where he
is going. He savors his work and perhaps does it well. He is enriched in
his close interpersonal relationships and feels a closeness on many sides.
A nursery rhyme from childhood recurs in his thinking, this time with
a new perspective—"Why does the lamb love Mary so? Mary loves the
lamb, you know." In surrendering, in choosing and in caring, his life
acquires increasing meaning.

For the person whom we call "character disorder" life is somehow
different. Things are connected because they occur together, not because
they are tied to one another by a life stream. As Straus (1958) has said
of the schizophrenic patient, life becomes "sensory." Feelings of the
moment rule one's existence. Rightness and wrongness in the world are
related more or less exclusively to feeling states. Variant symptomatology notwithstanding, this estrangement from a unifying awareness of
history and potentiality is inevitably present. And he may be too passive, too angry, too loving, too withdrawn, too active or too inert; he
may never marry or may marry often; he may never leave home and
parent or may leave in early adolescence. He may never love, may love
a much older woman, or a much younger girl. He may posture as if the
most virile of men or may wear the clothing of a woman. He may ingest
alcohol, dope, candy or may ascribe to the cultist adoration of the
human body. If one can see through the fog of symptoms (and the often
obscuring concept of visitation by the forces of disease) the essential
meaning of "being a character disorder" as a mode of living without
choosing from among one's potentialities in the world can be seen.

The relationship of symptomatology to the delineation and the maintenance of this characteristic mode of life is intricate and fascinating.
One man may "bind tension" poorly and thus a moment may seem an
eternity. He may be unable to wait, to hold back, to "control his instincts." Unable to tie together moments in time, he never develops a
sense of future and history, lives instead a mode of existence which is
marked by its impulsiveness and discontinuity.

---

about three billion females on the planet.

"Making the world disappear" and the passage of time with it is another life style which obscures the relationship of one moment to the next. Thus, for the alcoholic, there is a kind of timelessness, since one keeps time only with regard to the last drunk or the next period of sobriety. Somehow all potentialities in the world acquire a pivotal dependency upon the maintenance of sobriety. Similarly, the fat woman or man may evolve a kind of idiosyncratic mode of telling time which has to do with the undertaking of a diet, thence thinness and then time will begin. Similar mechanisms are observed in some who are somatically or sexually preoccupied. For other individuals, the passage of time is experienced in a fashion akin to the way events are related by the "old hands" at a fishing resort. One hears of "that tall fellow who caught a muskie the first time he ever fished and caught it on a line which didn't have any bait on it," only to learn that this event happened (or maybe happened) 28 years before. So it is with some old soldiers, old athletes long after the season and old fraternity brothers at reunions. So also with the angry and prejudiced people who sustain an injustice through the years, thereby denying the passage of time, the loss of potential, the uniqueness of the human capacity for enriching discovery and enhanced perspective. It is the same with some of those now separated from the great master and teacher who see time in the intervening days and years as equivalent to a "portal-to-portal" interval.

How does it happen that some individuals grow up without developing an awareness of the significance of temporal characteristics of life? How primordial is a disturbance in the appreciation of time in life as compared with other defects of feeling or behavior? Importantly, how do these vulnerabilities develop?

Although this paper has concerned itself in substantial part with the matter of certain aspects of the experience of time, it is not simply an "informational defect about a clock or a calendar" which will explain "character disorder." For psychic functioning is not compartmentalized and experience of the significance of temporal relationships is intricately a part of all aspects of what we sense and know. A deepening intimacy with the others and with the objects of our world is attained as the years pass and it is precisely as we live along a continuum of achieving intimacy—in space—over time that the richness and significance of our personal life unfolds. Such descriptive aspects of our day to dayness as "closeness," "cherished," "valued," "intimate," "trusted" all have a clear temporal as well as spatial component. Maturing requires the development of a personal world which can encompass closeness, values, intimacy. It encompasses as well the necessity of awareness of the temporal limitations of life (Wheelis, 1958).

What is growth? What is maturity? Such definitions are always elusive, but the writer suggests that the matters discussed earlier in this paper seem germane to these questions. A mature person will demonstrate an appreciating openness and curiosity to the many potentialities for life experience and at the same time will possess an awareness of his own limitations in time and space. Understandably, he would want to be the one to select and surrender from his own potentialities and would demonstrate as well an awareness of the special significance of these matters, not only in his own life, but in the lives of his fellows as well. Immaturity (failure of growth) results from those interpersonal, biological and social phenomena which prevent an individual from coming to know about such matters. Thus, immaturity represents a failure to know, a deficit in learning, undiscovered potentials dormant, never developed.

As an example, events accompanying the paradigm period of "toilet training" may be explored. The matter at hand during these moments, learning to be "toilet trained," represents only one of the learning possibilities. Facts about "that significant other human" may emerge at this time, a particularly important fact being that "she returns." Or, an awareness of "her returning nature" may come later, perhaps on average days of infancy and early childhood or perhaps when siblings come, or later still with teacher, or with difficulty, with kids in the club. Later still, though only with great difficulty, the trustworthiness and returning nature of people may be learned with the love mate, or even later perhaps with that person called "doctor." Certainly, there must be critical cutoff periods beyond which the richness, meaning and general applicability of what might have been learned is lost or sharply curtailed. Thus, if an individual has not learned that "the loved other returns" and, in adult life, for this or some other associated reason, consults a doctor, a disappointing discovery is often made. It often evolves that the most which can be learned (taught, experienced) is that this doctor, in contrast to all other human beings, so far at least, returns. Unhappily, although doctor returns, he may do so because "he is paid," or because "he is a saint," or because "he doesn't know the real me."

An earlier awareness that "the significant other returns" provides the basis for a wide variety of associated and exponentially growing experiences. Some first-person statements may serve as examples: "I am the kind of person who lives in the kind of world where people do return." "I'm worth returning to." "There is a preciousness of our time together." "Parting is a sweet sorrow." "We may choose to stay together or we may part." Finally, "In the beginning, each time you went away I was terrified that you would not come back. I was helpless, thought only of myself and my abandonment. Later I came to believe that you would always return, I was happy and carefree. I took you for granted. Now, I know that you would always return if you could. The word 'always' doesn't belong. This knowledge has changed me in a puzzling way. I feel enriched, sad, freer than before, able to appreciate and love, yet, most of all, I feel aware." This awareness is one of the crucial ingredients of maturity.

It goes without saying that many complex events, individual and interwoven, may serve to interfere with a development of this kind of past–present–future awareness (Deiter and Chotlos, 1961; Heidegger, 1962). Biological and hereditary defects may be important. Undoubtedly, a heightened susceptibility to severe anxiety may result from some structural impediment or deficit within the perceptual channels of the central nervous system. Nor is there reason to doubt the particular significance of disordered early maternal–child relationships. For it is with and from the mother that the new child learns the joy and safety of making discoveries, the essential rightness of what he may feel and want to do. From her he derives the pride which comes from being an appreciated individual zestfully making discoveries, enlarging and enriching his world. He learns (in the words of Dr. William Fey) "to trust his guts" because she trusts him. That there are indelible qualities of personality established very early in life seems undisputed and points to probable neurochemical representation within the CNS which results from early maternal–child interaction.

Events beyond infancy and childhood are also important in growth towards maturity. The social structure of family and community seem significant, at least in determining symptom choice in those who develop severe character problems. The high incidence of asocial-antisocial forms of character disorder in low socioeconomic groups is contrasted with that specific form of passive, ever expecting, never really trying, unappreciating, shallow and spoiled individual endemic within certain parts of the upper classes. An adequate understanding of the development of a given individual's character problem will continue to require detailed study and elaboration of the experiences and the experiencing of the developing person.

Finally, there is a paradox which becomes apparent during consideration of character disorder. Importantly, that disordered mode of existing in the world which is so pervasively present in these individuals is also, for most of us, at times something of our own. Psychoanalysts speak of the character neuroses of our time and from many sides we hear of a societal loss of authenticity and purpose. Writers like Fromm (1955), Whyte (1958), and Wheelis (1960) stress our culture's estrangement from its history and our individual uneasiness with the vagueness ahead. These writers emphasize the necessity for modern man to begin to accept and treasure his freedom to be who he can be and to choose where he may go.

REFERENCES

Deiter, J. & Chotlos, J. (1961). Motivation from a phenomenological viewpoint. *J. Existential Psych.*, 2:35–48.

Fromm, E. (1955). *The Sane Society.* New York: Rinehart.

Gendlin, E. T. (1962). *Experiencing and the Creation of Meaning.* New York: Free Press of Glencoe: Macmillan.

Heidegger, M. (1962). *Being and Time.* New York: Harper & Row.

Johnson, A. M. & Szurek, S. A. (1952). The genesis of antisocial acting-out in children and adults. *Psychoanal. Quart.*, 21:323.

Rogers, C. R. (1957). The necessary and sufficient conditions of therapeutic personality change. *J. Consult. Psychol.*, 21:95–103.

Straus, E. W. (1958). Aesthesiology and hallucinations. In: *Existence*, ed. R. May, E. Angel & H. Ellenberger. New York: Basic Books, pp. 139–169.

Wheelis, A. (1958). *The Quest for Identity.* New York: Norton.

Wheelis, A. (1960). *The Seeker.* New York: New American Library.

Whyte, W. H. (1958). *The Organization Man.* New York: Simon & Schuster.

11

Psychopathy, Freedom, and Criminal Behavior

Seymour Halleck

This paper by the forensic psychiatrist Seymour Halleck was first published in the *Bulletin of the Menninger Clinic* in 1966. His fundamental hypothesis is that psychopathy is a defensive search for painless freedom from objects. His premise is thought provoking and was partially stimulated by the previous work by Miller. To be sure, the scientific evidence concerning psychopathy points toward an object-relational world that is preoedipal and dyadic, not absent—a biology that predisposes the psychopath to be both underaroused and less influenced by bad consequences. His behavioral degrees of freedom are quite limited. He paradoxically exercises less choice, certainly less meaningful choice, than normals. The appearance of greater freedom in the psychopath is often caused by some observers' wishful projections, as is noted in this study. They are reminiscent of Norman Mailer's idealization of Gary Gilmore and Jack Abbott, two unrepentant but talented psychopaths. Nonetheless, Halleck's paper sheds light on the phenomenology of the psychopath, his psychodynamics, and society's morbidly curious reaction to him.

The subject of psychopathy always seems to create confusion and dissension. Few laymen are willing to acknowledge that the psychopath is a sick person. Even within psychiatry there is widespread disagreement as to whether psychopathy is a form of mental illness, a form of evil or a fiction. Most of the major arguments which have characterized psychiatric criminology have originated in efforts to understand and treat the psychopathic personality.

This article will review some of the historical problems of defining psychopathic behavior. The many inconsistencies in traditional approaches will be noted and a new concept of psychopathy based on phenomenological and psychoanalytic insights will be presented.

155

Finally, the relevance of psychopathy to the problem of criminality will be described.

HISTORY AND DEFINITIONS

The great humanitarian psychiatrist Pinel was the first to suggest that an individual who repeatedly involved himself in aimless antisocial behavior might be mentally ill. Shortly afterwards, the English psychiatrist J. C. Prichard (1837) described a syndrome in which the "moral and active principles of the mind are strongly perverted or depraved." His description of this condition, which he labeled "moral insanity," is quite similar to current descriptions of the sociopathic or psychopathic personality. From the beginning, the inclination of some psychiatrists to include selected forms of antisocial behavior under the category of mental illness was vigorously resisted. Philosophers, clergymen, attorneys, social scientists and other psychiatrists repeatedly warned of the dangers inherent in defining individuals who regularly transgress our laws as mentally ill and nonresponsible. Nevertheless, by the latter part of the 19th century, psychiatrists were becoming more active in redefining some forms of antisocial behavior as illness. The "morally insane" were now being described as "constitutional psychopathic inferiors" (McCord and McCord, 1956), a term more in keeping with a medical as opposed to a moralistic orientation.

In 1930, Alexander utilized psychoanalytic concepts of character formation and alloplasticity to describe certain antisocial individuals as "neurotic characters." According to Alexander, the neurotic character was a conflicted individual who, instead of developing psychic symptoms, resolved his conflict through alloplastic activity. Alloplasticity was believed to be related to a greater predisposition to violate the legal code. While the provocative quality of such an individual's behavior was recognized, his behavior was also seen as self-injuring. He was pictured as a guilt-ridden person who ultimately suffered "just like the neurotic." This concept made it easier for psychiatrists to describe problems of unacceptable or illegal behavior in terms of familiar psychoanalytic knowledge.*

---

*Alexander also postulated a condition in which both the expression of conflict through behavior and lack of guilt or self-punishment might exist simultaneously. He referred to this state as "pure criminality" and thought of it as an abstract condition. Alexander doubted that the "pure criminal" actually existed and insisted that, on closer examination, most offenders would turn out to be neurotic characters.

In 1956, William and Joan McCord, on the basis of an exceptionally thorough study of the literature, described psychopathy as an emotional disorder or syndrome and listed the characteristics of the psychopath as follows: "He is an antisocial, aggressive, highly impulsive person who feels little or no guilt and who is unable to form lasting bonds of affection with other human beings." They distinguished the psychopath from the neurotic character and contended that while psychopathy could predispose the individual to crime it could *not* be equated with criminality. For the McCords, psychopathy is a specific syndrome which rates an important place in psychiatric classification and nomenclature. Many psychiatrists are in agreement with this view and the official nomenclature manual of the American Psychiatric Association (1952) includes the term sociopathic or psychopathic personality as an acceptable diagnosis.

In the current literature the term psychopathy is defined vaguely and because of arbitrary usage tends to assume multiple meanings. At its worst the term becomes an invective to describe people who are personally disliked or whose values differ from our own. Another unscientific use of the term equates all criminality with psychopathy. Generally, however, two major usages predominate. There are those who would agree with the McCords that psychopathy is a personality disorder, a discernible clinical entity which can be isolated from other disorders and diagnosed with clarity. There are others who see the psychopath as similar to Alexander's neurotic character or "pure criminal" and visualize psychopathy as an abstraction, as a quantitative excess of alloplastic personality structures existing in individuals who utilize defense mechanisms which are similar to those employed by the neurotic. Psychiatrists who support this latter usage argue that one does not see real psychopaths, only individuals who are more or less psychopathic. Unfortunately, these two meanings of the term, one referring to a distinct emotional disorder and the other to an abstract condition are often used interchangeably.

Whichever concept of psychopathy we may choose to explore, perplexing inconsistencies are encountered when we think of psychopathic behavior as mental illness. The traits listed in any definition of psychopathy are derived entirely from the values or morals of our culture. This diagnosis is not based on the presence of pain or communication of personal suffering. The psychopath does not communicate personal

The idea of "pure criminality" is interesting, however, insofar as it is a description of a personality type that roughly coincides with descriptions others have made of the psychopath.

anguish unless we restrain him and he rarely experiences himself as being unable to control his behavior. When psychiatrists encounter him in a state hospital we are never sure that he really belongs there.*

The case for defining psychopaths as sick people must be made on the basis of their unreasonable behavior. Yet, it is not always easy to discern the unreasonableness of the psychopath. There are times when his goals and his efforts to obtain his goals appear to be entirely reasonable. When psychiatrists insist that psychopathy is a form of mental illness it is with a quality of overdetermination, almost as if they have to reassure themselves and others that people who commit objectionable acts and do not seem to be guilty about it must be suffering from an affliction.**

The concept of psychopathy as a disease is put on even more tenuous grounds when we consider the surprising versatility and flexibility the psychopath is able to demonstrate in certain circumstances. Henderson (1939) initially described a type of psychopathic state which was associated with genius and unusual creativity. In his classification, a brilliant but erratic person such as Lawrence of Arabia was considered a "creative psychopath." Even if creative individuals are rejected as not meeting the usual definitions of psychopathy, there remain many less colorful psychopaths who are still able to demonstrate peculiar and unusual strengths. Much depends on the social situation. People described as psychopaths are often able to function better under wartime conditions than many who would be considered normal. On the athletic field the relatively nonself-conscious psychopath may perform better than his neurotic teammate. The psychopath's capacity for success with women has been frequently noted, sometimes with a restrained note of envy. In frontier societies or under conditions of relative lawlessness, the psychopath has a higher survival potential than many other individuals. Even in the prison or mental hospital many psychopaths have

---

*Even when we agree that he is a legitimate object of psychiatric scrutiny, we have considerable difficulty in deciding what to call him. Repeated efforts to replace the phrase psychopathic personality with friendlier terms, such as sociopathic personality, neurotic character, or simple adult maladjustment, have met with limited success. The term "psychopath" seems to be retained because it has communicative value.

**Psychopaths have not always brought out the best in physicians. Even the most nonjudgmental of psychiatrists is at times unable to restrain feelings of hostility toward a psychopath, feelings that he seldom expresses as freely and casually toward other patients.

the capacity to create a comfortable niche for themselves and survive with grace under circumstances that would overtax the resources of a "healthier" person. Admittedly, the gains accrued through utilization of these strengths may later be dissipated through impulsive or inappropriate behavior. A high capacity for adjustment and survival for a limited time under adverse circumstances remains, however, an aspect of psychopathy that has never been adequately explained.

The individual diagnosed as a psychopath is often a charming and exciting person. While it is tempting to dismiss this charm as superficial or manipulative it is still intriguing. Moments of involvement with the psychopath are often remembered as moments of pleasure, excitement and even exhilaration. The literature of Western society abounds with characters akin to the psychopath. Many of them are pictured as totally villainous and unlovable. On the other hand, the major characters of some novels, such as *The Rainmaker, The Music Man,* or *One Flew Over the Cuckoo's Nest,* are people who, though "afflicted" with the traits of psychopathy, are, nevertheless, alive and exciting. They are people who have the capacity to bring excitement, fun and even love into the lives of others.

Psychiatrists have not been unaware of this quality, and have showed an unusual degree of interest in these troubling people. In his paper on the neurotic character, Alexander (1930) describes the fascinating qualities of these individuals in terms that could also be applied to the psychopath. He states:

> The eternal struggle between man and society is exemplified not in elusive intrapsychic processes, but in the visible drama of their own lives. That is why they are born heroes who are predestined to a tragic fate. Their defeat is the victory of society and the spectator who has had some conflict within his breast (and who is without it?) is able to live out both the rebellious and the social tendencies of his personality by sympathetically feeling themselves into the lives of the vanquished.

In this dramatic and sensitive description, Alexander has perhaps grasped a major reason for society's fascination with the psychopath.

A THEORETICAL CONCEPT OF PSYCHOPATHY

The following theoretical discussion is offered in the hope of shedding a new light on three basic issues: (1) the phenomenology of psychopathy,

(2) the psychodynamics of the psychopathic "syndrome", and, (3) society's reaction to the psychopath. Throughout this discussion psychopathy will be defined as an abstraction rather than as a definite syndrome. Pure psychopathy is considered to be a theoretical state lying at the end of a continuum of behavior and personality traits. Certain individuals who are usually labeled as psychopaths may on occasion approach the end point but no one ever reaches it. Stated differently, the pure psychopath does not exist, but there are individuals who are more or less psychopathic.

Using this frame of reference, psychopathy can be defined as *the search for a painless freedom from object relations*. The word "search" is important, because implicit in this concept is the idea that "painless freedom from object relations" can never be found in humans and must remain an abstraction. The adjective "painless" is included to distinguish psychopathy from autistic withdrawal, a condition in which the individual may seek freedom from object relations, but where he does so only with great anguish.

The psychopath is a person who constantly seeks to be free of meaningful involvements with other people. He perceives the normal ties of affection, dependency, trust and love as fetters or traps which must be avoided at all costs. He seeks a type of freedom in which what he does, who he is and where he goes is independent of the appraisals of others. The alternatives to his way of life are all seen as leading to helplessness. His constant search for a painless freedom is a defense against this intolerable emotion.

This concept is best illustrated by clinical example. The author, like so many other psychiatrists, has long been intrigued with the problem of psychopathy, and for years has searched for the "pure psychopath," the individual who is completely free of guilt, who takes what he wants without discomfort and who seems totally uninterested in relating himself to others. Such an individual might correspond to Alexander's concept of the pure criminal or to Karpman's (1941–42) concept of the idiopathic psychopath or anethopath. The patient to be described comes close to fitting this clinical picture.

The patient was a 22-year-old white male who was seen initially in a staff conference at a state reformatory. He was serving a five-year sentence for fraud and swindling. His family background was similar to that of many delinquents. The father was an inadequate individual, an alcoholic, who absented himself from the home for long periods. The mother was described as a long-suffering, "martyred" type of person who, in spite of her protestation of affection toward the patient, was often irresponsible. She would frequently leave the children alone in order to pursue extramarital escapades and drinking activities.

Throughout his school years, the patient was well liked by teachers and friends. His academic performance was slightly better than average. He was active in athletics and when he reached adolescence was unusually successful in attracting women. He left high school during his senior year and went to work in an auto shop. Finding this work too boring he became a used car salesman and even at the tender age of 18 had little difficulty in breaking most of the sales records of his firm. He chose not to linger at this position, however, and moved on to a series of sales jobs. In all of these he repeated a pattern of marked success followed by lack of interest, boredom and moving on to what appeared to be a "greener pasture." During this period he had many heterosexual involvements. For about three years prior to incarceration he had been engaged in a number of "confidence games" designed to swindle the unsuspecting. He was far more successful than most criminals and managed to lead a financially comfortable life until apprehended.

After reviewing the history, the patient was invited into the conference room to be interviewed. He entered with poise and dignity, an unusually handsome individual who, although dressed in prison garb, managed to be neater and better groomed than anyone else in the room. He stated that he was pleased to have the opportunity to talk to a group of intelligent men and throughout the conference remained disturbingly at ease. The initial part of the interview focused on his adjustment to prison. He revealed that he had become interested in journalism while at the reformatory and had recently been made editor of the prison newspaper. His success in this role had already led to a promising offer of a position on the town newspaper at the termination of his sentence. His casual observations that he was accepted and respected by guards and other inmates were easily confirmed.

When the author pointed out to him that he seemed to have found quite a comfortable place for himself in the prison setting, he replied, "Why shouldn't I? A man can be happy wherever he is if he has faith in himself, is confident and is interested in life." The author was, of course, intrigued with such comments and the next day spent several hours interviewing the patient in private. He talked freely and obviously enjoyed conversation with a psychiatrist. In discussing his viewpoint of life he stated: "Most people seem to have to believe in something to survive. Me, I have learned to believe in myself. My goal is to make myself as happy as I possibly can and to experience life to the fullest. To most people this sounds selfish, but to me it makes real sense." He could offer little explanation for having adopted this philosophy of life except for the following:

> Life was pretty hard for our family when I was little and until I was nine years old, I was worried and nervous most of the time. Then things really got bad. My father disappeared and one day when my mother was going out and planning to leave me alone, I felt that I just couldn't stand it anymore. I thought to myself that I would cry and plead with her to stay and maybe she wouldn't leave me. Then suddenly it came to me that no matter what I did, no matter how much I cried or pleaded, it wouldn't make any difference, she would leave anyway. At that moment, somehow or other, I was a free person. I didn't need her and I didn't need anybody. I stopped worrying and I started having fun. Since that time life has been easy and I can be happy even though I am in prison.

Two other items of information which the patient revealed are of interest. He admitted that at one time he had sought psychotherapy at the institution, partly "because I was curious" and partly

> because people were beginning to suspect I was different from them and I was afraid that if they ever realized what I am, they would find some way of hurting me. Going into psychotherapy was like masking myself. It was a little bit like going underground. I tried it for several weeks, had some interesting chats with the therapist and then figured that I had had enough.

When asked as to situations which made him uncomfortable, he replied, "The only danger I can see for myself is if I ever feel I really need to become involved with others. When I borrow a pack of cigarettes from another inmate, I try to return it as soon as possible so that I don't think I need him for anything." Then he stated, "Sometimes I think I would like to change and be like other people and sometimes I worry that maybe they have something that I don't. Then I start to think that I might lose so much of my strength if I ever became like the others. I have to hold on. I can talk to people, use them and enjoy them, but I can't let them mean anything to me."

This history is, of course, edited in a way that focuses mainly on those issues which are relevant to the thesis of this article. If this patient is kept in mind, however, together with the concept of psychopathy as a search for painless freedom from object relationships, various aspects of what most psychiatrists would consider psychopathic behavior will begin to take on a new meaning.

The antisocial character of the psychopath can be understood more clearly if we think about him in terms of his apparent lack of need for others. If an individual experiences interpersonal relationships as stultifying and dangerous, and if he really strives to deny his involvement in what others might think or say, then for that individual any sort of behavior is permissible. If a person does not care about the appraisals of others, the concept "antisocial" itself becomes meaningless. Antisocial behavior becomes only that behavior which is defined by law as punishable if one is unfortunate enough to be caught.

The apparent aggressiveness of the psychopath also takes on a different quality. Actually in this frame of reference, the psychopath is no more or no less aggressive than any other person. If others are truly insignificant there is simply less need to mask aggressiveness through feigned passivity. Similarly, the impulsiveness of the psychopath becomes more understandable. The ability to delay gratification is a strength that is for the most part contingent on learning experiences with other human beings. Impulses are restrained with the expectation of ultimately receiving greater rewards from others. This obedience to the reality principle can exist only so long as one really wants to gain the love and respect of others. If it is possible to approach a state of freedom from caring, the advantages of restraining immediate gratification are certainly less apparent.

The apparent inability of the psychopath to form bonds of lasting affection with others should be considered not only as an inability but also as an aversion. To a certain extent the psychopath consciously and unconsciously seeks to avoid such relationships. He is a person who has been hurt by others. His inability to maintain relationships based on mutual respect can be visualized in part as an unwillingness to try. He avoids situations which are painful and feels safe in relating himself to others only when he does not need them.

The psychopath has also been described as a person who does not experience guilt in the same way as other people. This can be understood by considering that he is a basically ahistoric individual for whom the past and the future are meaningless and for whom only the existing moment is important. Miller (1964) has described the psychopath poetically as a person who can "walk through snow without leaving footprints." History, however, must be written in terms of people and in terms of meaningful interactions between people. The psychopath, to the extent that he is successful in freeing himself of a need for others, can approach an ahistoric condition. His lack of commitment to people, causes or ideas allows him to slip through life with little impact upon the world. On the other hand, this same lack of commitment provides him with unlimited maneuverability, freedom from guilt and the sometimes enviable quality of being able to comfortably experience a wide variety of situations. Since the psychopath travels lightly, it is possible for him to visit a great deal of the world.

The charm of the psychopath, his bewildering comfort in stressful situations, and the observation that we at times envy, admire or even hate him are clarified if we consider his behavior in the light of a search for freedom. Allen Wheelis (1960) in his novel *The Seeker* describes the intense feeling of pleasurable release his major character experiences when he makes an almost conscious decision to cease to care about others. The hero of the book, a psychoanalyst, finds that he is then able to maintain a lucrative practice, gain professional acclaim through superficial accomplishments, overcome many of his anxieties and experience new success in seducing desirable women. The behavior of the major character is clearly psychopathic. But what fun he has while suffering from this disease!

Wheelis recognizes that if a man can disentangle himself from involvement with others he is free to develop qualities in his own personality which are socially useful. Other people will be attracted to the psychopath because he holds out the possibility of sharing his freedom. Women in particular are fascinated by his straightforwardness and apparent lack of dependency.

While most of us may personally deplore the behavior of certain entertainers, business people or even psychiatrists who live excitingly above and beyond the codes we hold to be dear, we would be dishonest if we did not occasionally consider the possibility that "these people have something." Perhaps it is not, as Alexander suggests, only rebelliousness which explains our fascination with the psychopath. More likely it is his apparent freedom. We can argue that this is an immoral freedom, that it is an unsatisfying freedom or that it is basically an inhuman freedom. It is still a commodity sufficiently lacking in the lives of most of us, so that it is often coveted.

Approaching the problem from this frame of reference may explain psychiatry's urgency in considering psychopathy as a mental illness, but it also exposes some of the defects in the medical model. Psychopathy is an illness only in the sense that it seeks a basically inhuman kind of existence which if allowed to prevail in a great number of people would make the continuation of organized society impossible. To the extent that we become more rational in describing and judging psychopathy, we are forced to look at other aspects of psychopathy that would come under the heading of "non-illness." From some frames of references and in some value systems, psychopathy "can't be all bad." Obviously for the psychopath himself his behavior may be sustaining and gratifying. He is always a little puzzled when society reacts toward him with such great anger.

PSYCHOPATHY AND CRIMINALITY

In describing the psychopath we have been listing a group of traits which are defenses against a subjective feeling of helplessness. The psychopath defends against oppression even when it is no longer present. His personality structure makes it difficult for him to find a conforming or mental illness adaptation. The psychopath is an activist who, in his efforts to suit the world to his own needs, often finds that is necessary to violate the law.

Two points must, however, be reemphasized. First, the psychopath is not necessarily a criminal and certainly need not be an unsuccessful criminal. If a really "pure psychopath" could exist his success in the world would probably preclude his ever coming to the attention of a psychiatrist. Second, true psychopathy is an abstraction and it is doubtful if any person could ever achieve a painless freedom from object relations. Even the prisoner we described earlier could not be called a "pure psychopath."

Still, it must be noted that those criminals whom the psychiatrist is allowed to examine seem to show a high degree of psychopathic behavior. What is important about this behavior, however, is that it is ineffective. The criminal is likely to be a poor or mediocre psychopath. He may seek a painless freedom from object relations but he has great difficulty in finding it. The criminal is unable to deny or overcome his need for the love and affection of others, and is capable of sustaining psychopathic behavior for only brief periods of time. His antisocial acts are often preceded or followed by periods of exaggerated conformity and dependency.

This phenomenon is observed in almost pure form in adolescent delinquents. The adolescent delinquent is a person who at times develops intense, dependent and even worshipful feelings toward adults. He is incapable, however, of sustaining these feelings. Eventually he is frightened by closeness and rebels, sometimes against the very individual with whom he was so deeply involved.

Some adult criminals find comfort only when they accept a certain amount of helplessness and receive gratification of dependency needs in a familial or institutional setting. Like the adolescent, however, this type of criminal cannot sustain his comfort. Relationships soon become contaminated with fears of helplessness and he adapts in the only way he knows. He strikes out against the world by committing an antisocial act. In so doing he seems to be saying, "I don't really need you people. I don't really need anybody." For most criminals this is a pathetic cry. A temporary state of freedom is obtained but the criminal's inept behavior usually guarantees that he will soon return to a familiar state of dependency.

SOME FURTHER DYNAMIC SPECULATIONS

Most of the psychoanalytic writers who have examined the problem of criminal behavior have concluded that the criminal is a masochistic person who unconsciously seeks punishment (Alexander and Staub, 1956; Freud, 1915; Friedlander, 1947). It is assumed that the criminal is ineffective because he unconsciously intends to be ineffective. This hypothesis seems to ignore the adaptive value of crime and can only be partially true. The criminal's ineffectiveness can also be understood as an inability to free himself from his need for others or an inability to be a "good psychopath." At the moment a provocative act is committed he may be seeking freedom as well as punishment. There is no way of determining if his failure resides in an unconscious masochistic wish to fail or if it is a maladaptive by-product of an ineffectual search for freedom. Both explanations may be valid but the latter explanation is usually given insufficient consideration.

If we examine maladaptive criminal behavior solely in terms of the ineptness of the psychopathic defense it can be explained without invoking the difficult concept of masochism. Such an explanation, however, must also consider the factors which encourage the criminal to seek the psychopathic defense but to use it so ineffectively. These factors have already been described. The criminal seeks freedom in order to maintain organismic integrity but he cannot find it because he cares too much about others and needs them too much to be a "good psychopath." If he were really a "good psychopath" he would be able to handle situations of oppressive stress more gracefully. Consider the following grotesque but illuminating clinical vignette.

The author, as part of his prison consultation duties, was asked to examine a 22-year-old male inmate who had been in solitary confinement for 30 days. This unusual length of stay had been provoked by repeated episodes of verbal and physical aggressiveness directed toward the prison guards. His aggression seemed boundless and even when physically restrained he would spit and curse. Although his intellectual functions were intact, his obviously self-destructive behavior had aroused the concern of the guards, who were beginning to tire of their struggle with this man and hoped that the psychiatrist would send him to the state hospital.

When interviewed, the patient expressed almost global aggression toward his jailers, toward those who had imprisoned him and even toward members of his own family, whom he felt had abandoned him. He swore revenge and though the hopelessness of his struggle was apparent to him he gave no indication of wishing to call it off. His physical condition was deplorable. He had lost weight, was unshaven, unkempt and beginning to show signs of vitamin deficiency. He nevertheless refused an offer of hospitalization, stating, "I am not crazy and even if you transfer me out of here sooner or later I'll come back and I'm going to get these guys." Although overt symptoms of psychosis were not obvious, the patient was transferred against his wishes to the state hospital simply on humanitarian grounds. As anticipated, he improved quickly, was returned to the prison and, of course, was soon experiencing further difficulty.

The apparently unresolved situation of this man while in solitary confinement was similar to that of a helpless child trying to influence a cruel and depriving mother. He was confronted with an authority which was in complete control, but which was at the same time nongiving, arbitrary and from his standpoint, cruel. Yet he needed his torturers for they supplied him with food, clothing, cigarettes and on rare occasions even bits of affection. The patient seemed inextricably bound up in a struggle with a rejecting and depriving maternal structure which he could control only in a negative direction, i.e., he could induce his captors to punish him, but he could not force them to help him. He would attack, feel relieved while attacking and then he would be punished.

While interviewing this man, the writer was preoccupied with alternative solutions by which the patient might handle his grievous situation. The prison authorities had not really been too unfair. They were simply performing their duties as instructed by prison protocol. It was obvious that the patient's own paranoid attitudes had helped to bring him to his plight. Why couldn't the patient see this? Why couldn't he accept himself as a deviant, aggressive and perhaps bad person and make an effort to live up to the expectations of conformity that others were trying to impose upon him? He was obviously too angry and rebellious, had been too deeply wounded to accept this kind of solution.

The writer then began to wonder why the patient simply did not "go crazy." Certainly many neurotic individuals could not have stood the abuse and isolation this individual had endured for more than a few days. When the writer verbalized this thought he was met with the reply of "I thought about that, Doc, and I know my behavior seems crazy but I'm not. I know who I hate and I hate them too much to ever go crazy."* Finally, the writer hit on what seemed to be the best way out and communicated this thinking to the prisoner.

> Why not pretend to conform, why not pretend to go along with what these people say, do what they want you to do until they leave you alone and then do as you please and live your life as you please from there on in. You don't really have to give a damn about them. Just pretend you like them and then you are free to do as you please the rest of the time.

This suggestion was the first one that both moved and troubled the patient. It also troubled the writer. What had been suggested as the most healthy means of handling a gruesome situation was actually cynical, dishonest and psychopathic.

If we return to our consideration of psychopathy and related traits we can ask if the depriving or rejecting mother (or world) really offers the growing child many more alternatives than those available to our unfortunate inmate. If mother, parents, or authority are consistently visualized as all powerful, cruel or arbitrary what behaviors are available to the individual? A direct attack upon a maternal structure which is perceived as oppressive implies that the individual still cares. At the same time that he seeks freedom, he is hopeful that his behavior will bring him the love and recognition he so desperately craves. But the "healthiest" resolution for the individual exposed to this kind of unfortunate situation would be possible only if he could cease to care. If one really does not care about others he can then "fake it." He can pretend to conform while allowing himself complete freedom to satisfy basic needs. This, of course, would be pure psychopathic behavior.

Our prisoner obviously did not have the strength to behave in a truly psychopathic manner. Whether or not he unconsciously sought the

---

*Editor's Note: The psychoanalyst Glen Gabbard described one who hates as intrapsychically holding on to an object in an unforgiving way. See G. Gabbard (1996). *Love and Hate in the Analytic Setting*. Northvale, NJ: Aronson.

suffering which was imposed upon him is debatable. What is clear, however, is that his quests for freedom took the form of an ineffective and futile rebellion. Actually our prisoner cared too much about the reactions of others to really find the freedom he craved.

Many criminals use the psychopathic defense far more effectively than the prisoner we have been discussing. Even they, however, cannot use it consistently. Sooner or later their needs for others lead to rebellious behaviors which have an implied message of caring and they become increasingly ineffective. Ultimately the psychopathic defense does not free the criminal; it only sustains him.

REFERENCES

Alexander, F. (1930). The neurotic character. *Internat. J. Psycho-Anal.*, 11: 292–311.

Alexander, F. & Staub, H. (1956). *The Criminal, the Judge and the Public*, rev. Glencoe, IL: Free Press.

American Psychiatric Association (1952). *Diagnostic and Statistical Manual of Mental Disorders*. Washington, DC: American Psychiatric Association.

Freud, S. (1915). Some character types met with in psychoanalytic work. In: *Collected Papers*, 4:318–344. London: Hogarth Press, 1949.

Friedlander, K. (1947). *Psychoanalytic Approach to Juvenile Delinquency*. New York: International Universities Press.

Henderson, D. (1939). *Psychopathic States*. New York: Norton.

Karpman, B. (1941–1942). On the need of separating psychopathy into two distinct clinical types. *J. Crim. Psychopathol.*, 3:112–137.

McCord, W. & McCord, J. (1956). *Psychopathy and Delinquency*. New York: Grune & Stratton.

Miller, M. (1964). Time and the character disorder. *J. Nerv. Ment. Dis.*, 138:535–540.

Prichard, J. C. (1837). *A Treatise on Insanity and Other Disorders Affecting the Mind*. Philadelphia: Haswell, Barrington & Haswell.

Wheelis, A. (1960). *The Seeker*. New York: Random House.

12

The Psychology of Wickedness
Psychopathy and Sadism
J. Reid Meloy

On occasion one writes a paper that instills a sense of pride, even years later. This is mine. It appeared in a thematic collection of papers on "wickedness" edited by Ansar Haroun in *Psychiatric Annals* in 1997. Although morality is outside the paradigm of psychology, psychiatry, and psychoanalysis, the psychodynamics of the psychopath and the sadist, often causing fear and anger in others, stimulate a reactive countertransference to idealize or condemn—evoking the literary stature of the Marquis de Sade or the mythic evil of Charlie Manson. Moralizing about psychopathy is an ever-present potential contaminant of scientific research on psychopathy, especially since the principal impairment in psychopaths is one of empathic judgment. Can we think objectively about a clinical problem that by its very nature is partially defined by community morals?

Since I come from a long line of Presbyterian ministers and have myself earned a graduate degree in theology, I approach the question of wickedness in psychology with an abundance of curiosity, but perhaps an insufficiency of humility. For wickedness, or evil, is outside the paradigm of science and, I think, should remain so. It is, instead, the default of morality, or moral choice, and occupies the paradoxical position of being known to the science of psychology yet not of it.

In the clinical practice of psychiatry and psychology, moreover, we cannot avoid occasionally coming face to face with patients who stimulate in us the thought that they are mean, wicked, or in some cases *ra*, the Hebrew for evil. Such patients live, in Oscar Wilde's words, "to give rebellion its fascination, and disobedience its charm," and truly frighten us as clinicians. Fortunately, their numbers appear to be few, since we have now entered the diagnostic and psychodynamic landscape of the evildoers, the wicked ones, in psychology: psychopaths and sadists. If we think about the psychology of wickedness, these are the men we must study and understand, yet fear.

171

THE PSYCHOPATH

The construct "psychopathy" was disavowed with the publication of DSM-II (American Psychiatric Association, 1968) but regained a tenuous foothold in DSM-IV (American Psychiatric Association, 1994). Subsumed by the psychodiagnosis of antisocial personality disorder, it is a much older and more clinically complex term that originated in late 19th-century German psychiatry, wherein such a patient would have been labeled a "constitutional psychopathic inferior," a phrase that interweaves both the Lombrosian notion of a bad seed and the common moral judgment that such people are less than human (Meloy, 1988). A century later, a substantial and growing body of research argues that habitual criminality does, in fact, have a heritable genetic loading (Raine, 1993).

Following the classic and resurrective work of Cleckley (1941), psychopathy has been carefully and empirically defined by Hare (Harpur, Hakstian, and Hare, 1988) as a constellation of traits and behaviors characterized by two factors: a callous and remorseless disregard for the rights and feelings of others and a pattern of chronic antisocial behavior. This two-factor loading can be reliably assessed using the 20-item *Psychopathy Checklist–Revised* (Hare, 1991). Such an assessment requires both a clinical interview and scrutiny of independent historical data because of the mendacity of such patients. At a certain quantitative threshold, the severe psychopath can be clinically identified, and predictive validity studies indicate that the construct is not useless psychobabble. Psychopaths are not amenable to treatment (Meloy, 1995) and in one study were found to be *more* violent 10 years after immersion in a therapeutic community before release (Rice, Harris, and Cormier, 1992). They are also more dangerous than other criminals and habitually engage in *predatory*, rather than *affective* violence (Serin, 1991). The former refers to planned, purposeful, and emotionless violence, usually toward strangers. The latter describes the reactive, emotional, and defensive violence that is the commonplace hurtful aggression that most male members of our species act out, on occasion. Usually the victims and the perpetrators of affective violence are bonded to some degree (Meloy, 1992). In maximum-security prisons, approximately three fourths of inmates will meet the criteria for antisocial personality disorder (DSM-IV), but at most only one third will be psychopaths (Hare, Hart, and Harpur, 1991).

Some of the psychodynamics of the psychopath bring us closer to his evil, or his wish to destroy goodness. Psychopaths are aggressively narcissistic, and this aspect of their character pathology is often behaviorally expressed in their repetitive devaluation of others, not just in fantasy, as we see in narcissistic personality disorder, but in real life. The psychopath generally does this for two reasons: first, to maintain his grandiosity, or sense of being larger than life; and second, to repair perceived insults or emotional wounds by retaliating against those he holds responsible. This repetitive devaluation of others, which may range from verbal insults to serial homicide, also serves to diminish envy, an emotion highlighted by Klein (1975) and later explored by Berke (1988). Envy is the wish to possess the goodness perceived in others. And, if it cannot be possessed, destruction of the good object renders it not worth having. This theorizing may, at first blush, seem quite theoretical, but not if we imagine a very empathic and loving psychotherapist who extends her caring—and perhaps violates her own professional boundaries—to help a psychopathic patient. Her perceived goodness may, in fact, stimulate the patient's envy and place her in great danger, both emotionally and physically. Psychotherapists particularly at risk are those who narcissistically invest (take great pride) in their capacity to heal others or love others unconditionally. They consequently engage in counterphobic denial of real danger (Lion and Leaff, 1973): for instance, the psychiatrist who sees a psychopathic patient in his home office or at unusually late clinic hours when no other staff are around to accommodate the patient's schedule.

Another psychodynamic of psychopathy that contributes to his evil propensities is his chronic emotional detachment from others (Gacono and Meloy, 1991). The psychopath's relationships are defined by power gradients, not affectional ties. This biologically based deficit in bonding capacity, which may be acquired or inherited, or both, was first noted by Bowlby (1944) in his study of delinquent adolescents, some of whom he labeled "affectionless." Instead of seeking proximity to others as a way to feel affection and closeness, and to ward off loneliness, the psychopath appears most concerned with dominating his objects to control them. This domination reduces threats to him and stimulates his grandiosity, but also diminishes the probability of any empathy and inhibition of aggressive impulse. It is phylogenetically a prey–predator dynamic (Meloy, 1988), often viscerally or tactilely felt by the psychiatrist as an acute autonomic fear response in the presence of the patient without an overt behavioral threat: the hair standing up on the neck, so-called goose bumps, or an inexplicable "creepy" or "uneasy" feeling. These are atavistic reactions that may signal real danger and should never be ignored; they necessitate a careful and thorough psychodiagnostic workup and treatment plan.

The third psychodynamic of the psychopath that is often a facet of his evil deeds is his deception of others. Psychopaths are chronic liars, and research indicates that we are most likely to be misled by the special skill we think we possess to detect lying (Ekman, 1985). The psychopath lies for many reasons, the most common to experience the feeling of contemptuous delight when he successfully carries out his deception (Bursten, 1972). This purpose sharply contrasts with normal lying, which is usually done to reduce the anxiety surrounding possible rejection by an angry object to whom one is bonded.

Without conscience, there is no guilt. And without guilt, the positive feeling aroused by deception both fuels the psychopath's grandiosity—his belief, for example, that he is smarter than most—and acts as an intermittent positive reinforcement. He is therefore more likely to deceive again. The mendacity of the psychopath is enormous and is usually best uncovered through scrutiny of the known details of his behavior and history independently of his self-report. The best psychometric assessment of deception concerning psychiatric disorder, what we normally diagnose as malingering, is a combination of the validity scales of the MMPI-2 and the *Structured Interview of Reported Symptoms,* a relatively new clinical interview (Rogers, 1992).

These three aspects of the psychopath—behavioral devaluation of others, chronic emotional detachment, and mendacity—are the catalyzing agents of his wickedness. The historical path of his life is marked by the hurt, wounded, and angry people he leaves behind, sometimes unwittingly stripped of their own capacity for goodness.

THE SADIST

The term "sadism" was coined by Krafft-Ebing (1886) and is based on the life and writings of the Marquis de Sade, who, surprisingly, lived to the respectable age of 74 (Lever, 1993). Notwithstanding its multiple meanings and often confusing and speculative literature (Mollinger, 1982), I am using the term to describe people who derive pleasure from the control, domination, and suffering of others. I treat *sexual sadism* as a more channeled variant (Shapiro, 1981), characterized by sexual arousal stimulated by the psychological or physical suffering of another. The DSM-IV has simplified things for us by eliminating sadistic personality disorder, but burning the map does not eliminate the territory. As Michael Stone (personal communication, March, 1996) said, "Sadistic Personality Disorder: not in the DSM, but still in the USA." The most comprehensive analysis of the sadistic personality has been done by Millon (1996).

The derivation of pleasure through the subjugation and control of others and their consequent pain is an impulse-affect that has received very little empirical attention and far more theoretical speculation. A review of the 1967–1992 extant research that I conducted (Meloy, 1992) yielded 70 citations, of which only one in four were empirical studies. There was a virtual absence of any measurable treatment studies: only three uncontrolled case studies, which focused on sexual sadism. One study used cyproterone acetate (Bradford and Pawlak, 1987); another used an olfactory aversion procedure (Laws, Meyer, and Holmen, 1978); and the third employed self-administered covert desensitization (Hayes, Brownell, and Barlow, 1978). All three showed positive treatment outcomes.

We clinically know characterological sadism, however, when we see it. The antisocial inpatient incessantly teases others and derives pleasure from their discomfort. The spouse batterer smiles broadly as he shamelessly recounts his assault on his wife. And most disturbing is the child who does not angrily kick his pet, but instead tortures animals with detached pleasure. We also know that the latter behavior, cruelty toward animals, correlates with adult violence (Felthous and Kellert, 1986), but the causative factors of sadism, whether biogenic or psychogenic, are unknown.

There is a growing body of empirical work on both consensual and criminal *sexual* sadism. The subculture of consensual heterosexual and homosexual sadomasochism has been explored through surveys. Spengler (1977) conducted the first study of male sadomasochists in Germany. In another study, sadomasochistic women appeared to be more extroverted, less neurotic, more psychopathic, and more sexually active than controls (Gosselin, Wilson, and Barrett, 1991). Self-defined sadomasochists are predominantly heterosexual, well educated, relatively affluent, and interested in both domination and submission; they engage in a wide range of sexual activities (Moser and Levitt, 1987). Breslow (1992) conducted the largest survey study to date in the United States and found that consensual sadomasochists included both men and women who were predominantly Caucasian, had a wide range of education, did not hide their proclivities from their significant other, had had an average of six partners during the past year, mostly engaged in oral sex and spanking, and were remarkably free of self-reported depressive and negative feelings about their sexual interests.

It appears that this abnormal expression of sexual behavior does not evoke wickedness or evil. I will instead focus on criminal sexual sadism, which by definition (DSM-IV) requires the paraphilia, a nonconsensual object, usually an abducted or captured victim, and psychological or physical torture. Here the paths of sadism and psychopathy cross and our species' capacity for evil is most apparent.

Two studies have scrutinized the offender and offense characteristics of the criminal sexual sadist for the first time. Dietz, Hazelwood, and Warren (1990) conducted an exploratory, descriptive study of a small, nonrandom sample (N = 30) of criminal sexual sadists, the majority of whom had murdered three or more victims. Virtually all the subjects were Caucasian males; the majority had not experienced parental infidelity or divorce, physical abuse, or sexual abuse as children. The banality of their known histories was surpassed only by the extraordinary cruelty of their offenses. The majority of the subjects had carefully planned their offense, taken the bound, blindfolded, or gagged victims to a preselected location, kept the victim in captivity for at least a day, and proceeded to rape anally, force fellatio, beat, and vaginally rape them (in descending order of frequency) before murdering them and concealing the corpses. Most of the sexual sadists also recorded their offenses, presumably to memorialize their victims' suffering and to use for masturbatory stimulation between offenses. There were sufficient data to conclude that virtually all the subjects remained unemotional and detached during their torturing and murdering.

Gratzer and Bradford (1995), mindful of the risks of uncontrolled research, conducted a comparative study of the Dietz sample, their own sample of criminal sexual sadists (N = 28) from the Royal Ottawa Hospital (ROH), and a sample of nonsadistic sexual murderers (N = 29). The sadistic murderers as a combined group had a significantly greater frequency of physical abuse, cross-dressing, voyeurism, exhibitionism, and homosexual experiences in their history than did the nonsadistic sexual murderers. They were also significantly more likely to plan their offense, preselect a location, and beat, anally rape, bind, and force fellatio on their victims. Emotional detachment and sexual dysfunction also distinguished them. Eighty-six per cent of the sexually sadistic murderers (ROH sample only) were antisocial personality disordered, and the majority had measurable neurological impairments.

Neither study (Dietz, Hazelwood, and Warren, 1990; Gratzer and Bradford, 1995) measured psychopathy, but the convergence with sexual sadism is strongly suggestive and expectable: both the psychopath and the sexual sadist share a desire and will to control and dominate their objects, a chronic emotional detachment that dehumanizes their objects, an aggressive narcissism that entitles them to do what they want to their objects, and a mendacity that both delights them and facilitates their abduction of their objects. We have recently found empirically that psychopathy and sadism are significantly and positively correlated, with a sufficient magnitude (effect size) to warrant further study (Holt, Meloy, and Strack, 1999).

CONCLUDING REMARKS

If we are to manage the wickedness of psychopathy and sadism clinically, we must first accept its reality. Regardless of the biogenic and psychogenic roots of these human disorders, we must look upon them with a scientific objectivity unfettered by a naive optimism that all psychopathology is treatable or, if not, will ameliorate in time. We must also be willing, at the same time, to exercise moral choice and judgment of those who act in such nefarious ways. For the most difficult decisions in life are moral. And the most difficult acts in life are those which demand moral courage.

If we lose sight of these complementary and distinct aspirations—to seek scientific objectivity and to also exercise moral choice and judgment—then we risk contaminating our scientific advancements with bias or abdicating moral responsibility in the service of scientific achievement. Without such aspirations, that "morning-star of evil," in Wilde's words, may begin to believe in us.

REFERENCES

American Psychiatric Association (1968). *Diagnostic and Statistical Manual of Mental Disorders*, 2nd ed. Washington, DC: American Psychiatric Association.

American Psychiatric Association (1994). *Diagnostic and Statistical Manual of Mental Disorders*, 4th ed. Washington, DC: American Psychiatric Association.

Berke, J. H. (1988). *The Tyranny of Malice*. New York: Summit Books.

Bowlby, J. (1944). Forty-four juvenile thieves: Their characters and home-life. *Internat. J. Psycho-Anal.*, 25:19–53, 107–128.

Bradford, J. & Pawlak, A. (1987). Sadistic homosexual pedophilia: Treatment with cyproterone acetate: A single case study. *Canadian J. Psychiat.*, 32:22–30.

Breslow, N. (1992). *Sadomasochism: A Report of a 10-Year Study into Sadomasochism Among Consenting Adults*. Los Angeles: Oceanside Press.

Bursten, B. (1972). The manipulative personality. *Arch. Gen. Psychiat.*, 26: 318–321.

Cleckley, H. (1941). *The Mask of Sanity.* St. Louis, MO: Mosby.

Dietz, P., Hazelwood, R. & Warren, J. (1990). The sexually sadistic criminal and his offenses. *Bull. Amer. Acad Psychiat. & the Law,* 18:163–178.

Ekman, P. (1985). *Telling Lies.* New York: Norton.

Felthous, A. & Kellert, S. (1986). Violence against animals and people: Is aggression against living creatures generalized? *Bull. Amer. Acad. Psychiat. & the Law,* 14:55–69.

Gacono, C. B. & Meloy, J. R. (1991). A Rorschach investigation of attachment and anxiety in antisocial personality disorder. *J. Nerv. Ment. Dis.,* 179: 546–552.

Gosselin, C., Wilson, G. & Barrett, P. (1991). The personality and sexual preferences of sadomasochistic women. *Personal. & Individ. Differences,* 12:11–15.

Gratzer, T. & Bradford, J. (1995). Offender and offense characteristics of sexual sadists: A comparative study. *J. Forensic Sci.,* 40:450–455.

Hare, R. D. (1991). *The Hare Psychopathy Checklist,* rev. manual. Toronto: Multihealth Systems.

Hare, R. D., Hart, S. D. & Harpur, T. J. (1991). Psychopathy and the proposed DSM-IV criteria for antisocial personality disorder. *J. Abn. Psychol.,* 100: 391–398.

Harpur, T., Hakstian, A. R. & Hare, R. (1988). Factor structure of the psychopathy checklist. *J. Consult. & Clin. Psychol.,* 56:741–747.

Hayes, S., Brownell, K. & Barlow, D. (1978). The use of self-administered covert sensitization in the treatment of exhibitionism and sadism. *Behav. Ther.,* 9:283–289.

Holt, S., Meloy, J. R. & Strack, S. (1999). Sadism and psychopathy in violent and sexually violent offenders. *J. Amer. Acad. Psychiat. Law,* 27:23–32.

Klein, M. (1975). *Envy and Gratitude and Other Works 1946–1963.* New York: Free Press.

Krafft-Ebing, R. von. (1886). *Psychopathia Sexualis: A Medico-Forensic Study.* New York: Putnam, 1965.

Laws, D., Meyer, J. & Holmen, M. (1978). Reduction of sadistic sexual arousal by olfactory aversion: A case study. *Behav. Res. & Ther.,* 16: 281–285.

Lever, M. (1993). *Sade/A Biography.* New York: Farrar, Straus & Giroux.

Lion, J. & Leaff, L. (1973). On the hazards of assessing character pathology in an outpatient setting. *Psychiat. Quart.,* 47:104–109.

Meloy, J. R. (1988). *The Psychopathic Mind: Origins, Dynamics and Treatment.* Northvale, NJ: Aronson.

Meloy, J. R. (1992). *Violent Attachments.* Northvale, NJ: Aronson.

Meloy, J. R. (1995). Antisocial personality disorder. In: *Treatments of Psychiatric Disorders, Vol. 2,* ed. G. Gabbard. Washington, DC: American Psychiatric Press, pp. 2273–2290.

Millon, T. (1996). *Disorders of Personality: DSM-IV and Beyond*. New York: Wiley.

Mollinger, R. (1982). Sadomasochism and developmental stages. *Psychoanal. Rev.*, 69:379–389.

Moser, C. & Levitt, E. (1987). An exploratory-descriptive study of a sadomasochistically oriented sample. *J. Sex Res.*, 23:322–337.

Raine, A. (1993). *The Psychopathology of Crime*. San Diego: Academic Press.

Rice, M., Harris, G. & Cormier, C. (1992). An evaluation of a maximum security therapeutic community for psychopaths and other mentally disordered offenders. *Law & Human Behav.*, 16:399–412.

Rogers, R. (1992). *Structured Interview of Reported Symptoms*. Odessa, FL: Psychological Assessment Resources.

Serin, R. (1991). Psychopathy and violence in criminals. *J. Interpers. Viol.*, 6:423–431.

Shapiro, D. (1981). *Autonomy and Rigid Character*. New York: Basic Books.

Spengler, A. (1977). Manifest sadomasochism of males: Results of an empirical study. *Arch. Sex. Behav.*, 6:441–456.

Section II

Treatment, Risk Management, and Psychodiagnosis

13

Introduction to Section II

J. Reid Meloy

Psychoanalysts tend to make their diagnostic formulations by beginning treatment. The interaction between themselves and their patients, principally through transference and countertransference, provides them with a sense of the patients' personality organization and their amenability to treatment. This reversal of the medical model—which calls for diagnosis first, treatment second—also captures the evolutionary history of our understanding of psychopaths. Psychoanalysts have studied the psychic architecture of psychopaths during the past century by continuous interaction with them through treatment efforts. Relatively recently we have begun to make diagnostic formulations, both clinical and empirical, to spell out similarities and differences when such patients are compared to various other groups of narcissistic individuals.

The four treatment papers in this section—incisive works by August Aichhorn (chapter 15), John Lion (chapter 18), Neville Symington (chapter 19), and Larry Strasburger (chapter 20)—are the best offerings among the very few analytic treatment papers on psychopathy that exist. As one would expect, rather than focusing on technique, these papers offer a psychoanalytic way of knowing the psychopath—through the countertransference, or internal reactions of the analyst. The absence of papers on technique is easily explained: there is no clinical or empirical evidence that psychopaths will benefit from any form of psychodynamic therapy, including the expressive or supportive psychotherapies, psychoanalysis, or various psychodynamically oriented group psychotherapies (Meloy, 2001).

Why would we, then, pay attention to countertransference in reaction to an untreatable patient? Precisely because psychopathy is not just present or absent, black or white, but varies in degree from one patient to another. Countertransference, along with objective measures such as psychological tests, becomes our barometer for gauging the severity of psychopathy and therefore the treatability of any one patient. The lesser the psychopathy (imagine, if you will, a mild form of diabetes), the more effective the treatment and the better the prognosis.

TRANSFERENCE

Psychopathic patients, true to their core narcissistic personality traits, will emotionally seek to establish one of four transference positions with their analysts. In Kohut's (1971) terms, a psychopathic patient will seek to idealize (I want to worship), to mirror (I want to be worshiped), to twin (I want to imitate), or to merge (I want to control). What differentiates the psychopathic transference from that of other narcissistic patients, however, is the *behavioral*, rather than the fantasized or verbalized, expression of these transference positions and the relatively rapid emergence of the most developmentally primitive of the four: the need and desire to control the analyst. This transference will be experienced by the analyst as the discomfort of "being under his thumb" or as a compelling need to "walk on eggshells" to avoid what is catastrophically imagined as rageful, explosive, and potentially violent affect (perhaps a complementary and fearful identification with how the psychopath felt as a child; see Racker, 1968).

Other predictable resistances in the psychopathically disturbed patient include manipulative cycling, deceptive practices, malignant pseudoidentification, and sadistic control.

Manipulative cycling was first identified by Bursten (chapter 17) and is a cognitive-behavioral sequence that is highly rewarding to the patient: there is a goal conflict, an intent to deceive, a successfully carried out deceptive act, and a subsequent feeling of contemptuous delight in the deceiver. The process unconsciously defends against envy and oral rage, which is likely felt when the analyst is initially idealized. It purges devalued introjects that are then projectively identified *into* the analyst and thus retain the homeostatis of the grandiose self-structure (Meloy, 1988). *Deceptive practices* are a component of most manipulation and are to be expected when one is working with psychopathically disturbed patients. Deceptive practices are consciously used to devalue the analyst by deceiving him and unconsciously ward off any persecutory anxiety. Often, acknowledging suspiciousness toward the patient can be a first step in the analysis of the need to deceive.

Malignant pseudoidentification refers to the conscious imitation and unconscious simulation of various identifications by the psychopath. They are typically short lived, resonate most easily with the narcissism of the analyst, and are used to hurt and control. Pseudoidentification will be apparent clinically in the imitation of certain emotions during analysis, usually through words that imply a certain feeling, and the unconscious simulation of analytically desirable emotional states without insight into the meaning of such emotions. The analyst will often be left feeling distant and skeptical, befuddled by the absence of any empathic resonance in herself. The patient does not gradually recompensate from intense emotion; instead the performance ends, the curtain has dropped, and the audience of two awaits another scene.

Sadistic control has been discussed by Kernberg (1984) as a component of malignant narcissism, along with paranoid regression in the transference, chronic self-destructiveness, and dishonesty. In analysis it may range from verbal devaluation of the process to blatant forms of psychological and physical aggression. It is a clinical manifestation of the prey–predator dynamic in which all relationships, including the one with the analyst, are defined by dominance and submission. The analytic question is the degree to which the desire for sadistic control by the patient is ego syntonic, or riddled with conflicts and dependencies. Heroic attempts to treat a sadism that is not ego dystonic will usually result in a profound dehumanization of the analysis and may place the clinician in actual danger.

COUNTERTRANSFERENCE

Lion (chapter 18), Symington (chapter 19), and Strasburger (chapter 20) spell out in detail a number of explicit countertransference reactions to the psychopath that help us diagnose the severity of his character pathology and our reaction to it.

Therapeutic nihilism, appropriate to the true psychopath, can spread to become a pervasive cynicism whenever the analyst encounters a patient with even the most mild antisocial history. It is a dismissive or derogatory attitude toward any patient who reports an illegal act or has been accused, or convicted, of a crime. The counterpoint to therapeutic nihilism is the mistaken belief that a patient has formed an attachment to the psychoanalyst, when, in fact, only an illusory treatment alliance exists. Such a false belief, often containing the wishful projections of the analyst that the patient has a *capacity* to form a bond, will be reinforced by the psychopath feigning affection for the analytic process and fawning attention on the analyst.

A fear of assault or harm is another countertransference reaction that is often felt as a physical sensation of goose bumps, piloerection, the skin "crawling," or a sense of hotness or coldness when one first meets with a psychopathic patient—even though he is not overtly threatening in any way. These are phylogenetically old, biologically based autonomic signals of impending predatory danger. They may prompt a variety of systemic disturbances in the analyst, including gastrointestinal and cardiopulmonary reactivity, and may be signaling an actual future threat. In a large survey study of mental health and criminal justice professionals, we found that this countertransference response occurred in a *majority* of those surveyed when first encountering a psychopath (Meloy and Meloy, submitted).

Denial and deception by the clinician in this context are often counterphobic responses to the real danger a psychopathic patient may pose toward the analyst. For instance, the clinician visiting a psychopath in prison might insist that the inmate be unshackled during the interview despite the correctional staff's dire warnings that the prisoner has assaulted two medical professionals in the past week. Deception may be the clinician's response to anticipatory fear of an angry reaction by the patient, such as lying about a personal fact that the patient has demanded to know, instead of refusing to provide the information for both therapeutic and safety reasons.

The analyst feels helpless and guilty when treatment fails with the psychopathic patient. Young clinicians may be particularly vulnerable to this reaction, especially when captivated by their own "Midas touch"— their belief in their ability to heal others (Reich, 1951), often a facet of unresolved narcissistic issues. The loss of belief in one's Midas touch is a blow. One psychology intern, when faced with the limits of his own therapeutic skill in helping a psychopathic patient, responded to his supervisor with exasperation, but also with insight into the true situation obtaining between him and the patient: "Why would I want to know about the patient's inner life anyway?"

Devaluation and the loss of professional identity may follow. Psychopathic patients continuously devalue treatment to shore up their own grandiosity, and this takes a toll on the self-esteem of the analyst. They are also skilled in "gaslighting," using persuasion and coercion to convince others that their values, beliefs, and perceptions are wrong or misguided (Calef and Weinshel, 1981), leaving the clinician confused and feeling that his mind has been "worked over."

Feelings of hatred and a wish to destroy others, including patients, may also be felt by the analyst in his treatment of the psychopathically disturbed individual. Such feelings and wishes may be quite disconcerting and often signal the analyst's identification with the aggressive narcissism, if not sadism, of the patient. The analyst's spontaneous fantasies of destroying the patient may emerge during contact with the patient or following a treatment session:

A colleague spent 16 hours over two weeks evaluating a primary psychopath who had committed a particularly brutal sexual homicide of a 12-year-old girl. At the end of the evaluation, the patient was asked if he remembered the doctor's name. He responded, "No, but I bet you won't forget mine." Later that evening the colleague had a graphic and violent fantasy of taking a .45 caliber pistol from his brief case during the evaluation and shooting the man in the chest and head. In the fantasy he then left the examining room quite exhilarated, turned over the firearm, and was arrested, tried, and unanimously acquitted by a jury. The colleague also reported several traumatic symptoms for two weeks after the examination.

The false assumption of psychological complexity in the psychopathically disturbed patient is the last countertransference reaction, often stimulated by his glibness and superficial charm. It may be enhanced by wishful projections on the part of the analyst that the patient be treatable and therefore be in possession of the requisite intelligence and ego strength to benefit from analytic work. There is a propensity for such an assumption when the psychopathic patient's IQ is in the superior range. Unfortunately, intelligence can mask a severe character pathology. Theodore Bundy was admitted to two law schools, served as a crisis counselor on a suicide "hot line," and was a rising young star in Republican political circles, while he was abducting, killing, raping, and dismembering young women in Washington and Utah (Rule, 1980).

The frequency and intensity of these countertransference reactions appear to correlate directly with the severity of psychopathy in the patient. Such intuitive signals should prompt careful and comprehensive psychological testing of the patient, ideally before psychodynamic psychotherapy or psychoanalysis begins. Data from other collateral sources should also be sought, with the patient's permission, since chronic lying and deception—to maintain control, not to manage anxiety—are repetitive behaviors of the psychopath.

TREATMENT OR RISK MANAGEMENT

Treatment can proceed when the presence of psychopathy is *measurably* mild to moderate (Psychopathy Checklist–Revised; Hare, 1991); there is a genuine motivation for treatment and palpable emotional pain that is not primarily caused by the demands of others; there is a history of attachment to others, even if quite pathological, and concomitant evidence of some anxiety; there is evidence of some superego development, both within and outside of the consulting room; and there is enough intelligence and psychological insight to warrant the initiation of a course of treatment.

Treatment should not proceed if the patient is a primary psychopath. Interpersonal and intrapsychic features that contraindicate any form of treatment include sadistic behavior in the patient's history that resulted in serious injury, maiming, or death of a victim; the need to justify or rationalize such behavior or a complete absence of any remorse; intelligence greater or less than two standard deviations from the mean; a historical absence of attachment without depression; and the presence of an atavistic fear of predation felt by clinicians when with the patient (Meloy, 1988).

PSYCHODIAGNOSIS

Psychoanalytic formulations of the psychopath depend on various maps of the mind, considered as a guide to behavior. But, as Korzybski (1954) noted, the map is not the territory. Psychoanalysis has always been enamored with maps, but also suspicious of them, since maps cannot describe the exact territory of the mind, nor are they strongly predictive of actual behavior. Thus, the generation of many psychoanalytic "maps" or models of the mind since Freud's tripartite structure of mental functioning and the contentious debates among their adherents, which continue to this day.

Empirically based psychodiagnosis—in contrast to one or another theoretical map—has also never been wholly accepted in the psychoanalytic profession for similar reasons; it is typically used only for billing purposes or scholarship (Schafer, 1954; Lerner, 1998). Psychodiagnosis categorizes and classifies to order phenomena and thus facilitates, indeed enables, further communication among professionals—as typologies do for all scientific disciplines—but it is derived from nomothetic, large sample research. Its aim is to discern what is the same and different among *groups* of individuals. In the midst of such endeavors, individual differences that make each patient unique are diluted or washed out. Nomothetic reasoning subsumes idiographic reasoning, and the case study is lost, awash in a sea of correlations, regression equations, and large Ns.

It appears, then, that we do need our maps, both to understand individuals and to sort out the meanings to be derived from large-scale research. The goal, as Eysenck (1947) noted over a half-century ago, is to recognize the importance of both nomothetic and idiographic research. Inductive and deductive reasoning dynamically interplay within all scientific thought, just as data shape theory, and theory helps us to understand new data.

While most analysts were observing psychopaths, sometimes interacting with them in their practices and occasionally documenting both transference and countertransference reactions, a few were attempting to spell out the structural and dynamic qualities that could be used to diagnose these patients. The remaining four papers in this section are replete with psychodynamic formulations, as one would expect; but each author—Wilhelm Reich (chapter 14), Betty Joseph (chapter 16), Ben Bursten (chapter 17), and Otto Kernberg (chapter 21)—attempts to tackle the descriptive classification problem of psychopathy and how it can be differentiated from other pathologies. These authors help us locate psychopathy within our current psychodiagnostic systems.

PSYCHOPATHY AND LEVEL OF PERSONALITY ORGANIZATION

Kernberg (1970) formulated an approach to instinctual development that he evolved into a theory of personality organization at three levels: psychotic, borderline, and neurotic (Kernberg, 1984). He theorized that character pathology cut vertically across these horizontal levels of organization, the last distinguished by certain object relations, defenses, and reality-testing capacities. He thus shifts the clinician's attention from characterologic features indicating, for example, hysteric or narcissistic styles to the level of psychic organization underlying the characterologic presentation.

In a series of Rorschach studies (Gacono and Meloy, 1994) we found that antisocial personalities (defined by DSM-III-R [American Psychiatric Association, 1987] criteria for antisocial personality disorder) and psychopaths (defined by the Psychopathy Checklist–Revised; Hare, 1991) were organized at a borderline level of personality. These studies, both nomothetic and idiographic, found part-object representations, preoedipal defenses (primarily devaluation, denial, and projective identification), and impairments in reality testing consonant with developmental object relations theory.[1] Although we did find some psychopaths

---

[1]Defenses were measured using Cooper, Perry, and Arnow's (1988) defense mechanisms scale. Reality testing was measured using the X-%, the proportion of poor form quality responses in a Rorschach protocol. Object relations were measured by the ratio of whole human percepts ("it's a person") to part or quasi-human percepts ("it's an arm, it's a humanoid") seen in a Rorschach protocol. Defenses were usually preoedipal, X-% averaged 22, which is high, and H:(H)+Hd+(Hd) averaged 2:2.5, which reverses the ratio of "whole to part" found in normals (Gacono and Meloy, 1994).

organized at a psychotic level, usually carrying a comorbid diagnosis of schizophrenia or bipolar disorder, we did not find psychopaths organized at a neurotic level of personality. Psychopathy in its most severe form did not coexist with Rorschach measures of neurotic personality organization (whole-object representations, mature defenses, and normative levels of reality testing). These empirical studies were among the first attempts to test Kernberg's (1984) model of personality organization within a particular character pathology.

PSYCHOPATHY AND NARCISSISTIC PERSONALITY

Other analytically derived maps do not differentiate levels of organization from character style so sharply; rather they combine them in different ways. Thus, in chapter 17 in this section, Bursten differentiates personality into three general domains: complementary, narcissistic, and borderline. The aim of the narcissistic personality, of which he identifies four types, is to regain a state of blissful union between the grandiose self and the idealized parent image, what Rothstein (1980) described as a "felt quality of perfection" (p. 4). One of his types is the phallic narcissistic, a direct descendant of Reich's "phallic-narcissistic" character, spelled out in chapter 14 in this section.

The exhibitionism and masculine striving of this personality type, however, though not identical with, is closely related to the manipulative type, Bursten's term for the psychopath who exploits and deceives others. This behavior serves his intrapsychic need to devalue others ("put something over on them") both to enhance his grandiosity and to ward off impulses of greed and feelings of envy. This impulse–feeling–defense triad (greed, envy, and devaluation) is also the centerpiece of Joseph's (chapter 16) case study in which the psychopath spoils that which he wants—the goodness in others—therefore rendering it worthless. This is an adaptive aspect of his aggression as a predator[2] and maintains his psychological homeostasis.

Similarly, vis-à-vis antisocial behaviors considered as a focus for diagnostic scrutiny, Kernberg theorizes a range of antisocial types

---

[2]There is a growing body of research that indicates psychopaths are much more inclined to predatory violence than are normals: a mode of violence that is planned, purposeful, and emotionless (Cornell et al., 1996).

(juxtaposing both continuums and categories) in chapter 21, in descending order of severity of psychopathology:

1. Dyssocial reaction
2. Antisocial behavior as part of a symptomatic neurosis
3. Neurotic personality disorder with antisocial features
4. Other personality disorders with antisocial features
5. Narcissistic personality disorder with antisocial behavior
6. Malignant narcissism
7. Antisocial personality disorder

What links the Reich, Joseph, Bursten, and Kernberg papers together is a clinical opinion to which I strongly adhere: pathological narcissism is a necessary core, but insufficient component, of psychopathy. The differential diagnosis of the psychopath from other, less severe forms of pathological narcissism can be difficult but psychodynamically centers on seven intrapsychic differences (Meloy, 1988).

First, aggressive drives predominate, and their gratification is the only significant means of relating to others, usually through the establishment of a dominance–submission (sadomasochistic) relationship with objects. Henderson (1939) noted both an "aggressive" and a "passive-parasitic" type of psychopath. In the latter, these aggressive drives are passively expressed by denying the importance of all object relations and, instead, idealizing receptive-dependent needs. The entitlement is to take what one wants from others while ignoring them—without being discovered.

One psychopath of this passive-parasitic type married a very wealthy woman and remained with her for a decade. He had received an MBA but was never employed during the marriage. What he did successfully was to impregnate his wife and produce four female offspring, whom she nursed continuously for seven years. He was uninvolved with the children and remained indifferent to them after her separation and divorce. He had once assaulted her, continued to threaten her life through third parties, and litigated alimony. She relocated to another state, changed her identity, and retained 24-hour protection.

Second, there is an absence of benign modes of narcissistic repair. This phrase, first used by Kernberg (1975), captures the narcissistic personality disordered-patient's ability to repair emotional wounds through fantasy by devaluing the object of the felt or anticipated aggression and humiliation. The following vignette describes not a psychopath but a narcissistic personality:

> A successful attorney in his early 40s remained single but desper-
> ately wanted to find "the right woman" to marry. His dating took
> a predictable course. Within months of beginning a new relation-
> ship, he would devalue the woman in fantasy—at least a certain
> aspect of her—until he was certain she was "wrong" and then
> would break off contact. The women never measured up to his
> idealized object of destiny, which partially served as a defense
> against much anger toward, and fear of, his own overbearing and
> intrusive mother. Although conscious of his devaluing, he felt
> powerless to do anything about it and resisted psychoanalysis.

This continuous repair of old emotional scars and anticipation of newly anticipated wounds also maintain the grandiose self-structure of the narcissist. Fortunately, no one is physically hurt or irreparably dam-aged, but he does remain lonely and isolated, always falling back on devaluation or intense competition to manage the envy he feels toward others' happiness.

The psychopath, however, engages in an *aggressive* mode of narcis-sistic repair, wherein real objects must be behaviorally devalued to heal internally. The inability of the psychopath to do this in fantasy means that he will leave a trail of hurt, wounded, and angry people behind him as he moves through life. If one needs to know where the psychopath has been, one searches for the damage. This aggressive mode of narcis-sistic repair can range from teasing and incessant humiliation of others, to fraudulent business practices, to sexual murder. The following report is from a colleague:

> About a decade ago my wife and I took a biking trip in the
> Canadian Rockies with a professional outfitter. There were about
> 20 of us, but the one who commanded the most attention was a
> gynecologist from Orange County, California. He carried himself
> with great confidence, almost arrogance, and I began to notice two
> disturbing behaviors: first, he was inappropriately suggestive and
> erotic in his conversations with the women on the bike trip,
> couched in a desire to "help them" professionally; and second,
> each day he would single out one vacationer to humiliate in front
> of others. The group dynamic took shape quickly, with many of
> the people sidling up to him so he wouldn't humiliate them, and
> the rest of us alienated from him, angry, and on guard. The trip

ended, and I was glad to see him for the last time. Six months later
he was sued civilly and criminally charged with multiple counts
of sexual battery and rape of many women in his professional
practice, a lead story on the television program *60 Minutes*.

The third intrapsychic difference between psychopaths and narcissists is sadistic behavior, implying the presence of primitive persecutory
introjects or "sadistic superego precursors" (Kernberg, 1984, p. 281),
which may at times be sexualized. Sadistic behavior most often occurs
when objects are perceived as the embodiment of goodness and stimulate envy; or objects are perceived as helpless and dependent and
stimulate hatred. We found in one study that various measures of
sadism significantly correlated with psychopathy in both violent and
sexually violent criminals (Holt, Meloy, and Strack, 1999). The relationships also showed a moderate-to-large effect. In related research among
serial murderers, the diagnosis of sexual sadism and antisocial personality disorder show high degrees of comorbidity (Geberth and Turco,
1997). Sadism—pleasure derived from the dominance and suffering of
another—is a logical affective outcome, given the psychopath's primary
mode of relating through dominance–submission and the absence of
other, more affectional capacities.

Fourth, the presence of a negative idealized object (e.g., taking pride
in one's father's criminality) that has its roots in a cruel and aggressive
parent distinguishes the psychopath from the narcissist. This "identification with the aggressor" (A. Freud, 1936) may be due to traumatic
bonding (Dutton and Painter, 1981) with an intermittently abusive
parent or simply imitation of a criminal parent whose aggression toward others was observed by the child.

A serial sexual murderer recalled watching as a boy his biological
father's reaction at a party when his mother put an ice cube down
his father's shirt. The father grabbed the ice cube, tackled his wife
in the living room, and, in front of the party guests, forced his hand
down her dress, into her underwear, and shoved the ice cube into
her vagina. The son did not consciously find this behavior shock-
ing or disturbing when recalling it as an adult 30 years later.

Fifth, there is an absence of a desire or need morally to justify one's
behavior, which, if present, would imply some superego development
or at least some awareness of socially acceptable behavior. Righteous
anger or fear when "caught" engaging in criminal or antisocial behavior
is evidence that a modicum of social values has been internalized,

although probably not as an identification. Complete indifference to the judgment or moral outrage of others is an important clinical marker for the absence of conscience, as is likely to be seen in psychopaths: a shrug of the shoulders and silence may be the psychopath's only response to confrontation, dashing the clinician's hope that the patient might at least attempt to rationalize his nefarious activities. By contrast, narcissistic personalities with antisocial features, as Kernberg notes in his chapter, will show strong affective responses when their illegal, immoral, or criminal activities are challenged.

Sixth, anal-expulsive (ridding the self of devalued objects) and phallic-exhibitionistic (showing others one's idealized objects) themes will be evident in a "manipulative cycle," as Bursten notes in his chapter, in which the psychopath will repetitively have goal conflicts with others, intend to deceive, carry out the deceptive act, and feel contemptuous delight. This pattern is both an intermittent positive reinforcement for the psychopath, and therefore will be repeated, and a means by which he can psychodynamically maintain his narcissism by contemporaneously devaluing others ("They were really stupid to let me con them") and idealizing the self ("I am certainly clever and shrewd").

Other, less psychopathic individuals will display this pattern, but the emotional outcome of contemptuous delight will be spoiled by concurrent feelings of guilt or remorse, thereby decreasing the risk of repetition and diminishing its usefulness to the grandiose self-structure.

The seventh and final differential criterion is evidence of paranoia when the psychopath is under great stress, rather than the depression expected when narcissistic personalities come under characterological fire. This is most dramatically evident in charismatic psychopaths, such as David Koresh and Jim Jones, two cult leaders who killed hundreds of their followers in Waco, Texas, and Jonestown, Guyana, respectively.[3] In both cases these men became increasingly paranoid over time as their cults came to the attention of state and federal authorities. Their paranoia was effectively communicated to their followers and led to

---

[3]The Guyana mass suicide-homicide occurred in 1978 when 914 followers of Jones, including 294 minors, drank a cyanide-laced fruit drink or were shot to death. The incident in Waco, Texas, involved the burning of the Branch Davidian compound on April 19, 1993, which claimed the lives of 52 adults and 21 children. On March 19, 2000, a similar event was reported from Kanungu, Uganda, in which 780 members of a millennial sect, the Movement for the Restoration of the Ten Commandments of God, were either burned to death in their church or shot to death. Joseph Kibwetere, 68, founded the sect but was not among the dead victims.

increased grandiosity, cohesiveness, fear, and a group belief in a shared, final Armageddon-like destiny involving mass death. Unfortunately, government authority in both cases contributed to the conflagrations through tactical probes that confirmed the seeds of their paranoia and increased stress through physiological deprivation and social isolation.

These seven factors should help discriminate the psychopath from other narcissistically disordered individuals when the clinician's theoretical framework is psychoanalytic. They allow us to discern certain forms of aggressive and malignant narcissism that preclude treatment since therapeutic engagement is not possible.

PSYCHOPATHY AND DSM-IV

The diagnosis in DSM-IV (American Psychiatric Association, 1994) that comes closest to psychopathy is, of course, antisocial personality disorder. This term represents a relatively recent "social deviancy" research tradition that has its roots in a book by Lee Robins (1966). Her study was the first longitudinal attempt to chart the nature and course of delinquency in children as they matured, and her work changed American psychiatry's understanding of chronic antisocial behavior.

The first edition of DSM in 1952 subscribed quite closely to Cleckley's (1941) ideas of psychopathy without using the term, but Robins's (1966) work redefined antisocial behaviors by focusing on the degree to which such behaviors deviated from social, moral, and legal norms. Robins was a sociologist, not a psychologist, and therefore had little interest in the internal world of these individuals.

Although DSM-II in 1968 officially adopted the term antisocial personality and relegated the term sociopathy to the dustbin of psychiatric nomenclature, Robins's work did not strongly influence the taxonomy until DSM-III in 1980. This edition ushered in the five-axis system of diagnosis, placed the personality disorders on Axis II, and defined antisocial personality disorder in behavioral, rather than personality, terms, unlike most of the remaining personality disorders. Its most recent incarnation in DSM-IV (American Psychiatric Association, 1994) identifies seven criteria, of which any three—a polythetic formula— must be present to meet the diagnostic threshold:

1. Failure to conform to social norms with respect to lawful behaviors.
2. Deceitfulness.
3. Impulsivity or failure to plan ahead.

4. Irritability and aggressiveness.
5. Reckless disregard for safety of self or others.
6. Consistent irresponsibility in work or financial obligations.
7. Lack of remorse.

The only criterion that implies an emotional state, or the absence of one, is "lack of remorse," which is then defined behaviorally. The advantage of the DSM model of antisocial personality disorder is its interjudge reliability: it is often the only personality disorder used in epidemiological studies because its reliability coefficients are the highest among the personality disorders. The disadvantages, however, are many. The diagnosis casts a wide net (approximately 5% of adult American males will meet the criteria), and it is confounded by education, social class, and intelligence, but not race (Robins and Regier, 1991). It purports to measure a final behavioral pathway that undoubtedly could have many internal causes. The antisocial personality disorder diagnosis in DSM-IV leaves clinicians yearning for more nuanced and refined descriptors of the psychological dynamics of these patients.

Conduct disorder, the necessary prelude to an antisocial personality disorder diagnosis in adulthood, makes things worse. Only three out of fifteen criteria are necessary to meet the threshold; the descriptors are largely behavioral; and arguably the most useful subcategories of conduct disorder (CD) were eliminated in DSM-IV.[4] Instead, the age of ten now demarcates early and late onset conduct disorder, the former having a much worse prognosis.

Conduct disorder also overlaps with other mental and emotional disorders. Studies indicate that only 25% to 50% of conduct-disordered children/adolescents will grow up to become antisocial personality disorders: the earlier the onset, the more likely the antisocial personality disorder outcome. Cultural differences also abound. Rates of antisocial personality disorder are 20 times higher in the United States than in Taiwan, for instance (Compton et al., 1991), and studies suggest that the more "individualistic" a society is, the greater the rates of this diagnosis. "Collectivistic" societies, a sociological term for cultures that place the interests of the group before the individual, have typically low rates of antisocial personality disorder (Reavis, 1999). Phenotypic expression of

---

[4]These subcategories parsed CD children and adolescents along two dimensions: aggression and socialization. The so-called solitary aggressive CD children of DSM-III were probably the fledgling psychopaths of their diagnostic time.

antisocial personality disorder[5] appears to be largely influenced by the expression of certain social values, such as the availability of multiple attachment figures for children and the provision of close supervision regarding acceptable social behavior. Gender differences also exist, with antisocial personality disorder rates five times greater in males than in females, although this ratio seems to have been decreasing in the United States during the past 20 years.

Where does this leave the psychoanalyst? The greater the number of DSM-IV criteria met, the greater the likelihood the clinician is evaluating Kernberg's "antisocial personality" proper, or what I would refer to as a primary or severe psychopath. Morey (1992) has found, however, that the majority of people with one diagnosable personality disorder will meet criteria for another diagnosable personality disorder when DSM-IV is used. In other words, discriminant validity among personality disorders, especially within clusters, is poor. If a patient is diagnosed with antisocial personality disorder, for example, there is a better than even chance that he will also meet criteria for histrionic, narcissistic, or borderline personality disorder.

One can see this overlap in the contributions in this volume. Reich's "phallic-narcissistic" character is likely to meet narcissistic personality disorder criteria in DSM-IV. Moreover, Bursten's "manipulative" type of narcissistic personality is likely to meet criteria for antisocial personality disorder if there is sufficient information to establish a pattern of conduct disorder before age 15. Bursten's "craving" subtype suggests both histrionic and dependent personality disorders in DSM-IV.

Gabbard (1989) reported two subtypes of narcissistic personality disorder that bear mentioning. The "oblivious narcissist" is consistent with the aggressive and exhibitionistic narcissistic personality in DSM-IV. His second subtype, the "hypervigilant narcissist," refers to the more introverted, self-absorbed individual who is highly sensitized to criticism and empathic failures from others. This quieter adaptation to early deficiencies in narcissistic supplies may find antisocial expression in Henderson's (1939) "passive-parasitic" psychopath: the criminal who engages in indirect exploitation of others, such as burglary or fraud, and idealizes his sense of entitlement and disavows his hostility toward a world that chronically disappoints. His passive-aggressive stance

---

[5]Phenotype should be distinguished from the theorized psychopathic *genotype*, which may be stable in our species and unaffected by the values of any particular culture due to a paucity of internalizations.

toward others is a behavioral means of exploiting without being confronted and criticized.[6]

PSYCHOPATHY AND THE HARE CHECKLISTS

Twenty years ago Hare (1980) published for the first time his Psychopathy Checklist (PCL). Based on Cleckley's (1941) 16 clinical criteria for psychopathy, which appeared 40 years earlier, Hare's unidimensional scale, subsequently reduced by two items (Hare, 1991), ushered in a dramatic increase in psychopathy research throughout the world. The items of the PCL–Revised (PCL–R) include glibness/superficial charm; a grandiose sense of self-worth; a need for stimulation and proneness to boredom; pathological lying; conning/manipulation; a lack of remorse or guilt; shallow affect; callousness and lack of empathy; a parasitic lifestyle; poor behavioral controls; promiscuous sexual behavior; early behavioral problems; lack of realistic long-term goals; impulsivity; irresponsibility; failure to accept responsibility for own actions; many short-term marital relationships; juvenile delinquency; revocation of conditional release; and criminal versatility.[7] There are now different versions of this scale for various clinical and nonclinical applications,[8] and they all represent an empirically reliable and valid method to determine the *degree* of psychopathy in any particular patient.

Items of the PCL–R illustrate how this older tradition for understanding chronic antisocial behavior differs from the social deviancy model of DSM-IV. It is a personality tradition that germinated in late 19th-century German psychiatry through the work of Emil Kraepelin

---

[6]This psychodynamic is situationally apparent in the professional or employee who believes he is grossly underpaid and therefore engages in fraud or thievery to assuage his angry entitlement. Examples of these cases include a psychologist who billed Medicare for group therapy since he was treating a patient with multiple personality disorder, now called dissociative identity disorder.

[7]The PCL–R contains 20 items. Copyright 1990, 1991 by Robert D. Hare, Ph.D., under exclusive license to Multihealth Systems Inc. 1990, 1991. All rights reserved. In the USA, 908 Niagara Falls Blvd., North Tonawanda, N.Y. 14120-2060, 1-800-456-3003. In Canada, 3770 Victoria Park Ave., Toronto, ON M2H 3M6, 1-800-268-6011. Internationally, +1-416-492-2627. Fax, 1-416-492-3343.

[8]The Psychopathy Checklist: Screening Version, the Psychopathy Checklist: Youth Version, the Psychopathy Screening Device, and the P-SCAN are four of the additional marketed instruments.

and J. L. Koch. The history of this avenue of research, emphasizing the internality of the antisocial patient, can be found in Millon (1996) and Meloy (1988).

The checklists themselves are quantified observational instruments that are scored on the basis of interviews and a review of collateral documents. A clinical interview alone is insufficient owing to the mendacity of the psychopath. Individuals who score ≥30 on the PCL–R are considered psychopaths for research purposes. The scale, moreover, can be viewed as a continuum to define a degree of disturbance: mild (10–19), moderate (20–29), and severe (30–40). Severity of psychopathy has been shown to predict treatment failure, violence and sexual violence risk, and recidivism when measurements use different criterion variables, samples, and settings in the United States, Canada, and Europe (Millon et al., 1998).

Factor analysis of the PCL–R variables indicates two factors, or clusters of items, that correlate 0.50. Factor I has been labeled "aggressive narcissism" (Meloy, 1992) and contains eight of the items. Factor II has been labeled "chronic antisocial behavior" (Hare, 1991) and contains nine of the items. Three items load equally on both factors. Recent research employing item-response theory (Cooke and Michie, 1999) has identified three factors: affective, interpersonal, and behavioral. Factor analysis is a statistical method similar to an inductive psychoanalytic inference: for example, the psychoanalyst's assumption of a mature superego, based on the patient's many statements concerning his realistic aspirations and prohibitions, parallels the researcher's statistical grouping of various items on a test to reach a "higher order" concept or factor.

Although the factors that constitute psychopathy are statistically distinct, the items within each factor may be predominately psychodynamic or psychobiologic. For instance, item 2 (grandiose sense of self-worth) is one facet of the psychopath's pathological narcissism and is maintained through the behavioral devaluation of others, often using the "manipulative cycle" identified by Bursten (see chapter 17). Item 3 (need for stimulation/proneness to boredom) is biologically rooted in the chronic cortical underarousal (Raine, 1993) and peripheral autonomic hyporeactivity (Hare, 1970) of the psychopath. Both items load on separate factors, but overall there is no simple equivalence between the two factors and a biological/socialization distinction.

In our series of Rorschach studies using the PCL–R to divide incarcerated criminals into psychopaths and nonpsychopaths (Gacono and Meloy, 1994), we found that the former are significantly more pathologically narcissistic, less attached, and less anxious than the latter. In other

words, our Rorschach studies found important psychodynamic differences, even among criminals, when the psychopaths were studied as a
separate group.

Paradoxically, the more severe the psychopathy, the less severe are
the internal conflicts—a state of mind we would predict given a dynamic context of no attachments and little anxiety—and the greater the
likelihood of a "pure" alloplastic character (Ferenczi, 1930). One of our
important, although counterintuitive findings, was that psychopaths do
not produce an "aggression" response when taking the Rorschach: an
articulated percept in which an aggressive act is occurring in the present, for example, "It's two people fighting." At least 50% of normals
produce one of these responses when taking the test, and our finding of
less "aggression" responses in virtually all the antisocial samples, including conduct-disordered children, was unexpected. As we scrutinized the psychodynamic meaning of aggression responses to the
Rorschach, we found that Rapaport and his colleagues (1946) and Holt
(1967) all considered such responses indicative of *tensions* of aggressive
impulses, which were then symbolized and stated. In the absence of
such tensions of ego-dystonic aggressive impulses in psychopaths, a
population who would act out rather than channel or bind such drive
derivatives, there would be no need to symbolize and verbally express
aggression; our unexpected finding lends empirical support to the
widely accepted clinical notion of alloplasticity in psychopaths.

Subsequent research by others has found that psychopaths in particular, and antisocial individuals in general, *do produce* more aggressive
content—"It's a gun"—than do normals; and this score, which we
developed, is partially diagnostic of antisocial personality disorder
(Baity and Hilsenroth, 1999). Aggressive content of this kind in Rorschach protocols may be indicative of a static, hard-object identification
for the antisocial person, a facet of his identification with the aggressor,
the predator part-object. Such an internalization may be more ideation-
ally stable, and therefore more diagnostic, than the presence or absence
of aggressive movement, a more affectively based Rorschach measure.

Although the Psychopathy Checklists were empirically derived and
the items are not psychodynamically defined, Cleckley's (1941) clinical
work, on which most of the items are based, was decidedly psychodynamic. He emphasized a number of differential criteria, including a lack
of remorse, pathologic egocentricity and an incapacity for love, and
general poverty in major affective reactions. He wrote that the object-
love deficits and "feebleness" of affect in the psychopath, "makes it all
but impossible for an adequate transference or rapport situation to arise

in his treatment and is probably an important factor in the therapeutic failure that, in my experience, has been universal" (p. 396).

PSYCHOLOGICAL TESTING

Although the psychodiagnosis of psychopathy from a psychoanalytic perspective is clinically important, and the location of such an endeavor among various diagnostic frames is theoretically useful, the task of diagnosis is often given short shrift by psychoanalysts. It is absolutely essential that it be done thoroughly and competently.

The diagnostic task, moreover, can be efficiently accomplished through the use of psychological testing, particularly with instruments that do not readily convey what they are measuring; or, if they do, there are measures of distortion and deception built into the instruments for appraisal by the clinician. The Rorschach, the Minnesota Multiphasic Personality Inventory–2, and the Millon Clinical Multiaxial Inventory–III meet these criteria and will provide the psychoanalyst with a wealth of data in a time-efficient manner to accept or reject the efficacy of treatment in any particular case. The primary reason for the use of psychological testing when psychopathy is considered is that the psychopath's mendacity cannot be detected without it other than through multiple clinical consultations, or perhaps psychotherapy sessions, which may eventually place the analyst at risk by the time he discerns the truth. Risk may come in many forms with the psychopathic patient, usually involving money, emotion, or physical safety. Without the efficiency and depth of psychological testing, an unwanted and difficult-to-unravel transference may already be under way.

Despite the absence of controlled outcome data, certain treatment modalities have shown effectiveness with antisocial personality disordered patients who are not severely psychopathic.[9] These modalities include pharmacotherapy for anxiety, depression, or impulsivity; family therapy with conduct-disordered children; milieu and residential therapy, such as token economies, therapeutic communities, and wilderness programs for adolescents; and cognitive-behavioral therapy (Meloy, 2001). The last method of treatment works best when there are clear and unambiguous rules and consequences; skills that are taught

---

[9]These are typically people who score below 30 points on the Psychopathy Checklist–Revised (Hare, 1991).

are commensurate with developmental level; cognitive distortions and criminal lifestyle patterns are identified and modified; tolerance for affect and its impact on others is stressed; and treatment continuity among providers is established (Gacono et al., 2001).

Treatment experience with psychopaths has historically preceded diagnostic competence. Unfortunately, the atmosphere of patient freedom, self-determination, mutuality, and honesty—hallmarks of psychoanalytic work—are rendered toxic by the mendacity and aggression of the psychopath. Analytic knowing, moreover, has charted the expectable but invariably malignant course of transference and countertransference and also contributed to empirical diagnosis to discern the patient for whom psychoanalysis offers no hope. As Partridge (1928) wrote, "The psychopath is one whose conduct is satisfactory to himself and to no one else" (p. 159).

REFERENCES

American Psychiatric Association (1968). *Diagnostic and Statistical Manual of Mental Disorders*, 2nd ed. Washington, DC: American Psychiatric Association.

American Psychiatric Association (1980). *Diagnostic and Statistical Manual of Mental Disorders*, 3rd ed. Washington, DC: American Psychiatric Association.

American Psychiatric Association (1987). *Diagnostic and Statistical Manual of Mental Disorders*, 3rd ed. rev. Washington, DC: American Psychiatric Association.

American Psychiatric Association (1994). *Diagnostic and Statistical Manual of Mental Disorders*, 4th ed. Washington, DC: American Psychiatric Association.

Baity, M. & Hilsenroth, M. (1999). Rorschach aggression variables: A study of reliability and validity. *J. Personal. Assess.*, 72:93–110.

Calef, V. & Weinshel, E. (1981). Some clinical consequences of introjection: Gaslighting. *Psychoanal. Quart.*, 50:44–66.

Cleckley, H. (1941). *The Mask of Sanity*, 3rd ed. St. Louis, MO: Mosby, 1955.

Compton, W., Helzer, J., Hwu, H. & Yeh, E. (1991). New methods in cross-cultural psychiatry: Psychiatric illness in Taiwan and the United States. *Amer. J. Psychiat.*, 148:1697–1704.

Cooke, D. & Michie, C. (1999). Psychopathy across cultures: An item response theory comparison of Hare's Psychopathy Checklist–Revised. *J. Abn. Psychol.*, 108:58–68.

Cooper, S., Perry, J. & Arnow, D. (1988). An empirical approach to the study of defense mechanisms: I. Reliability and preliminary validity of the Rorschach defense scale. *J. Personal. Assess.*, 52:187–203.

Cornell, D., Warren, J., Hawk, G., Stafford, E., Oram, G. & Pine, D. (1996). Psychopathy in instrumental and reactive violent offenders. *J. Consult. & Clin. Psychol.*, 64:783–790.

Dutton, D. & Painter, S. (1981). Traumatic bonding: The development of emotional attachments in battered women and other relationships of intermittent abuse. *J. Victimol.*, 6:139–155.

Eysenck, H. (1947). *Dimensions of Personality*. London: Routledge & Kegan Paul.

Ferenczi, S. (1930). Autoplastic and alloplastic. In: *Final Contributions to the Problems and Methods of Psychoanalysis*. New York: Basic Books.

Freud, A. (1936). *The Ego and the Mechanisms of Defense*. New York: International Universities Press, 1966.

Gabbard, G. (1989). Two subtypes of narcissistic personality disorder. *Bull. Menninger Clin.*, 53:527–532.

Gacono, C. B. & Meloy, J. R. (1994). *Rorschach Assessment of Aggressive and Psychopathic Personalities*. Hillsdale, NJ: Lawrence Erlbaum Associates.

Gacono, C. B., Nieberding, R., Owen, A., Rubel, J. & Bodholdt, R. (2001). Treating juvenile and adult offenders with conduct disorder, antisocial, and psychopathic personalities. In: *Treating Adult and Juvenile Offenders with Special Needs*, ed. J. Ashford, B. Sales & W. Reid. Washington, DC: American Psychological Association, pp. 99–130.

Geberth, V. & Turco, R. (1997). Antisocial personality disorder, sexual sadism, malignant narcissism, and serial murder. *J. Forensic Sci.*, 42:49–60.

Hare, R. D. (1970). *Psychopathy: Theory and Research*. New York: Wiley.

Hare, R. D. (1980). A research scale for the assessment of psychopathy in criminal populations. *Personal. & Individ. Differences*, 1:111–119.

Hare, R. D. (1991). *Manual for the Psychopathy Checklist–Revised*. Toronto: Multihealth Systems.

Henderson, D. K. (1939). *Psychopathic States*. London: Chapman & Hall.

Holt, R. (1967). *Psychoanalytic Essays in Honor of David Rapaport*. New York: International Universities Press.

Holt, S., Meloy, J. R. & Strack, S. (1999). Sadism and psychopathy in violent and sexually violent offenders. *J. Amer. Acad. Psychiat. & the Law*, 27:23–32.

Kernberg, O. (1970). A psychoanalytic classification of character pathology. *J. Amer. Psychoanal. Assn.*, 18:800–822.

Kernberg, O. (1975). *Borderline Conditions and Pathological Narcissism*. New York: Aronson.

Kernberg, O. (1984). *Severe Personality Disorders.* New Haven, CT: Yale University Press.

Kohut, H. (1971). *Analysis of the Self.* New York: International Universities Press.

Korzybski, J. (1954). *Time-Binding.* Lakeville, CT: Institute of General Semantics.

Lerner, P. (1998). *Psychoanalytic Perspectives on the Rorschach.* Hillsdale, NJ: The Analytic Press.

Meloy, J. R. (1988). *The Psychopathic Mind: Origins, Dynamics, and Treatment.* Northvale, NJ: Aronson.

Meloy, J. R. (1992). *Violent Attachments.* Northvale, NJ: Aronson.

Meloy, J. R. (2001). Antisocial personality disorder. In: *Treatments of Psychiatric Disorders,* 3rd ed., ed. G. Gabbard. Washington, DC: American Psychiatric Press.

Meloy, J. R. & Meloy, M. J. (submitted). Autonomic arousal in the presence of a psychopath: A predictable response in mental health and criminal justice professionals.

Millon, T. (1996). *Disorders of Personality: DSM-IV and Beyond.* New York: Wiley.

Millon, T., Simonsen, E., Birket-Smith, M. & Davis, R. (1998). *Psychopathy: Antisocial, Criminal, and Violent Behavior.* New York: Guilford.

Morey, L. (1992). *The Personality Assessment Inventory.* Odessa, FL: Psychological Assessment Resources.

Partridge, G. (1928). Psychopathic personalities among boys in a training school for delinquents. *Amer. J. Psychiat.,* 8:159.

Racker, H. (1968). *Transference and Countertransference.* New York: International Universities Press.

Raine, A. (1993). *The Psychopathology of Crime.* San Diego: Academic Press.

Rapaport, D., Gill, M. & Schafer, R. (1946). *Diagnostic Psychological Testing,* ed. R. Holt. New York: International Universities Press, 1966.

Reavis, J. (1999). Individualistic cultures, predatory aggression, felony theft, and psychopathy. Manuscript submitted.

Reich, A. (1951). On countertransference. *Internat. J. Psycho-Anal.,* 32:25–31.

Robins, L. (1966). *Deviant Children Grown Up: A Sociological and Psychiatric Study of Sociopathic Personality.* Baltimore, MD: Williams & Wilkins.

Robins, L. & Regier, D., eds. (1991). *Psychiatric Disorders in America.* New York: Free Press.

Rothstein, A. (1980). *The Narcissistic Pursuit of Perfection.* New York: International Universities Press.

Rule, A. (1980). *The Stranger Beside Me.* New York: Norton.

Schafer, R. (1954). *Psychoanalytic Interpretation in Rorschach Testing.* New York: Grune & Stratton.

14

The Phallic-Narcissistic Character
Wilhelm Reich

Wilhelm Reich first read this paper to the Vienna Psychoanalytic Society in October 1926. It appeared as a portion of a chapter in his magnum opus, *Charakteranalyse*, in 1933. Although the seeds of his own paranoid and narcissistic decompensation are evident in this brief work, Reich made a major contribution to our diagnostic understanding of psychopathy by specifying the clinical behavior of aggressive narcissism. His etiological formulations, however, should be taken with a large grain of salt. They are suffused with his own prejudice toward homosexuals and women and have been superseded by more thoughtfully composed developmental object relations theory and our selfobject understanding of the narcissistic transference positions. Many of the current DSM-IV criteria for narcissistic personality disorder are also evident in Reich's clinical descriptors.

The designation of the "phallic-narcissistic character" resulted from the necessity of defining character forms which stand between those of the compulsion neurosis and those of hysteria. They exhibit circumscribed traits which differ sharply, in both the way they originate and the way they become manifest, from those of the other two forms, so that the distinction is justified. The term "phallic-narcissistic character," sometimes less accurately referred to as "genital-narcissistic character," has been incorporated into psychoanalytic terminology in the course of the past few years. The description of this type was first presented in a previously unpublished paper read at the Vienna Psychoanalytic Society in October 1926.

The phallic-narcissistic character differs even in external appearance from the compulsive and the hysterical character. The compulsive is predominantly inhibited, reserved, depressive; the hysteric is nervous, agile, fear ridden, erratic. The typical phallic-narcissistic character, on the other hand, is self-assured, sometimes arrogant, elastic, energetic, often impressive in his bearing. The more neurotic the inner mechanism is, the more obtrusive these modes of behavior are and the more blatantly they are paraded about. In terms of physique, the phallic-narcissistic character is predominantly an athletic type, hardly ever an asthenic type and only in isolated cases a pyknic type (as defined by Kretschmer). His facial features usually exhibit hard and sharp masculine lines. Very often, however, despite his athletic habitus, we find feminine, girlish features (the so-called baby face). Everyday behavior is never cringing, as in the case of the passive-feminine character; it is usually arrogant, either coldly reserved or contemptuously aggressive. And sometimes his behavior is "bristly," as a representative of this type once put it. The narcissistic element, as opposed to the object-libidinal element, stands out in the attitude toward the object, including the love object, and is always infused with more or less concealed sadistic characteristics.

In everyday life, the phallic-narcissistic character will usually anticipate any impending attack with an attack of his own. The aggression in his character is expressed less in what he does and says than in the way he acts. Particularly, he is felt to be totally aggressive and provocative by those who are not in control of their own aggression. The most pronounced types tend to achieve leading positions in life and are ill suited to subordinate positions among the rank and file. When such is the case, as in the army or similar hierarchal organizations, they compensate for the necessity of having to subordinate themselves by dominating those beneath them. If their vanity is offended, they react with cold disdain, marked ill-humor, or downright aggression. Their narcissism, as opposed to that of other character types, is expressed not in an infantile but in a blatantly self-confident way, with a flagrant display of superiority and dignity, in spite of the fact that the basis of their nature is no less infantile than that of the other types. A comparison of their structure with the structure, for example, of a compulsive character, yields the clearest insights into the difference between pregenital and phallic-based narcissism. Notwithstanding their overwhelming concern for themselves, they sometimes form strong relationships to people and things of the world.* In this respect, they show a close resemblance to the genital character. They differ from the latter, however, in that their actions show a far deeper and broader tendency to be influenced by irrational motives. This type is encountered most frequently among

---

*Editor's Note: The distinction between attachments to animate and inanimate objects (e.g., loved ones vs. weapons) can be an important clinical marker for degree of psychopathy in the "phallic-narcissist."

athletes, pilots, military men, and engineers. Aggressive courage is one of the most outstanding traits of their character, just as temporizing caution characterizes the compulsive character and the avoidance of dangerous situations characterizes the passive-feminine character. This courage and pugnacity of the phallic-narcissistic character have, as opposed to the genital character, a compensatory function and also serve to ward off contrary impulses. This is of no special importance as far as their respective achievements are concerned.

The absence of reaction formations against his openly aggressive and sadistic behavior distinguishes the phallic-narcissistic character from the compulsive character. We shall have to demonstrate that this aggressive behavior itself fulfills a function of defense. Because of the free aggression in the relatively unneurotic representatives of this type, social activities are strong, impulsive, energetic, to the point, and usually productive. The more neurotic the character is, the more extravagant and one sided the activities appear—although they are not necessarily that extravagant and one-sided in actual fact. Between these actions and the creation of paranoic systems lie the many variations of this character type. The behavior of the phallic-narcissistic character differs from that of the compulsive character in its demonstration of greater boldness and less thoroughness with respect to details.

In phallic-narcissistic men, erective potency, as opposed to orgastic potency, is very well developed. Relationships with women are disturbed by the typical derogatory attitude toward the female sex. Nonetheless, the representatives of this character type are looked upon as eminently desirable sexual objects because they reveal all the marks of obvious masculinity in their appearance. Though not a rarity, the phallic-narcissistic character among women is far less frequently found. The neurotic forms are characterized by active homosexuality and clitoral excitability.* The genitally healthier forms are characterized by enormous self-confidence that is based on physical vigor or beauty.

Almost all forms of active male and female homosexuality, most cases of so-called moral insanity, paranoia, and the related forms of schizophrenia, and, moreover, many cases of erythrophobia and manifestly sadistic male perverts, belong to the phallic-narcissistic character type. Productive women very often fall under this category.**

Editor's Note: Reich did not have the benefit of Masters and Johnson's scientific investigation of the female orgasm.

**Editor's Note:* Reich shows a bit of his own phallic-narcissism in this arrogant and inaccurate condemnation through psychopathological labeling and lumping.

Now let us turn our attention to the structure and genesis of this character. First of all, we have to distinguish those impulses which attain direct gratification in the phallic-narcissistic behavior from those which form the narcissistic defense apparatus, though the two are intertwined. One typical feature brought out through analysis is an identification between the ego as a whole and the phallus; in the case of phallic-narcissistic women, there is a very strong fantasy of having a penis. This ego, moreover, is openly vaunted. In erythrophobia, this impulse is repressed and breaks through in the form of an intensely neurotic feeling of shame and blushing. At the basis of and common to these cases is a fixation on that phase of childhood development in which the anal-sadistic position has just been left, while the genital object-libidinal position has not been fully attained, and is, therefore, governed by the proud, self-confident concentration on one's own penis. This explanation does not tell the whole story. The phallic-narcissistic character is characterized not only by this phallic pride but more so by the motives which compel him to become arrested at this stage of development.

Along with pride in the real or, as the case may be, fantasized phallus, there is a strong phallic aggression. Unconsciously, the penis, in the case of the male of this type, serves less as an instrument of love than as an instrument of aggression, wreaking revenge upon the woman. This accounts for the strong erective-potency characteristic of this type, but also for the relative incapacity for orgastic experience. In the childhood histories of the phallic-narcissistic character, the most severe disappointments in love are found with surprising regularity, disappointments precisely in the heterosexual objects, i.e., in the mother in the case of boys and in the father in the case of girls. And, in fact, these disappointments are experienced at the height of the striving to win the object by phallic exhibition. In the case of the male representatives of this type, the mother is very often the stricter parent, or the father died at an early age or was not married to the mother and was never present.

The inhibition of the further development to genital object-love in childhood because of a severe frustration of genital and exhibitionistic activities at the *height* of their development, typically by that parent or guardian on whom the genital interests had begun to focus, results in an identification with the genitally desired parent or guardian on a *genital* level. Boys, for example, relinquish and introject the female object and shift their interests to the father (active homosexuality, because phallic). The mother is retained as a desired object but only with narcissistic attitudes and sadistic impulses of revenge. Again and again such men seek unconsciously to prove to women how potent they are. At the same time, however, the sexual act constitutes a piercing or destroying—closer to the surface, a degrading—of the woman. In phallic-narcissistic women, genital revenge upon the man (castration) during the sexual act and the attempt to make him or have him appear impotent becomes, in an analogous way, the leading tendency. This is certainly not at variance with the sexual attraction exercised by these strongly erotic characters on the opposite sex. Hence, we often meet with a neurotic-polygamous inability to stick to one's partner, the active inducing of disappointments, and passive flight from the possibility of being deserted. In other cases, where narcissistic sensitivity disturbs the mechanism of compensation, we find a weak potency, which the individual will not admit. The more disturbed the potency is, the more unstable the general mood usually is. In such cases, there are sudden vacillations from moods of manly self-confidence to moods of deep depression. Capacity for work is likewise severely disturbed.

The phallic-exhibitionistic and sadistic attitude serves simultaneously as a defense against diametrically opposite tendencies. The compulsive character, following genital frustration, regresses to the earlier stage of anality and develops reaction formations here. The phallic-narcissistic character remains at the phallic stage—indeed, he exaggerates its manifestations; but he does this with the intent of *protecting himself against a regression to the passive and anal stages.* In the course of the analysis of such characters, we meet with more and more intense and concentrated, while at the same time rigidly warded off, anal and passive tendencies. However, these tendencies do not directly constitute the character. Rather, it is mainly determined by the defense against these tendencies in the form of phallic sadism and exhibitionism, a defense proceeding from an ego that has become phallic-narcissistic. There is a marked difference here between the passive-feminine and the phallic-narcissistic character. Whereas the former wards off his aggression and his genital impulses with the help of anal and passive surrender, the latter wards off his anal and passive-homosexual tendencies with the help of phallic aggression. We often hear analysts describe such characters as anal and passive homosexual. However, just as the passive-feminine character cannot be designated as phallic-sadistic because he wards off these impulses, the phallic-narcissistic character cannot be described as anal-passive because he successfully subdues these impulses in himself. The character is determined not by what it wards off but by the way in which it does it and by the instinctual forces which the ego uses for this purpose.

In cases of moral insanity, active homosexuality, and phallic sadism, as well as in sublimated forms of these types, e.g., professional athletes, this defense succeeds well; the warded-off tendencies of passive and anal homosexuality are merely expressed in certain exaggerations. In cases of paranoia, on the other hand, the warded-off tendencies break through in the form of delusions. Erythrophobia is closely related to the paranoic form of this character; the representation of pathological blushing is often found in the anamnesis of paranoid schizophrenia. A patient suffering from erythrophobia falls victim to a symptomatic breakthrough of the warded-off passive and anal homosexuality inasmuch as he gives up masturbation because of acute castration anxiety. The sexual stasis which builds up weakens the defense function of the ego and affects vasomotor activity.* Active homosexuality, phallic sadism, and moral insanity, on the other hand, have a strong ego defense, provided there is effective libido gratification. If, for one reason or another, this gratification is interrupted for any length of time, the passive and anal tendency also breaks through in these cases, either symptomatically or openly.

Among the phallic-narcissistic-sadistic characters, one often finds addicts, especially alcoholics. Not only warded-off homosexuality lies at the root of these addictions, but also another specific trait of this character type, likewise the result of phallic frustration. Let us take the case of the male. Along with the mother's frustration of phallic exhibition and masturbation, there is an identification with her. This has a provocative effect upon the recently relinquished anal position and, consequently, upon the passive-feminine behavior. This is immediately offset by an accentuation of the phallic-exhibitionistic and aggressive, i.e., masculine, impulses. However, when the identification with the woman takes place at the phallic stage, the woman is fantasized as having a penis and one's own penis become associated with the breast. We therefore find a tendency toward passive and active fellatio in the sexually active forms of this character type, in addition to a maternal attitude toward younger men in the case of the male, and to younger and feminine women in the case of the female. In alcoholism, there is also a regression to the oral position. Accordingly, the typical traits of the phallic-narcissistic character are effaced in the alcoholic.

In the phallic-narcissistic character, the transitions between the healthy, object-libidinal form on the one hand and the acutely pathological, pregenital forms of addiction and chronic depression on the other hand are far more numerous and diverse than they are in other character types. In psychopathology, much is said about the affinity between the

---

*Editor's Note: Reich's theory of erythrophobia makes no sense. Blushing is best understood as a peripheral autonomic hyperreactivity to the feeling of shame.

genius and the criminal. However, the type they have in mind is a product neither of the compulsive nor of the hysterical nor of the masochistic character; he derives predominantly from the phallic-narcissistic character. Most of the sex murderers of recent years belong to this character type, e.g., Haarmann and Kürten. Because of severe childhood disappointments in love, these men later exercised phallic-sadistic revenge on the sexual object. Landru as well as Napoleon and Mussolini belong to the phallic-narcissistic character type. The combination of phallic narcissism and phallic sadism accompanied by compensation of passive- and anal-homosexual impulses produces those psychic constitutions most strongly charged with energy. Whether such a type will turn his energy to active endeavors or crime on a large scale depends, first and foremost, upon the possibilities which the social climate and situation provide for this character to employ his energies in a sublimated form.

Next in importance is the extent of genital gratification. It determines the amount of surplus energy which the destructive impulses receive and, therefore, how urgent the need for revenge becomes and what pathogenic forms it assumes. In contrasting the social and libido-economic conditions, we do not want to obscure the fact that the inhibition of gratification is also dependent upon socio-familial factors. In terms of their constitutions, these character forms probably produce an above-average amount of libidinal energy, thus making it possible for the aggression to become that much more intense.

The analytic treatment of phallic-narcissistic characters is one of the most gratifying tasks. Since, in these patients, the phallic stage has been fully achieved and the aggression is relatively free, it is easier to establish genital and social potency, once the initial difficulties have been mastered, than it is in patients of other character forms. The analysis is always promising if the analyst succeeds in unmasking the phallic-narcissistic attitudes as the warding off of passive-feminine impulses and in eliminating the unconscious attitude of revenge toward the opposite sex. If this fails, the patients remain narcissistically inaccessible. Their character resistance consists in aggressive deprecation of the treatment and of the analyst in a more or less disguised form, in narcissistic usurpation of the interpretation work, in the rejection and warding off of every anxious and passive impulse and, above all, of the positive transference. The reactivation of phallic anxiety succeeds only through the energetic and consistent unmasking of the reactive narcissistic mechanism. The indications of passivity and anal-homosexual tendencies should not be immediately pursued in depth; otherwise the narcissistic defense will usually build up to a point of complete inaccessibility.

15

The Narcissistic Transference of the "Juvenile Impostor"

August Aichhorn

This is a chapter from August Aichhorn's seminal work, *Wayward Youth*, first published in 1935, for which Sigmund Freud provided a foreword reminding us that the three impossible professions are teaching, healing, and governing. Aichhorn was a teacher, but he also had considerable skill as a clinician, and his theoretical understanding of an idealizing narcissistic transference in this paper is outstanding. Through a series of vignettes, he shows the importance of establishing such a transference, if possible, during the first contacts with a juvenile delinquent. Control and authority are paramount in his treatment, but they are invoked to confront and interpret, not to castigate. Aichhorn's sensitivity to the grandiose mask of the antisocial youth, the latter's strong unconscious desire for an idealizing transference and dependency, and his resistance, stood alone as a guide to treatment in the psychoanalytic writings of his time.

Among the various types of wayward youth, one is striking because of the high degree of transference which is quickly developed. The relations to us of a youngster of this type remain through a long period of time so intensive and unmistakably positive that we feel greatly encouraged in our capacity as counselors, and we continue our work with entire confidence; indeed, we expect to see soon a full-fledged identification with us to develop from what had been so far merely an object relationship. This would mean that a very important phase of our pedagogic task is now completed. Yet we experience each time the same unpleasant surprise; just at this particular point, the young patient starts behaving not at all as he should behave according to our own best judgment. True, he does not relapse into his former misconduct; yet all his manifestations show us distinctly, to our utter amazement, that it is only now that the youngster begins to perceive us as a separate object, and to recognize us as an independent personality.

213

This implies that he is still far from being able to identify himself with us; because, in fact, during the entire period of our previous work, he had failed to develop any object-libidinal relationship to our person.*

In its purest form, this type of juvenile delinquent is represented by what we may call the "impostor" variety. It was in such "mountebanks" that we first recognized a peculiar psychic structure which makes them well-nigh incapable of forming object-libidinal relations of any kind. The dependence upon ourselves, into which we succeeded to bring them by purely intuitive means, must have been of an entirely different nature. Nevertheless, with the help of a progressively more refined psychoanalytic insight, we managed somehow to understand our previous conduct (which was correct in its own intuitive way) as well as the child's attitude to us, and his behavior. Indeed, we progressed in our understanding until we finally became able consciously to provoke those reactions required for successfully overcoming the emotional distress.

The following case will give a fair idea of our method. A mother, coming from a good middle-class milieu, visits our child guidance clinic with her 18-year-old son; she complains that the young man has broken open her jewel box, pilfered some jewels and pawned them. As the boy had never been guilty of anything like this before, and as "It could not be a case of bad upbringing" (according to his mother), the only conclusion which the parents were able to reach was that it might have something to do with mental sickness. A doctor was therefore consulted. The doctor questioned the youth in detail and learned that he needed a lot of money for his affairs with various girls: he had found no means of procuring it except by robbing his own mother. Thereupon the doctor insisted that the mother should bring her son to our child guidance clinic. We learn from the woman all relevant particulars about the family conditions, the childhood and the upbringing of the boy. After our conversation with the mother, we call in the young man.

This is the first impression he makes upon us: a youthful impostor who because of his peculiar psychic structure could not possibly have had those experiences with girls about which he boasted to the physician. Our attitude toward him is immediately, unambiguously determined by this first impression: we greet him with a handshake, in a matter-of-fact though not unfriendly way, without any words being spoken; and we motion him to take a seat.

Editor's Note: Aichhorn was referring to what we now call a whole-object relationship.

"Why did you make fun of the doctor?" This is the question with which our talk begins.

"Because he asked for it," replies the boy, and he shrugs his shoulders.

"How much money do you have left?"

"One hundred and fifty shillings."

"Where do you keep them?"

"Here, in my pocket."

"Put the money on the table!" He obeys the order without any hesitation.

"Would you give this money back to your mother?"

"No!"

"But would you give it to me?"

"Yes, certainly."

I take an envelope, put the money in it, seal the envelope, write out a receipt for the sum of 150 shillings, and hand this receipt over to the boy. While he takes it, I ask him:

"What are you thinking about, right now?"

"I think that it was silly of me to give you the money."

"Then why did you give it?"

"This I don't know."

"Try to think of a reason."

". . . Really, I don't know."

Without any transition, I start talking about school, and he tells me something of his life at home, while I just listen. After a few minutes, I interrupt him with the question:

"What are you thinking about now?"

"I cannot stop thinking how really stupid I was. Surely, I should not have given you that money."

"Then why did you give it? Ten minutes ago you did not even know me. Yet you gave it to me, and refused to give it back to your mother. I ask—why?"

"I don't know."

"Please think about it once more."

". . . Well, I have the feeling that you would have taken it out of my pocket anyhow. But now it is most annoying. I have promised two friends of mine to take them to the movies tonight, and now I have no money."

"Why don't you ask your mother to give you some?"

"That's out of the question. Now that she is so angry at me, I could not bring myself to ask her to pay the price of tickets to the movies."

"Don't you know any other way of getting some money?"

"No."

"Why can't you steal something again?"

"Are you joking?"

"I am not."

"But that's quite impossible!"

"Why not? Isn't there anything more that you might steal?"

"Well, in fact, there is. My sister's bracelet."

"Where is this bracelet?"

"In the drawer of the bedside table."

So now we start discussing this project of a theft in every detail, and I go even so far as to call his attention, at several points, to various ways of improving his method of stealing. This amazes him, but gradually his bad mood leaves him, when he sees a new possibility of getting money.

However, our conversation does not stop at that. The task of a child guidance worker can hardly consist in steering a juvenile delinquent toward actual thievery. So therefore I go on talking to him:

"All things considered, we shall not do it. We reserve the bracelet for such time when we might need more money. Meanwhile, may I ask you how much the tickets to the movie will cost?"

He mentions the figure; I take the sum out of my purse, and hand it to him. The young man is now completely disconcerted, for he has no idea where he stands with me. At first I had taken from him the remainder of his loot, then I had joined him on an imaginary expedition of robbery, and finally I give him the money he needs out of my own pocket.

I want to leave him for some time in this state of tension, and therefore I promptly send him away, while making another appointment with him for the next day.

On the next day, as soon as he enters our office, he makes the following cryptic remark:

"I must tell you something; or rather—no, I won't tell it to you."

I do not react, but only bid him to sit down. He takes a chair and starts again:

"Do you like Thomas Mann?"

"What have you read among the works of Thomas Mann?"

He mentions several titles and goes on:

"We are now reading in class *Minna von Barnhelm* [he is in the last year of high school], and I cannot get through it." He indicates the passage they are studying and expects me to comment upon it.

"Who wrote *Minna von Barnhelm*?"

"Lessing. Why do you look away from me at your books?"

At this point I feel the time has come to take more drastic action, and I ask:

"What are you driving at? Are you trying to prove me dumb?"

He is startled and exclaims:

"In your presence one is not even allowed to think for oneself."

"When you entered this room," I counter, "you wanted to tell me something; but then you forgot to tell me."

"That's true. It was about our cook. She told me to be careful with this man, he is a sly fox."

"Is she a shrewd person herself?"

"Not at all! She is quite stupid!"

"So how could she make such a remark?"

"Very simple: she was with us even before my birth, she likes me very much, and when mother found out about the theft, our cook sided with me wholeheartedly."

"And is your cook right as to the warning she gave you?"

"Oh, no, not at all!"

"Then tell me yourself [I now use the direct address, German second person *Du*] about your swindles which nobody has discovered as yet."

Thereupon, the youngster starts relating a long story of thievery, which goes back to when he was only 10 years old.

He had started with petty thefts at home, then he had pilfered costume jewelry and money from neighboring hotel rooms while traveling with his mother; or during summer vacations, from lockers in bathing establishments at the beach. There followed an uninterrupted series of misdeeds; his stealing became more ambitious in scope; and yet he was never caught at it, because nobody suspected "the well-bred boy from a respectable family."

These two interviews, just described, must now be considered from a psychoanalytic angle. Let us remember first of all what we have learned from Freud (1914) about an overflow of narcissistic libido.

Relations to the other person are not always of an object-libidinal nature. Under certain conditions there occurs a repression of object libido which is effective to a certain extent, with a corresponding setback of sensual impulses, and ultimately an overflow of narcissistic libido may result. Although the attitude toward the object becomes different in nature, this difference in the relationship is not recognized: the object is still perceived as if a libidinal object cathexis had actually taken place. Likewise, there is failure to recognize that this subject now serves the purpose of attaining the goals of one's own ego ideal. "One loves it for that perfection which should have crowned one's own ego, and which one tries now to reach by this round about way, for the satisfaction of one's narcissism" (Freud, 1914). If those desires that tend toward immediate sexual satisfaction are held back entirely, then the object keeps growing ever more grandiose, ever more valued. The object finally comes to take possession of the ego's entire self-love. Meanwhile, the functions which belong to the ego ideal are brought to a complete standstill. The critical faculty which is normally exercised by the ego ideal becomes silent; whatever is done or demanded by the person who serves as an object seems right and blameless. The voice of conscience is no longer heard in any occurrence where the outcome seems to favor the object. The entire situation may be summed up: the object has taken the place of the ego ideal.

How do we translate our theoretical insight into practical work? When we meet the type of juvenile delinquent described, then we do not attempt to establish an object-libidinal relationship at all. We behave from the beginning in a manner which incites the youngster to let his own narcissistic libido flow over to our person, so as ultimately to create that dependence of his total personality upon us, a situation parallel to the ego's dependency upon its ego ideal.

We follow this procedure because the practice of child guidance has taught us that for this type of wayward youth, there is no other way to reach a heightened degree of dependency relationship which we need in order to achieve our guidance task. We must take into consideration that any youngster who comes to the clinic finds himself in a psychic situation which is not the one we need: his attitude toward us is negative, often hostile; he feels uncertain, puzzled, irritated; he tries to show aloofness, or acts as if he were superior to us; sometimes he does not seem to be interested at all in what goes on. It is seldom that his posture is one of eager expectation.

One may think it important to establish from the outset, in each case, what is the patient's frame of mind, among these psychic states which we have just described. But we do not really need to know this because we can always provoke through our own behavior that labile state of tension required for our work.

A feeling of uncertainty must be induced in the patient at the first moment of meeting, by the very manner of our reception. Our way of receiving him is not always the same, for it depends entirely on the impression the youngster makes upon us. An example is given above, when we greeted the young man without uttering a word.

From the beginning, we put ourselves in the spotlight, we aroused the boy's interest in our person and awakened his desire to try his strength with us.

Hence our first question: "Why did you make fun of the doctor?" We asked this in order to resolve the labile situation in our favor. The content of the question informs the boy that we are wise to his tricks.

As to the specific shape and intonation of our sentence, it is designed to compel him to react as we wish. It is timed also to bring about the desired decision. This part of our work may be described as the "timely use of the factor of surprise." While the juvenile delinquent is still unprepared for whatever awaits him and finds himself in a quite uncertain state of mind, there follows the dramatic act of unmasking, but without that dreaded consequence which is the only one he could have imagined: punishment.

He now observes that we are not the obnoxious adult who is called upon to castigate him; neither are we a teen-age comrade, prone to admire his courage or his smartness; in fact, we now seem to him a quite undecipherable being, of a species previously unknown, a person who indeed understands him, perhaps even with a slight undertone of appreciation, and who must be superior to him, in some inconceivable but not necessarily unpleasant manner. All this debate goes on not in his intellectual but in his emotional ego; for we do not move in his direction by way of verbal statements; it is only our general attitude which enables him to interpret our behavior, and after all he feels the interpretation might well be false. He is unable to reach a satisfactory conclusion, either in his own mind or through open discussion with the counselor; yet there remains the possibility to try to enter into a relationship with us—which he strives to attain for the benefit of his own ego, because he recognizes the "superiority" of our person.* At this point, a careless observer might gain the false impression that an object-libidinal cathexis had actually taken place.

We take advantage of this situation immediately; we accept the privileged position being offered us, and we even strengthen it by asking about the money which was left over from the theft. We do so in a quiet, matter-of-fact manner, which excludes any contradiction.

In due time, there follows the question: "Would you give the money to me?" which is asked in order to find out whether the relation of dependency is already strong enough for active intervention on our part.

As to the receipt, we give it to him as a proof that the money remains his property, and that we consider him a fully responsible person; also, in order to avoid any suspicions he may entertain about our hidden intentions, such as the idea that we might hand the money back to his mother without his knowledge.

---

*Editor's Note: Aichhorn works initially to establish an idealizing narcissistic transference in the boy.

With the writing out of the receipt, the first phase of our work is completed. To proceed with our further task, we must find out what is his precise state of mind in the present moment. His answer to our question, "What are you thinking about, right now?" shows how necessary it was to establish that point.

The purpose of the conversation that ensues is to ascertain whether he still remains restless or whether he has become inwardly reconciled to the fact of not having the money any more. If we break off this talk so soon, and revert in our next questions to the previous theme, it is only because he evidently takes little interest in such topics as school and home, whereas his entire attitude shows plainly that he still thinks about the money which he has handed over.

"I have the feeling that you would have taken it out of my pocket anyhow"—this is an admission which seems to prove that his relationship to us has grown considerably closer, and that his dependence upon our person is now correspondingly stronger.

We learn, immediately thereafter, that he is greatly embarrassed at not having the money for buying movie tickets; and that he does not know how to procure this money. We refer him quite intentionally to his mother, on the obvious assumption that he will not dare ask her now for any favors. But this, in turn, must focus his attention on his own state of utter helplessness, while it makes us appear before his eyes as the unexpected savior, who without any prompting has brought him much-needed help.*

Although the young man's relations to us have already reached a fairly high level of intensity, we are still far from being satisfied with the results. We want to take over more and more of his narcissistic libido, we intend to substitute ourselves for his ego ideal, so as to deprive him entirely of his critical faculty. In short, we plan to create a situation of dependency which would amount to nearly complete subservience.

Here a further observation is in order, for the benefit of the child guidance worker. This maximum amount of relationship is necessary in the first phase of our work with this specific kind of delinquent, inasmuch and insofar as we treat him in our sole capacity as counselor; but such maximum can be reached only when the juvenile delinquent sees in our person a superlative image of his own particular world. He will not be able to follow what we prescribe for him, if we are content to look

---

*Editor's Note: Within the idealizing transference is the perception of omnipotence of the object.

upon his crime of stealing from the mere standpoint of our social superego. It is not even enough to show ourselves complacently tolerant in condoning his actions. Something more is required: we must "play the game without restrictions," we must accept the boy's own values, we must prove to him that we can live within his world, that we, ourselves represent a worthwhile ideal by the standards of this world—in other terms, that we are capable of stealing even more shrewdly than he.

We realize that all this puts us in a singularly dangerous position, and we dare to do this only because we know that it is this peculiar relationship with the wayward boy which may stop him, perhaps, from committing another theft.

If we give him a little money, it is only in order to prevent the necessity of some additional thievery. Moreover, our generous act arouses in him such a storm of contradictory feelings that he is overwhelmed and loses his bearings. We do not allow him to come to any clear conclusions during our first interview; we send him home regardless of whether the "lesson" has come to an end; and we make a further appointment with him.

Let us consider the second meeting. The remark which he makes upon entering our office shows quite distinctly that he is again mistrustful. Therefore, something must have occurred between yesterday and the present visit, something of which we are still ignorant. Consequently, we remain watchful, we do not press him to tell us what he does not wish to tell, we avoid arousing his opposition; and so again we invite him merely to take a seat.

But this time it is he who asks questions. He reverses the situation of the previous day: yesterday we interrogated him, now our turn has come to answer his queries. Of course we do not let ourselves be maneuvered; we counter his question with one of our own. Already after a few sentences, he abandons the pretense of talking about literature and reverts to the topic which brought us together. For he has noticed by now that we do not follow him, although he is still reluctant to give up his own line.

Our question, "What are you driving at? Are you trying to prove me dumb?" is the result of a parallel reasoning which was unfolding in our mind while the boy was putting his questions to us. We know that a juvenile delinquent of this type is extremely fond of displaying his smartness in front of everybody and on every conceivable occasion. He is very conceited about associating only with clever people.

The young man's demeanor and his questions make us aware that he wants to escape from the dependency which had been developed on the previous day. He tries to break out by luring us into a field, literature, where in his opinion we shall find ourselves at a disadvantage. Indeed, had we followed his leading questions, we would certainly have wasted our time, and perhaps given him an occasion to achieve his ends.* But we did nothing of the sort. Through our own rejoinders, we made him understand that we were still his superior, as one the day before. The irrefutable proof that he finds himself in the same state of dependence lies in his manner of reacting to our question. He is startled, and he admits: "In your presence, one is not even allowed to think for oneself." But if he is really enmeshed in a dependency relationship, then he must also have given up that feeling of distrust which was so noticeable at the moment of his coming. We want to watch our step and make quite sure of it, so as not to endanger the situation through any false move. Therefore we interject: "When you entered this room, you wanted to tell me something; but then you forgot to tell me." In order not to awaken again his mistrust, we put the stress on this word: "forgot."

The fight which we have to sustain against the cook is not hard to win. Is she not a "stupid person?" We need only to put our questions in such a way as to remind our clever, "intellectual" young man of that fact.

Of course, we could not have guessed in advance that this "silly" old woman, the cook, would enable us to get the boy's almost full confession as early as our second interview, a confession involving nearly all the thefts of which the delinquent was still consciously aware. Nor could we have foreseen that it would suffice, in these circumstances, to use the direct, familiar address (German second person *Du*) in order to clinch a highly strengthened web of relationship to our person.

To create an element of surprise in order to startle the patient is not, however, an easy task. One cannot prepare oneself in advance; the surprise should result from circumstances that are by their very nature instantaneous; and each situation must be absolutely mastered as soon as it arises. A correct estimate of actions and consequences, even before they are set in motion, as well as a capacity for swift combination and immediate decision, are the prerequisites for achieving those dramatic effects which will work out as factors of surprise.

Here is an example. A youngster who had received a suspended sentence for theft was kept for a very long time under welfare observation. One day, the social worker, a woman, brings the young man to our child guidance clinic, because she has been suspecting him for some time of manifest homosexual practices.

---

*Editor's Note: The idealizing transference stimulates fears of dependency, which the psychopath will diminish through behavioral devaluation.

This social worker has had considerable experience. She treats her charge in accordance with the situation. In her eyes he is a grownup, and she tries to influence him favorably by her own straightforwardness because she has discovered certain elements in his character which should readily respond to such treatment.

From her reports of the youngster's present conduct, it appears that she takes care even of his pocket-money needs, providing him each week with petty cash and receiving his expense accounts, which she checks with the boy against his personal daily records, a procedure that was started on her initiative. She is particularly happy that the boy writes down even superfluous and unjustified expenses which must mean that he has nothing to hide from his counselor.

The reception of this boy at our clinic turns out to be rather unusual: the social worker introduces us to each other as if we were at a society meeting. His attitude is not that of the juvenile delinquent who presents himself before a child guidance counselor; in fact, he behaves as if he were a superior person whom his friend, the social worker, had invited to see me, because I showed interest in him. Obviously, he does not know that this "invitation" was merely a pretense, to make sure that he would come.

Right after the introduction, the social worker excuses herself and is about to go, so as to leave me alone with the boy. But just before going, she takes him to a corner of the office. I do not know what they are talking about, but I can see that he is receiving some money from her, and that his lips twitch momentarily in a half-smile of disparagement, only to resume at once its friendly, noncommittal expression. The social worker, busy with her purse, does not notice anything.

When we are alone, I ask him immediately about his talk with the social worker and I ask it in a way as to make him aware that I have marked his smile. He retorts by asserting that she had merely asked whether he needed money for the trolley car, and then had given him the money. Moreover, he goes on to say the social worker had settled his accounts with him only the day before, and she knew therefore that he was out of money. I am not impressed by this remark, and I demand instead that he show me his purse—a demand which I make in a tone that admits no contradiction. He seems completely taken aback, produces the purse at once, hands it over to me after a moment of hesitation, and waits in utter embarrassment. In the purse I find about twenty shillings in silver and banknotes, as well as a slip of paper on which are marked the names and addresses of two men, with corresponding appointments. Without further examination, I reproach him bluntly with his manifestly homosexual practices, for which he even gets paid.

He is so surprised at being found out that he does not try to deny the facts, and admits everything. Later, however, in the course of the conversation, he regains some of his self-assurance, and his statements again become mendacious.

How clever this young man is in misleading people can be seen from the following remark, made in answer to my question as to why he was lying so brazenly to the social worker: "When, in checking my accounts with her, I show her that I have no money, she thinks that I must be a decent guy, she makes favorable reports to the authorities, and I am left alone to do as I please."*

Another example is a young man of twenty-two, who has been driven from home by his own family, because of repeated swindles and thefts, and sent away to live with some relatives abroad. But now they are complaining that the young man is guilty of new acts of swindling. Upon receipt of this additional information, the parents, in complete despair, decide to visit our clinic.

The counselor explains to the parents that he cannot take any steps without interviewing the young man personally; whereupon they arrange for his return. Meanwhile, there appears at the clinic a friend of the family who on behalf of the parents asks for instructions as to how they should behave upon their son's arrival. But the counselor, relying on what he knows of the mutual relationship between members of this family, deems it important to meet the young man himself, before his reunion with his parents. He therefore suggests that the family friend should go to the railway station instead of the parents, and that he should bring Franz directly to me. The suggestion is accepted and carried out. Franz remains in the waiting room at the clinic while the friend goes into my office and tells me the following news: "You cannot imagine how Franz behaves! His aloofness is indescribable, I cannot stand his demeanor of icy coldness, he has not spoken one word since I met him at the station."

Intentionally, I leave Franz alone for a full hour in the waiting room. Meanwhile, the family friend relates further information about the young man and his parents. My line of reasoning is this: should this remarkable behavior of my young patient prove to be only a "mask," then he will not be able to bear his solitude, in an alien environment, not knowing what will happen next; therefore he will break down and

---

*Editor's Note: This is an example of Bursten's manipulative cycle—goal conflict, intent to deceive, deceptive act, and then contemptuous delight (see chapters 13 and 17).

become more accessible. On the other hand, if his haughtiness happens to be genuine, it will certainly end in an emotional outburst, after such a long wait which he will interpret as neglect of his person and regard as an outrage. As to other possibilities, such as listening at the door out of sheer curiosity, or remaining uninterested and aloof, I could rule them out, because of all I had learned about the character of Franz.

At the end of this "hour of waiting," I open the door which leads to the anteroom, in order to show Franz into my office. He is no longer the same Franz, but a bundle of wretchedness, a young man who has lost every semblance of self-control, and who now cowers miserably in a corner.

I take him by the hand, I address him without transition in the direct second person [German *Du*], I lead him into my office with these few words: "Don't be ashamed, let yourself cry as much as you wish!" Franz dissolves in a stream of tears, and it takes some time to pull himself together. He starts telling me, still sobbing, the pitiful story of his life: about himself, his parents who never understood him, the circumstances at home and in school, and a childhood without joy. This first interview is enough to unfold the sad picture of a really unhappy child.

The transference is achieved immediately, and holds fast for the duration of the treatment.

One more example: An estate manager from abroad comes to our clinic for consultation, and brings his son, who is considered in his family as a swindler. Father and son walk together into my office; because of the peculiar attitude of the son I lack the opportunity of having a preliminary talk with the father alone. The demeanor of this young man, who seems to be around twenty-five, shows that he has no use for the entire procedure; he glances at us inquiringly, but with the most supercilious expression, as if to convey the idea that there is no point in our present meeting.

The father recounts at great length the offenses committed by his son, whose behavior displays only a growing boredom. The statements of the father concern him as little as if they were made about someone else. Obviously, he has only one desire: that this annoying conversation should come to a stop.

When the father finishes his report, I reply in a tone which, at first, seems to ignore the son's presence altogether: "I do not treat cases of swindling; it would be a pity to waste my time and your money; if your son commits no further offense, everything will be all right anyhow; and should he revert to his old tricks, then they will lock him up, and you shall be rid of him." Turning to the son, I then continue: "Or perhaps you prefer to shoot yourself, if you are not a coward. This is another way of closing the case." While I speak these words calmly, without emotion, in a tone which I keep intentionally on the level of a matter-of-fact observation, I stand up in order to show that the interview has come to an end.

The father looks nonplussed and utterly dismayed. But from the countenance of the son one may note that we have succeeded in causing that state of irritation we intended to provoke. At the exit door, I shake hands with the young man, and add these few words: "You shall find no treatment at my clinic, but if you wish to talk with me once more, you may come and see me tomorrow." I also indicate the exact time at which I shall be expecting him.

After a short while, the father returns alone and starts complaining bitterly about my unbelievable behavior, which he fails to understand. Of course my purpose, in behaving as I did, escaped him entirely. So I explain to him the necessity of my line of conduct, which was dictated by the attitude taken by the son. I insist that he must not in any way influence his son's decision whether he should visit me again. Finally, the father goes away with a much easier mind.

On the next day, at the appointed hour, the young man comes to my office in a quite different mood—he is much less tense, more open to argument, and full of expectation: the transference has begun to work.

REFERENCE

Freud, S. (1914). On narcissism. *Standard Edition,* 14:73–102. London: Hogarth Press, 1957.

16

Some Characteristics of the Psychopathic Personality

Betty Joseph

Betty Joseph, a British psychoanalyst, first read this paper at the 21st International Psychoanalytic Congress in Copenhagen, July 1960. It was published that same year in the *International Journal of Psychoanalysis*. Joseph relies on the work of Melanie Klein and illustrates, through the analytic case of a young, noncriminal psychopath, the impulse–feeling–defense triad of greed–envy–devaluation in such patients. If the psychopath spoils that which he hungrily wants—the goodness in others—it is not worth having. Joseph posits this dynamic as a defense against anxiety, guilt, and depression, which may be true in her example. However, neurotic personality organization must be achieved to nurture such socialized feelings; this level of personality will not exist in the more primitive, less conflicted primary psychopath, whose greed, envy, and derogation are adaptive aspects of his aggression and psychological homeostasis.

In this paper I shall discuss some characteristics of the psychopathic personality. I use the term here in the sense in which it is generally employed in the psychiatric and psychoanalytic literature. I cannot, in a paper of this length, discuss the analytic literature on the subject but would refer particularly to Alexander (1930), Bromberg (1948), Deutsch (1955), Fenichel (1945), Greenacre (1945), Reich (1925), and Wittels (1938). It will be seen that my approach to the problem is essentially dependent upon an understanding of the work of Melanie Klein (1935, 1946, 1957).

I shall limit myself to describing and discussing one psychopathic patient whom I have had in treatment for about three years. I shall then draw certain conclusions from this case which seem to me, both by comparison with other psychopathic patients and from a perusal of the literature, to be relevant to the psychopathology of the non-criminal psychopath in general.

X was 16 when he came into treatment. His family is Jewish. His father is a somewhat weak and placating man; he works in a large industrial concern, but originally trained as a lawyer. The mother, of French origin, is an anxious and excitable woman who looks younger than her age. She started running a small café a few months before treatment started. There is a daughter who is two years younger and is more stable than X. There seems considerable tension between the parents, but both are concerned about X. X was referred for restless, unhappy and unsettled behaviour. He could not stick to anything, had no real interests, and was doing badly at school. His mother was anxious about his precocious sexual development and interests.

X was breast-fed for about two months; he was then put onto the bottle, as the mother had insufficient milk. He cried a lot between feedings. He appeared to have become increasingly difficult with his mother since puberty, but was overtly fairly friendly with the father despite frequent flare-ups. He went to boarding-school at 13 and on his holidays had one or two vacation jobs but could not stick to them. He seemed interested only in earning a lot of money in the easiest possible way. At 16 he was moved from boarding school to a cramming college in London in order to come to analysis. At this period he started to mix with a group of restless, near-delinquent teenagers who had no regular careers, training, or jobs, and himself remained just on the outer fringe of delinquency. He and his friends went to endless parties where there was a lot of petting with girls until all hours of the night, and they had virtually no other interests.

At college he despised and mocked his teachers, did almost no work, and cut his lectures. His two ideas for his future career were to be a lawyer or to go in for catering (his parents' careers). Soon he added a third, that of being a psychoanalyst! He was extremely demanding and exploiting with his parents, getting everything he could out of them, money, food, training, and then manifestly throwing away his opportunities. About all this he showed no apparent sense of guilt, but was very bombastic, and maintained a picture of himself as being in some way special and unique. He seemed emotionally very labile and impulsive and was apparently easily influenced by his group. He would often talk in a somewhat maudlin and sentimental way. Although he considered himself universally popular, he had in fact no real friends. In appearance he was slim, with a rather effeminate gait.

It seemed to me that X was in fact clearly a psychopathic personality. His difficulties did not seem to be just those of normal adolescence; he lacked obvious neurotic symptoms; he was not psychotic and had a severely disturbed character formation. As I have suggested, he was impulsive, had a weak ego, and was apparently lacking in a conscious sense of guilt. His object relationships were primitive; he was shallow in affect and very narcissistic.

In analysis X attended regularly, but there were periods when he would become very aggressive, would twist my interpretations, throw them back at me, verbally attack and mock me, or would argue and cross-question like a sadistic lawyer. At other times he was on the whole co-operative, often very smooth to the point of being placating; but there was a shallow type of response to my interpretations. He seemed consciously to pay little attention to them, would vaguely say "Yes" and go on to something else, and would not from one session to another show any continuity or refer back to insight he might have gained.

I shall now discuss three interrelated characteristics which I believe to be fundamental to X's psychopathic state. First, his striking inability to tolerate any tension; second, a particular type of attitude towards his objects; and third, a specific combination of defenses with whose help he maintains a precarious but significant balance.

X constantly shows his difficulty in tolerating any kind of tension. On a primarily physical level, he tears at his skin and bites his nails when he experiences any irritation; he was unable to establish proper bladder control until well into latency. He reacts to any anxiety by erecting massive defenses. He cannot stand frustration and tends to act out his impulses immediately with little inhibition. Nevertheless, as I shall indicate later, a great deal that appears to be an uncontrolled acting out of impulses can be seen on further analysis to consist of complicated mechanisms to avoid inner conflict and anxiety.

As to the second point—his particular type of attitude to his objects—X is, as I have described, extremely demanding and controlling, greedy and exploiting. What he gets he spoils and wastes; then he feels frustrated and deprived and the greed and demands start again. I want to show how this pattern is based on a specific interrelationship between greed and envy. To give an example: he must have analysis, he must have the sessions at the times he wants, it does not matter how difficult it is for his parents to afford the fees, but when he has it he mocks, he disregards, and he twists the interpretations. As I see it, he knows that he wants something and will grab, almost to the point of stealing, but then his envy of the giver—of the analyst, teacher, at depth the good parents—is so intense that he spoils and wastes it, but the spoiling and wasting lead to more frustration and so augment the greed again, and the vicious circle continues. Melanie Klein in discussing an aspect of this problem says, "Greed, envy and persecutory anxiety, which are bound up with each other, inevitably increase each other."

As to my third point, I am suggesting that the nature of the anxieties aroused by this interrelationship between greed and envy leads to the establishment of a characteristic series of defense mechanisms. These I shall describe in more detail, and I shall suggest how they enable X to maintain a particular type of balance. I shall show how X, despite his greed, exploitation, and impulsiveness, is not a criminal; despite his envious, omnipotent incorporation of his objects, his cruelty towards them, his apparent lack of concern for them, and his resultant inner persecution, he has not become psychotic. The balance that X achieves is, as I see it, the psychopathic state—a state in which profound guilt and depression, profound persecution, and actual criminality are all constantly being evaded.

The group of defense mechanisms mainly used by X to keep this precarious balance is centered on the maintenance and actual dramatization of powerful omnipotent phantasies which are largely based on massive splitting and excessive projective and introjective identification. So long as these mechanisms are effective, X's balance can be held and breakdown warded off. I have given some instances, such as his inability to visualize any career for himself other than that of his parents or myself. Or, when he was attempting to study economics for his General Certificate of Education, he immediately saw himself as a future writer of textbooks or an economic adviser to governments—not as a beginner student. I have also instanced how, when he was attending college, early on in the analysis, he in fact did no work, cut lectures, and mocked and derided his teachers as he did myself in the transference. But when faced with the reality of exams he would firmly maintain that he could easily catch up in the two or three weeks that remained.

These defenses depend upon a total introjection of, and magical identification with, the idealized, successful and desirable figures—the parents, analyst, writers of textbooks. This type of introjection enables him to ward off the whole area of depressive feelings. He avoids any dependence on his objects, any desire for or sense of loss of them. In addition, since he has swallowed up these idealized objects, and in his feelings stolen their capacities, he avoids envy and all competitiveness, including his oedipal rivalry. He has all the cleverness—the teachers and I are stupid, not worth his while attending to, we are the failures. Thus he splits off his wasting, failing self, his failure to make good and use what is available, and projects it into the teachers and myself. He is also magically reparative, can put forth everything right, e.g. the exams. In this way, failure, guilt, and depression are completely obviated.

Similar mechanisms are at work in his choice of friends. I have stated how, for a long time, he mixed only with a group of unsuccessful, near delinquent young people. It became clear that he projected into them his own criminal self—they stole, they lied, not he; thus he avoids actual criminality and the guilt that could result. It is interesting to note, however, that on the one occasion when he did get arrested by the police, along with a delinquent friend—mistakenly as it turned out—he lived in a state of near collapse for days, confirming that in fact it is the intensity of his fear of persecution that prevents his being a criminal.

A similar method of avoiding actual criminality and persecution and yet living out his stealing impulses by projective identification can be seen in the following type of behaviour. He would give a friend 10s. to hand over to a storeman who would "lift" a coat from a warehouse and get it round to X. X is constantly having to evade his inner persecuting figures and superego. These he would project into the police and parents, or, at college, his teachers, and then he allied himself with his delinquent friends against them. At other times he would identify with his inner accusing figures and turn violent accusations against his erstwhile friends, containing his criminal self. At yet other times he would appear to do a great deal of wheedling, cajoling, and bribing of his internal figures as if constantly trying to prove that his criminal impulses were not what they seemed, as is indicated in the example of the coat "lifted" by the storeman.

Naturally the constant use of projective identification to rid himself of the bad parts of the self and inner objects leaves him feeling more persecuted externally. This he deals with either by flight—for example, he eventually could not face his college and teachers at all; or by a manic, mocking, controlling attitude, as I have described in regard to his behaviour with myself and his teachers.

The need to project these various internal figures into the external world to avoid both inner persecution and the possibility of guilt plays a role of great importance in motivating psychopaths to maneuver rows, brawls, and fights in their outside environment to get themselves noticed and punished and attacked for apparently petty reasons. X, when his environment did not persecute him and when he seemed to be more settled and happy to be getting more insight, became noticeably accident prone. He poured boiling oil on his foot and cut off the tip of his finger as if he now had to play out the role demanded by his slashing and burning internal figures. It was also obvious that he unconsciously felt that such attacks were justified. He managed in a striking manner to neglect his scalded foot. I shall later indicate how such unconscious guilt and inner persecution drove X into actual stealing and into actually being rejected.

I have so far been trying to show some of the main mechanisms that X constantly used to avoid guilt, depression, inner and external persecution, and actual criminality. I want now to mention a more extreme defensive process which may occur when these ordinary mechanisms of omnipotence and projective identification fail him, and when he is momentarily faced with psychic reality. This process—a massive fragmentation of the self and inner objects—could be seen at certain periods in the analysis when the nature and need for his omnipotence were being interpreted; then one might get a sense of immediate chaos. X might become extremely angry and abusive with me, shouting at me for being ridiculous, or he might appear to collapse, yelling "All right, all right, all right," as if he were falling completely to pieces. In these situations parts of the self and internal objects that had previously been split off and projected out and kept at bay by his holding on to the idealized omnipotent phantasies, are, by virtue of the interpretations, brought back into contact with the self. At this moment a new violent splitting and falling to pieces of projective identification takes place, since the patient feels overwhelmed by his impulses and by his emerging guilt and his internal objects; at once the bad, for example "ridiculous" parts, as well as his inner persecuting figures, are projected into the analyst, who is attacked and abused, or is placated in a desperate masochistic manner—as with X crying, "All right, all right, all right." This splitting is now of a diffuse fragmenting type, making one aware of his nearness to schizophrenic disintegration, and his absolute need for the omnipotent defences that prevent it. In the second part of this paper I shall bring more detailed material to illustrate some of the main points that I have been making—especially the interconnection between greed, envy, and frustration in X and the nature and functioning of his characteristic defenses.

The material I am quoting occurred about a month before a Christmas holiday. My previous patient had in fact just left, but X arrived early, and instead of going as usual to the waiting room, came straight to the consulting room, opened the door, looked in, realized his error, shut the door and then went to the waiting room.

At the beginning of the session he told a dream, which was that he was in a place like a bar which also served food; his penis seemed to have come through the zip opening of his trousers. He put it back, but then it was as if he pulled it out again; he thought that people would realize that he was a homosexual, or a pervert. There were other men, perhaps sailors, in the bar. His associations were to a bar in a village near a town D, where he had stayed during the previous summer holidays. The bars there were closed on Sundays, but everyone went to the bar in the nearby village which was really meant only for travellers passing through. The penis showing through the trouser opening refers to a party the previous weekend when X got a bit drunk and a boy had his trouser opening showing. X then described how he went into a public lavatory a week or so before: the notice on the door said "Vacant," but when he opened the door he saw a man's bag standing on the floor inside, then realized that there was a man in the lavatory saying something to him as if inviting him to come in. X was alarmed and fled.

Briefly, I am suggesting that X was showing his feelings about the coming Christmas holidays, when I was felt to be the shut bar, and he turned away to the open bar, the homosexual relationships with men, experienced as a drinking and feeding, which I connected with fellatio phantasies. As I was speaking he said that he was just thinking about masturbation phantasies he had had about sucking his own penis. He then seemed to trail off, saying that he had a heavy bag of school books with him and wished he could leave it here in my flat. I pointed out that he seemed to be turning my flat into the lavatory scene that he had experienced the previous week, for he had started the session by pushing open the door as if maintaining that it said "Vacant" and was proposing to push the bag in here too.

I shall now bring together the main points that I tried to convey to him and that I want to discuss here. First there is the dramatization of the whole situation in the transference. There is also the avoidance of the frustration and anxiety about my being shut, as the mother, unavailable over the Christmas holiday, by turning greedily to the ever-open bar. But the bar is run by men; he turns to the father inside the mother, my room being a combined parent figure. There is a reference to his greed: last weekend he was a bit drunk; but the greed leads at once to envy of the person who can feed, so he incorporates the feeding penis, which is equated with the breast, and omnipotently sucks from his own penis in his masturbation phantasies and will, apparently, feed the other men—the sailors. His trousers then become the ever-open bar. Thus, all feelings of anxiety about loss and possible rejection by the mother are obviated; his need and desire for her are in the men who are split-up aspects of the father. But now the father containing these bits of himself becomes an object of terror, as is seen in the association about the flight from the man in the lavatory. In the dream there is a breakthrough of persecutory fears; he puts his penis back again, as if afraid of the greed of the sailors. X achieves his omnipotent solution by becoming homosexual, meaning that he now contains the penis-breast. But the guilt and persecution about the stealing of the breast is evaded, since the actual homosexuality is projected into me as the father seducing him.

There are two further points I want to make. First, that the homosexual collusion with the men—there are no women in the dream—is mirrored in his placating relationship with his actual father, in which both quietly denigrate the mother. Second, I am trying to show here the depth of X's omnipotent phantasies.* I have already stressed his need to have both his parents' careers, and he finally chose the one based on his mother's, both her immediate one and her original maternal feeding one. In this material it becomes clear that at depth what X feels he must have is the mother's breast stolen by the father and fused with the father's penis.

I shall now bring material to illustrate more fully an aspect of what I described earlier as X's particular type of attitude to his objects. I shall show some of his ways of avoiding his deepest guilt towards his first object, especially his method of dramatizing a situation in which he is thrown out, and thus punished, for a petty crime, rather than enduring the deeper underlying guilt which would lead him to experience the depressive position.

X decided to take up catering as a career and by now was able to start in a realistic way; he was accepted at a catering college and found a job in the kitchen of a good hotel where he could get preliminary experience. He was good at the work, and, for the first time since he had been in analysis, very happy in what he was doing. Suddenly, after being there just a month, he arrived saying that the chef had given him the sack, but he did not know why, except that they were cutting down staff. This reason did not convince him. Throughout the session he spoke very restrainedly, kept telling how very helpful and nice everyone had been, the work place, the employment agency, adding frequently, "I didn't fall to pieces, I didn't fall to pieces," and then went back to everyone's niceness. When I showed him both his belief that the chef had now stolen his job and his potency, and his fear of facing his own despair, persecution, and hate, he suddenly said that he thought that the chef was a crook. He had once overheard a conversation which seemed to indicate that in a previous job the chef had stolen some hams. As he described this X became panicky, saying "My anger's coming out," and

---

*Editor's Note: Dragan Svrakic identifies two kinds of grandiose fantasies: *free floating* and *structured*. The former is "free" in the inner world and able to be temporarily projected into any feeling, thought or action; the latter is permanently attached, usually to a particular self-representation, such as physical appearance, or to a successful career. See D. Svrakic (1989). Narcissistic personality disorder: A new clinical systematics. *European Journal of Psychiatry*, 3:199–213.

went back to describing how nice and helpful everyone had been. Right at the end of the session when speaking of his fear of his anger he said "It's like when I went to the cinema on Saturday, they showed the film of a plane crash, where fourteen people were killed. Tears came right up behind my eyes—ordinarily you act as if you felt tearful, but this was real, it caught me by surprise, I stopped it, but in a way I was glad the feelings came."

I want to stress three points here: first, his fear of falling to pieces if the hate, the persecution and despair were allowed to come through and overwhelm him, just as he seemed to be liable to fall to pieces in the session that I instanced earlier when his omnipotence was being analyzed and he was momentarily facing psychic reality. Second, his attempt again to deal with the guilt by projecting the stealing parts of the self (as will emerge later) and the oedipal impulses towards the mother, and the robbing, castrating internal figures into the chef standing for the father, and at first even denying his fear about him. Third, the profound idealization of the self, being so quiet and constructive, and of the whole outside world other than the chef.

But this splitting and idealization are now aimed also at keeping his good objects alive and safe. This can be seen by the emergence of depressive feelings; for example, the strikingly sincere way in which he spoke of the plane crash, and his fear about the crashing of his constructive work, at depth his good internal objects. But he had in fact brought about this partial crash, the loss of the good job. The reason for this emerged more clearly three days later when in response to interpretations he said that he thought that he might have been given the sack for stealing food from the hotel. Three times he had taken sandwiches home with him. So the criticism of the chef for stealing became clear.

But as I shall now try to show, this petty stealing of the sandwiches, which almost certainly got him the sack was, as I suggested at the beginning of this paper, not just an acting out of greedy impulses, but a more complex method of avoiding the deeper guilt and anxiety about stealing by the spoiling of his good object—at depth the mother's breast. This was shown the following day, when he arrived complaining that although he had got a new job he had only been paid one pound to keep him going. "I can't manage, I have to pay rent. I can't manage, I shall have to borrow. At the hotel the menu is in French and I can't understand it." I suggested that what he could not properly understand was how he got into all these muddles with money, and I should add that there was an important connection here with the French menu, the French mother's food.

He spoke of plans for paying the money back and went on to say he had had a bad night; his hot water bottle had leaked, the stopper wasn't in properly, and the bed got damp. I suggested that the real problem was that he felt that the money, just like the analysis and his other opportunities, seemed somehow to leak away and not get used properly. He spoke about a difficulty in plans for the day; how to manage the suitcase he had with him. If he took it to work, the doorman would go through it when he left to make sure he wasn't stealing anything, and he would be so embarrassed as it was full of soiled linen. I showed him his anxiety about taking in stuff from me, the hotel, in a stealing way, that is, not to use it himself: for example, to have a good meal but to slip it out secretly and make it into a mess represented by the soiled linen, as he did with the analysis, when the sessions again and again got lost and chaotic. He said that at the previous job it was true he did get three good meals a day, but then went to the lavatory three times a day to defecate.

Thus, the real nature of his guilt, his self-accusations, here projected onto the doorman, concern his turning his good meals at once into feces, my good interpretations into disregarded stuff, which are then just defecated or leaked out.

There are two points that I want to stress here. First, I believe that it is this type of envious spoiling that is the really critical point of the guilt in these patients, leading in X to a fear of loss and rejection. This guilt and anxiety he avoids by getting himself actively thrown out of his job for apparently petty, greedy stealing. Second, it is this spoiling and wastage that leaves these patients always dissatisfied, feeling, as they express it, that "the world owes me something," and this stirs up greed again. Of course, this dissatisfaction is increased by their guilt, which also prevents them from feeling able to use and enjoy what they do get.

CONCLUSION

I am suggesting in this paper that the psychopathology of X might be considered to be typical for a large group of non-criminal psychopaths. It seems that he is particularly unable to tolerate frustration and anxiety; that he approaches his objects with an attitude of extreme greed and stealing; and that the greed and experience of desire lead immediately to feelings of intense envy of the object's capacity to satisfy him. He attempts to obviate his envy both by spoiling and wasting what he gets from the object, thus making the object undesirable, and by omnipotent incorporation of the idealized object. He is faced with profound anxieties on many levels. He cannot face and work through the depressive position both because of the intensity of the persecution of his internal objects and his guilt; and because he is partially fixated in the paranoid-schizoid position owing to the strength of his envious impulses and splitting. I have tried to show how, faced with these various anxieties and impulses, he manages to keep a precarious balance, avoiding criminality on the one hand and a psychotic breakdown on the other. I have discussed the nature of the defense mechanisms—based on omnipotence, splitting, and projective and introjective identification which keeps this balance going—and am suggesting that this balance is the psychopathic state.

REFERENCES

Alexander, F. (1930). The neurotic character. *Internat. J. Psycho-Anal.*, 11: 292–311.

Bromberg, W. (1948). Dynamic aspects of the psychopathic personality. *Psychoanal. Quart.*, 17.

Deutsch, H. (1955). The impostor. *Psychoanal. Quart.*, 24.

Fenichel, O. (1945). *The Psychoanalytic Theory of Neurosis.* New York: Norton.

Greenacre, P. (1945). Conscience in the psychopath. *Amer. J. Orthopsychiat.*, 15:495.

Klein, M. (1935). A contribution to the psychogenesis of manic-depressive states. In: *Contributions to Psycho-Analysis, 1921–1945.*

Klein, M. (1946). Notes on some schizoid mechanisms. In: *Developments in Psycho-Analysis.*

Klein, M. (1957). *Envy and Gratitude.* London: Tavistock.

Reich, W. (1925). *Der Triebhafte Charakter.* Vienna: Internationaler Psychoanalytischer Verlag.

Wittels, F. (1938). The position of the psychopath in the psycho-analytic system. *Internat. J. Psycho-Anal.*, 19.

17

Some Narcissistic Personality Types

Ben Bursten

Ben Bursten, an American psychoanalyst, wrote this diagnostic paper, which appeared in the *International Journal of Psychoanalysis* in 1973. His important but little-known book, *The Manipulator*, was published by Yale University Press the same year. Bursten sets forth his four types of narcissistic personality: the craving, the paranoid, the manipulative, and the phallic narcissistic. He discusses their common aim, reunion with the omnipotent object, and the different means by which they pursue it. Most germane to psychopathy is the manipulative type, chiefly defined by repetitive attempts to "put something over" on the object. Domination is achieved, contemptuous delight is felt, and once again the grandiose self is preserved through the behavioral devaluation of the other.

I

Human beings appear in such a rich assortment of personalities that attempts to classify them into types are difficult and must be to some degree arbitrary. Our classifications are based on our observations, but what we observe, what we attend to and how we see it depend on our theoretical assumptions and our particular interests. This was true of the ancient humoral classification of temperament based on blood, phlegm, and yellow and black bile; it is equally true of modern approaches, such as Fromm's (1947) receptive, exploitative, hoarding, marketing and productive types, and Riesman's (1950) tradition-directed, inner-directed and other-directed types.

If, indeed, our categories depend in great measure on the orientation from which we start, why is it so important that we categorize? At least two reasons come to mind; some ordering is necessary for us to cope with, or even to retain, the vast variety of personality data, and classification enables us to relate one set of observations to another and to apply to a new situation the knowledge gained from a former one.

In psychoanalytic thought, too, evolution of our theoretical concepts has led to changes in our categorization. The early characterology emphasized the stages of libidinal development as a basis for classification. Freud (1908, 1913) and Abraham (1921, 1924a, 1925), for example, stressed the instinctual underpinnings of character structure. In his 1913 paper, Freud acknowledged the incompleteness of a theory resting on only the stages of development of the libido; however, the corresponding phases of ego development were yet to be charted, for example by Erikson (1950).

As our understanding of the ego evolved, particularly with the formulation of the structural theory (Freud, 1923), other bases for classifying character arose. Fenichel (1945, pp. 470 ff), for example, described sublimative and reactive character types, and he separated the latter into pathological behavior towards the id, which leaned heavily on the stages of libidinal development, pathological behavior towards the superego and pathological behavior towards external objects. That this is essentially an ego classification can be recognized when we recall that these three targets of pathological behavior constitute the "dependent relationships of the ego" described by Freud in "The Ego and the Id." And as early as 1916, Freud had described some character types representing not libidinal fixation points (the relationship to the id), but in large measure the relationship to what was later to be called the superego.

In 1931, although Freud utilized structural concepts in his characterology, his biological orientation impelled him to maintain that "if we confine our effort to setting up purely psychological types, the libidinal situation will have a first claim to serve as a basis for our classification." Accordingly, he described narcissistic, obsessional and erotic types as well as mixtures of these three types. More recently, however, character classification based on stages of instinctual development does not seem to be fashionable. While Hartmann (1952), in discussing ego formation, proposed an *enlargement* of our scope from only considerations of instinctual development to include considerations of aggression and "the partly independent elements in the ego," nowadays we seem to hear more about the latter considerations and less about the former. Indeed, some analysts seem to have all but repudiated the importance of instinct theory as out of date. Guntrip (1969) maintained that "a dynamic psychology of the 'person' is not an instinct-theory but an ego-theory, in which instincts are not entities *per se* but functions of the ego. . . . Instinct-theory *per se* becomes more and more useless in clinical work, and ego-theory more and more relevant" (p. 124). And Kernberg (1970a), in his valuable contribution to characterology, rejects a classification based on the stages of libidinal development. The libidinal components he employs are conceived of as "levels" of instinctual development: genital, pregenital, and a pathological condensation of genital and pregenital with a preponderance of pregenital aggression.

In part, this underplaying of instinctual theory is due to some very solid advances in ego psychology. However, I cannot escape the concern raised by Stein (1969), who points out that, even among analysts, repression of instinctual life may affect our observations and our study of character differences. And I believe that, in contrast to ego theory, instinct theory is most vulnerable to such repression.

The issue may be further clarified by referring to the distinction between the aim and the object of an instinct (Freud, 1905, 1915). The aim of an instinct is satisfaction and its expression has reference to various bodily zones. The object, not originally connected to the instinct, "becomes assigned to it only in consequence of being particularly fitted to make satisfaction possible" (Freud, 1915, p. 122). Hoffer (1952) has warned us about the importance of keeping this distinction in mind. In terms of the present discussion, I am suggesting that instinctual development, as characterized by its aim, is of basic importance in the understanding of variations in character. I do not imply that objects, ego organization, superego considerations, etc., all of which have their instinctual aspects, are of lesser importance; they are of great significance, but not to the exclusion of aims.

II

We may approach the subject of narcissistic personality types through Freud's (1914) two categories of object choice—narcissistic and anaclitic. The term narcissistic object choice is generally well accepted; it refers to an object who represents what the person is, was in whole or in part, or would like to be. Oremland and Windholz (1971) discuss the narcissist as one whose relationships are characterized by a sense of identity with himself. As Pulver (1970) indicates, there is no implication that the narcissist does not relate to others; rather it is the type of relationship—one characterized by seeing himself in the other person—that is important.

The term anaclitic is, as Eisnitz (1969) points out, out of date, in that it refers to an earlier concept of instincts. What, then, shall we call the other type of object choice? Eisnitz suggests Freud's synonym, "attachment." I hesitate to adopt this term; it suffers from the same theoretical difficulty as "anaclitic." Further, it is ambiguous—what could be more attached than an object seen as a part of or extension of oneself? Other

sets of terms, such as "narcissistic v. object love" or "narcissistic personality v. transference neuroses" are also ambiguous. As we have seen,
narcissists do love objects, although the objects represent the narcissists
themselves. And in psychoanalysis, narcissists do form a transference
along the particular lines of their type of object relationships, although
identification might be a better term than transference. Thus I choose
the term "complementary relationship" to denote the other type of
object choice. This term implies a fitting in with the person's needs and
yet a sense of separateness from the other person which the narcissistic
relationship lacks.

Now the separation of persons with complementary object relationships (complementary personalities) from narcissistic personalities is
based on object choice, not instinctual aim. When Freud (1914) differentiated these two types of relatedness, he disclaimed that he was proposing a character typology: "We have not, however, concluded that human
beings are divided into two sharply differentiated groups, according as
their object choice conforms to the anaclitic or the narcissistic type; we
assume rather that both types of object choice are open to each individual, though he may show a preference for one or the other" (p. 88).
However, later in the same paper he mentioned certain kinds of people,
such as criminals and humorists who "compel our interest by the
narcissistic consistency with which they manage to keep away from
their ego anything that would diminish it" (p. 89). When a narcissistic
preference reaches such a consistency that it dominates the ego's reper-
toire of defences and adaptations, it may fairly be called a character type.
And subsequent writings (Freud, 1931; Kernberg, 1970b; Kohut, 1971)
have distinguished a type of person called a "narcissistic personality."

Narcissistic personalities are distinguishable not only from complementary personalities, but also from people with borderline personalities. And here again, the chief element in the distinction is not the
instinctual aims but consideration of the objects—or, more properly, the
internalized object representations. The borderline personality has a less
cohesive self; he is easily subject to fragmentation. Likewise, the bound-
ary between himself and others is less clear. The narcissistic personality
may have transient episodes of fragmentation, but he more readily
recovers his sense of self (Kohut, 1971, pp. 1 ff.).

Thus the broad group of narcissistic personalities may be distinguished, with reasonable if imperfect clarity, from complementary personalities on the one hand and borderline personalities on the other.
Kernberg (1970a), Frosch (1970), and Kohut (1971) among others have
elaborated on the distinguishing characteristics; I shall touch only very
briefly on them here.

In contrast to the borderline personality, the narcissistic personality has a firmer sense of self, feels (and is) in less danger of fragmenting and has a better sense of reality testing. As Kohut (1971, pp. 11 f.) has pointed out, narcissistic concerns, such as grandiosity and the need for omnipotent others, are prominent in borderline personalities, but the "narcissistic structures . . . are hollow . . . brittle and fragile." While the narcissistic personalities have a firmer, more cohesive and stable ego organization than borderline personalities, they are not so able to separate themselves from others as are complementary personalities. This is seen, of course, in the narcissistic object choice—a reflexion or extension of the narcissist himself, with little ability to respect the object as a person in his own right. The cohesiveness of the ego is firmer in the complementary personalities; repression rather than splitting is a fundamental defence mechanism, and complementary personalities are not subject to the fleeting, psychotic-like regressions which are experienced by narcissistic personalities. Complementary personalities are guided more by guilt; narcissistic personalities, more by shame. We may view narcissistic personalities, then, as more or less intermediate between borderline personalities and complementary personalities, and, as we shall see when we examine the gamut of narcissistic personalities, they tend to merge with these other groups at the ends of the range.

We may look at one other distinguishing aspect—that which Frosch (1970) calls "the nature of the conflict and danger" and I shall call the task of the character structure. The primary task of the complementary personality is to resolve the Oedipus complex—to combat the castration fear and overcome the guilt. The main task of the narcissistic personality is to achieve the bliss and contentment characteristic of the primary narcissistic state, and this implies the reunion of the self which must be very grand with an object which must be nourishing and powerful (Rado, 1928; Lewin, 1950; A. Reich, 1960). Self-esteem, the approval of others and the confirmation of one's sense of worth by the ability to use others are as I have described elsewhere (Bursten, 1973, pp. 100 ff.), derivatives of the earliest narcissistic state. The primary task of the borderline personality is to prevent disintegration and dissolution. It may be seen to be related to the task of the narcissistic personality, for dissolution and psychic death are, in a sense, a return to the primary undifferentiated state. However, the narcissistic personality is governed by a need to satisfy the later derivatives of this primary state (Kohut, 1966); the borderline personality must struggle to prevent a regression towards the primary state itself.

I should point out here what may be a difference in emphasis between my formulation and that of Kohut (1971, pp. 15 ff., 152 f.). He speaks of the "central vulnerability" of narcissistic personalities as the danger of fragmentation or disintegration when the narcissistic relationship is ruptured. Nonetheless, narcissists have a resilience which borderline personalities lack and they tend to "snap back" and repair their narcissism. Thus I think of their fragmentation as a consequence of the failure of the central task—the reunion. Whereas the threat of fragmentation is central (in the sense of exerting a prominent influence upon the character traits) in the borderline patient, I emphasize the threat of the rupture of the narcissistic relationship as central to the narcissistic personality.

These three broad personality groupings, then, are distinguishable primarily by criteria other than the instinctual aims to which I referred in the first section of this paper. Nonetheless, instinctual aims are important also. Complementary personalities have a primary task related to the oedipal phase of development. Borderline and narcissistic personalities have tasks expressive of orality. The role of the instincts in the differentiation of borderline from narcissistic personalities is more obscure, possibly because this differentiation occurs in a period when ego and id are so intertwined that it is difficult for us to separate the instinctual components from the more easily understandable ego components.

I shall not linger further over the differentiation of these three groups. Early in life a course seems to be set for the establishment of a personality type according to one of these three categories. Let us turn now to the group of narcissistic personalities to examine the particular character types within this group.

III

In the course of my work at a U.S. Veterans Hospital I have had the opportunity to observe a large number of narcissistic personalities. I have seen them in the context of the social situation of a psychiatric ward, in the context of direct interviews with them, and through the eyes of psychiatric residents under my supervision. I have been fortunate to have been able to supplement these "direct" observations with material from my psychoanalytic work with each of the narcissistic personality types I shall describe shortly with the exception of the paranoid personality. I draw my material from a predominantly male population; nevertheless, I believe that the formulations to be presented here are generally applicable to women as well as to men.

From these observations, I have come to classify four types of narcissistic personalities—the craving, the paranoid, the manipulative and the

phallic narcissistic personalities. These are not necessarily new classifications, although some of them do not exactly coincide with classifications of the current psychiatric nomenclature. These personality types
can often be distinguished on clinical grounds and I shall describe some
of their more obvious features at this point.

The craving personality includes many people who have been called
"dependent" or "passive aggressive." Indeed, their interpersonal relationships are characterized by the need to have others support them.
They are clinging, demanding, often pouting and whining. They act as
though they constantly expect to be disappointed, and because of their
extraordinary neediness, disappointment comes frequently. When not
given to, they often seem to lack the energy to function, except for the
function of increasing their demands in obvious or subtle ways. In social
situations, some of these people seem quite charming and lively; however, one can often discern a certain desperation behind their charm,
and their liveliness has a driven quality. Others are less socially inclined;
they may cling to one person, or to a very small group of people. The
essential features of their personalities can often be seen in their mar-
riages. Even in those cases where they seem to function adequately at
their jobs, they collapse at home unless their wives give them a great
deal of attention.

I do not feel that "dependent" or "passive aggressive" really grasps
the essential feature of this personality. Like Rosenfeld (1964) and
Kernberg (1967), I doubt whether these people can be dependent. It is
precisely because they cannot depend on anyone that they are so
clinging. But I have still another reason for rejecting these terms. Among
many of our psychiatric colleagues, there seems to be an inordinate fear
of patients' dependency needs or attempts to be passive. Activity (of a
socially approved type, of course) and independence are highly valued.
These psychiatrists view the therapeutic situation as a struggle in which
the therapist must constantly try to force the patient to be independent.
"Dependency" and "passive-aggressiveness" play into this struggle.

A better term was suggested to me by one of my patients. I was
talking about his constant state of neediness and he corrected me.
"Neediness," he said, "it isn't just neediness. It's craving. I'm like a little
bird with a wide-open beak."

The clinical features of the paranoid personality are well described in
the *Diagnostic and Statistical Manual of Mental Disorders* (American Psychiatric Association, 1968): This behavioral pattern is characterized by
hypersensitivity, rigidity, unwarranted suspicion, jealousy, envy, excessive self-importance, and a tendency to blame others and ascribe evil
motives to them. These people are not psychotic. They should be

differentiated from those patients with paranoid states (Cameron, 1959), who are delusional. Much of the literature on paranoid conditions refers to paranoid schizophrenia on the one hand and paranoid states on the other. These psychotic conditions occur when there is a failure of the more usual coping mechanisms; in the paranoid personality there is no such failure. In fact, many paranoid personalities lead active and productive lives—especially in vocations where skepticism, suspiciousness and criticism are important components. Often these people are litigious. They are generally argumentative. Their anger runs the gamut from querulousness and skepticism to jealous rages.

The manipulative personality has been previously described by me (Bursten, 1972, 1973, pp. 153 ff.). This personality type includes some, but not all, persons generally known as "antisocial personalities" or "sociopaths." I find the current designations inadequate because they rely on a combination of psychological and sociological criteria. Too often the diagnosis is made on the basis of a record of repeated offences and conflicts with the law. The clinical features of the manipulative personality center around manipulativeness, whether in the context of socially approved activities as in the case of some businessmen and administrators, or otherwise as in the case of confidence men.

I define manipulation in a restricted way (Bursten, 1973, pp. 8 ff.). It is an intrapsychic phenomenon and this is independent of whether the manipulation succeeds. The manipulator perceives that another person's goal conflicts with his own, he intends to influence the other person and employs deception in the influencing process, and he has the satisfying feeling of having put something over on the other person when the manipulation works. These components of manipulation are readily available to consciousness; the manipulator knows what he is doing. This criterion excludes a great many behaviors which other psychiatrists term "manipulative." The mere fact that a person's actions influence another to treat him in a certain way does not constitute manipulation. Indeed, wherever one person is expressive and another empathic, influence is likely to occur. It is the conscious existence of these four components—conflict of goals, intention to influence, deception, and the feeling of putting something over—which comprise manipulation.

In addition to his central feature of manipulativeness, the manipulative personality is characterized by a propensity for lying (deception), little apparent guilt, transient and superficial relationships, and considerable contempt for other people. Some of these people are aggressively antisocial. Because they repeatedly get into trouble it has been felt that they do not learn from experience. Cleckley (1959) wrote: "The psychopath often makes little or no use of what he attains as a result of deeds that eventually bring him to disaster." In order to understand the manipulative personality, we must focus not on the obvious rewards of his manipulations, but on the inner compulsion to manipulate.

The phallic narcissistic personality has been described by W. Reich (1933, pp. 200 ff.), although he includes a wider variety of personalities in this category than I do. These are the "men's men." Often they are called "passive-aggressive." They parade their masculinity, often along athletic or aggressive lines. In common with some manipulative personalities, they tend to be both exhibitionist and reckless. While the exhibitionism of the manipulative personality tends more to call attention to his "good behavior" and reputation, the phallic narcissist tends more to show himself off and to exhibit his body, clothes, and manliness. The manipulative person is more reckless in his schemes, deceptions and manipulations; the phallic narcissist tends more towards feats of reckless daring, such as driving automobiles at excessive speeds, in order to prove his power. Many phallic narcissistic men seem to have a dual attitude to women. On the one hand, they talk about them in the contemptuous terms of locker-room language. On the other hand, they are the defenders of motherhood and the sanctity of women.

This personality type is not limited to men, although, because of the nature of my work, I have seen many more men than women. Phallic narcissistic women are often confused with hysterical women because of their narcissistic exhibitionism. Like their male counterparts, they tend to be very conscious of their clothes, cars, etc. They are usually much colder and haughtier than hysterics. Arrogance, above all, is a feature of phallic narcissism.

The relationships of these personality types to each other have particularly attracted my interest. I shall discuss these relationships along three dimensions—the mode of narcissistic repair, the degree of self–object differentiation, and the value system.

It is the dimension of the mode of narcissistic repair which brings considerations of instinctual aims to the forefront. To understand this, we must return to the chief task of the narcissistic personality as outlined above. The primary narcissism of the undifferentiated state sets the tone for this task. As the infant develops and his mental apparatus begins to differentiate, the basic pattern takes on instinctual and ego aspects. Lewin's (1950) oral triad describes the instinctual component; the ego components are self-esteem and the affects—anxiety and depression when the instinctual aims are thwarted and self-esteem falls, and bliss, contentment and elation when the instinctual aims are gratified and self-esteem is maintained or restored (Bibring, 1953; Rapaport, 1959). Rado's (1928) formulation of the reunion of the self with the nourishing breast is a crucial part of this pattern, having both instinctual aspects (oral gratification) and ego aspects (reunion and fusion of self and object representations). Complete fusion, of course, expresses the state of primary narcissism; secondary narcissism is built on reunion. The ability to obtain oral gratification is the basis for self-esteem and the grandiose self; the notion of a powerful and nourishing breast with which to unite is the basis for the omnipotent object, or idealized parent imago.

The development of these two aspects of narcissism has been set forth in detail by Kohut (1966, 1971). As the child grows older, the nature of the reunion takes on different colorations. The basic narcissistic pattern, however, is laid down in early infancy. It is not simply a fixation on the oral level. From the instinctual side, the vicissitudes of early orality are very important; the frustrations and disappointments due to inadequate and unempathic mothering (Jacobson, 1946; Kohut, 1971, pp. 63 ff.) set the stage for susceptibility to narcissistic wounds. The ego aspects of this drama—reunion, self-esteem and the affects—set the stage for the narcissism itself, and the subsequent measures which will be employed to sustain and restore it.

For the person with a narcissistic personality, then, the essential task is that of maintaining and restoring the self-esteem which accompanies the reunion of a grandiose self representation with an omnipotent object representation. The manner in which these four personality types go about this task is what I call the mode of narcissistic repair—"repair" because their narcissism is so vulnerable that keeping it in repair is a lifetime project. And, if one listens very carefully to the complaints offered by all of these types, they have a common underlying theme of having been disappointed and betrayed by someone who was not powerful enough or ready enough to give when they needed it.

The mode of narcissistic repair employed by the craving personality is so beautifully illustrated by my patient's comment. When in danger, he opens his beak ever-wider. Here we can see very clearly the instinctual component of the character trait. The craving personality must be fed. He is devastated if supplies and nourishment are not forthcoming, and with the expression of his predominantly oral orientation, he sucks harder, and sometimes he bites and grasps. He does this not only for the instinctual satisfaction of being fed. His libido is also pressed into the service of narcissistic repair. While he is unfed, his self esteem suffers; where is his specialness and where are the nourishing objects? Reunion is effected mainly by crying out, "I'm hungry!, I'm starving!"

Let us look now at the role of aggression in the narcissistic repair. All narcissistic personality types are capable of flying into cold rages; they have this capability in common and it may represent a regression to a diffuse infantile rage in the face of severe feelings of narcissistic injury. However, the role of aggression is seen to be different among the various types when the wound is not so great as to call for the rage; when the aggressive discharge is modulated it becomes admixed with the libidinal elements of the narcissistic repair. Such admixture has been described (A. Freud, 1949). In the case of the craving personality, we see pouting and sulking. Adatto (1957) has described the oral nature of pouting. It is essentially an inactive form of angry appeal for supplies. No work is done on the object or the world in order to bring about satisfaction. Some psychiatrists, following the transactional method of analysis, refer to this behavior as extremely manipulative; however, several patients have made it clear to me that they do not see themselves playing an active part in the process (Bursten, 1973, pp. 58 ff.). One woman had a prolonged sulking attitude toward her mother. When the mother gave her a casserole dish as a present, she was delighted until her husband revealed that he had told the mother that she had needed a casserole dish. This spoiled the whole gift—it had to come spontaneously in response to her needs; it lost its value if she (or her husband) played an active role in getting it. This is the difference which Freud (1911b) distinguished in this manner:

> [The infant] betrays its unpleasure where there is an increase of [internal] stimulus and an absence of satisfaction, by motor discharge of screaming and beating about with its arms and legs and then it experiences the satisfaction it has hallucinated. [That is, mother, realizing the baby is hungry, feeds it.] Later, as an older child, it learns to employ these manifestations of discharge intentionally.

Pouting and sulking, while more modulated, have much of the aspect of expressions of discomfort rather than intentional demanding.

The same process was shown by another craving patient. He had moved in with his girlfriend and he fully expected that she would work, and that their combined income would be supplemented by her parents—regardless of the fact that they disapproved of their daughter's living with this man. He just could not understand why money was not forthcoming. On an intellectual level, he could see the problem, but it was clear that it had no real meaning to him. As time went on and no money arrived, he pouted and ran out of energy. Increasingly, he expected his girlfriend to anticipate his demands in some empathic way. For example, he would lie on his bed hoping the girl would perform fellatio. Seeing his unhappiness, she would ask what she could do for him. This made him furious. He felt she should know without his having to tell her.

The needs and demands of the craving personality can drain the object dry. This clinging attitude has been described by A. Freud (1949) as a fusion of erotic and aggressive tendencies on the anal level: "Whoever has dealt with toddlers knows the peculiarly clinging, possessive, tormenting, exhausting kind of love which they have for their mothers, an exacting relationship which drives many young mothers to despair." While this behavior must, of course, wait until the infant is more mobile, there is much here to suggest oral grasping and greed. I suggest that these are orally tinged behaviors rather than anal ones. They suck their mothers dry, and they hold on to the external object rather than retain or expel an internal one. As one patient put it, "I've gone through two women now who have said, 'I've taken, taken, taken, and I've given nothing.'" And, while he could understand their complaints intellectually, he really could not grasp why he was so unlucky that he couldn't find a "loving" woman.

One further clinical vignette, this time from a joint interview with a hospitalized patient and his wife, will illustrate the aggressive and receptive aspects of the sulking. This patient was describing his temper—he got so angry sometimes, particularly when his authority as a father was challenged, that he wouldn't speak to any of the family for several days. He and his wife were groping for the right word to express the anger. I said, "It sounds like you're sulking." Both of them seized the word; that was exactly it. The wife went on to say that she was the one who had to stop the sulk—by apologizing, by offering him sex, or by being especially nice to him.

The sulking and complaining of the craving personality takes on a much more hostile tone in the paranoid personality, whose mode of narcissistic repair is expressed through argumentativeness, jealousy and critical suspiciousness. As I mentioned earlier, these people are not psychotic, nor is this personality type necessarily the forerunner of paranoid psychotic conditions.

Like all narcissistic personalities, they feel a sense of disappointment and betrayal by those whom they felt had the power to give to them when they were in need. With paranoid personalities, one does not have to listen very hard to hear the complaint of betrayal. It is apparent in their jealousy and suspiciousness. Much of the critical attitude of this type of person says, "Why does he get things I don't? And he doesn't even deserve it." Although Jacobson (1971) says that none of her paranoid patients "ever complained about having felt 'betrayed' by his parents" (p. 315), I have seen several such patients, some of whom were so bitter that they refused to have anything to do with their parents.

We can hardly talk about the mechanisms used by paranoid personalities without at least a brief discussion of the content underlying the argumentativeness, etc. In the first place, content and form (mechanism) are intertwined; secondly, Freud's (1911a) classic formulation in the Schreber case of the content of the mechanisms in paranoia cannot be overlooked. In this formulation, the projections served as a defence against homosexual impulses. As White (1961) observed, although Freud spoke of the paranoia as a fixation on the narcissistic level of libidinal development, his was essentially a negative oedipal formulation. Knight (1940) and Bak (1946) emphasized the anal aspects of paranoia, especially in regard to its sadomasochistic features. White, in my view quite correctly, pointed out the oral underpinnings of the conflict in terms of fusion with the mother. And, if we examine the case material presented by Knight and Bak we can easily see the reunion fantasies which underlie the homosexual urges. Bak presented his patient's dream, just prior to his paranoid episode, where he "resolved the differences with his father and at the final reconciliation, they wept." This led to feelings of great power. Knight described his patient's feeling that he had a brilliant mind (grandiose self); he and Knight would sit together at seminars and exchange knowing nods (reunion with powerful object). The homosexual aspect of the suspiciousness and anger both in paranoid psychoses and paranoid personalities derives in great part from the need to reunite with a powerful and nourishing figure. In the paranoid psychotic, such a reunion would be a fusion which risks the dangerous loss of ego structure. In the paranoid personality, such a reunion should fortify the narcissism as it does in the craving personality.[1] His complaints and jealousy portray his need to be the special, selected one. Why, then, does he struggle against this reunion by suspicion, criticism, and arguing? These maneuvers only drive people away. And how do such maneuvers serve to repair and maintain his narcissism?

Whether it be a reunion with the representation of the father with its homosexual implications or a reunion with a representative of the mother with implications of weakness and/or incest (and usually it is both), the narcissistic personality struggles against it because of shame.

---

[1] This distinction is, of course, overdrawn for purposes of illustration. Some of the dynamics of the paranoid personality's struggle against reunion are also seen in the case of the paranoid psychotic.

Fantasies of humiliation, embarrassment, and mortification are common. Shame is the enemy of the grandiose self and it makes the narcissist feel unacceptable to the omnipotent object. Thus, the task of the narcissistic repair mechanism is to be rid of the shame.

The narcissistic repair mechanism of the paranoid personality, then, is involved in getting rid of his shame—or more nearly correctly, his shameful self concept. Waelder (1951) provides us with an important key to understanding this mechanism: paranoia rests on denial. The patient is making a statement, albeit in the negative. He is saying, "I do not love him or her" and "I am not shameful." The simple statement does not suffice; externalization and projection are necessary. Thus the statement "I am not shameful" becomes "he or she is shameful." The instinctual aspects of this mechanism are eliminative. Jacobson (1946) has shown that the forerunner of this mode is disgust, spitting and vomiting. That which has been taken in is thrown out again and devalued. As anal eroticism gains primacy, the expulsion of feces serves as the vehicle for getting rid of the worthless material. And, as Jacobson (1957) points out, denial is a relatively primitive mechanism, developed when thinking tended to be very concrete. Thus spitting and defecation could well serve as the basis for the expulsion of a shameful introject (Abraham, 1924b; Rosenfeld, 1964) and the denial and projection of a shameful self-concept.

Now the paranoid psychotic can sufficiently distort reality to cement his conviction; the paranoid personality must continually work at this mode of supporting his narcissism. Thus he is critical, argumentative, suspicious, and he constantly looks for signs of shameful conduct in others, both as a public repudiation of his own inner feelings (Waelder, 1951) and as external affirmation and support of his projections.

Jacobson (1971, pp. 302 ff.) has described another feature of paranoid patients which dovetails with this formulation: they often betray their former allies by playing other people off against them. My own observations of several paranoid personalities confirm her findings. The patient, ashamed of his subordinate and sometimes masochistic or passive homosexual position with one ally, will form a new alliance by helping the new friend hurt, and sometimes ruin, the old. This clearly shows the use of the paranoid criticism as a means of effecting a union (or in narcissistic terms, a reunion) with the anticipated source of power. It is a way of saying, "Don't classify me with the bad guys—I'm one of the good guys like you." It is also eliminative as the patient has literally got rid of the "bad guy"—the projected image of his shameful self.

With one paranoid personality, the eliminative mode was very graphic. Time after time, he could make new friends, only to become quickly "disillusioned." He would then devalue his "friend" and complain about him to others in the most fecal terms. On one occasion, he defecated into a box, wrapped it and sent it to a man with whom he had had a falling out.

Another narcissistic patient who was not predominantly a paranoid personality had been in analysis with me for several years. He had been quite unable to express any strong affect or acknowledge that there was anything more than a kind of intellectual collaboration between us.

The patient had a strong identification with his mother, who was crippled. From her wheelchair, she had wielded enormous influence, however, and, in the manner of many mothers of narcissists, she exploited her son. He was her legs; he pushed her chair, opened doors for her, and ran errands. Although he realized his resentment of this role, any move toward independence caused him enormous anxiety; he was certain his mother could not survive if he were severed from her.

As he began to become more acutely aware of this theme, and more particularly, as he became aware of its reactivation in the transference, he found it harder and harder to ignore me. When the next opportunity for self-assertion presented itself, he could no longer employ his usual passivity. Instead he became paranoid, not in a psychotic way but in the manner of a paranoid personality. This period was ushered in by his report of a fantasy of being on a podium where he was supposed to give a speech. Instead of words, he threw little pellets of feces at the audience and laughed at them. "Wait!" he said, becoming my intellectual collaborate again. "That's defensive. I feel humiliated so I humiliate them."

In the ensuing weeks he was argumentative and critical and he saw exploitative motives in everyone. Toward the end of this period, he pondered whether he could ever respect me. At first he said he could not because it was too risky to have feelings towards me; I might exploit and betray him. Then he revised his reason. "I can't drop my contempt for you," he said. "If I do, I'll feel humiliated with my little penis. I'll just be a shitty little boy." The danger of loving me made him feel weak, homosexual and shitty—truly a cripple. It was this shit which he expelled by projecting (throwing) it on to others. They were the devalued ones—and at the same time exploitative (a reprojection of the introject of his crippled mother).

It is not difficult to see the aggression fused with the eliminative mode of narcissistic repair used by the paranoid personality. Both Knight (1940) and Bak (1946) have described the anal-sadistic aspects of the paranoid mechanisms; they need no further comment here.

Now you will recall Jacobson's (1971, pp. 302 ff.) reference to the fact that paranoid patients often betray their former allies by setting up a situation where others will harm them. These "schemes" come very close to manipulations, and in a conceptual way, can be seen as a bridge between paranoid and manipulative personalities. Contempt and devaluation, so prominent in the paranoid personality, is also a central feature of the manipulative personality, although it is perhaps more subtle. The mode of narcissistic repair of the manipulative personality is "putting something over" on the other person. I have described this mechanism in detail elsewhere (Bursten, 1973, pp. 97 ff.). I shall sketch it briefly here. Putting something over involves contempt and a feeling of exhilaration when the deception succeeds in making the manipulation work. The instinctual component of the contempt is that described for the paranoid personality. It is a purging of a shameful, worthless self-image and its projection onto the victim. The exhilaration is the elation of the reunion fantasy when the "cleansed" self is now glorified and powerful. As a manipulative analysand put it, his parents expected him to put up a good appearance—which he interpreted as being clean and not obviously aggressive. He was plagued, however, with inner feelings of worthlessness. One day he felt particularly dirty. "The problem, I guess, is how to get rid of all that shit without letting on," he said. "That's what I do, I play tricks on them and they never really know they got shit on." And a few days later, when he was feeling exceptionally successful, he recalled with great exhilaration a childhood fantasy of lying in bed waiting for the sky to open up and God to take him. He shouted, "I'm the *one*, the brains, the best."

Thus the manipulative personality, while employing the eliminative mode of the paranoid personality, keeps up appearances by attenuating his aggression and applying it to being clever and tricky. He also enters more actively into competition with his victim. While the paranoid inclines toward destruction, the manipulator leans toward proving his superiority (and acceptability for reunion) by defeating the other person. Thus, in the manipulative personality, we see not only the eliminative mode, but also some phallic themes.

These phallic themes occupy center stage, of course, in the phallic narcissist. His sense of shame often comes from an identification with a father whom he felt was weak. One of my patients "saw through" his father's self-assurance; it was really his mother who wielded the power in the family. He was very moved and upset one day when he happened to see a former radio announcer who had been a boyhood idol of his. The announcer looked old, dissipated, and beaten down while his wife still had youth and verve. This scene was called to mind again and again in the analysis. The shame of being weak is repaired by arrogance, self-glorification, aggressive competitiveness and pseudo-masculinity.

The body, representing the phallus, is adorned with clothes and sometimes with insignia. Phallic narcissistic personalities, even more than manipulative personalities, are risk-takers, often engaging in foolish acts of "bravery." A. Reich's (1960) formulation describes the narcissistic repair mechanism. Constantly in fear of the shame of castration, these men deny the shame and unconsciously fantasize they have the greatest phallus possible. (Here, I insert a step: the disappointing father representation is also denied.) As his megalomanic self-image is reunited with the fantasied giant phallus of the father, nothing can stop him. He is powerful and is protected by a powerful, benevolent fate. Greenacre (1945) speaks to the same point when she points out how these risk-takers feel they will be miraculously saved.

When we turn to the area of self–object differentiation we begin to clarify a remark I made earlier. You will recall that I stated that early in life a course seems to be set for one of the three broad personality types. With regard to the narcissistic group, this course has its instinctual roots in early orality, although, as we have seen, it is modified by contributions from later libidinal stages as well. From the ego side, the processes of separation and individuation described by Mahler (1967) play a major role. Mothers of narcissistic patients, in varying degrees, have difficulty in letting their children separate. Their own narcissism so influences the child's object relations throughout his infancy that the libidinal stages take on the coloration of narcissistic object relationships. Lichtenstein (1964) describes the situation thus: the infant's primary identity is set down in the earliest attempts to emerge from the symbiosis. The mother serves as a mirror showing the infant what he is supposed to be. This same mother will bring her influence to bear throughout his infancy and the later transformations of his sense of identity will become variations on the theme of the primary identity.

Thus we may postulate that all narcissistic personalities share common features in the relationships of their separation-individuation process. However, there must also have been some differences among them which are reflected in the four personality types. Perhaps we might say that narcissism is the primary identity while the four types are variations on the theme.

It is my impression that the craving personality most often exhibits manifest features of symbiosis. The clinging and desperate seeking show the need for actual physical proximity. Some of these patients show "as if" types of relationships. Others crumble and are literally lost (with no self) if left alone. One of my patients could not function when her husband went to sleep. She demanded he stay up (not necessarily actually to help her) until her work was finished.

I believe that paranoid personalities represent features of negativism seen when the infant has begun actively to disengage from the mother–child symbiosis (Mahler and Gosliner, 1955). The effect of the paranoid behavior is to wall the patient off from someone toward whom he is drawn. This disengagement process can be seen in Jacobson's (1971, pp. 302 ff.) descriptions of how paranoid patients become disenchanted with their former allies and betray them.

The manipulative personality is more secure in his separation; he does not have to try so hard. Thus, he has more energy available for doing work on the world, and concomitantly, his appreciation of reality is firmer. A good manipulator can size up a situation and move people around in such a manner that his own wishes are gratified. The process of individuation and firmness of self can be seen in the area of suggestibility and influence (Bursten, 1972, pp. 81 ff.). The craving personality tends to be more suggestible; having no firm sense of self, when he empathizes with others, he cannot relinquish the trial identification (Fliess, 1942) and he becomes the other person. The successful manipulator has a firmer sense of self; he can relinquish the trial identification involved in sizing up a situation and use the knowledge gained from it to influence others.

Phallic narcissists seem even more firm in their sense of self. While still maintaining a predominantly narcissistic orientation, as W. Reich (1933) noted, "They often show strong attachments to people and things outside" (p. 201). There is a greater admixture of complementarity in the phallic narcissist than in the other narcissistic personality types, and this reflects the greater degree of individuation. The need to be admired as a competitor reflects the reunion motif and the earlier symbiosis where the infant can exist only in conjunction with a mother; however, whereas the craving personality needs this relationship almost continuously and on a direct basis, the phallic narcissist has more successfully internalized his sources of approval. While he still needs external sources of flattery, he can also flatter himself. In both personality types we can see evidence of mirroring as described by Elkisch (1957). However, the quality of the mirroring in the craving personality is much closer to the direct mirroring of the infant. The phallic narcissist can often carry his mirror around with him. He is also freer to work, to perform, to compete and then to check with his mirror, because his sense of self is not so urgently dependent on the mirror.

Let us now briefly consider the four personality types from the point of view of the value system. In our discussion of the mode of narcissistic repair we encountered the shame and humiliation of being weak. Bibring (1953) indicated that the basic problem of self-esteem in the infant is the shock of helplessness in the face of needs which are frustrated. All subsequent conditions of helplessness or diminution of his sense of power will injure his self-esteem.

I have only fragmentary data relevant to how this paradigm is translated into the different conditions causing shame among the four personality types. What will be shameful and how it will be counteracted depends in great measure on the values the patient has internalized from his family, for it is they who set up his ego-ideal and it is the internalized images of them with which he must reunite.

I believe that the mothers of craving personalities value their sons as babies. Therefore these sons can be openly weak, passive and demanding. The mother of one such patient preserved her intimate attachment to her son by developing a special language for them to use. Another mother applauded her child only when he was "cute." In both of these patients, the image of the "weak" father was quite conscious and identification with him provided a way of winning mother's love. When a younger sibling enters the picture, the child may soon learn to inhibit his aggressive and assertive rivalry in favor of becoming the "good" (i.e., weak) little boy.

One of my craving patients, who had an intense identification with his mother, said, "My mother doesn't concern herself with work. She's intuitive, not practical. With her, things will just happen. My father is practical—it's a whole world I can't understand. I can't write or publish, I just expect to be famous. I never learned how to work."

In the cases of the other three narcissistic personality types, the situation is somewhat different; weakness becomes a threat to the reunion and causes a loss in self-esteem. In some of these patients, it has been very clear that the mother saw the son as her phallus and that the patient's struggle between strength and weakness reflected the mother's conflict over having a phallus/son on the one hand while not being able to tolerate the notion that a man's penis really counted for anything on the other. These patients are caught between being strong and manly in order to be useful to (acceptable to) mother and yet not really strong and manly because basically they must be "mama's boys."

Jacobson's (1971, pp. 302 ff.) paranoid patients grew up in families where there was overt cruelty and fights between the parents. She emphasizes the sadomasochistic family atmosphere and marital infidelity which sets the stage for the development of the child's own sadism. While I have seen this atmosphere in the families of some paranoid personalities, it has not been overt or obvious in all. However, even where it is not obvious, this atmosphere (and consequently these values) may come across in subtle ways. In one such family the weak father adored his phallic wife; he was her tool. She was an active clubwoman and he would write her speeches for her while staying in the background. The patient's mother was over-concerned with her favorite son's control of his impulses with the result that he developed a harsh superego. It was only later in life that the subtle paranoid atmosphere broke through the surface. By that time, the son had a typical paranoid personality. His mother became actively psychotic in her advanced years; she was suspicious to the point of delusion, accused her probably innocent husband of infidelity, had a most cruel temper, and became a hoarder of useless newspapers.

The family of the manipulative personality plays out its conflicts on the stage of public image (Greenacre, 1945). Johnson and Szurek (1952) have described the double messages given to children in these families: the manifest message is "Be good and obey society's rules," while the latent message is "Have fun so we parents can enjoy it vicariously." The child is thus freed to engage in hidden mischief as long as his public image is clear. This sets the stage for deceptions. As I have explained elsewhere (Bursten, 1973, pp. 162 ff.), the manipulative personality is reasonably well aware that he is a liar, but it does not matter; in his family the public image counted more than the truth. With this latitude, he does not have to treat himself so harshly as the paranoid personality, and he is less destructive.

The family of the phallic narcissist has usually put a high premium on "masculinity." The theme may be "Be a man like your father" or "Be a man like I wish your father were." If the encouragement to manliness were genuine, the child might not be narcissistic at all. However, mother cannot let go—the child has to be *her* man, her phallus, and, as I mentioned earlier, she undercuts his manhood because she cannot tolerate a real or independent man. And this mother–son relationship, like all such relationships of narcissistic mothers with their children, is built upon earlier years of inadequate mothering, so that the child's sense of his self and his confidence in others has already been severely compromised.

These few remarks do not do justice to the complexities of the value systems of these personality types. What they are meant to convey is the fact that the family settings, prompted by the needs of the parents, dovetail with the levels at which the issues of shame and the restoration of pride are enacted, and that they become internalized to provide a value system which coordinates with the other factors determining just which type of narcissistic personality an individual will have.

IV

In clinical psychiatric practice, especially in a large hospitalized population, it is often easy to identify patients who predominantly display the features of one or another of these personality types. As with all our diagnostic categories, however, I have not seen a pure case of one type or another. Most often, although it is possible to classify a patient as primarily a particular type of personality, we see features of an "adjacent" type as well. Thus some manipulative personalities have a tendency to be competitively phallic, some craving personalities complain to the point of jealousy and querulousness, etc. Other patients, although exhibiting primarily one type of personality, show a remarkable fluidity in their use of features of all types. In addition, all of these narcissistic personality types exhibit some features of the craving personality from time to time; they can become very demanding and clinging. Often this behavior is seen when they are physically sick or drunk. Perhaps the craving personality is closest to the primary identity and the subsequent identity transformations melt away under stress.

As we examine the aspects of the four personality types I have described, we see a progression from the craving personality with its emphasis on features of early infantile life through the paranoid and manipulative personalities, to the phallic narcissistic personality which manifests features of later development. These four categories probably do not exhaust the types of narcissistic personalities, but they do serve as guideposts along this progression. It is in the sense of this progression that I have spoken above about "adjacent" types. And, as I mentioned in Part II of this paper, at the lower end, this progression blends into the borderline personality, while at the upper end, the phallic narcissist approaches the complementary personality types.

Kohut has distinguished two forms of narcissism: the grandiose self and the idealized parent image (here called the "omnipotent object"). At first glance, the clinical pictures presented by these personality types suggest that craving personalities are largely expressing omnipotent object fantasies, while phallic narcissists largely express the grandiose self, and the other two types lie somewhere in between. However, analysis reveals the enormous grandiosity of the craver and the fantasies of omnipotence which the phallic narcissist gives to his objects. Both forms of narcissism are active in all four personality types.

While the roles they play in the differentiation of the types are not clear to me, I do have some preliminary thoughts. In the earlier personality types, such as the craver, the omnipotent object has been less adequately internalized; this would go along with his greater structural vulnerability, for, as Kohut (1971, pp. 49 ff.) has indicated, structure building is dependent on this internalization. Thus he shows on the surface a greater need for an external source of supplies, mirroring, etc. The later-stage personality types, such as phallic narcissists, have firmer structure, as I indicated in Part III. There is evidence of greater internalization of the archaic omnipotent object and its transformation into goals and ideals which generally have to do with appearances. The archaic grandiose self of the later personality types is also transformed so as to be more useful to the ego, for example, as in ambition. As Kohut (1971) explains, "the structures built up in response to the claims of the grandiose self appear in general to deal less with the curbing of narcissistic demands but with the channeling and modification of their expression" (p. 187). Thus we can see the grandiose self showing through the ambition and competitiveness of the phallic narcissist, but the reliance on the omnipotent object is hidden in the internalized structures. In the paranoid personality, with less firm structuralization, we can see the omnipotent object in the complaints about "their" influence, albeit malevolent, and the frequent search for new alliances. The manipulative personality shows less of this; his contempt is attenuated and his sense of self-glorification is aided by his initiative.

V

I shall recapitulate some of the relationships developed in this paper. I have distinguished three broad personality groupings. The borderline group has as its central task the prevention of fragmentation and disintegration. The narcissistic group has reunion as the central task. The central task of the complementary group is the resolution of the Oedipus complex. The three groups are on a continuum which is derived from the development of self–object differentiation and the firmness of the sense of self.

Within the narcissistic group, I have distinguished four personality types—the craving, the paranoid, the manipulative and the phallic narcissistic personalities. These types represent a progression both in terms of the instinctual stages predominantly represented in the execution of the narcissistic central task (reunion) and in the degree of separation and individuation. The values held by each of these types represent parental values which have dovetailed with the particular stage of libidinal emphasis and degree of separation and individuation. I have discussed some of the theoretical implications of this progression.

REFERENCES

Abraham, K. (1921). Contributions to the theory of the anal character. In: *Selected Papers on Psycho-Analysis*. London: Hogarth Press, 1927.

Abraham, K. (1924a). The influence of oral erotism on character formation. In: *Selected Papers on Psycho-Analysis*. London: Hogarth Press, 1927.

Abraham, K. (1924b). A short study of the development of the libido viewed in the light of mental disorders. In: *Selected Papers on Psycho-Analysis*. London: Hogarth Press, 1927.

Abraham, K. (1925). Character-formation on the genital level of libido development. In: *Selected Papers on Psycho-Analysis*. London: Hogarth Press, 1927.

Adatto, C. P. (1957). On pouting. *J. Amer. Psychoanal. Assn.*, 5:245–249.

American Psychiatric Association (1968). *Diagnostic and Statistical Manual of Mental Disorders*. Washington, DC: American Psychiatric Association.

Bak, R. C. (1946). Masochism in paranoia. *Psychoanal. Quart.*, 15:285–301.

Bibring, E. (1953). The mechanism of depression. In: *Affective Disorders*, ed. P. Greenacre. New York: International Universities Press.

Bursten, B. (1972). The manipulative personality. *Arch. Gen. Psychiat.*, 26:318–321.

Bursten, B. (1973). *The Manipulator: A Psychoanalytic View*. New Haven, CT: Yale University Press.

Cameron, N. (1959). Paranoid conditions and paranoia. In: *American Handbook of Psychiatry, Vol. 1*, ed. S. Arieti. New York: Basic Books.

Cleckley, H. (1959). Psychopathic states. In: *American Handbook of Psychiatry, Vol. 1*, ed. S. Arieti. New York: Basic Books.

Eisnitz, A. J. (1969). Narcissistic object choice, self representation. *Internat. J. Psycho-Anal.*, 50:15–25.

Elkisch, P. (1957). The psychological significance of the mirror. *J. Amer. Psychoanal. Assn.*, 5:235–244.

Erikson, E. H. (1950). *Childhood and Society*. New York: Norton.

Fenichel, O. (1945). *The Psychoanalytic Theory of Neurosis*. New York: Norton.

Fliess, R. (1942). The metapsychology of the analyst. *Psychoanal. Quart.*, 11:211–227.

Freud, A. (1949). Aggression in relation to emotional development: Normal and pathological. *The Psychoanalytic Study of the Child*, Vols. 3–4. New York: International Universities Press.

Freud, S. (1905). Three essays on the theory of sexuality. *Standard Edition*, 7:130–243. London: Hogarth Press, 1953.

Freud, S. (1908). Character and anal erotism. *Standard Edition*, 9:167–175. London: Hogarth Press, 1959.

Freud, S. (1911a). Psycho-analytic notes on an autobiographical account of a case of paranoia (dementia paranoides). *Standard Edition*, 12:3–82. London: Hogarth Press, 1958.

Freud, S. (1911b). Formulations on the two principles of mental functioning. *Standard Edition*, 12:218–226. London: Hogarth Press, 1958.

Freud, S. (1913). The disposition to obsessional neurosis. *Standard Edition*, 12:317–326. London: Hogarth Press, 1958.

Freud, S. (1914). On narcissism: An introduction. *Standard Edition*, 14:73–102. London: Hogarth Press, 1955.

Freud, S. (1915). Instincts and their vicissitudes. *Standard Edition*, 14:117–140. London: Hogarth Press, 1955.

Freud, S. (1916). Some character-types met with in psycho-analytic work. *Standard Edition*, 14:316–331. London: Hogarth Press, 1955.

Freud, S. (1923). The ego and the id. *Standard Edition*, 19:3–63. London: Hogarth Press, 1961.

Freud, S. (1931). Libidinal types. *Standard Edition*, 21:215–222. London: Hogarth Press, 1965.

Fromm, E. (1947). *Man for Himself.* New York: Rinehart.

Frosch, J. (1970). Psychoanalytic considerations of the psychotic character. *J. Amer. Psychoanal. Assn.*, 18:24–50.

Greenacre, P. (1945). Conscience in the psychopath. *Amer. J. Orthopsychiat.*, 15:495–509.

Guntrip, H. (1969). *Schizoid Phenomena, Object Relations and the Self.* New York: International Universities Press.

Hartmann, H. (1952). The mutual influences in the development of ego and id. *The Psychoanalytic Study of the Child*, Vol. 7. New York: International Universities Press.

Hoffer, W. (1952). The mutual influences in the development of ego and id: Earliest stages. *The Psychoanalytic Study of the Child*, Vol. 7. New York: International Universities Press.

Jacobson, E. (1946). The effect of disappointment on ego and superego formation in normal and depressive development. *Psychoanal. Rev.*, 33:129–147.

Jacobson, E. (1957). Denial and repression. *J. Amer. Psychoanal. Assn.*, 5:61–92.

Jacobson, E. (1971). *Depression.* New York: International Universities Press.

Johnson, A. M. & Szurek, S. A. (1952). The genesis of antisocial acting out in children and adults. *Psychoanal. Quart.*, 21:323–343.

Kernberg, O. F. (1967). Borderline personality organization. *J. Amer. Psychoanal. Assn.*, 15:641–685.

Kernberg, O. F. (1970a). A psychoanalytic classification of character pathology. *J. Amer. Psychoanal. Assn.*, 18:800–822.

Kernberg, O. F. (1970b). Factors in the psychoanalytic treatment of narcissistic personalities. *J. Amer. Psychoanal. Assn.*, 18:51–85.

Knight, R. P. (1940). The relationship of latent homosexuality to the mechanism of paranoid delusions. *Bull. Menninger Clin.*, 4:149–159.

Kohut, H. (1966). Forms and transformations of narcissism. *J. Amer. Psychoanal. Assn.*, 14:243–272.

Kohut, H. (1971). *The Analysis of the Self.* New York: International Universities Press.

Lewin, B. D. (1950). *The Psychoanalysis of Elation.* New York: Norton.

Lichtenstein, H. (1964). The role of narcissism in the emergence and maintenance of a primary identity. *Internat. J. Psycho-Anal.*, 45:49–56.

Mahler, M. S. (1967). On human symbiosis and the vicissitudes of individuation. *J. Amer. Psychoanal. Assn.*, 15:740–763.

Mahler, M. & Gosliner, B. (1955). On symbiotic child psychosis. *The Psychoanalytic Study of the Child*, Vol. 10. New York: International Universities Press.

Oremland, J. D. & Windholz, E. (1971). Some specific transference, countertransference and supervisory problems in the analysis of a narcissistic personality. *Internat. J. Psycho-Anal.*, 52:267–275.

Pulver, S. (1970). Narcissism: The term and the concept. *J. Amer. Psychoanal. Assn.*, 18:319–341.

Rado, S. (1928). The problem of melancholia. *Internat. J. Psycho-Anal.*, 9:420–438.

Rapaport, D. (1959). Edward Bibring's theory of depression. In: *Collected Papers.* New York: Basic Books, 1967.

Reich, A. (1960). Pathological forms of self-esteem regulation. *The Psychoanalytic Study of the Child*, Vol. 15. New York: International Universities Press.

Reich, W. (1933). *Character-Analysis.* New York: Noonday Press.

Riesman, D. (1950). *The Lonely Crowd.* New Haven, CT: Yale University Press.

Rosenfeld, H. (1964). On the psychopathology of narcissism: A clinical approach. *Internat. J. Psycho-Anal.*, 45:332–337.

Stein, M. H. (1969). The problem of character theory. *J. Amer. Psychoanal. Assn.*, 17:675–701.

Waelder, R. (1951). The structure of paranoid ideas: A critical survey of various theories. *Internat. J. Psycho-Anal.*, 32:167–177.

White, R. (1961). The mother-conflict in Schreber's psychosis. *Internat. J. Psycho-Anal.*, 42:55–73.

18

Outpatient Treatment of Psychopaths

John R. Lion

This paper, by the psychoanalyst John Lion, was first published in William Reid's *The Psychopath: A Comprehensive Study of Antisocial Disorders and Behaviors* in 1978. With a clear and elegant style, Lion provides a primer for the outpatient treatment of psychopathically disturbed patients. His chapter addresses the patient who has sufficient anxiety and attachment capacity to make the treatment endeavor worthwhile. Lion discusses the importance of sadness, if not the emergence of depression, as the patient's narcissistic defenses are confronted over time; but, if the psychopathy is severe and biologically rooted, such emotional states will not occur. The therapist may find, instead, that his time has been squandered by a chameleon.

This chapter serves as a primer for the treatment of the psychopath. Existing literature by other workers deals with intensive psychoanalytic treatment of this type of patient (Eissler, 1950; Schmideberg, 1949) and with therapy within special inpatient and outpatient milieus (Aichhorn, 1925; Jones, 1953). More recent work has focused on the general clinical problem of manipulation (Bursten, 1973). In this section general principles of psychotherapy in an outpatient setting are presented.

GENERAL PRINCIPLES

Clinicians electing to treat psychopaths must be cognizant of the following principles. First, the therapist must be continually vigilant with regard to manipulation on the part of the patient. Second, he must assume, until proved otherwise, that information given him by the patient contains distortions and fabrications. Third, he must recognize that a working alliance develops, if ever, exceedingly late in any therapeutic relationship with a psychopath.

Developing Trust

The above cautions mitigate against disappointments and frustrations which all too often become converted into therapeutic nihilism by those involved in working with these types of character disorders, for the therapeutic contract is most imperfect. Almost inevitably psychopaths are referred by third parties such as probation officers, courts or lawyers. Even when psychopaths do enter treatment "voluntarily" they usually come under some duress such as that of a spouse who is threatening to leave; hence, covert coercion is present. Coercion and the presence of a third party are not conducive to developing trust. When the clinician is under some obligation to report to an outsider the "progress" of a psychopath, initial mistrust is bound to linger. The only recourse the therapist has is to openly describe the state of progress by sharing with the psychopath all impressions he has about him. I show psychopaths all correspondence generated and received concerning them. Complete frankness and honesty are the only hope for these relationships and often lead to fruitful dialogue in therapy.

There are two sets of magical expectations surrounding the treatment of psychopathy. The first occurs on the part of the third party referring the patient for treatment. If the patient is seen as charming, articulate, and intelligent, he automatically becomes a "good candidate for insight psychotherapy" in the mind of the referring agent. Hence, marvelous things are expected to happen in the treatment process. The second magical expectation comes from the patient himself, who, sensing the alternative of treatment to incarceration or other legal action, sees a chance to manipulate as well as to acquire new skills with which to outwit others. The clinician is immediately endowed with enormous perspicacity and a power of observation which he in fact does not possess. In the initial stages of treatment, psychopaths will "lay themselves bare" and reveal interesting tidbits of information relevant to sexual exploits, grandiose dealings with money, and other matters which are designed to intrigue therapists, particularly those in earlier stages of training. The therapist must constantly be on guard for these distractions; he should be alerted when he finds himself fascinated by the accounts of the psychopath whom he has opted to treat.

Psychopaths are also prone in the early stages of treatment to lavish praise upon the therapist as the person who "genuinely cares" or "understands" him and who will listen to him patiently, in contrast to "those others who always want something." The magnitude of praise and positive statement is proportional to the patient's attempt to seduce the therapist into a position of lowered vigilance, at which point deviant behavior may be forthcoming. At the same time, if he is successful in his seduction, the psychopath reassures himself of the fact that his skills and charms still work, even in the face of a critical professional; the patient thus gains positive reinforcement from his ability to subtly shape the course of therapy.

I have often found it useful to tell psychopaths who are in early treatment phases that their stories are most engrossing but have nothing whatsoever to do with the treatment process. Often such a remark is met with the question: "What do you want me to talk about?" Here one must educate the patient in some respect, since the only language he knows is the language of manipulation. I generally make some statement to the effect that my job is to help him to recognize true and spontaneous emotions, emotions not clouded by the need to win or triumph over others. I also state that I am not interested in issues of money, sexual prowess, or personal glory, but merely wish to learn something about his mundane day-to-day life. This kind of statement needs constant repeating, for it forms the basis for therapy and inevitably causes some discouragement in the patient in subsequent treatment.

Irrespective of the etiology of psychopathy, one may take as an operating premise for therapy the concept that the psychopath not only lacks a conscience, but is unaware of the subtleties of affect and fantasy (Lion, 1974) that are adaptive for a normal lifestyle. Coupled with these deficits is a general narcissistic posture which is prominent in all phases of treatment. Our job is to hold a mirror up to the patient so that he sees his self-centered ways of behaving which, without foresight and reflection, and unencumbered by guilt, are ultimately so destructive for him. Seeing this reflection time and again hopefully converts that which is syntonic into that which is dystonic. Few psychopaths enjoy this process. Introspection and insight are foreign exercises and alien to a lifestyle of impulsive and hedonistic behavior. The psychopath wants and does; he is loathe to look and think. The narcissism and need to win or "con" are defenses against involvement and means of devaluing other individuals, effectively precluding intimacy.

Thus, in time the psychopath is ultimately put into the position of viewing himself. He will later be confronted with the problem of identity, a crisis he has eluded for too long and dealt with by borrowing the identities of others. In some instances, paranoia develops as the next stage and much anger at the therapist is seen in the transference. Eventually *depression* develops as the narcissism is relinquished and the

patient begins to deal with his intrinsically low feelings of self-esteem.*
Such is a rough, basic synopsis of treatment.

The psychopath enters treatment in the same way he starts any new
endeavor. A gusto prevails during early sessions and a honeymoon
period ensues. The honeymoon period is concurrent with the time
during which the therapist is endowed with special qualities. Yet there
exist within the patient underlying feelings of inferiority which mobilize
him to take a position of attack. He is apt to launch himself into battles
regarding philosophical issues and the treatment process. The patient
may begin to read psychiatric texts. Discussions about styles of therapy
and schools of psychiatry may dominate the hour, allowing little chance
for the therapist to confront the patient with routine issues of affect and
behavior. Yet such intratherapeutic contests siphon off adverse behavior. Thus, during the honeymoon phase, the patient becomes quiescent
outside of the therapeutic hour and relatives or his spouse are quick to
comment that he is making enormous gains in a relatively short time in
treatment. These accolades of success, perhaps reported by the patient
himself, must basically be ignored.

Sooner or later, the psychopath will "test" the therapist by behaving
in some deviant manner at home or work. This "test" of deviance is
usually subtle and ambiguous, confronting both patient and therapist
with a new transgression in therapy and signaling the end of the
honeymoon period. Since there is ambiguity in the transgression, it is
difficult to analyze. Often the patient will have been fired from a job for
stealing but will claim that he was fired because of union difficulties.
Since the therapist cannot easily ascertain the validity of this claim, he
is at a disadvantage. The only solution is to begin the painful business
of discussing with the patient one's doubts about his credibility, a tactic
which ushers in the bilateral mistrust so prominent during the early
stages of treatment. The concomitant disillusionment subsequent to this
is reflected in anger on the part of the psychopath, accompanied by
dismay, rejection, and either feigned or genuine hurt with regard to the
therapist's betrayal and mistrust of him. At this point, it is necessary to
point out quite firmly to the patient that his primary difficulty is one of
mistrust and that it is sad, indeed, that the therapist cannot trust him
and that he in turn cannot trust the therapist. Since such general mistrust
must exist in outside relationships as well, it must be most unsatisfying
and may perhaps be a good focus of therapy.

---

*Editor's Note: I do not assume low self-esteem in psychopathy unless it is evident
from psychological testing.

Additional problems arise when spouses or third parties report deviations in behavior which reflect the return of psychopathic activities. Again, such unsolicited reports evoke the issue of confidentiality and the therapist must share with the patient such breaches, which are an inevitable part of the treatment process. The patient will accuse the therapist of being an agent of the court, etc., while the therapist must stand his ground and state that although his job is to sift the information given him while maintaining as much confidentiality as possible, he may indeed have some allegiance to the court, which places him in a precarious position. Many therapists do not like this and may share this dislike with the patient. Such a shared dislike does not preclude treatment but merely sets out in the open the unpleasantness of third party watchfulness. The following case example summarizes some of the issues involved in the early stages of treatment.

A 20-year-old psychopathic young girl was referred by her father, an attorney, because of pathological lying, shoplifting, and a general lifestyle of deceit. After the honeymoon period had been entered with magical results at home, the patient was mysteriously fired from her job. The details of this firing were obscure to me but, as often happens in these cases, I learned from a friend of the family that the patient had apparently stolen some money from the cash register and had been dismissed on those grounds. Not knowing what was the truth, and not wishing to act as detective, I confronted the patient with my ignorance of the basis for her firing but stated that I had heard from a third source—and named that source—that there had been some financial indiscretion which alarmed me greatly. I stated that while I was not a lawyer or detective, the patient needed to tell me what was going on. I had no choice except to believe her even though I doubted the veracity of her comments. The patient then launched into a thoroughly believable story about the incident, which led me to comment that her statement made sense but still left me with an uneasy feeling of mistrust, and that I would hope that trust could be reestablished at some time in the future. This made the patient unhappy but clearly stated my position in the treatment process.

In the foregoing case, the informer was a relative of the patient. These situations do indeed happen in treatment of psychopaths, since friends, family, and other third parties feel that the therapist may not "fully know the facts" and are eager to enlighten him with regard to actual behavior on the outside. I personally do not turn off such knowledge, although I do tell whomever calls that I will confront the patient with it and reveal the source. Such confrontations produce enemies, but open communication is the only salvation in the treatment of psychopathy and I cannot disregard outside messages. Again, the only ammunition the therapist has is direct and open honesty, even though the therapy is to some extent being performed in an arena with interested spectators. One can only hope that in time, as behavior returns to normal, the arena will empty and privacy will be restored.

Dealing with Anger and Absences

It is obvious that the therapeutic relationship is exceedingly fragile and delicate. The patient, sensing that the therapist has little faith in him or her, is often sullen and rebellious while alternately being grandiose, with a desire to please and manipulate. Anger is often a problem in the early course of coercive therapies, since a patient whose lifestyle is psychopathic becomes frustrated when he or she cannot cope with situations in the usual manipulative manner. The fragile alliance suffers even more when scheduled appointments are missed because of illness, holidays, or vacations. Psychopaths take any opportunity to break routine and throw the therapist off guard. Absences on the part of the therapist have a demonstrably negative effect upon trust and often weeks of therapy are required to recapture gains previously made. Retaliatory absences are not uncommon even when the clinician goes to great pains to work this through. The following example is illustrative.

A psychopathic patient had been making reasonable progress in therapy, coming to grips with object relations. After treatment of a year, I developed hematuria necessitating frequent visits to a urologist for radiographic studies and cystoscopy. During one absence, I told my secretary that she should telephone the patient and explain to her that I would be absent from a session because of a cystoscopic examination for what was then believed to be kidney stones. I emphasized to the secretary that the detailed explanation was very necessary and the secretary complied. Following this workup, sessions were restored with the patient, at which time the patient entered my office with questions as to how I was feeling and if my "flu" was all better. I replied that I did not have the flu and questioned as to what she had been told on the phone. The patient adamantly stated that she had been told that I had a cold and had missed the session because of this. Subsequently, the patient cancelled a session for no valid reason.

I believe that example illustrates what I felt to be an inability to tolerate the affect evoked by a detailed revelation of my illness. She used denial and distortion as a defense. The anger having to do with unexpressed alarm over my health was reflected in a retaliatory absence; however, these speculative issues were not amenable to confirmation as we had not reached a level of therapy and trust appropriate to discussion of transference feelings. The point is that the therapy is highly vulnerable, perhaps more vulnerable than one would imagine when first confronted with the apparent coldness of the psychopath. Viewing the patient as a person with a narcissistic personality disorder may make this phenomenon more understandable.*

Absences on the part of the patient create problems, since one can never be sure whether the patient is actually sick or is feigning illness to avoid what he or she senses will be a difficult session. The following is an example.

A patient telephoned me to state that his automobile was broken and that he could not attend the session. I told him that I had some time in the afternoon and that he could call me when he knew the state of repair of his car. The patient promised to call, but never did. In the following week's session, he stated that he had been tied up with the towing operations of his car and did not have the time to call me until late in the afternoon when he realized I could no longer see him. I told him that this explanation seemed plausible, but that there was some seed of doubt in my mind regarding the fact that he could not find the time to telephone and at least apprise me of the situation. Again, I reflected to him the issue of mistrust. The patient sat stonily and listened to me without acknowledgment, although I sensed he clearly understood my point.

While one cannot easily ascertain the causes of absences in patients, one can still share with them disbelief in a matter-of-fact way without accusation. It is wise to operate on a "gut level" in these instances, since

---

*Editor's Note: See Modell (1975) for a detailed exposition of the "affect block" and the illusion of self-sufficiency in narcissistic pathology: A. H. Modell. A narcissistic defence against affects and the illusion of self-sufficiency. *Internat. J. Psycho-Anal.*, 56:275–282.

there is little else to go on and therapists should refuse to be put in the position of being a detective. Patients who are psychopathic will often come armed with all kinds of ammunition and alibis, as though they were about to appear before a magistrate. The therapist should state that he is not equipped to handle evidence more appropriate for a court but must rely upon verbalizations rendered by the patient. He can believe or disbelieve these verbalizations according to his intuition, but this is all he has to go on. This makes it very clear to the patient that evidence plays little role in psychotherapy and that affect, not fact, is the issue at stake.

Early countertransference reactions on the part of the therapist fluctuate. During the honeymoon phase, many therapists become enthused with the apparent rapid progress being made by patients who are so verbal and articulate. Rescue fantasies become prominent, particularly with well-to-do psychopaths from influential families; but humility is called for. My own feelings about prognosis suggest that it takes a good working year of therapy in order to determine whether or not a patient is making any reasonable gains with regard to the development of true affective awareness, intimacy and trust.

Acting Out

Problems of acting out become important as the transference develops (Greenacre, 1947). Generally, the acting out is of an aggressive type having to do with authority figures. Patients who see the therapist as a parental figure may translate feelings into behavior on the outside against their own parents, personnel at school or employers in the job situation. In addition, sexual acting out may become problematic. Every attempt must be made to trace these behaviors to their transference source. This is very difficult for psychopathic patients, who appear to have some ingrained developmental difficulties in translating affective states to conscious and verbal awareness.

Acting-out behavior, particularly when deviant, poses problems in the therapy. Often the therapist is being "tested" to see how loyal he is. I have on occasion threatened psychopaths with the termination of therapy if acting out in the form of deviant behavior or absences from therapy does not cease. The injunction needs to be made very clearly; the patient must realize that the therapist will not tolerate certain behaviors and that limit setting will be imposed. The therapist must unambivalently set for himself a threshold for intolerable behavior. I have discharged patients whom I could not control with mutual acknowledgment of the poor therapeutic alliance; some have accepted the discharge while others clamor for return, espousing a new honesty which is certainly suspect.

Payment

Payment is an issue which must be discussed from the outset (Lion, 1974). Generally, I ask for payment prior to each session until such time as a therapeutic relationship is established. For some patients, this is several months; for others it may be longer. There are certain psychopathic patients who have problems with money; from these I accept only cash. Nonetheless, I have been misled on several occasions.

> A charming and handsome middle-aged psychopath with a history of check forging was sent to me for treatment by his wife, an earnest and tearful woman who desired treatment for her "unfortunate" husband. The woman agreed to pay for the husband's treatment and the husband came for three sessions with a check in hand written by his wife. All three checks were returned to me for insufficient funds. While the wife had indeed signed them, she had done so with inadequate bank assets.

That example illustrates the complexities of exacting payment and demonstrates the need for being firm with regard to money. This may be quite unpleasant for certain therapists who are used to billing monthly or having an agency or professional corporation bill for them. I explain to patients that their general behavior makes me more comfortable with regular weekly payments. Surprisingly, patients understand this, especially when roles are reversed in fantasy and they are asked to imagine how they would feel as the doctor treating a psychopath who is prone to skip payment.

Often patients will omit payment for one session to test the therapist; I allow two such sessions to occur and, if payment is not brought up-to-date, discharge the patient. I ask for cash or a money order from high-risk patients and accept checks from those deemed more trustworthy. In no case do I allow third-party coverage to reimburse me directly. Signed receipts should be given the patient for money and the money should be scrupulously counted, even though this appears an odious task. On several occasions, I have been underpaid and on one occasion overpaid by a patient who was testing to see whether I would return the extra money. Therapists have a tendency not to look at checks, as though it were a crass and mercenary act, but the amount written on the check should be noted and prompt discussion should ensue if it is incorrect.

Referrals

On occasion, the psychopathic patient may request referral to a lawyer or internist for consultation. In this case, I generally ask the patient to share his request for consultation and its reason with me. The following example illustrates the reasons for careful scrutiny and foresight with regard to a referral. Referrals should not be made casually.

> A 30-year-old psychopath asked me for referral to an accountant for help in preparing his income tax form. Since the patient had a history of excessive spending and falsifying expense statements at work, I decided that the best course of action was to refer him to my own accountant, whom I knew to be an exceedingly conservative man. I knew in this instance that the patient would not easily dupe or fool the accountant and I also felt that he would receive reasonable service. I told the patient this, and explained my reasons for the referral. He accepted both and appeared pleased with the result.

On another occasion, the patient asked to be referred to a dentist for both necessary repair of a cavity and some elective restorative work. Again, the general grandiosity of this patient made me apprehensive lest he accumulate a large bill which could not be paid. Accordingly, I chose my own dentist, with the same rationale as above. The patient went to him, settled for a reasonable amount of both elective and necessary dental work, and arranged reasonable terms of payment to which he adhered.

It will be recognized that the foregoing examples illustrate principles quite deviant from the traditional ones in psychotherapy. Upon examination, however, they appear quite logical given the premise of mistrust which is at the heart of all treatment with psychopaths. In another instance, and with a more traditional patient, one might urge the patient to seek his own accountant and dentist in order to foster autonomy and independence.

PROGRESS IN THERAPY: DEPRESSION AND DESPONDENCY

Gains in therapy with these patients are exceedingly slow and arduous. The therapist, rather than accepting the hollow "improvements" mentioned earlier, should wait for despondency and depression to occur since, as previously mentioned, narcissism and grandiosity are the hallmarks of most psychopaths who seek exploitative ways of manipulating themselves out of unpleasant situations. With persistent confrontation, introspection occurs in time. One eventually reaches a point in therapy at which nihilism appears in the patient and genuine sadness ensues. I have seen such depression develop to the point of requiring antidepressant medication; however, both the patient's capacity and his tolerance for depression must be learned and developed as an adaptive human trait (Lion, 1972b).

Psychopathic patients may come to sessions after therapy is well underway and verbalize such sentiments as "there is nothing for me to do." At this point repeated acknowledgments of the despair induced by the absence of manipulative ability are necessary. At this time, even more acting out of the depression—and anger at the therapist for its induction—is a possibility. The patient may quit his job and start a new business venture or enter a grandiose entrepreneurial scheme to avoid this boredom and despondency. Premature attempts at termination and absences from sessions occur. These matters must be monitored closely. The therapist should constantly strive to teach the patient the process of insight and contemplation; the development of an active ability to fantasize and anticipate the consequences of action, as well as an affective awareness, is a prerequisite to efficacious treatment (Lion, 1972b).

When the patient can visualize what can happen to him if he should engage in a socially deviant piece of behavior, he has shown progress in treatment; when he can recognize anger, fear, and nuances of affective expression, he has made some improvement. A capacity for intimacy and trust, as revealed both within and outside of the therapy, is indicative of positive change.

Use of Medications

The treatment of aggressive psychopaths differs in several respects from the treatment of non-aggressive psychopaths. With the aggressive psychopath, in contrast to, say, the check forger or the "con artist," problems in the direct handling of hostile urges are issues in therapy (Lion, 1972a). With the aggressive psychopath, depression is even more of a risk as the aggression abates and there is a dynamic shift from outwardly directed to inwardly directed anger. Medications may help in the reduction of impulsivity and lability of mood and affect associated with aggressive outbursts, but psychopaths quite often resist taking medication or abuse it.

For those patients who do show responsible willingness to accept drugs to curb aggressiveness and impulsivity, consideration should be made of anti-anxiety agents such as the benzodiazepines. This class of drugs reduces the tension which often propels patients into impulsive acts and can secondarily diminish the hypervigilance often seen as part of the paranoid symptoms shown by some psychopaths (Lion, 1975). The latter patients, in fact, will not usually tolerate antipsychotic agents even though suspiciousness is clinically evident, for these major tranquilizers markedly impair watchfulness and thus may heighten, rather than reduce, paranoia and the tendency to become aggressive. In addition, antipsychotic agents frequently produce subtle side effects intolerable to paranoid and narcissistic individuals.

The anticonvulsants have been shown to reduce aggressiveness in patients who demonstrate epileptoid outbursts of rage (Monroe, 1974, 1975). Confirmation of underlying brain dysfunction by electroencephalographic examination, neurological evaluation, and psychological testing may provide additional justification for the use of such drugs.

Lithium has also been shown to be of use in certain patients labeled "emotionally unstable." These patients' symptoms probably reflect variants of a bipolar affective disorder manifested not by typical mood swings but by fluctuations in levels of psychomotor agitation, irritability, and aggressiveness (Lion, 1975).

Two classes of experimental drugs bear mention. The central nervous system stimulants used with hyperkinetic children have been anecdotally reported to be of benefit in adults who show clinical pictures of impulsivity, aggressiveness, and antisocial behavior (Allen et al., 1975). Also, research with progestational agents on sexually deviant and aggressive patients has demonstrated positive effects of these drugs, which act by reducing sexual drive state and thus, secondarily, reducing aggressiveness (Blumer and Migeon, 1975). I have on one occasion administered reserpine to a patient with a severe character disorder with the hope of making him depressed to the point of introspection; such a tactic was experimental, in response to the intriguing question of how to induce depression in patients who deny it and handle it by behavioral means (Lion, 1975). I have felt the value of most psychopharmacologic agents in the treatment of psychopathy—such as the tranquilizers and anticonvulsants—to lie in the propensity of these agents to curb impulsivity and produce a mild state of depression conducive to reflection.

The "Burning Out" Process

Time is the greatest ally of the therapist. Thus it is observed that the longer an aggressive psychopath is kept locked up, the less likely he is to revert to his old manipulative and aggressive ways of behaving. This "burning out process" probably has to do with physiologic maturation and can be seen in impulsive and aggressive youths who show reduced impulsivity and hostility in their 30s and 40s, after having served comparatively long sentences within institution settings. Maturation is an important variable but one which is poorly understood. The burning out process most likely represents physiologic changes which have a general dampening effect on psychological parameters of lability and impulsivity. In the "natural experiment" one sees this in the differences between normal adolescents and adults. Maturation or burning out also plays a role in outpatient therapy, since the duration of treatment is long. It should be noted, however, that "burning out" may refer more to physically violent criminal activity than to antisocial behavior in general, since there are some data which suggest that psychopaths continue to be socially maladjusted as they age but are less often convicted of criminal activity (Maddocks, 1970).*

Development of Guilt

The development of guilt and a "superego" has been conceptualized as a major task of treatment for all psychopaths. Regrettably, the super-ego, a derivative of the ego, cannot be so easily shaped. It is felt by most clinicians that milieu treatment with 24-hour custodial and therapeutic care enables feedback to be present at all times so that some rudimentary forms of guilt develop, or, at the very least, the patient learns what is right and wrong. Many tactics in the treatment of psychopaths, including the precipitation of depression mentioned earlier, reflect the desire

---

*Editor's Note: As I have noted elsewhere, *nonviolent* criminality appears to lessen among psychopaths in their 40s, while *violent* criminality, for at least half, does not lessen. See R. D. Hare (1998). Psychopaths and their nature: Implications for the mental health and criminal justice systems. In: *Psychopathy: Antisocial, Criminal, and Violent Behavior*, ed. T. Millon et al. New York: Guilford, pp. 188–214.

on the part of clinicians to forcefully confront the patient with issues of good and bad and to induce a state of hopelessness conducive to therapeutic insight.

A psychopathic girl was hospitalized at a private facility. Outpatient treatment had produced little change in her behavior and it was decided on this occasion to keep her on suicide precautions with a one-to-one patient–staff ratio in order to always have a nurse with her. It was thought that this might foster some form of discomfort conducive to reflection and identification. The hospital course proceeded rather smoothly with gains made in introspection. In time she was discharged and later committed suicide.

Another patient prone to violent outbursts was treated on an outpatient basis with anticonvulsants. His violent behavior was markedly reduced but he, too, ultimately killed himself (Monroe, 1975).

A third patient was hospitalized. His wealthy family agreed to pay for two staff members who traveled on the hospital grounds wherever he went and always confronted him with any deviant piece of behavior he demonstrated. Few gains were made of any lasting value.

These various examples illustrate complex problems as well as equally complex and imperfect solutions and their hazards.

GROUP THERAPY

Group therapy forms an important treatment modality for psychopaths, since they are apt to be brutally honest with one another while being devious with the primary therapist. There is much peer confrontation in the group setting and it is a useful means of self-confrontation (Lion and Bach-y-Rita, 1970). Enhancement of psychotherapy by videotape playback of sessions may also be helpful.

Some groups form on the basis of self-help organizations such as Synanon and Daytop and are, of course, a prime modality of treatment within any hospital milieu. Within the group therapy, it may be useful to pick one particular psychopath as a therapist-leader. This tactic utilizes the dynamic of reaction formation, often most prominently seen in prison settings where there appears to be a thin line between the prisoner and the guard. By elevating a psychopath to the position of responsibility, he may identify with and adopt some values of the therapist, internalizing valuable ideas and norms which become part of his way of behaving. Obviously, this process takes considerable time to develop.

EXPLOITATION IN A HOSPITAL SETTING

Mention should be made of one facet of the inpatient treatment of psychopaths which demonstrates the exploitative power of the patient. The psychopath can create dissension on a hospital ward and actively manipulate events in such a way as to produce staff and patient distrust. Subtle and flagrant violations of ward rules confront everyone with issues of compliance and at the same time produce splits in staff allegiances. The psychopath is particularly skilled at generating conflicts over power and authority, and may become an uncontrollably defiant member of the patient population. Administrative problem solving may center around the psychopath when other issues and other patients are equally important.

Staff impotence must be acknowledged and discussed. Limits must be set and maintained. At the same time, caution must be exercised so that the psychopath does not exploit and exhaust the time that the staff has at its disposal. In time, some manipulation may require benign neglect to be extinguished. I have seen rare instances in which the ward could not tolerate the destructive manipulation of a psychopath and transfer to another facility was warranted. All of these points illustrate the constant need for the therapist to be vigilant and aware of his limitations. Consultation with colleagues is useful for the latter, since psychopaths, inpatient or outpatient, regularly mobilize feelings of helplessness in therapeutic staff.

THERAPEUTIC QUALITIES

The final question remains as to which kinds of therapists are best, or even suitable, for treating psychopaths. There exist in every therapeutic community physicians, psychiatrists and therapists who are particularly willing and able to deal with behavior disorders and psychopaths. Generally, these clinicians are those who have had experience in forensic matters and who are more skilled at detecting manipulation than their more psychoanalytically oriented colleagues, who depend heavily upon the self-reporting and spontaneous introspective processes which are part of the analytic process. In addition, it has been my observation that the therapists most skilled at treating psychopaths have some degree of entrepreneurial spirit which puts them in touch with the narcissism and grandiosity inherent in these patients. Without this "window" into the psychopath's tendency to exploit in a grandiose style, the clinician cannot understand and internally predict what the psychopath will do. He is thus almost constantly "off guard." Also, the less attuned therapist is apt to be entrapped by his latent exhibitionism vis-à-vis mankind's fascination with psychopathic entrepreneurs, as evidenced by many famous hoaxes and swindles.

The therapist who works with psychopaths carries burdens which require a balance of work with other types of patients—neurotic and psychotic—lest he become hardened in his style. The therapist must constantly suspect his patient's intentions and behavior and work toward the day when an open honesty appears, one which is paradoxically, but quite predictably, accompanied by a depression. This melancholy heralds the beginning of a guiltlike process which can eventually lead to appropriate affects, attachments, and a normal lifestyle.

REFERENCES

Aichhorn, A. (1925). *Wayward Youth.* New York: Viking Press.

Allen, R. P., Safer, D. & Covi, L. (1975). Effects of psychostimulants on aggression. *J. Nerv. Ment. Dis.,* 160:138–145.

Blumer, D. & Migeon, C. (1975). Hormone and hormonal agents in the treatment of aggression. *J. Nerv. Ment. Dis.,* 160:127–137.

Bursten, B. (1973). *The Manipulator.* New Haven, CT: Yale University Press.

Eissler, K. R. (1950). Ego-psychological implications of the psychoanalytic treatment of delinquents. *The Psychoanalytic Study of the Child,* 5:97–121. New York: International Universities Press.

Greenacre, P. (1947). Problems of patient–therapist relationship in the treatment of psychopaths. In: *Handbook of Correctional Psychology,* ed. R. M. Lindner & R. V. Selinger. New York: Philosophical Library.

Jones, M. (1953). *The Therapeutic Community.* New York: Basic Books.

Lion, J. R. (1972a). *Evaluation and Management of the Violent Patient.* Springfield, IL: Charles C. Thomas.

Lion, J. R. (1972b). The role of depression in the treatment of aggressive personality disorders. *Amer. J. Psychiat.,* 129:347–349.

Lion, J. R. (1974). Diagnosis and treatment of personality disorders. In: *Personality Disorders,* ed. J. R. Lion. Baltimore, MD: Williams & Wilkins.

Lion, J. R. (1975). Conceptual issues in the use of drugs for the treatment of aggression in man. *J. Nerv. Ment. Dis.,* 160:76–82.

Lion, J. R. & Bach-y-Rita, G. (1970). Group psychotherapy with violent outpatients. *Internat. J. Group Psychother.*, 20:185–191.

Maddocks, P. D. (1970). A five year followup of untreated psychopaths. *Brit. J. Psychiat.*, 116:511–15.

Modell, A. H. (1975). A narcissistic defence against affects and the illusion of self-sufficiency. *Internat. J. Psycho-Anal.*, 56:275–282.

Monroe, R. R. (1974). The problem of impulsivity in personality disturbances. In: *Personality Disorders,* ed. J. R. Lion. Baltimore, MD: Williams & Wilkins.

Monroe, R. R. (1975). Anticonvulsants in the treatment of aggression. *J. Nerv. Ment. Dis.*, 160:119–126.

Schmideberg, M. (1949). The analytic treatment of major criminals: Therapeutic results and technical problems. In: *Searchlights on Delinquency,* ed. K. R. Eissler. New York: International Universities Press.

19

The Response Aroused by the Psychopath

Neville Symington

The British psychoanalyst Neville Symington wrote this literary and clinical paper, which was published in the *International Journal of Psychoanalysis* in 1980. Although arguably he overestimates the emotional and moral development of psychopathic persons—implying love, guilt, and a rigid morality—he ventures with great clinical insight into the countertransference aroused by these patients. His exposition of our collusion, disbelief, and condemnation when encountering a psychopath is masterful. He shows especially keen insight into our disbelief and condemnation as superego defenses against our own sadism: impulses to be cruel and vengeful toward psychopathically disturbed patients, who often deeply hurt and betray others.

What do we mean by "psychopath"? We need to know this before we can understand the response which he arouses. The term psychopath or psychopathic covers a wide range of observable phenomena but there is one common denominator: the overriding determination to attain certain goals, and these by flouting the values which the society holds sacred. This was a point made succinctly by Edward Glover (1960): "Moral obliquity is in fact the hallmark of the psychopaths who engage the attention of the courts."

It was, for instance, a value of this country to accumulate wealth by hard work and saving and correspondingly taboo to obtain this by robbery or fraud. But this alone would mean that all revolutionaries are psychopaths, so there is another important diagnostic criterion: the criminal psychopath always acts in isolation. This is why Karl Marx saw the criminal as a reactionary and not a revolutionary.

On the subject of psychopathy, the standard psychiatric and psychological literature is unrewarding. The psychoanalytic writings are more helpful and in particular that of Freud, Melanie Klein, Glover and Hyatt

283

Williams, but an important aspect of psychopathy, though noted, is underemphasized. I think this lacuna is supplied by Emily Brontë in her novel *Wuthering Heights*. The protagonist of the book, Heathcliff, is a psychopath. Characters of his kind are often found in novels; the arch-villain is a well-known stereotype and in fact Emily's sister, Ann, writes about such a one: Lord Huntingdon in *The Tenant of Wildfell Hall*. But here the villain, as is usually the case, is described "from outside" and the writer's purpose is to arouse our disgust and condemnation. In *Wuthering Heights* the reader is left with no illusions about Heathcliff, but Emily's aim is to enlighten the reader and to evoke neither condemnation nor praise. I will give a resumé of the story for those who have forgotten it or do not know it:

The action takes place in two properties on the Yorkshire Moors—Wuthering Heights and Thrushcross Grange—which are separated from each other by a distance of three miles. Wuthering Heights is the estate of the Earnshaw family and has been in the family for some generations and similarly Thrushcross Grange belongs to the Linton family. One day old Mr. Earnshaw goes on a trip to Liverpool and while there picks up a young gypsy brat who is homeless. He is adopted by him and his wife, much to the latter's annoyance. His origin, background and name are unknown and so he is simply called "Heathcliff." He grows up together with the two Earnshaw children, Hindley and Catherine. Old Earnshaw has special affection for Heathcliff and he exploits his position. From Hindley he gets things he wants by blackmail. On one occasion old Earnshaw brings home two colts and gives one to Hindley and the other to Heathcliff. A few days later Heathcliff's becomes lame so he demands that Hindley swap, saying that he will show the old man the bruises Hindley has given him if he refuses. Hindley submits.

The children grow up, and Heathcliff, we discover, loves Catherine but when she is of age she decides to marry Edgar Linton. By this time old Earnshaw has died and Hindley, master of the home, humiliates Heathcliff and has reduced him to servant status. Catherine tells her confidante, Ellen Dean, an old family retainer, of her decision to marry Edgar Linton but Heathcliff overhears and disappears for three years. In the meantime Hindley's wife has a child called Hareton and she dies, and then Catherine marries Edgar Linton.

After three years Heathcliff, unexpected and uninvited, appears on the doorstep of Thrushcross Grange, having gone to lodge at Wuthering Heights. Although Hindley hates Heathcliff, his greed for money overcomes his natural sentiments. He is an expert at playing on people's weaknesses. He now has some money of his own and is a fully grown man. He becomes a regular visitor at Thrushcross Grange and Edgar allows it for Catherine's sake. It is not long before Heathcliff starts to flirt with Edgar's sister, Isabella, who becomes totally infatuated with him. Catherine sees them kissing in the garden and there ensues a row between Heathcliff and Catherine in which the former abuses the latter. Ellen Dean rushes off to fetch Edgar Linton, who rushes at Heathcliff, but Catherine, instead of defending her husband, goes to the defense of Heathcliff.

Eventually, with the help of two laborers, Heathcliff is ejected from the house and banished from it. Catherine, who is now pregnant, declares that if she cannot have Edgar and Heathcliff she will make sure that neither of them can have her and she determines that she will die and so she starves herself and becomes delirious. Heathcliff elopes with Isabella and marries her and then returns with her to Wuthering Heights. With the help of Ellen Dean, Heathcliff sneaks in to see the dying Catherine and they declare their love for each other. Catherine dies but not before a baby daughter is born to her and she is also named Catherine.

Heathcliff is now governed by one ruling passion: to possess everything that belonged to Catherine and to oust all other contenders. He is determined to become owner of both Wuthering Heights and Thrushcross Grange. When Hindley Earnshaw dies of drink it emerges that Heathcliff is now the owner of Wuthering Heights. Hindley had mortgaged his property to pay his debts incurred through gambling which Heathcliff had encouraged. The mortgagee of the property is, of course, Heathcliff, so on Hindley's death the property becomes his. Isabella flees from Heathcliff to the south of England and there she has a baby boy whom she names Linton.

Twelve years later Isabella dies and Edgar Linton goes to collect the young Linton and brings him to Thrushcross Grange, but hardly has he arrived in the house when Heathcliff sends to claim his son so the young Linton goes to his father at Wuthering Heights. Despite strict instructions from Edgar Linton, Heathcliff manages, when the two children are of age, to bring Catherine and Linton together through various deceptions. Then he captures the two and forces them to marry. Edgar Linton, now dying, realizes that unless he changes his will all his property will go to Catherine and therefore fall into Heathcliff's hands, so he sends messengers to summon his solicitors but Heathcliff sends contrary messages and so Edgar dies before the solicitors reach him. So now Heathcliff is also master of Thrushcross Grange. All that was associated with his beloved Catherine now belongs to him.

Now his goal is achieved but instead of satisfaction, life becomes an empty abyss and all he wants now is to die. Like his beloved Catherine he starts to starve himself but he first desecrates the grave and makes a place for himself next to Catherine. Then he dies and is buried next to his beloved tormentor, Catherine. His son, Linton, had died shortly before him so the final irony is that the whole estate of Heathcliff passes to Catherine Linton and Hareton Earnshaw, who marry at the end of the book.

Heathcliff's relationship with Catherine is key to understanding his character and makes Emily Brontë's formulation a precursor of object relations theory. Explanation which focuses on the death instinct, guilt, impulses and tension cannot be left out. It is impossible to give an account of psychopathy without taking account of this, and Emily Brontë was well aware of it. Where Heathcliff came from, what his parentage was and even his nationality is deliberately left unknown. The biological organism with its genetic inheritance, impulses and instincts is therefore given recognition but onto this foundation Emily grafts a character structure that is a product of his relationship with Catherine. The relations between Heathcliff and Catherine need to be understood both as symbolical of an intrapsychic conflict *and* the early relationship of infant with mother. The internal relations within the unconscious can only become literature by translating them into adult love relationships. In this way great novels frequently describe an intrapsychic conflict.

Heathcliff and Catherine become close friends when Hindley goes off to college for three years. The bond between them was all the stronger because Catherine's mother had died some years before. Catherine becomes quasi mother to Heathcliff. In the relationship of Heathcliff to Catherine is symbolized the bond between infant and mother at a very early developmental stage.

While in their early teens, old Earnshaw dies, and Hindley returns with a wife whom he has secretly married. He is now the master of Wuthering Heights and puts Heathcliff to work on the farm, treats him as a servant and humiliates him in various ways. Heathcliff swears revenge. Then comes the biggest blow for Heathcliff: Catherine decides to marry Edgar Linton of Thrushcross Grange and we get a crucial insight into the psychology of the relationship between the two. Ellen Dean, who narrates the story, asks Catherine why she is going to marry Edgar Linton and she answers that Edgar has position and money. Ellen Dean asks, "What about Heathcliff?"

Catherine's answer is staggering: "It would degrade me to marry Heathcliff, now; so he shall never know how I love him; and that's not because he's handsome, Nelly, but because he's more myself than I am. Whatever our souls are made of, his and mine are the same."

And a few minutes later she says,

I cannot express it; but surely you and everybody have a notion that there is, or should be an existence of yours beyond you. What were the use of my creation if I were entirely contained here? My great miseries in this world have been Heathcliff's miseries, and I watched and felt each from the beginning; my great thought in living is himself. If all else perished, and *he* remained, I should still continue to be; and if all else remained, and he were annihilated, the universe would turn to a mighty stranger. I should not seem a part of it. My love for Linton is like the foliage in the woods. Time will change it, I'm well aware, as winter changes trees. My love for Heathcliff resembles the eternal rocks beneath—a source of little visible delight, but necessary. Nelly, I *am* Heathcliff—he's always in my mind—not as a pleasure any more than I am a pleasure to myself—but as my own being—so don't talk of our separation again—it is impracticable.

And later in the book, when Catherine has just died, Heathcliff says of her, "I *cannot* live without my life! I *cannot* live without my soul."

Heathcliff, the psychopath, is merged psychologically with his primary love object and separation from it is unbearable. He says his love for Catherine is a thousand times stronger than the love Edgar Linton has for her but it is a love that will suffer any behavior in the beloved just because it is the product of the loved one. Heathcliff says that if his and Edgar's positions were reversed he would never have raised a hand against Edgar, even though he hated him, for as long as she had regard for him but then he says: "The moment her regard ceased, I would have torn his heart out, and drunk his blood!"

This can only mean that he is furious with Catherine for her attention to Edgar Linton, but he will always protect her from his own violently vengeful feelings. As soon as Catherine is dead he is determined upon Edgar Linton's downfall, and he also brutally attacks her brother Hindley, which he would not have done while she was alive. The revenge of the psychopath is so intense that he is terrified of experiencing it towards his primary love object with whom his own survival is so intimately bound up. The needs of survival do not allow him to attack his primary love object. Talking of the baby's dilemma Bion (1962) says, "Fear of death through starvation of essentials compels the resumption of sucking. A split between material and psychical satisfaction develops."

So desire for revenge becomes displaced from his primary love object onto other figures. He protects this one figure with all his strength and destroys all others in order to do so. What the world sees is the figures whom he destroys but not the invisible figure whom he protects. When treating a psychopath, the analyst frequently becomes this protected figure in the transference; and I think one of the reasons this type of patient is so difficult to treat is that if interpretations begin to bear on this protective screen, the analyst becomes a focus of paranoid fury which is not expressed verbally, but acted out, either towards people outside of the treatment situation or towards the analyst in some concrete way, like burgling his home or attacking him or a member of his family. Unless this paranoia is laid bare I do not think the patient's psychopathy can be treated more than superficially and this creates a difficult problem. But surely in prison the problem can be tackled with safety? But how many would allow themselves to become the focus of a determined vendetta that might not be worked through, a vendetta that might put the analyst's family at risk? It was no surprise that weapons were smuggled in to the Baader-Meinhof group at Stuttgart Prison. Officers protecting these prisoners would know that their families and themselves would be at risk from the group's confederates outside if they had not done so. I do not offer a solution, but it is healthier to recognize that very often we collude with the criminal psychopath for our own safety, and we should not deceive ourselves about it or blame others for doing so. In *Wuthering Heights* one of the most fateful aspects of the novel is that all, even Edgar Linton, submit to Heathcliff's undying determination.

It is often asserted that the criminal psychopath is amoral and not bound by any ethical system; nothing could be further from the truth. He is intensely moral and generally speaks in puritanical terms. Hatred for the primary love object is displaced and acted out in external behavior, so feelings of guilt are frequently displaced onto something quite venial. A criminal once borrowed £2 from a forensic psychiatrist; a few days later he battered an old lady and nearly killed her. Some time later he was enormously guilty at not having repaid the money to the psychiatrist, but had no apparent remorse about the elderly lady who was his victim. The criminal's ethical system is built around an internal figure. The end justifies any means, but there always is an end. In the story of Heathcliff we see an example of this where he marries Catherine's sister-in-law, Isabella, to take revenge on Edgar Linton. His ethical goal is individual, personal and remains unseen by those around him and by himself also. Klein (1934) has given expression to the way in which the positive factor is not seen by those in his social environment:

One of the great problems about criminals, which has always made them incomprehensible to the rest of the world, is their lack of natural human good feeling; but this lack is only apparent. When in analysis one reaches the deepest conflicts from which hate and anxiety spring, one also finds there the love as well. Love is not absent in the criminal, but it is hidden and buried in such a way that nothing but analysis can bring it to light.

I want to dwell further on internal objects and ethical systems. Within the psychical system there is a subject which is the ego and objects to which it relates with feelings of love, hate or a mixture of both. Subject and object are used in the grammatical sense of subject and object of a sentence; in fact objects are usually figures of people experienced internally. These are the significant caring figures of childhood but altered according to the infant's own perception and feelings so the internal mother may be quite other than that consciously experienced. So the psychopath consciously may proclaim his mother to be a saint but unconsciously feel her as a bitter, persecuting figure.

It is these internal objects or inner figures that mobilize energy; someone will cross the world in pursuit of a loved one and also in search of a hated enemy. Motivation flows from the presence of these inner figures but they have a conscious representative in the external world. So a man devoted to the improvement of conditions for some minority group, like the Maltese or Cypriots, has a loved figure within him that he wishes to care for and in analysis this can be traced to the minority group which becomes the conscious representative of the unconscious inner figure. Then there is the man who dedicates his life to combating some evil like racism which he vehemently hates, and again the emotional force comes from a persecuting inner figure. In these cases the internal object has undergone a process of sublimation, but with the psychopath, due to failure in symbol formation, this has not occurred. He is dedicated to an inner unseen figure and in pursuit of her destroys all objects in his path. All the world can see is that he sweeps aside the values which most people hold sacred as Glover (1960) has observed:

In order to obtain an accurate picture of the "criminal psychopath" it is essential to keep constantly in mind that the main feature of criminal psychopathy, viz. moral obliquity, is estimated by social rather than clinical considerations. The lack of "moral fibre" is measured by the degree to which the criminal psychopath ignores and contravenes social codes.

For Heathcliff, the motivating inner figure is the dead Catherine, who yet remains alive for him. When Catherine dies, his only way of taking hold of her is to possess entirely all the material possessions which were associated with her: Wuthering Heights and Thrushcross Grange. But the point is this: it is he who has killed her and he is so guilty that he has to keep her alive. By keeping her alive he does not experience the guilt for her death. When he does finally own all that belonged to Catherine he feels in an empty abyss and says, "Be with me always—take any form—drive me mad! Only do not leave me in this abyss, where I cannot find you! Oh God! it is unutterable!"

He has one last desire: to die and be buried next to Catherine, so he starves himself and makes sure that he will be buried beside her. What he pursues so ruthlessly is a lost object which has become persecuting to him. The persecuting figure is similar to the one Freud (1917) describes in "Mourning and Melancholia," but there are two important differences. The depressive persecutes his object mentally inside himself; all is conducted within the mental sphere. The depressive is suffering from a loss that has occurred later developmentally when symbolization has been satisfactorily established. The psychopath's loss has occurred earlier, when the infant is still stretching for his object and holding it to himself in a tactile way, and before he can internalize it within the unconscious. The psychopath has suffered a loss which occurred when mother and infant were still a unit. In Kleinian language, the infant has sustained a loss while in the paranoid-schizoid position. The projective and introjective mechanisms by which the infant separates himself from mother have not completed their work. So the infant has lost not just mother but a part of himself. It is precisely this which Heathcliff poignantly describes when Catherine dies.

The envy and destructive forces towards the primary love object are so powerful that they have to be deflected both from the self and from the object. The psychopath cannot say, "I feel I would like to kill my mother" because unconsciously he has killed her, and the guilt and depression about it is so enormous that it is projected powerfully into those significant others of his environment. He is mother and if for one instance the depression comes home, as it were, he kills himself.

How do people respond to the psychopath? Let us listen first to how those surrounding Heathcliff responded. Ellen Dean says of him as a child: "From the very beginning he bred bad feeling in the house."

One of the most evident signs of psychopathy is the presence of confusion and bad feeling. One person is set against another and suspicion is rife, but the cause is never rooted out. In these days when it is fashionable in institutions to analyse group phenomena on a systems theory basis the presence of psychopathy is often missed. It is thought that all can be resolved if everyone's role is clear and that by "talking through," harmony can be reached. This may work in the absence of a psychopath but not when one is present in a group. The psychopath scorns such genteel methods of dealing with problems. He will create more confusion out of it so that "talking through" will provide no solution.

Another time Ellen Dean says, "I wondered often what my master saw to admire so much in the sullen boy who never, to my recollection, repaid his indulgence by any sign of gratitude."

People expect that the psychopath will respond to goodness and kindness and show gratitude in the end. This is a pious wish; the experience of those working with psychopaths is the opposite. Experience belies the wishes and longings of those brought up to adhere to the Christian ethics of Western society. After the incident where Heathcliff blackmails Hindley, Ellen Dean says of him, "I persuaded him easily to let me lay the blame of his bruises on the horse; he minded little what tale was told since he had what he wanted."

He did not care as long as he got what he wanted. Material gain sweeps all other considerations aside. Ellen Dean also notes that he did not seem to mind being abused physically or verbally by Hindley and she says, "He complained so seldom . . . that I really thought him not vindictive—I was deceived completely, as you will hear."

The psychopath is extremely vindictive but does not show it in word or gesture at the time of the injury. He stores it up and responds in action later. When normal people tell a lie it is registered on a G.S.R., but not with the psychopath.* The psychopath does not belie his feelings. People around do not feel him to be vindictive and vicious. I once refused a request to a psychopath and he just said blandly, "Oh, that's alright, don't worry" and went off cheerily and the next day he burgled my flat. The rage and vindictiveness is so split off that people do not believe he has done what he has, even when the evidence is incontrovertible.

Even Catherine says of Heathcliff to Isabella, who was later to marry him, "He'd crush you like a sparrow's egg, Isabella, if he found you a troublesome charge. I know he couldn't love a Linton; and yet he'd be quite capable of marrying your fortune and expectations. Avarice is growing with him a besetting sin. There's my picture; and I'm his friend."

Editor's Note: The actual research on deception as measured by the polygraph in psychopaths and normals is limited and equivocal; more research is needed to test the ability of psychopaths to "beat" a polygraph exam in realistic settings.

And soon after Isabella has married him she writes to Ellen Dean and asks, "Is Heathcliff a man? If so, is he mad? And if not, is he a devil?"

It is possible to classify the responses aroused by the psychopath under three headings: *collusion, disbelief* and *condemnation*.

In the novel, after Isabella has married Heathcliff and is living at Wuthering Heights, Ellen Dean goes to visit her, in response to a forlorn letter from her. There she meets Heathcliff, now banned from Thrushcross Grange, but he persuades Ellen Dean to help him sneak in unseen to visit the dying Catherine; against her better judgement she agrees, because she feels that if she does not, worse will happen. She is also afraid of Heathcliff, who threatens her. The psychopath is so desperate that he persuades people with a pressing urgency to carry out his wishes. To obtain what he wants is all important, and he will seduce, cajole and threaten in order to obtain it. The despair and ultimate emptiness calls forth a collusive response in those to whom he appeals. A beseeching call for help which only you can answer is difficult to resist. It revives in us early feelings when we also were totally helpless. In treatment the psychopath will try every means to get us to do something, other than give interpretations. He makes a desperate appeal to us to lend him money, give him longer sessions, get him a glass of water, allow him to use our telephone and so on.

In themselves these requests are harmless enough, but to collude is to spell disaster; it is equivalent to agreeing that it is impossible for the patient to introject a good object, and ultimately, to give the analyst up. Once a patient tried to persuade me to go for a drink with him after the session, telling me he needed to feel I was human. I did not accede to his request. Later it was possible to analyze that he hated me for my happiness with my family and friends. In taking me for a drink he was wanting to lead me into drunkeness, then drugs, and so destroy the happiness I had. On this occasion the word "human" was not so benign as first appeared. In treatment the cry of the psychopath is frequently "You give me absolutely nothing—give me something concrete."

It is essential to help the psychopath pass through this "dark night of the senses" and that we do not, from our own anxiety, prevent him from doing so.

There is another type of collusion which is more difficult to define but it haunts the atmosphere of *Wuthering Heights* from start to finish. It is that ultimately it is hopeless to resist the determination of the psychopath. In the novel this is typified by Edgar Linton who becomes helpless in the face of his rival. He forbids Heathcliff entrance to his home yet he is defied; he forbids his daughter to go to Wuthering Heights but Heathcliff subtly interferes and thwarts his plans. He goes to fetch his nephew, Linton, when Isabella dies, but when Heathcliff demands the child he submits without a murmur. Finally Heathcliff kidnaps his daughter and forces her to marry his son. Edgar Linton's only response is to die. All the people close to him die: Catherine, Isabella, Edgar Linton, Hindley, and his own son, Linton.

The psychopath projects his own inner despair into those around him and achieves his short-term goals in this way. He controls those around him through powerful projective mechanisms. He makes others feel what he dare not feel himself. Only at the end of the book does Heathcliff himself cry out with despair and then it is his turn to die. When I have made an interpretation to a psychopath that gets in touch with his despair there is a momentary flash of horror accompanied by some statement such as: "I'd bloody kill myself if I thought that," and then the projective armor clashes to again. What he says is true: there is a symbolic equation between the ego and the hated object in the unconscious. If the depression comes home it leads to an actual killing, so he has to push it away.

Through strong projective mechanisms, the psychopath stirs our own primitive sadism and this leads to a twofold response: either disbelief or condemnation. These are two ways of dealing with our own sadism. This attitude of disbelief is expressed commonly enough in such exclamations as: "Surely he can't be as bad as that." Yet when Heathcliff elopes with Isabella, he gives her clear evidence as to his character. As the two are leaving Thrushcross Grange he takes her favorite dog, puts a rope around its neck and hangs it from a tree, and yet she still adheres to an illusory picture of him and he despises her for it.

The psychopath despises the person who holds on to an illusion that he is good; unconsciously he knows that it is a rejection of an important part of him. It is the renewed experience of a mother who could not contain his sadistic impulses in the first few weeks of life. Despite the evidence, Isabella keeps a protective screen around him. Just as Heathcliff maintains a protective screen around his Catherine, so he arouses the same response in relation to himself. Remember he *is* Catherine; that is not a literary metaphor but a psychological fact. Because the psychopath unconsciously hates the person who has an illusion about him, he will always give a strong clue about the hidden side of his character.

Some years ago my flat was burgled one weekend when I was away and it seemed certain to have been done by one or more ex-prisoners that I had been concerned with. Two men had been observed climbing up a ladder into my flat on the Saturday night so it was known that two men had been involved in the burglary. A day or two later an ex-prisoner came to see me, slapped me on the back and said, "Oh I know, Neville, we've had the odd rows but I really think it's diabolical when someone burgles your flat after all you do for us."

I had an immediate presentiment that he was one of the culprits. Consciously it was the old trick; I was bound to say to myself, "It can't be him," but unconsciously he was telling me the truth, using a reaction formation defense. Shortly afterwards the police arrested him for the crime. One of the objects stolen from my flat was a check book. Another man whom I knew quite well came to me and said with pride: "Look, I've opened a bank account and here's my check book," and he showed me his new check book. He was showing me that it was he who had stolen *my* check book. He was the other man who was arrested. This need to leave evidence of his real character is the unconscious determinant of clues left by the criminal that lead to his arrest.

To adhere to the evidence rather than disbelieve requires us to accept our own sadism which we deny all the harder when it is being stirred by the psychopath. Our disbelief is reinforced by the Christian value system which says that man, like God, is good. We are all familar with the counsels "Blessed are the Meek" and "Blessed are the Merciful." Our desire to be acceptable in terms of these standards puts additional pressure on us to deny our own sadism. If we accept what we see in the psychopath then we have to accept our own sadism. It may be more comfortable to believe that he and ourselves are good.

When *Wuthering Heights* was first published in 1847 the critics complained of the stark brutal quality of Heathcliff. Even Charlotte, Emily's sister, tried to persuade her to temper her characterization of Heathcliff for propriety's sake, but Emily refused. She was not going to moderate the way she saw things. The public wanted an illusion and not the real psychopath whom Emily portrayed. The uncompromising way in which revered values and standards are swept aside by the psychopath shocks us today just as it did our Victorian forebears.

The other reaction is to deny our sadism by projecting it back onto the criminal psychopath. Frequently criminals feel that they are being victimized and their perception is accurate. They are particularly suitable scapegoats onto which we can project our own sadism, but to relate with neither disbelief nor condemnation is extremely difficult. The two sets of reactions could be clearly seen in the debate as to whether Myra Hindley should be given parole or not.* The same split can be seen in

---

Editor's Note: This was the infamous "Moors murders" case in Britain in 1966. See F. Harrison (1986). *Brady and Hindley: Genesis of the Moors Murders.* Bath: Ashgrove Press.

the response aroused by the psychopath who goes into a psychiatric hospital where he is met with disbelief and in the prison where he meets condemnation.

Both disbelief and condemnation are products of the same emotional neglect: the failure to accept the psychopath *as he is*. The foundation stone of any treatment is to respond with neither disbelief nor condemnation. To be present to the psychopath as he is becomes the *sine qua non* for successful treatment. The psychopath does stir our sadism and tries to induce our disbelief or provoke our condemnation. When we come to terms with this in him and in ourselves we have laid a basis for a fruitful analysis. Of course it must not remain in the mental sphere but be demonstrated actively in the treatment situation. Only then do we reach the unconscious phantasies wherein his difficulties lie.

SUMMARY

Heathcliff, the protagonist of Emily Brontë's novel *Wuthering Heights*, is a psychopath, and the article analyzes his character from an object relations perspective. It highlights the powerful ambivalent feelings towards the primary love object as the source of the psychopath's determination and energy. The loving feelings are kept hidden and the hatred is displaced onto suitable objects in the environment. The loving feelings emerge in an analysis, as they do in Emily Brontë's characterization of Heathcliff. The cause of his condition is traced to an object loss that has occurred before symbolization has taken place.

The response which the psychopath arouses is considered under three aspects: collusion, disbelief and condemnation. The psychopath is desperate for concrete goods that he can tangibly lay hold of. People collude with him because their own infantile longings are aroused. Disbelief in the psychopath's greed and destructiveness is a defense against sadism in those who treat him. So also is condemnation, which occurs when people project their cruel and vengeful feelings onto the psychopath. The foundation for a successful treatment is to be present to the psychopath as he is.

REFERENCES

Bion, W. R. (1962). *Learning from Experience*. London: Heinemann.
Brontë, E. (1847). *Wuthering Heights*. London: Penguin Books.

Freud, S. (1917). Mourning and melancholia. *Standard Edition*, 14:243–258. London: Hogarth Press, 1975.

Glover, E. (1960). *The Roots of Crime*. London: Imago.

Klein, M. (1934). On criminality. In: *Love, Guilt and Reparation and Other Works*. London: Hogarth Press, 1975.

20

The Treatment of Antisocial Syndromes
The Therapist's Feelings
Larry H. Strasburger

The Boston psychoanalyst Larry Strasburger contributed this paper as a chapter in William Reid's book, *Unmasking the Psychopath*, in 1986. Building on the work of John Lion and Gerald Adler, he empathically captures the therapist's feelings when attempting treatment of an antisocial person. Strasburger first defines the requisite "maturity" necessary for such work and then elucidates six countertransference responses: fear of assault or harm, helplessness and guilt, loss of professional identity, denial of danger, rejection of the patient, and the rageful wish to destroy. This is a clinically rich and sophisticated, yet realistic paper that captures the sometimes frozen, and often frightening, landscape of therapeutic engagement with a psychopathically disturbed patient.

The psychopath is the least loved of patients. Patients with antisocial syndromes traditionally have been considered untreatable (Cleckley, 1964). Even a quick review of the literature suggests that a chapter on effective treatment should be the shortest in any book concerned with psychopathy (Suedfeld and Landon, 1975).

There are some valid reasons for therapeutic pessimism. These people are impulsive, unable to tolerate frustration and delay, and have problems with trusting. They take a paranoid position or externalize their emotional experience. They have little ability to form a working alliance and a poor capacity for self-observation. Their anger is frightening. Frequently they take flight. Their relations with others are highly problematic. When close to another person they fear engulfment or fusion and loss of self. At the same time, paradoxically, they desire closeness; frustration of their entitled wishes to be nourished, cared for, and assisted often leads to rage. They are capable of a child's primitive fury enacted with an adult's physical capabilities, and action is always in the offing.

297

Much therapeutic pessimism arises from the feelings psychopaths engender in their caretakers and treaters. It is difficult to be sympathetic toward delinquent, substance-abusing, and sometimes violent individuals. Therapists are likely to regard the coping behavior of psychopaths as sin more than sickness. They are bad, not mad. "The defense mechanisms that underlie sociopathy seem . . . as unbearably gross to the observer as a strong cigar in a crowded elevator" (Vaillant, 1975). Indeed, psychiatrists are involved in the same unconscious rejection of psychopaths that society openly admits through its punitive attitudes (Bromberg, 1953).

Psychopaths are people with primitive personalities who for some reason have avoided facing inner dysphoria through antisocial forms of enacting or sharing displeasure. They are not simply bad, hopeless, incorrigible people. They can be worked with in therapy like other primitive personalities if one understands and can utilize the effects the patient has on an average therapist.

There is, however, a depreciatory attitude toward individuals burdened with a character diagnosis. In many training institutions personality disorders are not regarded as "good treatment cases." They may sarcastically be referred to as "PDs," with knee-jerk suspiciousness about their motivation and treatability. They are, in effect, often extruded from a clinic's teaching population (Lion and Leaff, 1973). Clinical staff do not like their repeated demands for help, coupled with their insistence that their troubles always originate outside themselves. Their infantile manner, omnipotent demands, and lack of introspection cause them to be rejected. Their hedonism and requirements for instant gratification often clash head-on with the personal values of clinical staff.

The antisocial veneer does have a curious attraction. Clinicians often focus on it, treating these individuals superficially, as though they had no inner dynamics. The inner desolation or chaos may be intolerable to doctor as well as patient. Since the behavior is repugnant, however, the patient is dismissed as a "psychopath" and the opportunity to understand his underlying psychopathology is lost (Protter and Travin, 1983). This antipsychological attitude—ignoring an individual's inner world— is dehumanizing, but mirrors the way the therapist is treated by the patient. It is an essential element in the traditionally pessimistic attitude toward treatment of the antisocial syndromes.

Although the individuals exhibiting antisocial syndromes may be depersonalized in this way by those who deal with them, their psychology can reveal familiar, often manageable, human processes. When avenues of escape through action are cut off, these people show the dynamics of other, more treatable primitive personality disorders. "This pejorative term, psychopath, is accurate only insofar as it describes the back of a patient fleeing therapy. If a psychiatrist sees the same patient in a prison hospital, he may doubt that such a disorder exists" (Vaillant, 1975). Underlying the antisocial epithets are familiar clinical syndromes. Depression, for example, often lies behind the behavior of the aggressive personality disorders (Lion, 1972). This depression, produced by ordinary frustrations, accompanied by a sense of personal weakness and helplessness, leads to the violence these people manifest. In the presence of a facilitating environment and a therapist who is a match for the task, the depression is treatable.

SUCCESSFUL THERAPISTS

Before looking more closely at the pathological collusions the psychopath tends to enact with his surroundings, trying to articulate the relevant processes in the therapist, and, where possible, suggesting techniques for managing them, let us examine certain characteristics of therapists who successfully deal with antisocial patients. The ideal therapist is a readily perceptible, accessible person, differentiated by sharply defined characteristics, so that the patient can form a clear picture of him as a model for identification (Adler and Shapiro, 1973). The therapist can usefully adopt an informal, self-revealing style (Lion, 1981). He must be warm and understanding, but not uncritical, because he needs to confront maladaptive behavior. "I'm OK, you're not OK" may have some therapeutic value, according to Lion, who advises, in appropriate context, a direct confrontation of the patient's lack of success using his pathological style.

At the same time, the therapist must help his patient define "problem areas" rather than accept the patient's picture of himself as totally bad. It is very helpful to particularize problems, as these people usually have had very little realistic, nonpunitive feedback in their lives. Often they have experienced a pathological acceptance of their actual badness, along with unrealistic attributions. The therapist, therefore, must not collude in their black–white, polarized, global thinking. "Frank descriptions of one's own reaction to violent [individuals], given spontaneously, have the remarkable therapeutic effect of helping them separate themselves from . . . an illusionary omnipotence and to see themselves in a realistic mirror" (King, 1976).

The treatment of the antisocial syndromes requires active involvement rather than an expectant or nondirective approach. Therapist passivity has been correlated with a negative outcome for incarcerated delinquents. Those who respond positively to therapy judge their therapist to be firm, as well as warm and understanding (Persons and Pepinsky, 1966). "The effective therapist will make it clear that he sees through the manipulative attempts of the patient, and will continue to be realistically rather than gullibly supportive" (Suedfeld and Landon, 1975). The therapist must have the capacity to set clearly defined limits, well explained to the patient. The rules must be enforced firmly and promptly, otherwise the treatment structure is disrupted and essential respect for the therapist is lost.

Latent antiauthoritarian attitudes of the therapist quickly become manifest and are exploited (Macdonald, 1965). Patients may vicariously gratify unconscious wishes or fantasies of the therapist, which may be one reason therapists choose to work with such persons in the first place. Inmates do things to others about which therapists cannot allow themselves even to have conscious fantasies. When the therapist is intrigued with such stories of crime, inmates correctly perceive that they are admired or envied for their badness. Obviously, this jeopardizes treatment.

It is particularly important that the therapist be able to modulate and constructively discharge his own anxiety. Psychopaths, "brought up to believe that anxiety is too dreadful to be borne and too awful to confess [are] reassured that someone can be anxious and yet in control" (Vaillant, 1975). One must show the capacity to bear intrapsychically what the patient cannot—this is the model for identification.

Therapeutic modesty is a prerequisite. How little we really know about the treatment of personality disorder, despite the wealth of material which has been written on the subject! Therapeutic omnipotence, even enthusiasm, may lead to severe disappointment for both patient and therapist. Some individuals do benefit from treatment; many do not.

In sum, that elusive and difficult-to-define characteristic, maturity, is a critical element in the personality of those who would attempt the frustrating task of treating antisocial patients. One wonders how this is to be found in therapists who have led a relatively sheltered academic life in the long process of earning a doctoral degree. Psychopaths have lived more in the world, and have learned from it. Is it any wonder that the streetwise psychopath is such a difficult challenge to a therapist during training or the early professional stages of his career?

THE THERAPIST'S FEELINGS

Despite the emergence of theoretical knowledge and treatment modalities for the antisocial syndromes, one of the primary roadblocks to successful treatment is the therapist's own feelings. The treatment of neurotic patients does not arouse such strong feelings. This emotional constellation, this countertransference, poses a unique set of problems which must be resolved if treatment is to be useful.

Freud introduced the term "countertransference" in 1910 to refer to the neurotic conflicts of the therapist which were reactivated within the therapeutic setting by the transferences of the patient.

> We have become aware of the "counter-transference," which arises in [the physician] as a result of the patient's influence on his unconscious feelings, and we are almost inclined to insist that he shall recognize this counter-transference in himself and overcome it. We have noticed that no psychoanalyst goes further than his own complexes and internal resistances permit.

Subsequent writers have developed a view of countertransference less as a flaw in the therapist and more as a rich source of information about nonverbal communication. The less rigorous popular usage of the term, which will be employed here, defines countertransference broadly as any emotional reaction the clinician has toward his patient. It includes reactions to the patient's reality, his transference, and the setting in which he is treated—the totality of the therapist's reaction to his patient.

While countertransference reactions may represent the reemergence of neurotic character traits of the therapist, and thus be quite individualized, there is a set of reactions which are more universal. These reactions occur as a result of the patient's primitive defenses, such as splitting, denial, projection, and acting-out—defenses against poorly tolerated feelings. The reactions are based in the character pathology of the patients and are to be expected in the treatment of the antisocial syndromes.

The phenomenon of countertransference was originally viewed pejoratively; it was an aberration in the therapist, something basically wrong that had to be overcome. Current therapeutic technique, however, involves the active use of countertransference reactions as a part of the treatment rather than just things to be "overcome." It is not the countertransference or the feeling that interferes, but the therapist's use of it—whether it is unrecognized and collusively enacted or recognized and looked upon as a source of data.

Because countertransference is a reenactment of unrecognized elements of a patient's earliest relationships as he perceived them, it has the potential of providing valuable information about the nature of the patient's early formative relationships. These have not been internalized in such useful forms as memories and awareness. In situations in which words are not available or memories fail to describe the nature of early life, countertransference serves as a vivid, if primitive, mode of communication to the therapist about the emotional flavor of that early life. Countertransference, if the information can be decoded, becomes an invaluable tool for understanding the patient. "It is often the other people in contact with the patient who find themselves experiencing the affect he is avoiding" (Frosch, 1983). Problems, however, arise from repression of countertransference and, at the opposite pole, from becoming overwhelmed by it (Racker, 1957). When unconscious, countertransference may generate well-rationalized but destructive acting-out by the therapist.

Countertransference can prevent the therapist from being his best therapeutic self, interfering with his perceptions and thinking, as well as making him exquisitely uncomfortable. Immature characterologic defenses are contagious. "In the presence of a drug addict liberals become prejudiced; the masochist elicits our own latent sadism, and the malingerer our passive-aggression. When baited by their adolescent children, even the most reasonable and staid parents become hopelessly involved and utterly unreasonable" (Vaillant, 1975).

In addition to complicating the treatment of individuals, countertransference contributes to the attrition of personnel at institutions dealing with antisocial syndromes. The work is hard, more so because of the personal myths the inexperienced have about therapeutic work. Countertransference often undermines the staff's feelings of competence and self-respect, adding to the phenomenon known as "burnout."

Often rationalized as a realistic assessment of treatment results, the traditional therapeutic pessimism about psychopaths may be regarded as a countertransference response in itself. The bias against treating psychopaths is rationalized as well as reinforced by the myth of untreatability; in turn, the myth of untreatability is both a cause and an effect of countertransference.

SPECIFIC COUNTERTRANSFERENCE REACTIONS

Fear of Assault or Harm

Fear may be rational or irrational. Some anxiety is therapeutic wisdom, leading the therapist to monitor the relationship. When fear is rational, the first priority is safety rather than further analysis. Such fears must be carefully assessed, clarifying differences between fantasy and reality, between feeling and acting. Real dangers must not be minimized or denied.

Rarely, the patient may be so determined to provoke a rejection that in fact he gives the psychiatrist the choice of withdrawing or being destroyed. To persist in the treatment of a patient where there are substantial risks of this order is to fall into the ultimate snare of one's own narcissism, namely the unrealistic belief that one is physically invulnerable [Maltsberger and Buie, 1974].

Fears of physical assault may be less rational. The therapist's frustration can produce anger, which is projected as a fear of ambush. A revival of memories of past events of violence in a therapist's life may lead to overestimation of the patient's potential for violence. Fear can lead to the abandonment of talking in favor of seclusion, restraint, or medication.

Fears of assault on the therapist usually diminish with experience. Although fantasies of the paranoid patient who kills his psychiatrist are common, in fact life-threatening assaults on therapists are very rare (Strasburger and Eddy, 1985). Learning to read the advance warnings of imminent danger and to determine what to do about them is part of developing clinical judgment. Although patients with aggressive impulses fear losing control of them and may become more agitated when they sense fear in others (Lion and Pasternak, 1973), the therapist who does not provoke or disclose his own difficulty with aggression will promote the patient's confidence in the stability required for treatment. Familiarity with the environment of the treating institution may also reassure one that security is adequate.

An unusual handling of countertransference fear was reported by Whitaker (1975):

One day in an initial interview with an adult veteran, I became terrified lest he kill me then and there. I excused myself, went across the hall and got Dr. John Warkentin and brought him back into the interview. I told him and the patient of my fear. He said to the patient with a perfectly straight face and in a serious tone, "I don't blame you a bit; I've often wanted to kill Whitaker myself!" This confused me but it made the patient's anger much more controllable, and we went on with a comfortable interview.

Wishnie (1977) describes a mismanagement of patients at a drug treatment center, where staff members were terrified and sought to appease patients rather than confront and deal with their fears in more productive ways. Unacknowledged fear reactions should be suspected when there are unusual staff behavior patterns, such as calling in sick, forgetting appointments, using excessive seclusion and restraint or higher medication doses than needed, or early discharge of patients. In order to enhance staff capacity to cope with fear-producing situations, staff members, as a group, must be allowed to openly express fear.

Fears can also include fears of litigation (Haldipur, Dewan, and Beal, 1982), increasingly so in the post-Tarasoff era, as courts sometimes hold therapists responsbile for the behavior of their patients. Paradoxically, when this fear is not acknowledged, it can produce its own cause, as through the premature discharge of potentially violent patients.

Helplessness and Guilt

Psychotherapy with antisocial patients is a difficult, slow-moving task. The therapist cannot assume the existence of a collaborative alliance. It is more probable that he will feel his efforts to help rejected while he himself is devalued. The therapist often feels impotent in his quest for change in the patient. Here the problem has to do in part with the therapist's wish to do something to the patient rather than to help him make more enlightened choices. Helplessness and guilt about the patient's lack of improvement may lead to rage at the patient. This can become manifest either as emotional withdrawal or (by reaction formation) as overresponsibility for what happens to the patient, with rescue attempts or "smothering."

Therapists in training or at the beginning of their professional careers are particularly vulnerable to feelings of helplessness (Adler, 1972). Patients project their own helplessness. The beginning therapist who feels inadequate due to his lack of experience believes his feelings are representative of the true state of affairs, rather than reflective of the countertransference.

Anticipatory guilt over harm to others as a result of inadequate or insufficient treatment is a common phenomenon. Beyond the rational concerns about patients who threaten others is the fantasy that the patient will commit a murder and the therapist will be held responsible. The anxiety is, of course, aggravated by legal decisions holding therapists responsible for injuries to third parties. This situation may actually represent the therapist's difficulty differentiating himself from the patient and his inappropriately holding himself responsible for the patient's behavior. It is a pervasive problem, for the therapist and the institutional setting have actually taken over some responsibility for the patient, when their task is, instead, to show the individual his responsibility for himself, his choice points, and their consequences.

Feelings of Invalidity and Loss of Identity

The therapist's idealized self-image as strong, loving, kind, etc., is threatened as the patient defends against assault on his fragile identity by producing a similar dilemma for the therapist. In a general sense, as the patient disowns his problems and ascribes them to the therapist, the therapist may come to feel that *he* owns them. Unwilling to experience this dysphoria, the therapist may engage in an unconscious counterprojective game of "you touched it last" as he attempts to wriggle free of the patient's attributions.

All therapists, whatever their level of professional experience, require validation (Adler, 1970). Devaluation is devastating, producing feelings of worthlessness, depression, fear, rage, guilt, shame, and envy. It represents an acceptance of the patient's projected badness. The devaluation experienced in the treatment of personality disorders removes our sense of "wholeness" about our own personality. The neophyte therapist is particularly vulnerable. He has little confidence in his abilities as he stands at the threshold of professional identity formation, a process which will lead to self-awareness as a person with skills and knowledge of the worth and limits of his work. The patient who tells the therapist that his personal and professional doubts are correct touches a particularly vulnerable spot.

A more subtle problem occurs as a result of the cognitive styles of many patients who manifest antisocial syndromes. The literal, concrete conversation of such patients is often confined to monosyllabic responses to questions. The thinking of these patients is nonpsychological, reflecting an inner world without imagination or subtle nuances of feeling. They do not free-associate and often seem incapable of forming fantasies. Although impulsive, they seem at the same time to operate entirely on the basis of secondary process thinking. This style clashes with the therapist's modus operandi and thereby with his professional identity.

The therapist often feels as though something is keeping him from working in his usual way, something which threatens his professional autonomy. Since it may be hard for the therapist to identify the source of the trouble, it produces a subtle upset of his equilibrium. These patients, suffering from identity problems, lack a well-defined self-image, and view themselves basically as worthless, unlovable persons. "Their fundamental identity is unformed, and is essentially an amorphous, hollow shell, consisting mainly of the feeling of nonexistence. It is this vacuum that they project onto the therapist" (Giovacchini, 1972). The resultant painful feeling produces an existential anxiety in the therapist, which is often as persistent as it is difficult to decipher. It may take the form of professional rationalization, in which the patient is condemned as untreatable because he is too rigid and resistant.

Denial

"Denial is the most ubiquitous defense against anxiety generated by a violent patient" (Lion and Leaff, 1973). It may lead to a failure to elicit information about weapons, lethal skills, past criminal or violent acts, or even driving habits. "To face the issue of dangerousness is very threatening to the physician, much as it is to face the seductiveness of a female patient; the therapist's human vulnerability emerges" (Lion and Leaff, 1973).

The therapist may counterphobically place himself in a dangerous position. One inexperienced resident known to the author responded to two adolescents bullying a female patient by calling them "chicken." His chivalrous indiscretion was rewarded by their attempt to throw him from a third-story window.

Rejection

The patient deals with all transactions as current, conscious, and deliberate. The coin of interchange is action, struggle. Language is assaultive, locked in the moment, and nonreflective. "They blunt the unconscious, obviate the sympathetic, race past the rational, and exhibit no evidence of conscience" (King, 1976). It is easy to moralize about manipulation, impulsivity, and flouting of social conventions, yet an attitude of acceptance without moralizing is important. The therapist who treats this type of patient must maintain a delicate balance between a talion rejection of the patient and a "masochistic submission to unreasonable demands" (Frosch, 1983).

Rejection may take subtle forms, such as a lack of emotional investment on the part of the therapist. Boredom can be one sign of emotional withdrawal, with the therapist projecting his feelings at the expense of contact and activity with the patient.

Hatred

Transference hatred provokes countertransference hatred, a combination of aversion and malice. The patient may provoke countertransference hatred to substantiate his own projections. His basic questions about the reliability, worth, and integrity of other people amount to a transference assault on the therapist. Such assaults on the therapist's self-esteem arouse hatred. The narcissistic aspirations of the therapist to heal all, to know all, and to love all make him especially vulnerable.

Although the danger of a patient's suicide may be heightened by ignoring countertransference hatred (Maltsberger and Buie, 1974), the generation of that hatred may be a positive accomplishment for the patient (Winnicott, 1947). "If the patient can experience an affect such as hatred, and if he can provoke others to hate him, he is creating a situation where love can also exist. To hate someone means that his existence is acknowledged" (Giovacchini, 1972).

Rage and the Wish to Destroy

Rage tends to be a final common pathway for the emotions of both therapist and patient. Whether it be through reactively mirroring the emotion of his patient or through the more complex route of identification with the aggressor, the therapist will find anger to be a constant companion in the treatment of antisocial syndromes. Some of this has to do with the primitive interpersonal world of such people, in which the experience of pleasure in mutuality is nonexistent: I live; you die.

Often the rage is only perceptible through an awareness of the defenses against it. The patient's defiant, remorseless, threatening attitude provokes its punitive reaction, with which the therapist may deal outside his awareness. When there is a loss of the therapist's own ego boundaries, he often attempts to control the patient as though he were a dangerous aspect of himself (the therapist). The largest single problem in the work can be "the appearance in the dyad of an oppositional stance due to countertransference rage in the therapist stirred up by the patient—a stance that can lead, in turn, to fruitless struggle, recapitulation of infantile modes of relating, and suspension of useful investigation" (Gutheil, 1985).

Those interested in the treatment of antisocial syndromes are often people who have difficulty with their own expression of aggression, people who tend to internalize anger (Lion, 1981). As patients become demanding and manipulative, and as they begin to act out their thoughts and feelings, therapists become aware of their own irritation and anger. This is a distinct therapeutic challenge. What is needed is "an effective therapist who is comfortable with his own anger so that he is aware of it, can stand it without projecting it, can test how much really belongs to the patient, and does not lose his ability when faced with a frightened and frightening patient who never had that capacity or has lost it" (Adler and Shapiro, 1973).

SPECIAL PROBLEMS OF SETTINGS

The setting in which treatment of antisocial syndromes occurs can have a significant role in evoking countertransference responses, separate and apart from the role of therapist–patient interaction. Treatment often occurs in prisons or settings where a punitive philosophy is at odds with professional training emphasizing empathic caring and respect for others. Correctional personnel inevitably test mental health personnel, frequently with jibes and "jokes," in order to check their resilience, to see if they will retaliate, or to find out "whose side they really are on." Identification with this "sadism" is all too easy for mental health staff, who bring their own set of problems and issues to work with them at such institutions. At the opposite pole, anger at being witness to the cruelty which inmates suffer may produce an overidentification with them; this overidentification makes it hard to clarify the role inmates play in incidents or to help them accept responsibly (Adler, 1984).

The therapist working in a prison setting cannot avoid being characterized by his patients as an agent of the authoritarian system. Inmates externalize their sense of their own badness, generalizing about the badness of the world and of people in authority. There is an implicit question: Will the therapist act dishonestly, like a criminal? "An encounter with workers who acknowledge that they represent the authority in power, and, as a part of it, are honest, empathic, and nonpunitive can provide a new kind of experience that discourages [such] primitive generalization" (Adler, 1984).

Outside prison settings, the institution can still have a role in countertransference formation (Gendel and Reiser, 1981). When a chronically ill individual has a stable, sustaining relation with an institution, institutional countertransference can block change and contribute to hopelessness about treatment. In these situations the patient is often treated by a succession of trainees who never really get to know him. The therapist usually feels the patient is well-known to the clinic, even though little information about him may be available in the record.

Because the patient's primary relationship is with the facility, the therapist often believes that he cannot be important to the patient. He may see no richness to the patient's inner life, fail to work toward developing his particular potentials, and believe that management of the institutional transference is the only important function of therapy. A banal form of "cookbook therapy" follows.

SOLUTIONS TO COUNTERTRANSFERENCE PROBLEMS

Solutions to the problems posed by countertransference can be found outside the therapist as well as in the therapist's inner world. The use of secure facilities has already been recommended. Some assistance with the intensity of countertransference may be found through treatment dilution, without withdrawing from the patient or giving up on him. The use of treatment groups, as opposed to individual treatment, is often recommended (Lion and Bach-y-Rita, 1970). Reduction of patient–therapist contact through infrequent meetings or the use of walk-in clinics has also been recommended. Short-term treatment, centered on specific task-oriented issues, has been proposed as a way of reducing countertransference issues. This approach has been attempted in a unique way in wilderness experience programs (Matthews and Reid, 1981). Some advocate simple incarceration as a treatment mode. This, of course, removes the issue of countertransference. It also avoids the patient's inner reality and is indistinguishable from punishment.

When the countertransference problem is institutional, the periodic staff conference may provide an opportunity to integrate and modulate countertransference reactions, as well as to improve overall morale within the institution. It provides an opportunity for staff reality testing of the countertransference, as well as for peer supervision. Staff awareness and agreement about limited goals and restraint of therapeutic omnipotence helps prevent pessimism, hopelessness, and the "burnout" phenomenon.

The inner world of the therapist—the locus of the countertransference experience—is perhaps the most fruitful place to focus efforts at countertransference resolution. Winnicott (1947) emphasizes self-knowledge: "However much he [the psychiatrist] loves his patients he cannot avoid hating them and fearing them, and the better he knows this the less will hate and fear be the motive determining what he does to his patients."

The therapist must learn to use his own personality as an instrument in the treatment process. Because his reactions to the patient are a means of understanding how the patient treats important others and how he feels treated by them, the countertransference can lead to identification and verbalization of the patient's previously inaccessible feeling states. Reacting to such transference–countertransference situations with interest rather than anxiety or anger is most helpful. This requires a capacity for reflection and self-observation. The therapist may feel anxious or angry, "but his attitude about his fear and anger is non-anxious and benevolent. He is reacting and at the same time is analytically interested in his reactions" (Giovacchini, 1979, p. 488).

In his article on taking care of the "hateful" medical patient, Groves (1978) offers some suggestions which may be usefully applied to the treatment of the antisocial syndromes. He has grouped these individuals and the reactions which they evoke into four categories: "Dependent clingers" evoke aversion in the physician, with which he must deal by limiting his expectations of the treatment. "Entitled demanders" evoke anger and a wish to counterattack, which should be dealt with by acknowledging the patient's entitlement to good care. "Manipulative help-rejecters" evoke depression, which should be confronted through an acknowledgment to the patient that his pessimism is empathically shared. "Self-destructive deniers" evoke the physician's malice. In this situation the clinician must reduce his expectations that he can give perfect care and be willing to accept the possibility of suicide by his patient as ultimately beyond his control.

Giovacchini (1972) believes that honesty is especially useful in one's approach to these patients. Again, in terms of identification, if the therapist acknowledges his mistakes and takes responsibility for them, he provides a model for the patient to do the same.

> To admit that it is possible that the patient may be correct and to investigate further what might have occurred shows respect for the patient's integrity as a sensitive observer, who is concerned about his self-esteem. Furthermore, it also demonstrates that the therapist is not ashamed of the irrational within himself, making the patient more accepting of his own inner primitive forces. A calm acceptance of the possibility of a countertransference reaction and a willingness to investigate further represent an active demonstration of the therapeutic process and a convincing example of the faith one has [in one's treatment method.] . . . Honesty is a pragmatic approach that makes sense in the therapeutic process [Giovacchini, 1972].

This is especially true with dishonest individuals.

Kernberg believes that the therapist's capacity to experience concern is important in overcoming the effects of aggression and self-aggression. Concern manifests itself in an awareness of the serious nature of destructive and self-destructive impulses in the patient. It is present in the authentic wish and need to help the patient in spite of his transitory "badness."

> In concrete terms, concern implies ongoing self-criticism by the analyst, unwillingness to accept impossible situations in a passive way, and a continuous search for new ways of handling a prolonged crisis. It implies active involvement of the therapist as opposed to narcissistic withdrawal, and realization of the ongoing need of consultation with and help from one's colleagues. The last point is important: willingness to review a certain case with a consultant or colleague, as contrasted with secrecy about one's work, is a good indication of concern [Kernberg, 1965].

Kernberg's conception of concern would appear to have ethical as well as pragmatic value, as ethics depend for their base on an affirmation of life and caring feelings for others (Ciccone and Clements, 1984).

The treatment process which has been described is clearly a difficult one. Why would a therapist want to undertake it? Is it simply an exercise in masochism or martyrdom?

I think not. Many antisocial patients are fascinating people. They have things to teach about life in general, as well as about psychotherapy in particular. The benefits both to them and to society from their rehabilitation can be most gratifying to those who treat them. Is it absolutely necessary for the therapist to have such adverse feelings? They are an integral part of an intimate relationship with people who commit antisocial acts. Not to be adversely affected by such people would be a denial of one's humanity. However, "being human includes having failings. Possibly without such failings there would be no treatment of patients who have so often been used by persons who have to deny their own failings" (Giovacchini, 1979).

REFERENCES

Adler, G. (1970). Valuing and devaluing in the psychotherapeutic process. *Arch. Gen. Psychiat.*, 22:454–461.
Adler, G. (1972). Helplessness in the helpers. *Brit. J. Med. Psychol.*, 45: 315–326.

Adler, G. (1984). Correctional (prison) psychiatry. In: *Comprehensive Textbook of Psychiatry*, ed. H. I. Kaplan & B. S. Sadock. Baltimore, MD: Williams & Wilkins.

Adler G. & Shapiro, L. N. (1973). Some difficulties in the treatment of the aggressive, acting out patient. *Amer. J. Psychother.*, 27:548–556.

Bromberg, W. (1953). The treatability of the psychopath. *Amer. J. Psychiat.*, 110.

Ciccone, J. & Clements, C. (1984). Forensic psychiatry and applied clinical ethics: Theory and practice. *Amer. J. Psychiat.*, 141:395–399.

Cleckley, H. (1964). *The Mask of Sanity*. St. Louis, MO: Mosby.

Freud, S. (1910). The future prospects of psycho-analytic therapy. *Standard Edition*, 11:139–151. London: Hogarth Press, 1957.

Frosch, J. (1983). The treatment of anti-social and borderline personality disorders. *Hosp. & Community Psychiat.*, 34:243–248.

Gendel, M. & Reiser, D. (1981). Institutional countertransference. *Amer. J. Psychiat.*, 138:508–511.

Giovacchini, P. (1972). Technical difficulties in treating some characterological disorders: Countertransference problems. *Internat. J. Psychoanal. Psychother.*, 1:112–127.

Giovacchini, P. (1979). *Treatment of Primitive Mental States*. New York: Aronson.

Groves, J. (1978). Taking care of the hateful patient. *New Engl. J. Med.*, 298:883–887.

Gutheil, T. (1985). Medicolegal pitfalls in the treatment of borderline patients. *Amer. J. Psychiat.*, 142:9–14.

Haldipur, C., Dewan, M. & Beal, M. (1982). On fear in the countertransference. *Amer. J. Psychother.*, 36:240–247.

Kernberg, O. (1965). Notes on countertransference. *J. Amer. Psychoanal. Assn.*, 13:38–56.

King, C. (1976). Countertransference and counterexperience in the treatment of violence prone youth. *Amer. J. Orthopsychiat.*, 46:43–53.

Lion, J. (1972). The role of depression in the treatment of aggressive personality disorders. *Amer. J. Psychiat.*, 129:347–349.

Lion, J. (1981). Countertransference and other psychotherapy issues. In: *The Treatment of Antisocial Syndromes*, ed. W. H. Reid. New York: Van Nostrand Reinhold.

Lion, J. & Bach-y-Rita, G. (1970). Group psychotherapy with violent patients. *Internat. J. Group Psychother.*, 20:185–191.

Lion, J. & Leaff, L. (1973). On the hazards of assessing character pathology in an outpatient setting. *Psychiat. Quart.*, 47:104–109.

Lion, J. & Pasternak, S. (1973). Countertransference reactions to violent patients. *Amer. J. Psychiat.*, 130:207–210.

Macdonald, J. (1965). Acting out. *Arch. Gen. Psychiat.*, 13:439–443.

Maltsberger, J. & Buie, D. (1974). Countertransference hate in the treatment of suicidal patients. *Arch. Gen. Psychiat.*, 30:625–633.

Matthews, W. & Reid, W. (1981). A wilderness experience treatment program for offenders. In: *The Treatment of Antisocial Syndromes*, ed. W. Reid. New York: Van Nostrand Reinhold.

Persons, R. & Pepinsky, H. (1966). Convergence in psychotherapy with delinquent boys. *J. Counsel. Psychol.*, 13:329–334.

Protter, B. & Travin, S. (1983). The significance of countertransference and related issues in a multiservice court clinic. *Bull. Amer. Acad. Psychiat. & Law*, 11:223–230.

Racker, H. (1957). The meanings and use of countertransference. *Psychoanal. Quart.*, 26:303–357.

Strasburger, L. & Eddy, S. (1985). Violence to the therapist. Unpublished manuscript.

Suedfeld, P. & Landon, P. (1975). Approaches to treatment. In: *Psychopathic Behavior: Approaches to Research*, ed. R. Hare & D. Schalling. New York: Wiley.

Vaillant, G. (1975). Sociopathy as a human process. *Arch. Gen. Psychiat.*, 32:178.

Whitaker, C. (1975). Psychotherapy of the absurd with a special emphasis on the psychotherapy of aggression. *Family Process*, 14:1.

Winnicott, D. (1947). Hate in the countertransference. In: *Collected Papers*. New York: Basic Books, pp. 194–203, 1958.

Wishnie, H. (1977). *The Impulsive Personality*. New York: Plenum.

21

The Narcissistic Personality Disorder and the Differential Diagnosis of Antisocial Behavior

Otto F. Kernberg

Otto Kernberg, an influential and well-known American psychoanalyst, has contributed much to a developmental object relations understanding of antisocial personality, his preferred term. This paper, which first appeared in *Psychiatric Clinics of North America* in 1989, draws heavily on the object relations theory of Edith Jacobson to formulate a diagnostic understanding of various antisocial psychologies. Kernberg underscores the centrality of pathological narcissism, superego deficits, and sadism in psychopathy. He also mentions some important treatment and transference guidelines that should be helpful to most clinicians.

The purpose of this article is to focus on the intimate relationship between the narcissistic personality disorder and the antisocial personality disorder. In essence, I propose that practically all patients with an antisocial personality disorder present typical features of the narcissistic personality disorder plus a specific pathology of their internalized systems of morality (their "superego functions") and a particular deterioration of their world of internalized object relations. The only significant exception to the rule that antisocial personality disorders present narcissistic personality disorders plus severe superego pathology is the relatively infrequent and prognostically grave clinical syndrome of "pseudo-psychopathic schizophrenia," typically, chronic schizophrenic patients with periodic improvement (with or without treatment) and severe, chronic antisocial behavior during such periods of "improvement" that disappears only when the patient again becomes psychotic. I also describe an intermediary group of patients between the narcissistic personality disorder and the antisocial personality disorder characterized by what I have called the syndrome of "malignant narcissism" (Kernberg, 1984). This syndrome is characterized by the combination of (1) a narcissistic personality disorder, (2) antisocial behavior, (3) ego-syntonic aggression or sadism directed against others or even expressed in a particular type of triumphant kind of self-mutilation or suicidal attempts, and (4) a strong paranoid orientation.

By implication, I am describing a dimension of antisocial behavior that links the narcissistic personality disorder with the antisocial personality disorder, and the syndrome of malignant narcissism as an intermediary personality constellation. This dimensional characteristic linking these three disorders may also be found in other dimensional links connecting other personality disorders among each other, such as, for example, the schizoid personality disorders' relationship with the schizotypal personality disorder, and the hysterical personality disorders' relationship with the histrionic, hysteroid, infantile and borderline personality disorders (Kernberg, 1984).

One important complication of this discussion derives from the shortcoming of the description of the antisocial personality disorder in DSM-III-R, where the use of excessively concrete, behavioral criteria instead of personality traits—psychological, intrapsychic criteria—and the heavy emphasis on criminal behavior all risk coming to an improper diagnosis.* The DSM-III-R (American Psychiatric Association, 1987) criteria for the antisocial personality disorder are certainly broad enough to include practically all patients with antisocial personality disorders who present predominantly aggressive interactional patterns and criminal behavior. In this area, sensitivity is high although specificity is probably low.** By stressing the severity of the criminal behavior, these criteria override the philosophical problem of what is antisocial from the viewpoint of particular value systems, and in their stress on childhood antecedents they appropriately direct the clinician to the childhood origins of this character pathology. Unfortunately, however, in this very stress on the criminal aspect of antisocial behavior they include delinquents with very different personality makeup, and blur the distinction between sociocultural and economic determinants of delinquency on the one hand and psychopathology of the personality on the other. Thus, these criteria contribute to causing what Rutter and Giller (1983) have described as the indiscriminate lumping together of

---

*Editor's Note: Dr. Kernberg's criticism is no less relevant to DSM-IV.

**Editor's Note: In fact, most self-report and structural interview measures of personality disorder show higher rates of specificity (true negatives) than of sensitivity (true positives).

delinquent behavior, which, in their view, interferes with discovering predisposing factors for those with a specific personality disorder. These criteria also lead to the critical questions raised by Stone (1984). Another problem with the DSM-III-R (American Psychiatric Association, 1987) criteria is that they neglect the nonaggressive variety or the predominantly inadequate or passive type of antisocial personality disorder, in which chronically parasitic and/or exploitive behaviors predominate rather than directly aggressive ones.

What I find most striking about the description of the antisocial personality disorder in DSM-III-R is the remarkable absence of the focus on pathological personality traits as opposed to direct antisocial behaviors, a criticism that Millon (1981) so cogently formulated.

The problem of the diagnosis of the antisocial personality disorder is complicated by the vicissitudes of the terminology that has confused this field. Unresolved conceptual problems emerge in the context of a historical analysis of the clinical descriptions and terminology.

DSM-I (American Psychiatric Association, 1952) shifted from the traditional term "sociopathic personality," that stressed the socially maladaptive aspects of these patients and the interplay between personality and social determinants, to the term "sociopathic personality disturbance" for this field. DSM-I differentiated the "antisocial reaction" from the "dissocial reaction," the first referring to the psychopath in a strict sense, and the second to patients who disregard social codes and develop within an abnormal social environment, but are still able to display strong personal loyalties. Throughout all these years, Cleckley's (1941) The Mask of Sanity, the fourth edition of which was published in 1964, remains, in my view, the basic text describing what we now call the antisocial personality disorder. DSM-II (American Psychiatric Association, 1968), in an effort to circumscribe the diagnosis of psychopathy to the antisocial personality in a restricted sense, shifted the terminology to "antisocial personality," and proposed a capsule definition that, in essence, derived from Henderson's (1939) and Cleckley's (1941) work:

This term is reserved for individuals who are basically unsocialized and whose behavior pattern brings them repeatedly into conflict with society. They are incapable of significant loyalty to individuals, groups or social values. They are grossly selfish, callous, irresponsible, impulsive and unable to feel guilt or to learn from experience and punishment. Frustration tolerance is low. They tend to blame others or offer plausible rationalizations for their behavior. A mere history of repeated legal or social offenses is not sufficient to justify this diagnosis.

From a clinical viewpoint, this is a brief but remarkably relevant and meaningful definition. It also contains references to the narcissistic personality features of these patients. DSM-III (American Psychiatric Association, 1980) maintained the same term—antisocial personality—adding the characteristic label "disorder" at the end, but shifted its approach to the broader, criminal-behavior–oriented focus. The epidemiological research carried out by O'Neal et al. (1962), Guze (1964a, b), and particularly Robins (1966) was the crucial determinant of this approach.

In my view, psychoanalysis has contributed to both confusing the diagnostic issues and to clarifying the structural characteristics of the antisocial personality. Alexander and Healy (1943), in this country, developed the concept of the "neurotic character" to refer to severe character pathology, including here character pathology with antisocial features, thereby implicitly blurring the distinction between the antisocial personality disorder proper and the other personality disorders. Eissler (1950), in applying the term "alloplastic defenses" in contrast to "autoplastic defenses," also contributed to a homogenized approach to character pathology that blurred the differential diagnosis of the antisocial personality. The overemphasis in the psychoanalytic literature of the 1940s and 1950s on Freud's (1916) description of "criminals from (an unconscious) sense of guilt" interpreted antisocial behavior (naively, I think, from the viewpoint of contemporary psychoanalytic thinking) as a reaction formation against unconscious guilt rather than an expression of severe deficits in the development of the normal superego.

It was only with Johnson (1949) and Johnson and Szurek's (1952) description of "superego lacunae" that psychoanalytic thinking began to focus on the structural—rather than the dynamic—aspects of antisocial personalities. Their relatively simple formulation was rapidly overtaken by the more sophisticated description of severe superego pathology linked to the narcissistic personality by Rosenfeld (1964) and Jacobson (1964, 1971), whose work has influenced my own views on the origins and nature of superego pathology in narcissistic personalities, and the relation of this pathology to the antisocial personality proper (Kernberg, 1984, 1986).

Rutter and Giller's (1983) book *Juvenile Delinquency: Trends and Perspectives* reviews comprehensively the epidemiological studies dealing with the relationship between juvenile delinquent behavior and abnormal personality functioning, reevaluating in the process our present knowledge regarding the etiology of these conditions. From the viewpoint of the ongoing debate regarding biological, psychological, and sociological factors influencing the development of antisocial behavior, they point to the evidence of a clear relation between specific constellations of early childhood development in the family and the individual's later degree of social compliance, but state that the mechanisms by which the familiar factors are associated with delinquency are still unclear. They also point to a relation between social change and increase in delinquency, again stressing our current lack of available knowledge regarding the corresponding mechanisms. They conclude that multiple causes appear to be active in codetermining juvenile delinquency, including peer group influence, social control and social learning, biological factors influencing extreme types of antisocial behavior, and situational factors. They propose that it is absurd to look for a single explanation for juvenile delinquency and emphasize that no clear strategy of prevention is yet available.

Lewis et al.'s (1985) study of childhood antecedents of children who later commit murder pointed to the prevalence, in these cases, of psychotic symptoms, major neurological impairment, psychotic first degree relatives, violent acts witnessed during childhood, and severe physical abuse, thus strongly highlighting biological and psychosocial antecedents to antisocial behavior.

Dicks's (1972) book *Licensed Mass Murder* reports the investigation of the background and personality development of a series of SS mass murderers before and after their concentration camp functions. It provides dramatic evidence that these criminals, while suffering from severe personality disorders with a predominance of narcissistic, paranoid, and antisocial features from early childhood on, only engaged in the most repugnant criminal behavior in the context of the social facilitation of the SS training and death camps, reverting to their previous, nondelinquent personality functioning during and after their prison terms, thus illustrating what amounts to an almost empirical study of social facilitators of severe and chronic criminality (obviously, the "burn-out" tendencies of middle aged delinquents also need to be taken into consideration here).

A PROPOSED DIAGNOSTIC FRAME

Antisocial behavior should ideally be defined in terms of its psychological meanings rather than in behavioral and/or legal terms. For example, "ran away from home overnight at least twice while living in parental or parental surrogate home (or once without returning)"—one of the criteria for antisocial personality disorder in DSM-III-R—is a descriptive term that omits considering whether a child is running away from an impossible home with physically abusive parents or from a well-constituted home. Again, "has never sustained a totally monogamous relationship for more than one year"—another DSM-III-R criterion—includes a vast spectrum of late adolescents and early adults, whose dating behavior may be influenced by multiple neurotic inhibitions, culturally determined patterns, and practically any of the personality disorders.

Sexual promiscuity has different implications within different social environments and within the context of different personality structures (masochistic versus narcissistic) (Kernberg, 1988). The presence of obviously marked and chronic delinquent behavior may overshadow such subtleties, but, by the same token, shifts the diagnostic focus to delinquency per se rather than to the specificity of a personality disorder.

I have found that, regardless of the degree of delinquent behavior or even its absence, from a clinical perspective the first indication of the possibility of the existence of an antisocial personality disorder is the presence of a narcissistic personality disorder. In fact, the clinical profile of the antisocial personality described by Cleckley (1941) falls naturally into three categories: first, some basic characteristics that differentiate the antisocial personality from psychosis and organic brain syndromes—"absence of delusions and other signs of irrational thinking" and "inadequately motivated antisocial behavior" (the dominant immediate symptom); second, a series of characteristics found in severe narcissistic character pathology: "sex life impersonal, trivial, and poorly integrated," "unresponsiveness in general interpersonal relations," "general poverty in major affective reactions," "pathological egocentricity and incapacity for love"; third, what amounts to manifestations of severe superego pathology: "unreliability," "untruthfulness and insincerity," "lack of remorse or shame," "poor judgment and failure to learn by experience," and "failure to follow any life plan."

Only four of Cleckley's clinical profile listings, namely, "absence of 'nervousness' or psychoneurotic manifestations," "fantastic and uninviting behavior with drink and sometimes without," "suicide rarely carried out," and "superficial charm and good intelligence" are, in my view, questionable. There are many antisocial personalities who do present psychoneurotic symptoms, and impulsive suicide can be observed in these patients (as well as in patients with the syndrome of malignant narcissism, to which I shall return); and inappropriate behavior with drink and sometimes without seems to me rather nonspecific. Many patients with antisocial personality disorder, particularly those within the criminal population, do not show superficial charm, and one finds antisocial personality disorders at all levels of intelligence.

But antisocial behavior linked with a narcissistic personality disorder is not enough to make the diagnosis of an antisocial personality disorder. As I mentioned before, there exists an intermediary group between the narcissistic personality disorder and the antisocial personality disorder, the syndrome of malignant narcissism, characterized by the presence of antisocial behavior in a narcissistic personality structure, while the patient still presents a capacity for non–self-serving investment in others, for authentic concern for others and for himself, for experiencing authentic guilt feelings, and for identification with non–self-serving value systems in some areas while such capacity is lost in others.

Antisocial behavior may emerge in the context of other personality disorders, so that the practically much neglected differential diagnosis among personality disorders becomes highly relevant in evaluating this symptom. This differential diagnosis, in my experience, has fundamental prognostic and therapeutic importance. Antisocial behavior in a non-narcissistic personality structure is prognostically favorable, in contrast to the extremely poor prognosis of antisocial behavior in the antisocial personality proper.

Antisocial behavior also may be a consequence of a normal or pathological adaptation to a highly pathological social environment, such as the "culture of the gang," and while this is a clinically infrequent condition, the "dyssocial reaction" of DSM-I was a useful reminder of this group of patients. By the same token, sometimes antisocial behavior may be the equivalent of a neurotic symptom: for example, neurotic adolescent rebelliousness may take the form of occasional antisocial behavior.

Antisocial behavior should be explored in the light of a patient's general level of organization of superego functions. Here we may reexamine the question of the "criminal out of an unconscious sense of guilt." Antisocial behavior that derives from an unconscious sense of guilt and a corresponding unconscious search for punishment has to be differentiated from the vast majority of cases in which self-destructiveness and self-provoked punishment are a consequence of the antisocial behavior but do not reflect such an unconscious motivation. In fact, the psychoanalytic hypothesis of an unconscious sense of guilt can be demonstrated as valid only if it becomes conscious as a result of psychoanalytic exploration. This is definitely not the case in intensive, long-term efforts of psychoanalytic psychotherapy with most patients presenting severe antisocial behavior. In addition, on purely theoretical grounds, given all the other evidence of severe deterioration or unavailability of basic superego functions in the large majority of patients with antisocial behavior, the assumption of an unconscious sense of guilt in these cases is highly questionable.

In clinical practice, there are patients with neurotic personality organization (in contrast to borderline personality organization), or, in simple terms, with "high level" personality disorders (hysterical, obsessive-compulsive, and depressive-masochistic personalities) (Kernberg, 1984) who may present antisocial behavior unconsciously geared to self-punishment or to obtaining punishment from external sources. The type of the dominant personality disorder points to this rather infrequent etiology.

In this connection, a relatively infrequent symptom, namely, *pseudologia fantastica*, should also be explored in the light of the personality disorder within which it emerges. Pseudologia fantastica may be found with hysteroid, histrionic, or infantile personalities, prognostically is less severe than both chronic lying and pseudologia fantastica in narcissistic and antisocial personality disorders. Once again, pinpointing the dominant character pathology emerges as a crucial issue in the differential diagnosis of antisocial behavior.

One issue that very frequently complicates the differential diagnosis of antisocial behavior is the presence of alcoholism and/or drug abuse, and of symptoms secondary to these disorders. Another related and often complexly interwoven psychopathology is that of antisocial behavior and a well-structured perversion or sexual deviation, "paraphilia" in DSM-III (American Psychiatric Association, 1980) and DSM-III-R (American Psychiatric Association, 1987) terminology. For practical purposes, here the main issue is the extent to which ego-syntonic aggression is built into the deviant sexual pattern: the more the personality structure shifts from the narcissistic into the antisocial, the more such aggressive behavior may become life threatening, and a subgroup of aggressive antisocial personalities may center their criminal behavior on sexual assaults and murder (Kernberg, 1985, 1986).*

CLASSIFICATION AND DIFFERENTIAL DIAGNOSIS

What follows is a classification of personality disorders in which antisocial features are prominent, from the most severe to the least severe

*Editor's Note: See R. Stoller (1975). *Perversion: The Erotic Form of Hatred.* Washington, DC: American Psychiatric Press; and J. R. Meloy (2000). The nature and dynamics of sexual homicide: An integrative review. *Aggression and Violent Behavior,* 5:1–22.

of these disorders. For practical purposes, in all patients presenting antisocial behavior, it is helpful to first rule out the diagnosis of an antisocial personality proper. For this reason, I also investigate systematically the potential presence of antisocial behavior in all patients with narcissistic personality disorder.

The Antisocial Personality Disorder

These patients typically present a narcissistic personality disorder. The typical symptoms of the narcissistic personalities are, in the area of *pathological self-love:* excessive self-reference and self-centeredness; grandiosity and the derived characteristics of exhibitionism, an attitude of superiority, recklessness, and overambitiousness; overdependency on admiration; emotional shallowness; and severe bouts of insecurity alternating with a predominant grandiosity. Regarding the area of *pathological object relations,* these patients' predominant symptoms are inordinate envy (both conscious and unconscious); devaluation of others as a defense against envy; exploitativeness reflected in greediness, appropriation of others' ideas or property, and entitlement; an incapacity to truly depend on others in a mutual relationship; and a remarkable lack of the capacity for empathy with and commitment to others. The *basic ego state* of these patients is characterized by a chronic sense of emptiness, evidence of an incapacity to learn, a sense of aloneness, stimulus hunger, and a diffuse sense of meaninglessness of life.

In addition, all of these patients present some degree of *superego pathology.* Ordinary superego pathology of narcissistic personalities includes the incapacity to experience mournful, self-reflective sadness; the presence of severe mood swings; a predominance of "shame" as contrasted to "guilt" in their intrapsychic regulation of social behavior; and a lack of an integrated adult value system, reflected in the persistence of childlike values. Their self-esteem depends on physical beauty, power, wealth, and admiration from others, in contrast to such adult values as personal capabilities, achievements, responsibility, and relation to ideals.

The antisocial personality disorder proper presents more severe superego pathology. The antisocial behaviors that these patients present include lying, stealing, breaking in, forgeries, swindling, and prostitution—all in a predominantly "passive-parasitic" type—while assault, murder, and armed robbery are typical of the aggressive type (Henderson, 1939; Henderson and Gillespie, 1969). In other words, clinically one may differentiate between the behaviorally aggressive, sadistic, and usually also paranoid orientation of some patients with antisocial personality disorder from the passive, exploitative, parasitic type of others.

It needs to be stressed that, with intelligent patients from a favorable socioeconomic and cultural background who present a predominantly passive-parasitic type of antisocial behavior, the childhood antecedents of such behavior may be apparently mild or even go unnoticed, particularly in some highly pathological yet socially adaptive families. For example, one patient was a brilliant student through elementary school, high school, and college, and was socially successful and well-liked as a young man. His occasional stealing was generously forgiven by his parents, and his lack of a sense of responsibility was adjudicated to his having been spoiled and overprotected by an admiring mother and grandparents. He was able to obtain a postgraduate degree, he married a woman with whom he kept an apparently normal marital relationship for over 15 years, and he was kind to his children. At the same time, he was embezzling funds from associates and from his family business. While running up inordinate debts, he also gave expensive gifts to friends and associates, appeared to be a year-round "Santa Claus," and was brought to consult by his family only when he was threatened by a potential jail sentence because of tax evasion.

The crucial differentiation of both passive and aggressive antisocial behavior as part of a narcissistic personality disorder from an antisocial personality disorder proper depends on the absence, in the latter, of a capacity for authentic guilt feelings and remorse. Thus, even after being confronted with the consequences of their antisocial behaviors and in spite of their profuse protestations of guilt or regret, there is no change in their behavior toward those they had attacked or exploited, nor any spontaneous concern over this lack of change in their behavior. The absence of guilt is central in this disorder. While the differential diagnosis of the capacity for experiencing guilt and concern requires the inferential step of evaluating a patient's reaction to confrontation and the breakdown of his omnipotence, other characteristics reflecting this incapacity for guilt and concern may become directly evident in the interviews.

For example, the patient with an antisocial personality disorder is unable to imagine an ethical dimension in others and therefore in the diagnostician's mind. After reiterating his truthfulness to the therapist, and after subsequently being caught in lying to him, he may react sheepishly but is not able, when asked, to empathize with the therapist's reaction to him except with a sense that the therapist must feel fooled and angry with the patient. Or an antisocial patient may "confess" his actions but only in those areas where he has been caught, thus entering into a flagrant contradiction with simultaneously professed remorsefulness over his past behavior.

The lack of investment in nonexploitative relations with others may be reflected in transient, superficial, indifferent relations with others, lack of capacity to emotionally invest in people as well as in pets, and the absence of any internalized moral value, let alone the capacity to empathize with such values in others. The deterioration of these patients' affective experience is expressed in their intolerance of any increase in anxiety without developing additional symptoms or pathological behaviors, their incapacity for depression with reflective mourning or sadness, and their incapacity for falling in love or experiencing any tenderness in their sexual relations.

The lack of a sense of the passage of time, of planning for the future, and of contrasting present experience and behavior with aspired ideal ones are usually striking in these patients, so that planning extends only to an immediate improvement of present discomforts and to a reduction of tension by the achievement of immediately desired goals. Their failure to learn from past experience is an expression of the same incapacity to conceive of their life beyond a short, immediate time span. Their manipulativeness, pathological lying, and flimsy rationalizations are well known. Paulina Kernberg (personal communication) has coined the term *holographic man* to refer to patients who create a vague, ethereal image of themselves in the diagnostic sessions that seems strangely disconnected from their present reality or their actual past, an image that changes from moment to moment in the light of different angles of inquiry, and leaves the diagnostician with a disturbing sense of unreality.

Again, once the diagnosis of a narcissistic personality structure is obvious, the crucial diagnostic task is to evaluate the severity of any presenting antisocial features, their past history and childhood origins, and then the patient's remaining capacity for object relations and superego functioning. The practically total absence of a capacity for non-exploitative object relations and of any moral dimension in personality functioning, reflected in the clinical characteristics mentioned before, are the key elements in the differentiation of the antisocial personality proper from the less severe syndromes of malignant narcissism and the narcissistic personality disorder. This diagnosis may be arrived at by taking a complete history, exploring carefully the patient's narrative, tactfully confronting the patient with contradictory and obscure areas in this narrative, evaluating the patient's interaction with the diagnostician, and exploring his reactions to being confronted with contradictions between objective information from the patient's past, his present narrative, and his behavior.

The exploration of the patient's reactions to inquiry about potential antisocial behavior that might follow from what he has said but has not acknowledged may be very helpful. For example, to raise a question with a patient whose history would show a natural tendency to engage in prostitution: "What prevented you from engaging in prostitution?," or, similarly, with a patient involved with drugs, "Why would you not be dealing?" may test the patient's superego functions as well as his honesty in relating to the therapist. Obviously, patients who are lying to the therapist without acknowledging that they are lying (many antisocial personalities may acknowledge to the therapist that they are lying to him but continue doing so after such an acknowledgment)ʹ require that we take history from the relatives, sophisticated social work interventions, and reports from institutional settings with which the patient has been involved in the past.

The reasons for consulting a psychiatrist, the manipulative efforts involved in obtaining a "certificate of health" or a certificate for "reinstatement in school," and, in many cases, the more or less obvious efforts to avoid facing legal procedures by means of psychiatric interventions may serve diagnostic as well as prognostic purposes. Usually the investigation into all these factors requires several interviews, returning again and again to areas of uncertainty and confusion, and repeated evaluation of the patient's reaction to confrontation with whatever deceptive maneuvers or contradictions he presents.

The countertransference to patients with severe antisocial behavior may provide what might be called a second line of information: the therapist may react with a sense of confusion, the temptation to either accept uncritically the patient's statements or to reject them with a paranoid stance in the countertransference, a protective "pseudoneutrality" that conceals an underlying devaluation of the patient, or the wish to escape from an intolerable relationship with a patient who implicitly attacks the most basic values of human relations so dear to the therapist. In my view, a therapist's oscillation between moments of a paranoid stance and others of concern, in other words, a true ambivalence in his reaction to these patients, constitutes a healthy response. It is helpful for the therapist to be able to present himself as moral but not moralizing, as fair but not naive, and as confronting but not aggressive. Confrontation as a technical device implies the tactful bringing together of contradictory or confusing aspects of the patient's narrative, behavior, and/or past; it is not an aggressive display of criticism or disagreement with the patient.

Usually, a major affective disorder may be ruled out by careful history-taking and mental status examinations, but psychological tests may provide additional help in ruling out an organic mental disorder, such as temporal lobe epilepsy or a limbic lobe syndrome, disorders that may present with explosive aggressive behavior. They may also help to rule out an atypical schizophrenic disorder, such as "pseudopsychopathic schizophrenia." When antisocial behavior develops in middle or late adulthood in the context of a loss of memory and higher abstract reasoning, many chronic organic mental disorders may have to be ruled out, and in addition to psychological testing, may require neurological, EEG, and radiological studies.

If an antisocial personality proper can be ruled out, the next diagnostic category to be considered is that of a narcissistic personality disorder with the syndrome of malignant narcissism, or an ordinary narcissistic personality with predominantly passive-parasitic antisocial trends.

Malignant Narcissism

As mentioned before, these patients are characterized by a typical narcissistic personality disorder, antisocial behavior, ego-syntonic sadism or characterologically anchored aggression, and a paranoid orientation. In contrast to the antisocial personality proper, patients with malignant narcissism still have the capacity for loyalty to and concern for others or for feeling guilty; they are able to conceive of other people as having moral concerns and convictions; and they may have a realistic attitude toward their own past and in planning for the future.

Their ego-syntonic sadism may be expressed in a conscious "ideology" of aggressive self-affirmation but also, quite frequently, in chronic ego-syntonic suicidal tendencies. These suicidal tendencies do not emerge as part of a depressive syndrome, but rather in emotional crises or even "out of the blue," with the underlying fantasy that to be able to take one's life reflects superiority and a triumph over the usual fear of pain and death. To commit suicide, in these patients' fantasy, is to exercise sadistic control over others or to "walk out" of a world they feel they cannot control.*

The paranoid orientation of these patients (which psychodynamically reflects the projection onto others of unintegrated sadistic superego

---

Editor's Note: I have described this phenomenon as an acute dysphoric plunge in which suicide represents a final, rageful act of omnipotent control. The life and death of Andrew Cunanan, the killer of Gianni Versace, captured this psychopathic attitude (see M. Orth [2000]. *Vulgar Favors.* New York: Dell).

precursors) is manifest in an exaggerated experience of others as idols, enemies, or fools. These patients have a propensity for regressing into paranoid micropsychotic episodes in the course of intensive psychotherapy, and illustrate most dramatically the complementary functions of paranoid and antisocial interactions in the interpersonal realm (Jacobson, 1971; Kernberg, 1984). Some of these patients may present what, from the outside appears as frankly antisocial behavior, for example, as leaders of sadistic gangs or terrorist groups: an idealized self-image and an ego-syntonic sadistic, self-serving ideology rationalizes the antisocial behavior, and may co-exist with the capacity of loyalty to their own comrades.

Narcissistic Personality Disorders with Antisocial Behavior

These patients present a variety of antisocial behaviors, mostly of the passive-parasitic type, and show remnants of autonomous moral behavior in some areas and ruthless exploitativeness in others. They do not evince the ego-syntonic sadism or self-directed aggression or an overt paranoid orientation typical of the syndrome of malignant narcissism. They have a capacity for experiencing guilt and concern, loyalty to others, an appropriate perception of their past, and they may realistically conceive of and plan for the future; in some cases, what appears from the outside as antisocial behavior is simply a manifestation of lack of capacity for commitment in depth to long-range relationships. Narcissistic types of sexual promiscuity, irresponsibility in work, and emotional or financial exploitation of relatives are prevalent here, while these patients are still able to care for others in some areas and to maintain ordinary social boundaries of honesty in more distant interpersonal interactions.

Other Severe Personality Disorders with Antisocial Features

The next level of pathology, with less negative prognostic and therapeutic implications, is the presence of antisocial behavior in personality disorders other than the narcissistic personality. In terms of the classification of personality disorders that I have proposed in the past (Kernberg, 1975, 1984), these are patients with borderline personality organization and nonpathological narcissism. Typical examples are the infantile, histrionic, hysteroid, or Zetzel type III and IV personality disorder (not to be confused with a hysterical personality proper)

(Kernberg, 1986), and the paranoid personality disorder: these are the two most frequent personality disorders of this group that present with antisocial behavior. In the infantile personality, pseudologia fantastica is not infrequent; the "paranoid urge to betray" described by Jacobson (1971) illustrates treacherousness in a paranoid context. In my experience, most patients with factitious disorder with psychological and/or physical symptoms, pathological gambling, kleptomania, pyromania, and malingering, if they do not present a typical narcissistic personality disorder, form part of this group of personality disorders with antisocial features.

Neurotic Personality Disorders with Antisocial Features

Here we find the criminals from (an unconscious) sense of guilt (Freud, 1916). These patients are of great clinical interest because, in spite of what sometimes appears as dramatic antisocial behavior, this behavior occurs in the context of a neurotic personality organization and has an excellent prognosis for psychotherapeutic and psychoanalytic treatment.* As a typical example, I saw a research scientist who compulsively falsified experimental data, only to recheck them again and again until the experiments with the correct results would neutralize and eliminate the findings of the experiments he had tampered with. This dangerous, seemingly purposeless, self-defeating behavior, which gravely threatened his research career, was fully resolved in a four-year psychoanalytic treatment that at the same time also resolved a severe depressive-masochistic personality disorder. The patient presented no antisocial behavior outside the specific pattern I mentioned, and he had a history of pseudologia fantastica in his childhood.

Another patient with an obsessive-compulsive personality disorder would steal minor objects in public places within the organization where he worked, exposing himself to embarrassing and humiliating experiences of being caught and threatened with immediate dismissal. Fortunately, a sophisticated psychiatric evaluation by a colleague provided the information that protected this patient's future while treatment was initiated. While such cases are relatively rare, the enormous difference in their prognosis from that of the groups previously mentioned warrants a careful assessment of the personality structure in each case of antisocial behavior.

*Editor's Note: See J. R. Meloy and C. B. Gacono (1994). A neurotic criminal: "I've learned my lesson . . ." *Journal of Personality Assessment*, 63:27–38.

Antisocial Behavior as Part of a Symptomatic Neurosis

This category refers to occasional antisocial behavior as part of adolescent rebelliousness, in adjustment disorders, and/or in the presence, in many cases, of a facilitating social environment that fosters channeling psychic conflicts into antisocial behavior.

Dyssocial Reaction

This clinically relatively infrequent syndrome refers to the normal and/or neurotic adjustment to an abnormal social environment or subgroup. In clinical practice, most of these patients do present some type of personality disorder that facilitates their uncritical adaptation to a social subgroup with antisocial behaviors.

PROGNOSTIC AND THERAPEUTIC CONSIDERATIONS

The treatment of antisocial behavior is essentially psychotherapeutic, except, of course, when it is symptomatic of an organic mental disorder or of a psychotic illness. The levels of severity of antisocial behavior I have described correspond to the prognosis for psychotherapeutic treatment, with the first of these levels, the antisocial personality disorder proper, having the poorest prognosis to the extent that practically all of these patients are not responsive to ordinary psychotherapeutic approaches. The treatment of the antisocial personality disorder in childhood, however, the "conduct disorder" in DSM-III-R (American Psychiatric Association, 1987), has a more favorable prognosis, and encouraging results with treatment of these children in specialized residential settings (Diatkine, 1983) have been reported. "Unsocialized aggressive conduct disorder," however, seems to have the least favorable prognosis. This diagnosis corresponds to what is called "solitary aggressive type" in DSM-III-R.

Regarding adult patients, outpatient psychotherapy with antisocial personality disorders has been very discouraging. I believe that it is too early to conclude whether specialized therapeutic community settings for patients with antisocial personality disorders may be effective in the long run. Extended inpatient treatment in specialized closed hospitals or prison systems would seem to be effective in some cases, particularly if a firm and incorruptible environmental control is combined with the opportunity for group therapy in groups constituted by delinquent patient-prisoners (Kernberg, 1985).

The first task of the psychiatrist evaluating patients with antisocial behavior under ordinary outpatient conditions is to establish carefully the differential diagnosis elaborated before, and then to separate out the prognostically more favorable personality disorders with antisocial behavior from the antisocial personality proper. The second task for the psychiatrist is to protect the immediate social environment of the patient with an antisocial personality disorder from the consequences of his antisocial behavior, help the patient's family protect themselves, and provide tactfully but openly full information and counsel regarding the nature of this psychopathology and its prognosis to the family. The fact that, as many researchers and clinicians have pointed out, the antisocial personality disorder tends to "burn out" in middle and later adult years may provide some long-range hope, or at least some consolation to the family (Glueck and Glueck, 1943).

The psychiatrist's third task is to create realistic conditions for whatever treatment is attempted, eliminating all secondary gains of treatment—treatment used to escape from the law, for example, or for ongoing parasitic dependency on parents or other social support systems. The therapist needs to establish reasonable minimal preconditions that will safeguard any treatment effort from secondary exploitation by the patient.

The prognosis for the treatment of malignant narcissism, while reserved, is significantly better than that of the antisocial personality proper, and, in the course of intensive, long-term, psychoanalytic psychotherapy some of these patients may achieve a gradual transformation of their antisocial behavior and the corresponding manipulative, exploitative behavior in the transference into predominantly paranoid resistances. Such paranoid resistances may even lead to a paranoid transference psychosis, but also, if and when such regression can be contained and managed in the psychotherapy, to further gradual transformation into more ordinary transferences characteristic of severe narcissistic personality disorders. One potential limit to such treatment efforts is presented by patients whose aggressive behavior is potentially threatening to others, including the psychotherapist, so that the possibility of dangerous violence connected with severe paranoid transference reactions should be evaluated before an intensive psychotherapy is undertaken.

The treatment of patients with narcissistic personality and antisocial features may follow the ordinary stages of intensive psychotherapy with this personality disorder. These patients usually have an indication for psychoanalytic psychotherapy rather than psychoanalysis proper, which is also true for the next category, namely, other severe personality disorders with antisocial features. Antisocial behavior as an expression of unconscious guilt, that is, in neurotic personality organization, has an indication for psychoanalytic treatment.

THE PSYCHODYNAMICS OF MALIGNANT NARCISSISM AND OF THE ANTISOCIAL PERSONALITY

In my view, the psychodynamic findings of patients with malignant narcissism (Kernberg, 1984) open the way for a psychoanalytic understanding of the intrapsychic structure and the internal world of object relations of the antisocial personality disorder proper.

The transferences of patients with malignant narcissism reflect the vicissitudes of both faulty early superego formation and the failure to consolidate total object relations in the context of integration of ego identity. In essence, these patients are so dominated by the earliest sadistic superego precursors that the subsequent idealized superego precursors cannot neutralize them, superego integration is blocked, and the more realistic superego introjects of the oedipal period are largely unavailable. These patients convey the impression that their world of object relations has been transformed malignantly, leading to the devaluation and sadistic enslavement of potentially good internalized object relations on the part of an integrated yet cruel, omnipotent, and "mad" self (Rosenfeld, 1971). This pathological grandiose and sadistic self replaces the sadistic precursors of the superego, absorbs all aggression, and transforms what would otherwise be sadistic superego components into an abnormal self-structure, which then militates against the internalization of later, more realistic superego components.

These patients experience external objects as omnipotent and cruel. They feel that loving, mutually gratifying object relations not only can easily be destroyed but contain the seeds for an attack by the omnipotent, cruel object. One way to survive is by total submission. A subsequent route is to identify with the object, which brings to the subject a sense of power, freedom from fear, and the feeling that the only way to relate to others is by gratifying one's aggression. An alternative route to escape is by adopting a false, cynical way of communication and to totally deny the importance of object relations, to become an innocent bystander rather than to identify with the cruel tyrant or to submit masochistically to him.

The limited experiences I have had in attempting a psychodynamic exploration of patients with antisocial personality proper, together with the findings derived from the intensive psychotherapy and psychoanalysis of patients with malignant narcissism, lead me to propose the following tentative considerations regarding the psychodynamics of the antisocial personality proper.

These patients convey past experiences of savage aggression from their parental objects, and frequently report violence both observed and experienced in their early childhood. They also convey a dramatic conviction of the impotent weakness of any good object relation: the good are weak and unreliable by definition, and the patient shows rage, devaluation, and contempt against those vaguely perceived as potentially good objects. The powerful, in contrast, are needed to survive, but are unreliable in turn; and they are invariably sadistic. The pain experienced in having to depend upon powerful, desperately needed but sadistic parental objects is transformed into rage, and expressed as rage mostly projected, thus worsening the sadistic image of powerful bad objects who become towering sadistic tyrants. In this world, which is reminiscent of Orwell's (1977) novel 1984, aggression is prevalent but unpredictable, and this unpredictability precludes even a secure submission to the sadistic tyrant and prevents the patient from idealizing the sadistic value system of the aggressor.

This failure to achieve any idealization of objects differentiates the antisocial personality proper from the "self-righteous" aggression of the patient with malignant narcissism who has at least found some possibility of condensing sadism and idealization by identifying himself with an idealized, cruel tyrant. The failure of this idealization also prevents the antisocial patient from attempting a masochistic submission to a predictable although sadistic authority. The patient is deeply and totally convinced that only his own power itself is reliable, and the pleasure of sadistic control the only alternative to the suffering and destruction of the weak. In such a world, there exists the need (to paraphrase Paul Parin) to "fear thy neighbor as thou fearst thyself" and to devalue all the weakening linkages with them.*

So far, I have focused on dynamics of the predominantly aggressive antisocial personality disorder. The passive-parasitic antisocial personality disorder, in contrast, has found a way out of gratification by means of sadistic power into the denial of the importance of all object relations, and into the regressive idealization of the gratification of receptive-dependent needs—food, objects, money, sex, privileges—and symbolic power exerted over others by extracting such gratifications from them. To extract the supplies needed while ignoring others as persons and protecting oneself from revengeful punishment is the meaning of life. To eat, to defecate, to sleep, to have sex, to feel secure, to take revenge, to feel powerful, to be excited—all without being discovered by the surrounding dangerous though anonymous world—permits an adaptation of sorts to life. This adaptation is the adaptation of the wolf disguised to live among the sheep while the real danger comes from other wolves similarly disguised, against whom a protective "sheepishness" has been erected. This psychological structure permits the denial of aggression and its transformation into ruthless exploitation.

In malignant narcissism, some idealized superego precursors have been drawn into the aggressively infiltrated, pathological grandiose self, facilitating at least a consolidated sense of self, of self-continuity throughout time, and, by means of projection, a sense of stability and predictability of the world of powerful and dangerous others as well. The pathological narcissism, ego-syntonic grandiosity, antisocial behavior, and paranoid alertness of these patients jointly permit them to control their internal world of object relations. At the same time, this same pathological grandiose self protects them from the unbearable conflicts around primitive envy that torment the less pathologically protected narcissistic personality. The antisocial personality proper, in contrast, is protected from rageful envy only by aggressive, violent appropriation or passive-parasitic exploitation of others.

Dicks's (1972) study of SS killers illustrates the facilitation and induction of criminal behavior under particular social circumstances. Zinoviev (1984) has made a study of the moral characteristics of social groups and institutions in totalitarian political regimes whose moral authority images are projected onto the top hierarchy of the system as external "persecutory" figures.* He stresses the generalized social corruption that is a consequence of such a social structure and that may

---

*Editor's Note: Jerold Post's work on malignant narcissism and national leadership is also relevant and instructive. See, for example, J. Post (1993). Current concepts of the narcissistic personality: Implications for political psychology. *Political Psychology*, 14:99–121.

affect the public behavior of large segments of the population. His dramatic descriptions of the general corruption of public life under such circumstances illustrate the dependency of the individual's moral behavior upon the social structure that surrounds him. Milgram's (1963) famous experiments indicate how uncritical obedience to authority may easily bring about guiltless participation in sadistic behavior even at high levels of psychological organization and in an atmosphere of social freedom. The antisocial personality's reality is the normal person's world of nightmares; the normal person's reality is the nightmare of the psychopath.

REFERENCES

Alexander, F. & Healy, W. (1935). *The Roots of Crime*. New York: Knopf.
American Psychiatric Association (1952). *Diagnostic and Statistical Manual of Mental Disorders (DSM-I)*. Washington, DC: Mental Hospitals Service.
American Psychiatric Association (1968). *Diagnostic and Statistical Manual of Mental Disorders (DSM-II)*. Washington, DC: American Psychiatric Association.
American Psychiatric Association (1980). *Diagnostic and Statistical Manual of Mental Disorders (DSM-III)*. Washington, DC: American Psychiatric Association.
American Psychiatric Association (1987). *Diagnostic and Statistical Manual of Mental Disorders, 3rd ed. rev. (DSM-III-R)*. Washington, DC: American Psychiatric Association.
Cleckley, H. (1941). *The Mask of Sanity*. St. Louis, MO: Mosby.
Diatkine, G. (1983). *Les Transformations de la Psychopathie [The Transformations of Psychopathy]*. Paris: Presses Universitaires de France.
Dicks, H. V. (1972). *Licensed Mass Murder: A Socio-Psychological Study of Some SS Killers*. New York: Basic Books.
Eissler, K. R. (1950). Ego-psychological implications of the psychoanalytic treatment of delinquents. *The Psychoanalytic Study of the Child*, 5:97–121. New York: International Universities Press.
Freud, S. (1916). Some character-types met within psychoanalytic work. *Standard Edition*, 14:309–333. London: Hogarth Press, 1957.
Glueck, S. & Glueck, E. (1943). *Criminal Careers in Retrospect*. New York: Commonwealth Fund.
Guze, S. B. (1964a). Conversion symptoms in criminals. *Amer. J. Psychiat.*, 121:580.
Guze, S. B. (1964b). A study of recidivism based upon a follow-up of 217 consecutive criminals. *J. Nerv. Ment. Dis.*, 138:575.

Henderson, D. K. (1939). *Psychopathic States*. London: Chapman & Hall.

Henderson, D. K. & Gillespie, R. D. (1969). *Henderson and Gillespie's Textbook of Psychiatry: For Students and Practitioners*, 10th ed., revised by Batchelor ERC. London: Oxford University Press.

Jacobson, E. (1964). *The Self and the Object World*. New York: International Universities Press.

Jacobson, E. (1971). *Depression*. New York: International Universities Press.

Johnson, A. M. (1949). Sanctions for superego lacunae of adolescents. In: *Searchlights on Delinquency*, ed. K. R. Eissler. New York: International Universities Press, pp 225–245.

Johnson, A. M. & Szurek, S. A. (1952). The genesis of antisocial acting out in children and adults. *Psychoanal. Quart.*, 21:323.

Kernberg, O. F. (1975). *Borderline Conditions and Pathological Narcissism*. New York: Aronson.

Kernberg, O. F. (1984). *Severe Personality Disorders: Psychotherapeutic Strategies*. New Haven, CT: Yale University Press.

Kernberg, O. F. (1985). The relation of borderline personality organization to the perversions. In: *Psychiatrie et Psychanalyse: Jalons pour une fécondation réciproque*. Quebec: Gaetan Morin Editeur, pp. 99–116.

Kernberg, O. F. (1986). A conceptual model for male perversion. In: *The Psychology of Men: New Psychoanalytic Perspectives*, ed. G. I. Fogel, F. M. Lane & R. S. Liebert. New York: Basic Books, pp. 152–180.

Kernberg, O. F. (1986). Hysterical and histrionic personality disorders. In: *Psychiatry 1*. New York: Basic Books, pp. 1–11.

Kernberg, O. F. (1988). Clinical dimensions of masochism. *J. Amer. Psychoanal. Assn.*, 36:597–625.

Lewis, D. et al. (1985). Biopsychosocial characteristics of children who later murder: A prospective study. *Amer. J. Psychiat.*, 142:1161–1167.

Milgram, S. (1963). Behavioral study of obedience. *J. Abn. & Soc. Psychol.*, 67:371–378.

Millon, T. (1981). *Disorders of Personality: DSM III: Axis II*. New York: Wiley.

O'Neal, P. et al. (1962). Parental deviance and the genesis of sociopathic personality. *Amer. J. Psychiat.*, 118:1114.

Orwell, G. (1977). *1984*. New York: Harcourt Brace Jovanovich.

Reid, W. H., ed. (1981). *The Treatment of Antisocial Syndromes*. New York: Van Nostrand Reinhold.

Robins, L. N. (1966). *Deviant Children Grown Up: A Sociological and Psychiatric Study of Sociopathic Personality*. Baltimore, MD: Williams & Wilkins.

Rosenfeld, H. (1964). On the psychopathology of narcissism: A clinical approach. *Internat. J. Psycho-Anal.*, 45:332–337.

Rosenfeld, H. (1971). A clinical approach to the psychoanalytic theory of the life and death instincts: An investigation into the aggressive aspects of narcissism. *Internat. J. Psycho-Anal.*, 52:169–178.

Rutter, M. & Giller, H. (1983) *Juvenile Delinquency: Trends and Perspectives.* New York: Penguin Books.

Stone, A. A. (1984). Psychiatry and the Supreme Court. In: *Law, Psychiatry, and Morality: Essays and Analysis.* Washington, DC: American Psychiatric Press, 5:99–131.

Zinoviev, A. (1984). *The Reality of Communism.* New York: Schocken Books.

Index

Abraham, K., 115, *131*, 240, 252, *261*
Acklin, M., 17, *22*
acting out, 229, 272–273
    psychoanalytic technique and, 100
    types of, 272
    unwittingly encouraged by therapist, 99–100
Adatto, C. P., *261*
addiction, 210
Adler, G., 299, 304, 305, 308, *311–312*
adoption, 26–29
    case material, 26–28
affect block, 271
affect hunger, 26–29
    prognosis of children with, 29–30
    psychodynamics, 32
    treatment of children with extreme, 30–31
    types of response to, 33–34
affectionless characters, 35–41
affectionless psychopathy, 4
affective factor of psychopathy, 199
affects, 16–19
aggression. *See also specific topics*
    infantile, 57, 60
    object seeking and, 139
aggression responses on Rorschach, 200
aggressive courage, 207. *See also* risk taking
aggressive impulses, 35–37
    absence of ego-dystonic, 200
aggressive modes of narcissistic repair, 192–193
aggressive narcissism, 8, 199
aggressiveness, 163
aggressor, identification with, 10–11, 193, 200
Aichhorn, A., 49n, 79, 85, *90*, 92, 97, 103, 104, 109, *112*, 115, *131*, 265, *280*
Ainsworth, M. D. S., 3, 4, *19*
alcoholism, 210
Alexander, F., xi, *xi*, 92, 99, *112*, *113*, 156, 159, *166*, *169*, 227, *237*, 318, *335*
Allen, J., 5, *19*
Allen, R. P., 276, *280*

anal-expulsive themes, 194
anal-passive stage, defense against regression to, 209
anger, in treatment, 270–271
animals, cruelty to, 16
antisocial behavior
    aggressive vs. passive-parasitic, 191, 197, 317, 323–324. *See also under* psychopaths, types of
    as Factor II of PCL–R, 199
    as part of symptomatic neurosis, 330
    vs. psychopathy, 8, 316–317
antisocial character formation, 80
antisocial personality disorder, 323–327
    psychodynamics, 333–335
    sociodemographics, 196–197
antisocial tendency, 133
    case material, 133–135
    nature of, 135–137
    treatment of, 143
antisocial types. *See also* psychopaths, types of
    Kernberg's range of, 190–191
anxiety, 57
    absence of, 7–8, 200
    drug therapy for, 276
    inability to tolerate, 229
    paranoid *vs.* depressive response to, 194
    persecutory, 229–230, 233
    in therapist, 300
anxiety disorders, 8
anxious avoidant attachment, 4
Arnow, D., 189n, *203*
arousal, 5–7
as-if personalities, 126, 130
as-if qualities, 59, 75, 255. *See also* imposters
assessment. *See* diagnosis; testing and assessment
attachment, 3–5, 7, 241, 256
    to animate *vs.* inanimate objects, 206n
    aversion to, 163
    capacity for, 185
    defined, 4
    dismissing, 4–5

denial
of patient's dangerousness, 173, 206
and self-deception, 186
as diagnostic tool, 326
early, 272
fear
of assault or harm, 185–186, 302–304
of being deceived, 105
feeling controlled, 10, 184
feelings of invalidity and loss of identity, 305–306
hatred, 307
loss of professional identity, 186
countertransference problems, solutions to, 309–311
courage, aggressive, 207
Covi, L., 276, *280*
craving personality, 245, 248–250, 255, 257, 259
creativity, 158
criminality
age and, 277
psychopathy and, 165–166
"pure," 156n, 157, 160
Cunanan, Andrew, 327

dangerousness, 288, 302–304
denial of patient's, 173, 306
signs of, 173
Davis, R., 199, *204*
death, fear of, 287
deception, 173–174, 246, 254, 326. *See also* manipulation
of therapist, 105, 108
deceptive practices, 184
defenses, 17–18, 230–232
mature/neurotic *vs.* primitive, 17
Rorschach analysis of, 189n
Deiter, J., 152, *153*
delinquency
constitutional *vs.* environmental factors in, 90
latent, 79–80, 82, 89
Demera, Ferdinand, 123–125
denial, in therapist, 173, 186, 306
deniers, self-destructive, 310
dependency, 245
fear and avoidance of, 221–222, 230
lack of capacity for, 245

"dependent clingers," 310
dependent transference, 218, 220–222
depression and depressive feelings, 194, 290, 299. *See also* sulking
defenses against, 230, 235
experienced in treatment, 267–268, 275, 276
depressive position, 137, 234
deprivation in childhood, emotional, 65, 136–137, 142
Derrick O'C., case of, 39–40
detachment, 4, 173
Deutsch, H., 58, *60*, 74, *77*, 125, 126, *131*, 227, *237*
devaluation, 12, 172–173, 186, 190, 194, 230, 293
developmental markers of psychopathy, 8
devouring. *See* incorporation
Dewan, M., 304, *312*
diagnosis, 188, 320. *See also* testing and assessment
differential, of personality disorders with antisocial features, 318, 320–330
Diagnostic and Statistical Manual of Mental Disorders (DSM), 195–198, 316–318, 316n
diagnostic frame, proposed, 319–322
Diatkine, G., 330, *335*
Dicks, H. V., 319, 334, *335*
Dien, J., 7, *20*
Dietz, P., 15, 20, 176, *178*
dismissing attachment, 4–5
dominance–submission, 10, 12, 173, 185, 191, 193, 332
drive theory, 240–241
drives, 138–139, 244
drug addiction, 210
drug intoxication, 57n
drug therapy, 275–277
DSM (Diagnostic and Statistical Manual of Mental Disorders), 195–198, 316–318, 316n
Dufree, H., 66, *77*
Dunn, W. H., 59, *60*
Dutton, D., 193, *203*
dyssocial reaction, 330

Eddy, S., 303, *313*
educational phase of therapy, preparatory, 103
ego, nonego *vs.* true, 128

Permissions

Chapter 2

David Levy (1937). Primary affect hunger. *American Journal of Psychiatry,* 94:643–652. © 1937, the American Psychiatric Association. Reprinted by permission.

Chapter 3

John Bowlby (1944). Forty-four juvenile thieves: Their characters and home-life. *International Journal of Psychoanalysis,* 25:121–124. Reprinted by permission. © Institute of Psychoanalysis and Juliet Hopkins, Literary Executor to Dr. John Bowlby.

Chapter 4

Phyllis Greenacre (1945). Conscience in the psychopath. *American Journal of Orthopsychiatry,* 15:495–509. © 1945 by the American Orthopsychiatric Association, Inc. Reprinted by permission.

Chapter 5

Lauretta Bender (1947). Psychopathic behavior disorders in children. In R. Lindner and R. Seliger (eds.), *Handbook of Correctional Psychology.* New York: Philosophical Library, pp. 360–377. Reprinted by permission of Peter Schilder, M.D., Ph.D.

Chapter 6

Kate Friedlander (1949). Latent delinquency and ego development. In K. Eissler (ed.), *Searchlights on Delinquency,* pp. 205–215. Reprinted by permission of International Universities Press.

Chapter 7

Adelaide M. Johnson (1949). Sanctions for superego lacunae of adolescents. In K. Eissler (ed.), *Searchlights on Delinquency,* pp. 225–245. Reprinted by permission of International Universities Press.

Chapter 8

Helene Deutsch (1955). The impostor: Contribution to ego psychology of a type of psychopath. *Psychoanalytic Quarterly,* 24:483–505. Reprinted by permission of Martin Deutsch, Executor of the Helene Deutsch estate.

Chapter 9

Donald Winnicott (1956). The antisocial tendency. *Through Pediatrics to Psychoanalysis.* London: Hogarth Press, pp. 120–131. Reprinted by permission of Basic Books, a member of Perseus Books.

Chapter 10

Milton H. Miller (1964). Time and the character disorder. *Journal of Nervous and Mental Disease,* 138:535–540. Reprint permission granted by Lippincott, Williams and Wilkins, and Milton Miller, M.D.

Chapter 11

Seymour Halleck (1966). Psychopathy, freedom and criminal behavior. *Bulletin of the Menninger Clinic,* 30:127–140. Reprint permission by The Guilford Press.

Chapter 12

J. Reid Meloy (1997). Psychology of wickedness: Psychopathy and sadism. *Psychiatric Annals,* 27:630–633. Reprint permission granted by SLACK, Inc.

Chapter 14

Wilhelm Reich (1933). The phallic-narcissistic character from "Some Circumscribed Character Forms" from *Character Analysis* by Wilhelm Reich, translated by Vincent R. Carfagno. © 1945, 1949, 1972 by The Wilhelm Reich Infant Trust. Reprinted by permission of Farrar, Straus and Giroux.

Chapter 15

August Aichhorn (1964). The narcissistic transference of the "juvenile impostor." In O. Fleischmann, P. Kramer & H. Ross (eds.), *Delinquency and Child Guidance: Selected Papers by August Aichhorn,* pp. 174–191. Reprint permission granted by International Universities Press.

Chapter 16

Betty Joseph (1960). Some characteristics of the psychopathic personality. *International Journal of Psychoanalysis*, 41:526–531. Reprinted by permission © Institute of Psychoanalysis.

Chapter 17

Ben Bursten (1973). Some narcissistic personality types. *International Journal of Psychoanalysis*, 54:287–300. Reprinted by permission © Institute of Psychoanalysis.

Chapter 18

John R. Lion (1978). Outpatient treatment of psychopaths. In W. H. Reid (ed.), *The Psychopath: A Comprehensive Study of Antisocial Disorders and Behaviors*. New York: Brunner/Mazel, pp. 286–300. Reprinted by permission of John Lion, M.D. Reproduced by permission of Routledge, Inc., part of The Taylor & Francis Group.

Chapter 19

Neville Symington (1980). The response aroused by the psychopath. *International Review of Psychoanalysis*, 7:291–298. Reprinted by permission © Institute of Psychoanalysis.

Chapter 20

Larry H. Strasburger (1986). The treatment of antisocial syndromes: The therapist's feelings. In W. H. Reid, D. Dorr, J. Walker & J. Bonner III (eds.), *Unmasking the Psychopath: Antisocial Personality and Related Syndromes*. © 1986 by William H. Reid, Darwin Dorr, John I. Walker, and Jack W. Bonner. Reprinted by permission of W. W. Norton and Company, Inc.

Chapter 21

Otto F. Kernberg (1989). The narcissistic personality disorder and the differential diagnosis of antisocial behavior. *Psychiatric Clinics of North America*, 12:553–569. Reprinted by permission of W. B. Saunders Publishing Company.